ILYA KATSOV

INTRODUCTION TO
ALGORITHMIC MARKETING

Introduction to Algorithmic Marketing
by Ilya Katsov

Visit the book's website at https://algorithmicweb.wordpress.com
for additional resources.

ISBN 978-0-692-14260-8

"At a time when power is shifting to consumers, while brands and retailers are grasping for fleeting moments of attention, everyone is competing on data and the ability to leverage it at scale to target, acquire, and retain customers. This book is a manual for doing just that. Both marketing practitioners and technology providers will find this book very useful in guiding them through the marketing value chain and how to fully digitize it. A comprehensive and indispensable reference for anyone undertaking the transformational journey towards algorithmic marketing."

—Ali Bouhouch, CTO, Sephora Americas

"If you're tired of the vague fluff about AI in marketing, and you want to understand the real substance of what's possible today and how it works, then you must read An Introduction to Algorithmic Marketing. This is the best book in the field of marketing technology and operations that I've read yet."

—Scott Brinker,
Author of Hacking Marketing, Editor of chiefmartec.com

"Its all possible now. This book brings practicality to concepts that just a few years ago would have been dismissed as mere theory. It features principled framing that captures what the best marketers innately feel but cannot express. Elegant math articulates the important relationships that are so elusive to traditional business modeling. The book is unapologetic for its lack of spreadsheet examples – much of the world can not be represented linearly in just a few dimensions and devoid of uncertainty. Instead, the book embraces rigorous framing that yields better insights into real phenomenon. It's written neither for the data scientist nor the marketer, but rather for the two combined! Its this partnership between these two departments that will lead to real impact. This book is where that partnership should begin."

—Eric Colson, Chief Algorithms Officer, Stitch Fix

"This book is a live portrait of digital transformation in marketing. It shows how data science becomes an essential part of every marketing activity. The book details how data-driven approaches and smart algorithms result in deep automation of traditionally labor-intensive marketing tasks. Decision-making is getting not only better but much faster, and this is crucial in our ever-accelerating competitive environment. It is a must-read for both data scientists and marketing officers–even better if they read it together."

—Andrey Sebrant, Director of Strategic Marketing, Yandex

"Introduction to Algorithmic Marketing isn't just about machine learning and economic modeling. It's ultimately a framework for running business and marketing operations in the AI economy."

—Kyle McKiou,
Sr. Director of Data Science, The Marketing Store

"This books delivers a complete end-to-end blueprint on how to fully digitize your company's marketing operations. Starting from a conceptual architecture for the future of digital marketing, it then delves into detailed analysis of best practices in each individual area of marketing operations. The book gives the executives, middle managers, and data scientists in your organization a set of concrete, actionable, and incremental recommendations on how to build better insights and decisions, starting today, one step at a time."

—Victoria Livschitz, founder and CTO, Grid Dynamics

"While virtually every business manager today grasps the conceptual importance of data analytics and machine learning, the challenge of implementing actual competitive solutions rooted in data science remains quite daunting. The scarcity of data scientist talent, combined with the difficulty of adapting academic models, generic open-source software and algorithms to industry-specific contexts are among the difficulties confronting digital marketers around the world. This book by Ilya Katsov draws from the deep domain expertise he developed at Grid Dynamics in delivering innovative, yet practical digital marketing solutions to large organizations and helping them successfully compete, remain relevant, and adapt in the new age of data analytics."

—Eric Benhamou,
founder and General Partner, Benhamou Global Ventures;
former CEO and Chairman of 3Com and Palm

"This book provides a much-needed collection of recipes for marketing practitioners on how to use advanced methods of machine learning and data science to understand customer behavior, personalize product offerings, optimize the incentives, and control the engagement – thus creating a new generation of data-driven analytic platform for marketing systems."

—Kira Makagon, Chief Innovation Officer, RingCentral;
serial entrepreneur, founder of RedAril and Octane

CONTENTS

ACKNOWLEDGEMENTS

This book would not have been possible without the support and help of many people. I am very grateful to my colleagues and friends, Ali Bouhouch, Max Martynov, David Naylor, Penelope Conlon, Sergey Tryuber, Denys Kopiychenko, and Vadim Kozyrkov, who reviewed the content of the book and offered their feedback. Special thanks go to Konstantin Perikov, who provided a lot of insightful suggestions about search services and also helped with some of the examples.

I am indebted to Igor Yagovoy, Victoria Livschitz, Leonard Livschitz, and Ezra Berger for supporting this project and helping with the publishing. Last, but certainly not least, thanks to Kathryn Wright, my editor, who helped me shape the manuscript into the final product.

1

INTRODUCTION

In 1888, Vincent van Gogh, a little-known Dutch artist at that time, wrote to his brother, Theo, that *the painter of the future would be a colorist the like of which has never yet been seen.* Leaving the artistic aspect aside, the very way in which Van Gogh poses the question about the painters of the future and answers it is striking and admirable. Van Gogh, no doubt, was right in anticipating that the artists of the upcoming century would develop skills that have never yet been seen and questioning the ways of doing art. What if we ask the same question about marketing practitioners who live in the era of digital media and abundance of data? Who will be the marketers of the future? Will they be artists of client communications? Statisticians the like of whom have never yet been seen? Software engineers who create marketing systems? Experts in economic modeling?

The history of marketing can be viewed as the evolution of principles, techniques, and best practices for a certain kind of business optimization. It has always been recognized that this optimization problem can be approached in a scientific way and that rigorous mathematical methods can be applied to a wide range of marketing applications. Adopters of such methods, however, traditionally struggled with challenges related to incompleteness of data, complexity of real-life marketing settings, inflexibility of business processes, and software limitations. The challenges were especially overwhelming in areas that required far-reaching strategic decisions, where human judgment was often the only viable solution for practical applications.

The advancement of digital marketing channels changed the game and created an environment that requires millions of *micro-decisions* to be made, which simply cannot be done efficiently without intelligent marketing software and algorithms. Targeted sales promotions, dynamic pricing in brick-and-mortar and online stores, e-Commerce search and recommendation services, online advertising – all of these applications require advanced methods of economic modeling, data science, and software engineering to realize the potential of the digital environment. For instance, this potential cannot be fully achieved without tailoring personalized experiences for millions of individual customers, which, in turn, requires millions of unique decisions to be made. Moreover, ubiquitous digital media and mobile devices have empowered customers to go through the entire marketing funnel from research to purchase in seconds, anywhere and anytime, and this pervasive *micro-moment behavior* requires marketing decisions to be taken in microseconds as well. This environment introduces the challenge of building marketing systems that make decisions and act at an unprecedented level of autonomy, scale, and depth of analysis. In certain cases, not only can individual decisions and analytics be done in a data-driven way, but entire business processes can be planned, executed, measured, and optimized by an automatic software system.

Although the problem of marketing automation can be studied from different perspectives, including economics, management, statistics, and engineering, the creators of such systems have to line up all of these pieces into a cohesive set of methods that can be efficiently implemented in software to achieve the business objectives. Leading a modern marketing technology project is not unlike conducting an orchestra of diverse instruments and making them operate in concert. We take exactly this perspective on marketing throughout this book and put together the results of the vast experience gained by developers of marketing systems in retail, online advertising, and other industries over the last few decades, as well as the guiding theoretical principles. It should be noted that we deliberately focus on the results reported by industry practitioners that have proved to be useful in business solutions, rather then theoretical and academic studies. Fortunately, the number of methods, models, and architectures published by such practitioners is high and sometimes provides a great level of detail. Some of these publications are mainly focused on the technology and implementation aspects, whereas others dive deep into mathematical modeling, optimization, and econometrics. In practice, both aspects are important for the successful creation and operation of a marketing system. Many of these results are also based on or related to models developed in scientific marketing by academic researchers.

1.1   THE SUBJECT OF ALGORITHMIC MARKETING

One of the traditional definitions of marketing describes it as the activity of defining products and services offered by a company and communicating them to existing or potential customers. This activity can be broken down into several streams that are typically described as variations of the following categories [McCarthy, 1960]:

- Product – analysis of marketing opportunities, planning of product lines and product features, assortment planning.

- Promotion – all methods of communication between the company and its customers: advertisements, recommendations, customer care, and others.

- Price – pricing strategies, including posted prices, price discounts, and price changes over time.

- Place – historically, this refers to the process of making a product or service available to the end user through various distribution channels. More recent interpretations emphasize the role of product discovery and convenience to buy, with the argument that distribution is becoming less relevant with the rise of digital marketing channels [Lauterborn, 1990].

This categorization is well known as the *marketing mix*. The mix can be viewed as a set of variables that a marketing manager or marketing software can control to influence the position of products and brands in the market. Each component of the marketing mix represents a broad area that can be viewed and studied from different perspectives. The subject of algorithmic marketing can be better understood by distinguishing the following two aspects of marketing activities: *strategy* and *process*. We use the term *strategy* to label long-term top-level business decisions that define the value proposition of the company and set the overall direction for its marketing processes. For example, a retailer has to define its target market, customer services, and product lines as parts of the business strategy. The *process* is an implementation of the strategy that focuses on tactical decisions that support continuous functioning of the company. Continuing the example with a retailer, high-level pricing and promotional strategies require numerous decisions about how to select consumers for promotional campaigns or how prices for individual products should change over time.

Although the scope of neither strategy nor tactical processes can be rigorously defined, and there is no clear boundary between these two counterparts, we can argue that the strategy side is more focused on exploration, analysis, and planning involving human judgment, whereas the process side is more focused on execution, micro-decisioning, and, most importantly, automation. This makes the process side of marketing especially attractive for our study, although both strategy and process can be described from the viewpoint of data science and clearly benefit from data-driven methods. The short summary is that the subject of algorithmic marketing mainly concerns the processes that can be found in the four areas of the marketing mix and the automation of these processes by using data-driven techniques and econometric methods.

1.2   THE DEFINITION OF ALGORITHMIC MARKETING

We define *algorithmic marketing* as a marketing process that is automated to such a degree that it can be steered by setting a business objective in a marketing software system. This implies that the marketing system should be intelligent and knowledgeable enough to understand a high-level objective, such as the acquisition of new customers or revenue maximization, to plan and execute a sequence of business actions, such as an advertisement campaign or price adjustment, with the aim of achieving the objective, and to learn from the results to correct and optimize the actions if needed. This basic principle is illustrated in Figure 1.1. In this book, we also use the term *programmatic* to refer to highly automated marketing software systems and services, and the terms algorithmic and programmatic are used interchangeably in most contexts.

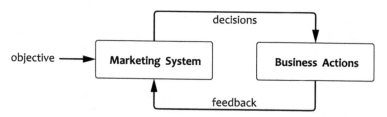

Figure 1.1: A conceptual view of the algorithmic marketing ecosystem.

Although it would be ideal for a programmatic system to be perfectly automated and autonomous, we do not consider this a principal goal or design requirement. On the contrary, a programmatic system is typically maintained by many people, including data scientists, engineers, and analysts, who develop and adjust models and algorithms to improve the system's efficiency and capabilities. It can also consume the outputs of strategic analysis and planning done elsewhere with non-programmatic methods and, possibly, in connection with some other problems. However, the system's ability to understand the business objective and work through the entire process from the objective to measurable results is essential. Again, it is important to keep in mind the limitations and perils of automation in marketing. In many real-life applications, it is more appropriate to view programmatic systems as intelligent tools that enable marketers to efficiently achieve what they want, rather than as their replacements.

1.3 HISTORICAL BACKGROUNDS AND CONTEXT

There is no sharp boundary between algorithmic and non-algorithmic marketing. In some senses, it is even invalid to draw such a boundary because algorithmic systems are just a method of answering old marketing questions, not posing new ones. However, it is evident that the level of marketing automation differs sharply across industries, which indicates that some environments are more favorable in that regard than others. Conversely, successful acquisition of advanced algorithmic methods can drastically transform an industry and create increasingly better conditions for further development. Analysis of such favorable environments is a natural starting point for understanding algorithmic marketing. Let us briefly review several business cases that laid the foundation for algorithmic marketing in search of the patterns and characteristics that enabled the systematic approach.

1.3.1 *Online Advertising: Services and Exchanges*

The history of internet advertising can be traced back to May 3, 1978, when the first spam email was sent to 400 users of the computer network ARPANET, deployed at that time in just four locations: the University of Utah, UCLA, UC Santa Barbara, and Stanford Research. Fifteen years later, by 1993, when ARPANET had developed into the Internet and the spread of the Web enabled multimedia websites, the market of banner ads appeared. This new market originally relied on direct selling of banner slots offered by website publishers to advertisers, but this approach started to lose its efficiency very quickly when there was a surge in the number of websites. It became operationally difficult or even impossible for advertisers to run ad campaigns and manage budgets across thousands of publishers. On the other hand, publishers needed a robust and centralized way to sell their inventory at scale.

The challenge was taken up by ad networks that acted as brokers between publishers and advertisers. DoubleClick, launched in 1996, offered a platform that enabled advertisers to run ad campaigns across a wide network of websites, dynamically customize a campaign according to its performance, and measure the return on investment. This created a perfect environment for automatic decision making because the measurements and adjustments could be done dynamically. However, it was not really programmatic at that time.

The online search engines, meanwhile, were also struggling to improve their advertising capabilities. Advertisers paid for the number of times their ad was demonstrated by the search engine – the cost per thousand impressions (CPM) model – similarly to banner ads. This approach was inflexible from the pricing perspective, causing certain revenue losses for search engines, and also from the targeting perspective because irrelevant ads were not penalized in any way. The breakthrough happened in 1998 when the GoTo.com search engine introduced an automated auction model with two innovative features:

- Advertisers could bid how much they would be willing to pay to appear at the top of the results for specific search queries.

- Advertisers paid per click, not per impression.

The per-pay-click (PPC) model improved both revenues and ad relevancy because advertisers who were willing to pay for top ad spots for specific search queries generally offered more relevant and better resources. This model was adopted by Google in 2002 with one principal improvement: the ad was selected based on Google's expected revenue, not the bid amount. Google measured the click-through rate for each ad as a ratio between clicks and impressions, and the expected revenue was estimated as

$$revenue = bid\ price \times click\text{-}through\ rate$$

This was a programmatic self-learning technique that optimized the business objective, both in terms of revenue and relevancy, because click-through rates tend to be low for irrelevant ads, so even high-budget advertisers were not able to clog up the bandwidth.

The trajectories of ad networks and search engines converged in 2007–2009 with adoption of the auction model across the board. Advertisers and publishers became connected by ad exchanges that accepted real-time bids for individual ad impressions, and a new era of real-time bidding, commonly abbreviated as RTB, thus began. The advent of RTB exchanges gave impetus to programmatic tools for advertisers – data-management platforms (DMPs) and demand-side platforms (DSPs) – that provided the ability to collect data about the behavior of Internet users and make bids on RTB exchanges depending on the estimated propensity of a given user to respond. The success of RTB was impressive: the share of inventory sold by DoubleClick (acquired by Google by that time) through RTB rose from 8% in January 2010 to 68% in May 2011 [Google Inc., 2011].

Reflecting on the history of RTB, we can conclude that one of the most prominent achievements of programmatic advertising is a framework that enables owners of consumer bases, originally the publishers of web content, to provide personalized marketing services to parties who are limited in their ability to interact with consumers, originally the advertisers of products and services. The infrastructure that sits in between the publishers and advertisers is typically provided by an independent party and includes the following:

- *Advertising services* that enable advertisers to run advertising campaigns using the publisher's resources. These services are typically used to connect multiple advertisers with multiple publishers and resemble a marketplace where resources are sold and bought, often on a bidding basis.

- *Data services* that collect and store information about consumers, taking it from publishers, advertisers, and third parties. Advertising services take advantage of this data to run ad campaigns and make real-time automatic decisions on ads to be delivered.

Later on, this pattern started to spread across other industries. Other types of consumer-base owners, such as retailers and mobile operators, were also looking for an efficient way to commercialize their data and relationships with consumers, and other types of service users, such as banks, product manufacturers, and insurance companies, were willing to know more about their customers and have more channels for communication with them. For instance, a manufacturer of consumer packaged goods can use a retailer's channels, such as stores and eCommerce websites, to offer personalized discounts to consumers to promote new products and increase their market share.

Consequently, advertising services and data services started to transform into the more generic model illustrated in Figure 1.2, which represents a multipurpose marketplace of services and data that connects actors from different industries. The range of services offered by such a marketplace can go far beyond advertising, covering areas like credit scores and insurance premiums. The heterogeneity of this environment, where one constantly deals with someone else's data, often in real-time, leads to overwhelming complexity of data flows and operational decisions, and programmatic methods are probably the only way to tackle it.

1.3.2 *Airlines: Revenue Management*

Online advertising and data marketplaces are perhaps the most famous and successful cases in the history of programmatic marketing, but

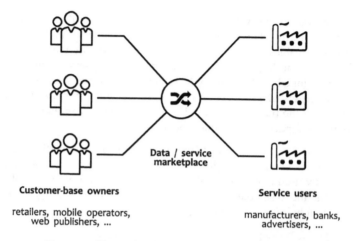

Customer-base owners

retailers, mobile operators,
web publishers, ...

Service users

manufacturers, banks,
advertisers, ...

Figure 1.2: The marketplace model for data and services.

definitely not the only one. Online advertising, to a degree, was a completely new environment that provided unprecedented capabilities for solving unprecedented challenges. Programmatic methods, however, can be successfully applied in more traditional settings. Let us consider a prominent case that, by coincidence, also began to unfold in 1978, the same year that the first spam email was sent.

The federal Civil Aeronautics Board had regulated all US interstate air transport since 1938, setting schedules, routes, and fares based on standard prices and profitability targets for the airlines. The Airline Deregulation Act of 1978 eliminated many controls and enabled airlines to freely change prices and routes. It opened the door for low-cost carriers, who pioneered simpler operational models, no-frills services, and reduced labor costs. One of the most prominent examples was PeopleExpress, which started in 1981 and offered fares about 70 percent lower than the major airlines.

The low-cost carriers attracted new categories of travelers who had rarely traveled by air before: college students visiting their families, leisure travelers getting away for a few days, and many others. In 1984, PeopleExpress reported revenue of $1 billion and its profits hit $60 million [Talluri and Van Ryzin, 2004]. The advent of low-fare airlines was a growing threat to the major carriers, who had almost no chance to win the price war. Moreover, the established airlines could not afford to lose their high-revenue business travelers in pursuit of the low-revenue market.

The solution was found by American Airlines. First, they recognized that unsold seats could be used to compete on price with the low-cost carriers, because the marginal cost of such seats was close to zero anyway. The problem, however, was how to prevent the business travelers from purchasing tickets at discounted prices. The basic solution was to introduce certain constraints on the discounted offers; for example, the tickets had to be purchased at least three weeks in advance and were non-refundable. The challenging part was that the surplus of seats varied substantially across flights and the optimal allocation could be achieved only by using dynamic optimization. In 1985, after a few years of development, American Airlines released a system called Dynamic Inventory Allocation and Maintenance Optimizer (DINAMO) to manage their prices across the board. PeopleExpress also used some simple price-management strategies to differentiate peak and off-peak fares, but their information technology system was much simpler than DINAMO and was not able to match its efficiency. PeopleExpress started to lose money at a rate of $50 million a month, headed straight to bankruptcy, and eventually ceased to exist as a carrier in 1987 after acquisition by Continental Airlines [Vasigh et al., 2013]. American Airlines, however, not only won the competition with PeopleExpress but also increased its revenue by 14.5% and profits by 47.8% the year after DINAMO was launched.

The case of American Airlines was the first major success of a revenue management practice. By the early 1990s, the approach had been adopted by other industries with perishable inventories and customers booking the service in advance: hospitality, car rentals, and even television ad sales. The success of revenue management in the airline industry is clearly related to the specific properties of the inventory and demand in this domain:

- The demand varies significantly across customers, flights, and time: the purchasing capacity of business travelers can be much higher than that of discretionary travelers, peak flights can be much more loaded than off-peak, etc.

- The supply, that is, the available seats, is not flexible. The airline produces seats in large chunks by scheduling flights, and once the flight is scheduled, the number of seats cannot be changed. Unsold seats cannot be removed, so the airlines' profit completely depends on its ability to manage the demand and sell efficiently.

We can conclude from the above that revenue management can be considered as a counterpart of supply-chain management or, alternatively, a demand-chain management solution that struggles with inflexible production and adapts it to the demands of the market (and, conversely, manipulates the demand to align it with the supply), as illustrated in Figure 1.3.

Figure 1.3: Revenue management as a counterpart of supply-chain management.

This friction between supply and demand can be found not only in air transportation but in other industries as well. Hotels and car rentals are clearly the closest examples, but advertising, retail, and others also demonstrate features that indicate the applicability of algorithmic methods for demand-chain management.

1.3.3 Marketing Science

The case studies of online advertising and airline ticketing give a general idea of how algorithmic methods advanced in the industry. Industrial adoption was backed by rapid developments in marketing science and, conversely, the development of scientific marketing methods was boosted and propelled by industrial needs. Marketing as a discipline emerged in the early 1900s, and, for the first five decades of its existence, it was mainly focused on the descriptive analysis of production and distribution processes; that is, it collected the facts about the flow of goods from producers to consumers. The idea that marketing decisions could be supported by mathematical modeling and optimization methods began to gain currency in the 1960s, a fact that can be attributed to several factors. First, marketing science was influenced by advances in *operations research*, a discipline that deals with decision-making and efficiency problems in military and business applications by using statistical analysis and mathematical optimization. Operations research, in turn, arose during World War II in the context of military operation planning and resource optimization. Second, the advancement of mathematical methods in marketing can be attributed to technological changes and the adoption of the first mainframes in organizations, which made it possible to collect more data and implement data analysis and optimization algorithms. Finally, marketing practitioners began to feel that the old ways of selling were wearing thin and that marketing needed to be redefined as a mix of ingredients that can be controlled and optimized; this is how the concept of the marketing mix appeared in 1960. Marketing science boomed in the sixties and seventies of the twentieth century when numerous quantitative models for pricing, distribution, and product planning were developed using advanced probabilistic and optimization techniques. Some of these methods were readily adopted in practice, as in the case of revenue management in the airline and hotel industries, but many others had limited practical applicability, so the overall level of marketing automation remained low in many industries [Wierenga, 2010].

The advancement of digital channels has changed the situation drastically. Digital media created the need and the opportunity to make millions of micro-decisions at the level of individual customers and provide totally new services, such as product search or real-time mobile notifications. This has created challenges that often go beyond economic modeling and optimization, which is the main theme in traditional marketing science, and require the use of advanced software engineering and data analysis methods that were not originally connected to marketing. In modern retail, for instance, a substantial part of the revenue can be generated by search and recommendations services that internally rely on text analysis methods, rather than economic models. Some of these methods came from areas as distant from marketing as biology and genome studies. To summarize, we can say that traditional economic modeling, data science, software engineering, and conventional marketing practices are all important for the creation of programmatic systems.

1.4 PROGRAMMATIC SERVICES

The marketing mix model defines four factors that can be controlled by a company to influence consumer purchase decisions: product, promotion, price, and place. As such, this categorization is very broad and provides little guidance on how exactly programmatic marketing systems should be built. So far, we have learned that a programmatic system can be viewed as a provider of one or more functional services that implement certain business processes, such as price or promotion management. Consequently, we can make our problem statement more specific by defining a set of services, each of which implements a certain function and has its own inputs (objectives) and outputs (actions). There are different options for how the marketing mix can be broken down into functional services depending on the industry and business model of a particular company. We choose to define six major functional services that are relevant for a wide range of business-to-consumer (B2C) verticals: promotions, advertisements, search, recommendations, pricing, and assortment. These six services are the main subject of this book, and we will spend the later chapters discussing how to design and build them. The applications and design principles are very different across the services, but there are many relationships between them as well. Let us briefly review these relationships and some common design guidelines that will be used in the rest of this book to streamline the detailed discussions of individual services.

The relationships between the six services we have defined, as well as their connections to the marketing mix, can be established as follows:

- The primary purpose of promotion and advertisement services is to match customers with offerings and convey the right message to them. This typically requires customers to be found who can be incentivized to do actions that contribute toward the desired business objective. The capability for identifying the right customers and offerings is the keystone of this service group. From the marketing mix perspective, these services directly address the Promotion domain of the mix and are also related to the Price domain through the costs and profits associated with promotion and advertising campaigns.

- The search and recommendation services solve the problem of finding the right products for a given customer, which naturally complements the previous service group. The principal goal of these services is to enable and simplify product discovery, which is related to the Place and Promotion domains of the marketing mix. This group of services requires an understanding of the purchasing intent of the customer, expressed either explicitly or implicitly, and the ability to find offerings that match it well.

- The goal of pricing and assortment services is to determine and optimize the set of offerings and their properties, including price. These services often rely on a capability to predict the demand as a function of assortment, prices, and other parameters, which enables what-if analysis and optimization of different options. This group mainly covers the Price and Product domains of the marketing mix.

This three-group classification, illustrated in Figure 1.4, is convenient because it reflects the similarities in the objectives and design principles shared across the services. We structure the rest of this book on the basis of these three groups to address both fundamental capabilities, such as identification of the right customers for an offering, and individual services.

The next question we can pose is what these services have in common from the design and implementation standpoints. Although the design principles and implementation methods are very different for the different services, the programmatic approach introduces common guidelines that can be explicitly or implicitly followed by all services.

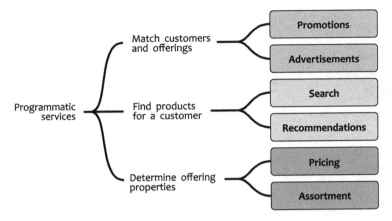

Figure 1.4: Programmatic services.

We can use these guidelines to define the basic terminology and components that can later be elaborated within the scope of the corresponding domains.

The concept of the programmatic method accentuates the objective-driven design approach, so we can attempt to define a common framework by starting with the notion of the business objective. In order to understand and execute the objective, a programmatic service is likely to include a certain set of functional components that can have different designs for different domains (see Figure 1.5):

- Since any automatic decision making is driven by data, the decision-making pipeline starts with data collection. Examples of input data for most marketing applications include customers' personal and behavioral profiles, inventory data, and sales records.

- The raw input data often has to be transformed into well-defined *features* that can be fed into analysis and decision-making algorithms. The reason is that programmatic services often rely on some measure of similarity between entities like products or customers to learn the patterns and make decisions, which requires the entities to be represented as comparable sets of attributes. Search services, for example, often rely on some similarity measure between a user query and the products to find the most relevant offerings, which requires both products and queries to be converted into well-defined comparable representations. The engineering of these attributes, referenced as features in many contexts, plays a critically important role in programmatic systems.

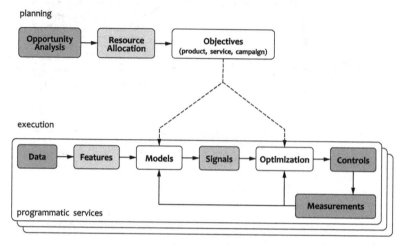

Figure 1.5: A high-level design framework for programmatic services.

- The most important step in the programmatic pipeline is to evaluate how well different action strategies fit the business objective. This generally requires the development of one or more models that consume a candidate solution and produce signals that indicate the level of fitness. For example, a promotion service can rely on a *model* that scores the customer according to their propensity to buy a certain product, a pricing service can score different pricing options according to expected profits, and a search service can score products by their relevance for a query.

- The *signals* generated by models carry information about the quality of different decisions that a marketer can make. A business action, however, often requires the combination of many signals and intermediate decisions into the final action plan. For example, a marketer can send promotions to the most valuable clients, which requires individual customers to be evaluated, but the final mailing list has to be constrained to the campaign budget. Thus, programmatic services typically contain an optimization or signal-mixing component that makes the final decisions.

- A programmatic service communicates with the outside world through *marketing channels* and integrates with other services. These channels determine a set of possible business actions that a service can take and action parameters that a service can control, such as price levels, discount values, email messages, or product order in search result lists. These controls are used by the programmatic service to execute its decisions, so the decisions should eventually be expressed as parameters for available controls.

- Finally, the feedback collected from the execution channels can be routed back to the models and optimization procedures to learn from the results and adjust the decision-making logic. The measurement stage is a mandatory part of all marketing services, and many marketing methods rely on a measurement-driven trial and error approach to optimization.

In practice, a marketer often wants to achieve multiple strategic goals and can leverage multiple services to do it. The programmatic infrastructure can support this by providing capabilities for market opportunities analysis and global *resource allocation* that help to elaborate the objectives and parameters for individual services, as well as consolidate the measurements. This planning functionality and the execution pipelines of individual services make up the complete programmatic ecosystem. The framework we have defined is very abstract at this point, but we will gradually elaborate design methods for all stages of the pipeline in the subsequent chapters.

1.5 WHO SHOULD READ THIS BOOK?

This book is for everyone who wants to learn how to build advanced marketing software systems. It will be useful for a variety of marketing and software practitioners, but it was written with two target audiences in mind. The first target audience is implementers of marketing software, product managers, and software engineers who want to learn about the features and techniques that can be used in marketing software products and also learn about the economic foundations for these techniques. The other target audience is marketing strategists and technology leaders who are looking for guidance on how marketing organizations and marketing services can benefit from machine learning and Big Data and how modern enterprises can leverage advanced decision automation methods.

It is assumed that readers have an introductory background in statistics, calculus, and programming. Although most methods described in the book use relatively basic math, this book may not be suitable for readers who are interested only in the business aspects of marketing: this book is about *marketing automation*; it is not a traditional marketing textbook. Overall, if you are comfortable with the following expression, you are probably good to go:

$$\mathbb{E}\left[X\right] = \int_{-\infty}^{\infty} x\, f_X(x)\, dx$$

This book is divided into six chapters. This first chapter, Introduction, outlines the main concepts and principles of algorithmic marketing and also discusses several inspiring case studies that illustrate the prerequisites and benefits of the algorithmic approach. The second chapter, Review of Predictive Modeling, focuses on the mathematical foundations of algorithmic marketing. The last four chapters cover four different domains of marketing – advertisements and promotions, search services, recommendations, and pricing – one domain at a time. These four main chapters follow the same algorithmic methodology and, thus, have the same structure: we start each chapter with a description of the environment to understand the constraints and variables that we can optimize, we then discuss business objectives to better define the optimization problem, and we finally work through decision automation methods for different tasks and scenarios that appear in the domain. As each of the four main chapters addresses its own domain, the chapters are relatively independent, and readers can thus use this book as a reference to read selectively about the areas that are most relevant for their needs or read sequentially from cover to cover.

Readers should feel free to skip parts that are not relevant to their background or intended use. For example, readers familiar with probability, statistics, and machine learning can just quickly scan through the second chapter or skip it completely. Readers who are primarily interested in the business applications and capabilities of the algorithmic approach can focus on sections that describe environments, business objectives, and optimization problems, and they can skip the mathematical details and numerical examples. On the other hand, readers who implement marketing systems should most likely examine the algorithms, numerical examples, and implementation details.

1.6 SUMMARY

- A programmatic approach to marketing focuses on creating highly automated marketing systems and processes that can be steered by business objectives. Programmatic methods can be applied to all of the domains of the marketing mix, namely, product, promotion, price, and place.

- Programmatic marketing can be viewed as services that provide insights into the market state and enable one to interact with the market. These services can be used internally by the company that owns the customer base or can be sold to a third party. Programmatic components should be self-contained, well-packaged, and able to implement a reasonably high level of abstraction to be sold as high-value services.

- A programmatic service often acts as a dynamic controller of demand and, consequently, a counterpart of supply-chain management. The efficiency of programmatic methods increases with variability of demand across consumers or over time and decreases with flexibility of production. Consequently, programmatic methods are most rewarding in areas with high diversity of consumer tastes and incomes and/or areas with inflexible production that creates a surplus of goods or services with low marginal cost if demand drops.

- The most important examples of programmatic services include promotions, advertisements, search, recommendations, pricing, and assortment. The design principles differ across the services, but a few functional capabilities and logical components are widely used across all service types. Examples of such components are scoring models that assess the fitness of candidate solutions for a selected business objective, optimization models that analyze and mix the scores to make the final decisions, and controls that are used to turn decisions into actions.

2

REVIEW OF PREDICTIVE MODELING

Algorithmic marketing, by definition, cannot exist without a methodology for the evaluation of possible business actions and corresponding outcomes based on the available data. In this chapter, we will review the basic methods of machine learning and economic modeling that enable predictive analysis and provide the building blocks that will be used in the rest of the book. Our primary goal here is to describe the main capabilities and limitations of predictive modeling, rather than to provide a comprehensive study of machine learning algorithms. We will describe only a few methods that are routinely used in marketing applications and provide mathematical details and examples only to illustrate the capabilities, limitations, and relationships with other methods. We will not go into the practical aspects of modeling, such as preparation of the input data and evaluation of the resulting models, in depth in this chapter; these details are left until later in the book.

2.1 DESCRIPTIVE, PREDICTIVE, AND PRESCRIPTIVE ANALYTICS

Before we proceed to predictive modeling, a brief note regarding the terminology used in the marketing domain. In business applications, data analytics methods are often categorized at a high level into three distinct types: descriptive, predictive, and prescriptive. *Descriptive analytics* refers to methods for data summarization, data quality assessment, and finding correlations. Examples of descriptive analytics are management reports providing aggregated sales data or market basket analyses yielding information about the products frequently bought together. Descriptive analytics does not aim to explain how the observed results can be influenced or optimized. *Predictive analytics* focuses on estimation of the likelihood of a potential outcome by using data that are observed or known prior to the outcome. Common examples of predictive analytics are the forecasting of demand and the propensity scoring used to determine the likelihood of customers responding to a promotion. Note that "predictive" does not necessarily mean a forecast of the future – it is used in the sense that the predictive model can estimate some output variable given some change in an input variable. Finally, *prescriptive analytics* refers to modeling of the dependency between decisions and future outcomes for optimal decision making. One of the basic examples of prescriptive analysis is price optimization where the profit is modeled as a function of the price, so that one can estimate how many dollars of profit would be generated by every dollar of price discount and determine the profit-optimal discount value.

In the marketing domain, data-related activities and processes are commonly viewed through the lenses of these three types of analytics, and all three types are important. In programmatic applications, where automated decision making is key, the main focus is on prescriptive analytics, which, in turn, uses predictive models as building blocks. Consequently, it should be kept in mind that programmatic applications only use a subset of marketing analytics methods.

2.2 ECONOMIC OPTIMIZATION

Marketing is an activity that aims to achieve certain business objectives by executing business actions of a certain type. The first step we need to take as we begin to discuss the algorithmic approach is to translate this business language into more formal models that describe the objective we are trying to achieve, the space of possible actions, and the constraints we should meet. Most marketing problems translated into this econometric language are naturally optimization problems that express business metrics, like revenue, as a function of possible actions, such as marketing campaigns or assortment adjustments, and require the optimal action to be found from among the various possible strategies.

The economic model is also a function of data in the sense that it uses properties and parameters estimated from past experience. For instance, consider a retailer planning a marketing mailing campaign. The space of possible actions can be defined as a set of send/no-send decisions with regard to individual customers, and the revenue of the campaign depends both on actions, that is, who will receive the incentive and who will not, and data, such as expected revenue from a given customer and mailing costs. This approach can be expressed in a more formal way as follows:

$$s_{opt} = \underset{s \in S}{\operatorname{argmax}} \ G\,(s,\,D) \qquad\qquad (2.1)$$

in which D is the data available for analysis, S is the space of actions and decisions, G is an *economic model* that maps actions and data to an economic outcome, and s_{opt} is the optimal strategy. The design of model G completely depends on the application. We will discuss the construction of different models in the next chapters in the context of particular marketing problems, but there are several basic considerations that should be taken into account in any model design.

First, we need to define the *business objective* and express it as a numerical metric that can be a subject of optimization. In many cases, it is reasonable to model and optimize the profit, but, as we will see later, other objectives can be set for particular applications. The design of the objective can be especially challenging if the objective represents a trade-off between the enterprise's profit and the usefulness to the consumer, for example, a search in an online catalog that should provide results both relevant to the query entered by the consumer and aligned with the merchandising goals and rules.

Second, we should account for available data or address the data collection problem. The role of data mining in problem 2.1 is crucial because model G, which links the actions with the outcomes, can be complex and may have to be determined from data by means of regression analysis or other data mining techniques. In some cases, the model cannot be completely specified, either because of high complexity (e. g., user behavior cannot be precisely predicted) or because it is impossible to extrapolate the existing data to the case in point (e. g., the action is to introduce a completely new product or service). In either case, the data should be treated as a business asset that might require investment, and there is a trade-off between the cost of data acquisition and the value delivered by the acquired data. For example, the real-life testing of multiple models in parallel is a simple way to trade economic efficiency (running different models simultaneously is obviously suboptimal) for acquisition of more data points and, sometimes, lower model complexity.

Third, the model can be created at different levels of granularity. We can express the same objective by using different models depending on the space of possible actions, available data, and our knowledge of the business constraints. One of the key considerations in model design is the level of data aggregation. Classic economic models often operate with a small number of high-level aggregates, such as the overall demand. This makes the models simple from the computational and data collection perspectives but limits their ability to model complex dependencies. Algorithmic methods assume the availability of a powerful data processing infrastructure and high-resolution data, which enables more granular modeling. The difference between these two approaches can be illustrated by the following simplistic example [Kleinberg et al., 1998]. Suppose that a retailer sells a product with the margin m, and q_u is the monthly amount of this product purchased by customer u. The monthly revenue can therefore be described as

$$G = \sum_u q_u m \qquad (2.2)$$

The retailer wants to run a promotion campaign that boosts sales by the factor of k, and the cost of each promotion is c. The retailer can control both k and c by choosing a more or less aggressive promotional strategy. Consequently, the optimization problem to be solved can be defined as

$$\max_s \sum_u k \cdot q_u m - c \qquad (2.3)$$

in which s is the promotional strategy determined by the pair of parameters k and c. We can see that the definition in terms of individual consumers is redundant, and the problem can be redefined in terms of aggregates, namely the total demand

$$Q = \sum_u q_u \qquad (2.4)$$

and the total budget of the campaign C. Thus, the problem is defined as

$$\max_s \ k \cdot Q \cdot m - C \qquad (2.5)$$

Let us now assume that the retailer wants to create two different consumer segments and assign the strategy $s_i = (k_i, c_i)$ to one of these segments and the strategy $s_j = (k_j, c_j)$ to the other segment. With the assumption that the strategies are selected from domain S, the optimization problem will be

$$\max_{s_i, s_j \in S} \sum_u \max\{ q_u k_i m - c_i, q_u k_j m - c_j \} \qquad (2.6)$$

This expression is not linear with regards to the k and c parameters, so we cannot easily redefine it in terms of aggregates. Consequently, more sophisticated data mining techniques might need to be used. This trade-off between aggregates and high-resolution data is a common pattern that arises in many problems because of nonlinear dependencies between the variables involved in the optimization.

Finally, it should be noted that optimization problem 2.1 as a whole is somewhat dependent on time because of environmental changes (new products appear on the market, competitors make their moves, etc.) and the enterprise's own actions. One possible approach for handling this dependency is to use a stateless model, treating it as a mathematical function, but allow for time-dependent arguments to account for memory effects. For example, a demand prediction model can forecast the demand for the next month by taking the discount levels for the last week, last two weeks, last three weeks, etc. as arguments.

2.3 MACHINE LEARNING

We stated in the previous section that the optimization objective can be defined as a function of the data and marketing strategy, $G(s, D)$. Our next step is to provide a more formal definition of data that will help to bridge the gap between the economic model and data mining methods.

The first thing we note is that the economic modeling process is concerned only with certain metrics of the company or consumer that are directly related to the modeled objective. Examples of such metrics are the demand for a certain product or the propensity of a consumer to respond to a promotion. In most cases, the marketing strategy and actions do not unconditionally determine these metrics but only influence them. A price discount, for instance, can increase the demand for a certain product, but this may not be the case if a similar discount is simultaneously offered by a competitor. Consequently, we are interested in finding the functional dependency between the controlled or uncontrolled factors and the metrics of interest. In probabilistic terms, this can be expressed as the conditional distribution

$$p(y \mid x) \tag{2.7}$$

in which x is the vector of factors and y is the metrics. In the example with discounts, x can include variables like the price of a given product, prices of related products, and competitor prices, and y is the demand measured in units sold. Each marketing strategy s then corresponds to a particular combination of factors, that is, some value of vector x, which we denote as $x(s)$. With the assumption that the distribution is known, the economic optimization problem can be rewritten in the terms introduced above as

$$\max_{s} \quad G(p(y \mid x(s))) \tag{2.8}$$

The data come into play if the conditional distribution $p(y \mid x)$ is complex and should be learned from the data as opposed to being manually defined. Consequently, we are interested in the data that contain pairs (x, y) that are drawn from the true but unknown distribution $p_{data}(y \mid x)$. We will refer to these pairs as *samples* or *data points*. The input data are often observed (collected) in a form that is not suitable or optimal for modeling, so vector **x** and metric y are typically constructed from the raw data by using cleansing and normalizing transformations. We will refer to the elements of such a prepared vector **x** as *features* or *independent variables* and to y as the *response label* or *dependent variable*. With the assumption that we have n samples and m features, all feature vectors can be represented as an n × m matrix, **X**, called the *design matrix*, and all response variables as an n-dimensional column-vector **y**. Each row of the design matrix **X** is a feature vector **x** and each element of **y** is a response label y. All data points can then be represented as an n × (m + 1) matrix, **D**, with the following structure:

$$
\mathbf{D} = [\mathbf{X} \mid \mathbf{y}] =
\begin{bmatrix}
- & x_1 & - & y_1 \\
- & x_2 & - & y_2 \\
  & \vdots & & \vdots \\
- & x_n & - & y_n
\end{bmatrix}
\tag{2.9}
$$

Our goal then is to create a statistical model that approximates the true distribution $p_{data}(y \mid x)$ with the distribution $p_{model}(y \mid x)$ learned from the data, so the economic model will actually be evaluated by using the following approximation:

$$
\max_{s} \quad G\left(p_{model}(y \mid x(s))\right) \tag{2.10}
$$

In many practical applications, we do not need to specify the distribution but rather need to estimate the most likely value of y based on **x**, that is, to learn the function

$$
\hat{y} = y(x) \tag{2.11}
$$

in which the left-hand side is the estimated value of the response variable. Estimation of the most likely value of y is easier than estimation of the entire distribution and, as we will see shortly, it can be done without accurate estimation of the actual probability values. The economic model can then be evaluated as

$$
\max_{s} \quad G\left(y(x(s))\right) \tag{2.12}
$$

In a general case, model G can use multiple data models derived from one or more data sets. This approach divides the original modeling problem into the following smaller tasks that can be explored separately:

- The distribution $p(y \mid x)$ should be estimated from the data. This is a standard machine learning problem that falls into the class of *supervised learning* tasks.

- In certain cases, appropriate x and y values are not explicitly present in the available data. However, it may be possible to find a transformation that maps the original data to a new representation that is more suitable for modeling. This task is known as *feature engineering*. In some cases, feature engineering can be done semimanually by using relatively basic methods. For example, it may be found that taking a logarithm of the input values improves the accuracy of the model. In other cases, one needs to use more advanced machine learning methods to find a proper representation. We refer to this problem as *representation learning*.

- Finally, the economic model that estimates the business outcomes from the distribution should be defined. This is an economic problem, rather than a machine learning one, so we will discuss it in detail in the subsequent chapters dedicated to particular marketing problems. However, there exist a number of standard models for fundamental problems, such as prediction of consumer choice behavior, that we will touch on later in this chapter.

We proceed with an overview of each of these three areas to describe the toolkit that is available for developers of applicable programmatic systems and to define a vocabulary of the building blocks that we will use throughout the book. Herein, we will focus on the conceptual problems and solutions and do not dive into the algorithmic and implementation details, which can be found in textbooks on machine learning, such as [Bishop, 2006], [Murphy, 2012], and [Zaki and Meira, 2014], to name a few.

2.4 SUPERVISED LEARNING

Previously, we have seen that the modeling task can be partially reduced to learning of the distribution $p(y \mid x)$ based on the available samples x and y. The function p, which maps an m-dimensional vector of features to the probability values, can be interpreted as a probability density function for continuous y or a probability function for discrete y. In many applications, we do not need to learn the entire distribution but only a function that predicts the most likely y response based on the input x. The task of learning such distributions or functions is known as supervised learning because the data contain the response variables that "guide" the learning process. This problem comes in two types. If the response variable is categorical, that is, y belongs to some finite set of *classes*, the problem is known as *classification*. If the response variable is continuous, the problem is known as *regression*.

In this section, we will first discuss how the problem of estimating the distributions and predictive models can be approached and the relationship between the true distribution $p_{data}(y \mid x)$ and the learned distribution $p_{model}(y \mid x)$, and we will then consider a few examples of how the actual models can be built.

2.4.1 Parametric and Nonparametric Models

One of the main considerations in predictive model design is the choice between parametric and nonparametric approaches. The parametric approach makes the assumption that the data distribution has a certain functional form specified by a fixed number of parameters, so the problem of distribution estimation can be redefined as the problem of *model fitting*, that is, the selection of model parameters θ so that the distribution model

$$p_{model}(y \mid x, \theta) \tag{2.13}$$

can be optimally fitted with the data. The optimality condition, of course, needs to be formally specified as well. The nonparametric approach assumes that the number of parameters can grow with the amount of training data, and, in some methods, each data point can be viewed as a parameter. One of the most commonly used nonparametric methods is the k nearest neighbor (kNN) algorithm. The idea is to estimate the response variable for the feature vector x based on the response variables of the data samples that are the nearest neighbors of x in the feature space. In a case of classification, the probability that the response variable y belongs to the class c can then be estimated as

$$\Pr(y = c \mid x, k) = \frac{1}{k} \sum_{i \in N_k(x)} \mathbb{I}(y_i = c) \tag{2.14}$$

in which k is the algorithm parameter that defines the neighborhood size, $N_k(x)$ is the neighborhood of k nearest data points in the training data set, and $\mathbb{I}$ is the indicator function equal to 1 if its argument is true and to 0 otherwise. The neighborhood of the input vector x can be determined by using any vector distance metric, such as Euclidean distance. The classification decision can then be made by choosing the most probable class as follows:

$$\hat{y} = \underset{c}{\arg\max}\, \Pr(y = c \mid x, k) \tag{2.15}$$

This process is illustrated in Figure 2.1. A regression model can be defined in a similar way by estimating the response as the average values of response variables in the neighborhood.

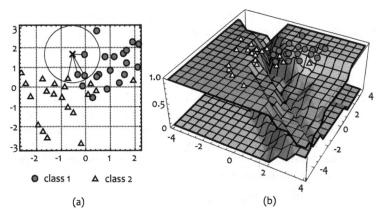

Figure 2.1: Classification of two-dimensional points by using the kNN algorithm. (a) Training data set with two classes of points. Each point
in the space is classified based on $k = 4$ nearest neighbors. (b) Class
probabilities estimated as functions of the features according to equation 2.14.

The nearest neighbor algorithm is one of the most basic supervised
learning methods; however, it can work quite well in many settings. For
example, it is widely used in recommendation algorithms, as we will
discuss in the appropriate chapter. The shortcoming of nonparametric methods is that the higher the dimensionality of data, the sparser
the space becomes, and we then have to look at neighbors that are so
far away from the given point that they do not really predict the dependency between inputs and outputs in the required region. In other
words, the model uses only local observations and cannot generalize
the patterns observed through the data set. This problem can be allevi-
ated by using parametric models, which provide less flexibility because
of the limited number of parameters but which learn these parameters
globally.

2.4.2 Maximum Likelihood Estimation

Model fitting is an optimization problem in its own right, so we need to
specify an objective function that will be optimized. Let us assume that
a set of n samples is drawn independently from the data distribution
$p_{data}(x, y)$. Each data example (x_i, y_i) can be interpreted as the input
x_i that results in the output y_i. The objective function can then be

defined as the probability of the observed response data given that the probability density specified by the parameter vector θ is known:

$$L(\theta) = p_{model}(y \mid X, \theta) \tag{2.16}$$

This function is referred to as the *likelihood function* or, simply, the likelihood. It is the probability of observing the training data under the assumption that these data are drawn from the distribution specified by the model with parameters θ. The logarithm of the likelihood function, often more convenient for analysis and calculations, is known as the log-likelihood $LL(\theta)$. Our goal is to find the parameter vector that maximizes the likelihood of the estimation:

$$\theta_{ML} = \underset{\theta}{\operatorname{argmax}} \ \log p_{model}(y \mid X, \theta) \tag{2.17}$$

By assuming that the examples are independent and identically distributed, we can split the likelihood probability into a product of n probabilities estimated for individual samples:

$$LL(\theta) = \log p_{model}(y \mid X, \theta) = \sum_{i=1}^{n} \log p_{model}(y_i \mid x_i, \theta) \tag{2.18}$$

We can divide the equation by n because the argmax operator is indifferent to rescaling. θ_{ML} is then expressed in terms of mathematical expectation over samples:

$$LL(\theta) = \mathbb{E}_{x,y \sim p_{data}} [\log p_{model}(y \mid x, \theta)] \tag{2.19}$$

Now we can show that the maximum likelihood principle leads us to minimization of the divergence between the data generation distribution and its estimation. The standard measure of divergence between two distributions is the Kullback–Leibler divergence, commonly abbreviated as KL divergence, which is defined as

$$KL(p_{data}, p_{model}) = \mathbb{E}_{x,y \sim p_{data}} \left[\log \frac{p_{data}(y \mid x)}{p_{model}(y \mid x, \theta)} \right] \tag{2.20}$$

As p_{data} does not depend on θ and cannot be the subject of the optimization, we only have to minimize the second term in order to minimize the divergence, which is equivalent to maximization of the log-likelihood defined in equation 2.19:

$$\underset{\theta}{\operatorname{argmin}} \ KL(p_{data}, p_{model}) = \underset{\theta}{\operatorname{argmin}} \ -LL(\theta) \tag{2.21}$$

The maximum likelihood can thus be viewed as optimization of the model parameters such that the model distribution matches the empirical distribution.

2.4.3   *Linear Models*

The maximum likelihood principle provides a common framework that can be used to derive applicable algorithms for the creation of data models. We will now describe how this principle can be used to build several basic but very useful predictive models. We will first look at the regression problem and derive a model that predicts the response y as a continuous linear function of the input x. Next, we will turn to the classification problem and discuss several models that predict a categorical response by fitting a hyperplane that splits the feature space into areas, each of which corresponds to some response class.

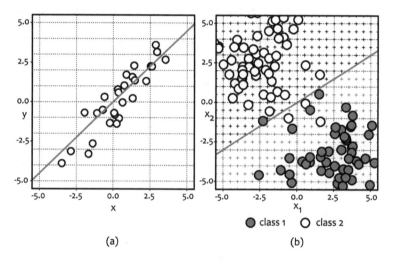

Figure 2.2: (a) Example of linear regression with one-dimensional feature space. (b) Example of classification with a linear decision boundary and two-dimensional feature space. Training points are shown as circles.

All of the models that we will consider are linear. The regression model is linear in the sense that the dependency between the features and response is modeled as a linear function, as shown in Figure 2.2. If the observed dependency is not actually linear, the model may not be accurately fitted to the data. The classification models are linear in the sense that the boundary between the classes is modeled as a hyperplane, so the data are *linearly inseparable*; that is, if the groups of points cannot be accurately separated by a hyperplane, the models may not be properly fitted to the data.

2.4.3.1 *Linear Regression*

The goal of a regression model is to map a continuous input $\mathbf{x}$ to a continuous output y. Linear regression models map this as a linear function of the input:

$$y(\mathbf{x}) = \mathbf{w}^T\mathbf{x} \tag{2.22}$$

in which $\mathbf{w}$ is the vector of model parameters to be learned. Thus, the estimation error will be

$$\epsilon = y - y(\mathbf{x}) = y - \mathbf{w}^T\mathbf{x} \tag{2.23}$$

With the assumption that the error has a normal distribution, the distribution of the estimate produced by the model is also described by a normal distribution, that is, the Gaussian with the mean $\mathbf{w}^T\mathbf{x}$ and the variance σ^2:

$$\begin{aligned}
p(y \mid \mathbf{x}, \, \mathbf{w}) &= \mathcal{N}\left(y \mid \mathbf{w}^T\mathbf{x}, \, \sigma^2\right) \\
&= \left(\frac{1}{2\pi\sigma^2}\right)^{\frac{1}{2}} \exp\left(-\frac{1}{2\sigma^2}\left(y_i - \mathbf{w}^T\mathbf{x}_i\right)^2\right)
\end{aligned} \tag{2.24}$$

By inserting this probability distribution into the definition of the log-likelihood defined in equation 2.18 and doing some algebra, we get the following log-likelihood expression that has to be maximized:

$$\begin{aligned}
LL(\mathbf{w}) &= \sum_{i=1}^{n} \log p(y \mid \mathbf{x}, \, \mathbf{w}) \\
&= \sum_{i=1}^{n} \log \mathcal{N}\left(y \mid \mathbf{w}^T\mathbf{x}_i, \, \sigma^2\right) \\
&= -\frac{1}{2\sigma^2} SSE(\mathbf{w}) - \frac{n}{2}\log(2\pi\sigma^2)
\end{aligned} \tag{2.25}$$

in which SSE is the sum of squared errors, defined as

$$SSE(\mathbf{w}) = \sum_{i=1}^{n}\left(y_i - \mathbf{w}^T\mathbf{x}_i\right)^2 \tag{2.26}$$

It is an intuitive result – maximization of the likelihood is equivalent to minimization of the estimation error. By assuming that the variance is fixed to some constant parameter σ^2 (in the general case, it can also be estimated), we can discard the second term in log-likelihood equation 2.25, so maximization of the log-likelihood can be performed with respect to the SSE only. We first rewrite the likelihood expression in a more compact vector form:

$$LL(\mathbf{w}) = -\frac{1}{2}(\mathbf{y} - \mathbf{X}\mathbf{w})^T(\mathbf{y} - \mathbf{X}\mathbf{w})$$
$$= \mathbf{w}^T(\mathbf{X}^T\mathbf{y}) - \frac{1}{2}\mathbf{w}^T(\mathbf{X}^T\mathbf{X})\mathbf{w} - \frac{1}{2}\mathbf{y}^T\mathbf{y} \qquad (2.27)$$

in which

$$\mathbf{X}^T\mathbf{X} = \sum_{i=1}^{n} x_i x_i^T \quad \text{and} \quad \mathbf{X}^T\mathbf{y} = \sum_{i=1}^{n} x_i y_i \qquad (2.28)$$

and we then take the gradient with respect to $\mathbf{w}$

$$\nabla_{\mathbf{w}}LL(\mathbf{w}) = \mathbf{X}^T\mathbf{y} - \mathbf{X}^T\mathbf{X}\mathbf{w} \qquad (2.29)$$

By equating this gradient to zero and solving the equation for $\mathbf{w}$, we obtain an estimation for the ML-optimal $\mathbf{w}$ in a closed form:

$$\mathbf{w}_{ML} = (\mathbf{X}^T\mathbf{X})^{-1}\mathbf{X}^T\mathbf{y} \qquad (2.30)$$

Linear regression is the most basic method of predictive modeling, but the way we have derived it here is a good illustration of how model fitting can be performed based on the maximum likelihood principle. We will show later that methods that are able to capture nonlinear dependencies can be derived from linear regression.

2.4.3.2 *Logistic Regression and Binary Classification*

The second example we consider is how the maximum likelihood principle can be used to build a binary classification model, that is, a model that maps the input $\mathbf{x}$ to one of two possible classes $y \in \{0, 1\}$. We follow the same path that we used for linear regression and first define the form of the model. The goal is to find a linear decision boundary (hyperplane) that separates two classes at the point where

$$Pr(y = 0 \mid \mathbf{x}) = Pr(y = 1 \mid \mathbf{x}) \qquad (2.31)$$

We can rewrite this equation in a logarithmic form as follows:

$$\log \frac{Pr(y = 0 \mid \mathbf{x})}{Pr(y = 1 \mid \mathbf{x})} = 0 \qquad (2.32)$$

As we are looking for a linear boundary, the boundary hyperplane can be described by a linear function of the input $\mathbf{x}$ with the coefficient vector $\mathbf{w}$:

$$\log \frac{Pr(y = 0 \mid \mathbf{x})}{Pr(y = 1 \mid \mathbf{x})} = \mathbf{w}^T\mathbf{x} \qquad (2.33)$$

This means that we assign the input to class 0 if $\mathbf{w}^T\mathbf{x}$ is positive and to class 1 if $\mathbf{w}^T\mathbf{x}$ is negative. Equation 2.33 is equivalent to

$$Pr(y = 1 \mid \mathbf{x}) = \frac{1}{1 + \exp(-\mathbf{w}^T\mathbf{x})} \equiv g(\mathbf{w}^T\mathbf{x})$$

$$Pr(y = 0 \mid \mathbf{x}) = \frac{\exp(-\mathbf{w}^T\mathbf{x})}{1 + \exp(-\mathbf{w}^T\mathbf{x})} = 1 - g(\mathbf{w}^T\mathbf{x})$$

(2.34)

in which g is known as a *logistic function*. This model is called a logistic regression. Note that this is a *classification* model, despite the confusing name. Next, we have to calculate the log-likelihood for this distribution:

$$\begin{aligned} LL(\mathbf{w}) &= \sum_{i=1}^{n} \log p(y_i \mid x_i) \\ &= \sum_{i=1}^{n} \log g(\mathbf{w}^T x_i)^{y_i} \left(1 - g(\mathbf{w}^T x_i)\right)^{1-y_i} \\ &= \sum_{i=1}^{n} y_i \log g(\mathbf{w}^T x_i) + (1 - y_i) \log \left(1 - g(\mathbf{w}^T x_i)\right) \end{aligned}$$

(2.35)

We can calculate the gradient of this expression, but, unfortunately, we cannot obtain the optimal solution for $\mathbf{w}$ in closed form by equating this gradient to zero and solving the equation with respect to $\mathbf{w}$. So numerical methods, such as gradient descent, should be used to maximize log-likelihood equation 2.35 and estimate the optimal weight $\mathbf{w}_{ML}$.

Logistic regression models the class probabilities by using a logistic function defined by equations 2.34. This function represents an S-curve, also known as a sigmoid curve, with the steepness controlled by parameter $\mathbf{w}$. Examples of logistic functions are shown in Figure 2.3 where two curves are fitted on the data. Note that the decision boundary between the classes, that is, the intersection of the two surfaces, is a straight line. This illustration uses the same data set as our previous example with the kNN classifier in Figure 2.1, so it is interesting to compare the probability surfaces. The surfaces of the kNN classifier have a more complex shape than those of the logistic regression because the kNN algorithm is a nonparametric method. The surfaces fitted by logistic regression have a much more simple shape determined by the logistic curve.

Logistic regression is one of the simplest classification methods that is unable to capture nonlinear boundaries between the classes. It is possible, however, to extend it and other linear methods in such a way that nonlinear decision boundaries can be captured, as we discuss later.

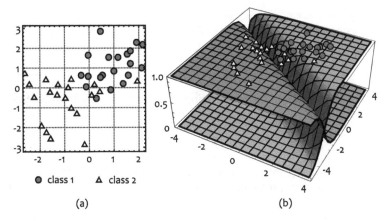

Figure 2.3: Classification of two-dimensional points by using logistic regression. (a) Training data set with two classes of points. (b) Class probabilities estimated as functions of the features according to equation 2.34.

2.4.3.3 *Logistic Regression and Multinomial Classification*

Logistic regression can be straightforwardly extended for cases with multiple classes. As we have multiple classes, we cannot use the convenient relationship

$$\Pr(y = 0 \mid x) = 1 - \Pr(y = 1 \mid x) \tag{2.36}$$

used in the binary case and one linear decision boundary is not sufficient. Instead, we can estimate the probability of each class c separately by using a dedicated coefficient vector $\mathbf{w}_c$. This means that equation 2.33 can be rewritten as follows:

$$\begin{aligned}
\log \Pr(y = 0 \mid x) &= \mathbf{w}_0^\mathsf{T} x - \log Z \\
\log \Pr(y = 1 \mid x) &= \mathbf{w}_1^\mathsf{T} x - \log Z \\
&\vdots \\
\log \Pr(y = c \mid x) &= \mathbf{w}_c^\mathsf{T} x - \log Z
\end{aligned} \tag{2.37}$$

in which $\log Z$ is a normalizing term that ensures that the resulting distribution over y is, in fact, a probability distribution that sums to one. The role of Z becomes more clear when equation 2.37 is written in the exponential form:

$$\Pr(y = c \mid x) = \frac{1}{Z} \exp\left(\mathbf{w}_c^\mathsf{T} x\right) \tag{2.38}$$

The normalizing factor thus scales the probability distribution. We can estimate Z from the fact that all class probabilities must sum up to one

$$\sum_c \Pr(y = c \mid x) = 1 \tag{2.39}$$

and, consequently, the normalizing factor can be found by substituting 2.38 into 2.39:

$$Z = \sum_c \exp\left(w_c^T x\right) \tag{2.40}$$

By substituting this result back into equation 2.38, we obtain a formula for the class probability estimation:

$$\Pr(y = c \mid x) = \frac{\exp\left(w_c^T x\right)}{\sum_i \exp\left(w_i^T x\right)} \tag{2.41}$$

This probability can be used to define the log-likelihood, and the coefficient vectors w_i can then be estimated by using numerical methods such as gradient descent.

It is important to note that resultant equation 2.41 can be interpreted as a generic method for mapping a vector of real values to a vector of class probabilities, regardless of the underlying model that produces these values. To see this, let us assume that some model, not necessarily a linear one, produces a vector of values v, where each value can be interpreted as a relative weight of the corresponding class. These weights are not necessarily normalized as probabilities: values v can be out of the $[0, 1]$ range or may not add up to one. To map these weights to normalized class probabilities, let us define a generic function, commonly known as the softmax function, that repeats equation 2.41 with a vector of real values as a parameter:

$$\text{softmax}(i, v) = \frac{\exp(v_i)}{\sum_j \exp(v_j)} \tag{2.42}$$

The normalized class probabilities can then be acquired by passing the class weights v through the softmax function. We will use this property in the later chapters to construct some predictive models.

2.4.3.4 Naive Bayes Classifier

The last model that we consider in this section is the Naive Bayes classifier. This method is widely used for text classification, so it will be very helpful later in building search and recommendation services. Recall that a classification problem with multiple classes can be defined as

$$\hat{y} = \operatorname*{argmax}_c \Pr(y = c \mid x) \tag{2.43}$$

By applying the Bayes rule to the conditional probability of class c, we get the following equation:

$$Pr(y = c \mid \mathbf{x}) = \frac{Pr(\mathbf{x} \mid y = c)Pr(y = c)}{Pr(\mathbf{x})} \qquad (2.44)$$

The probability of the feature vector in the denominator is the same for all classes, so it can be discarded for a classification problem:

$$\hat{y} = \underset{c}{\operatorname{argmax}} \, Pr(y = c)Pr(\mathbf{x} \mid y = c) \qquad (2.45)$$

The key assumption made by the Naive Bayes classifier is that each feature x_i is conditionally independent of every other feature, given the class c. This means that the probability of observing the feature vector $\mathbf{x}$, given the class c, can be factorized as

$$Pr(\mathbf{x} \mid y = c) = \prod_{i=1}^{m} Pr(x_i \mid y = c) \qquad (2.46)$$

in which m is the length of the feature vector. This assumption, called the *conditional independence assumption*, is rarely true in practical applications, but the Naive Bayes algorithm performs reasonably well in a wide range of such cases. For example, this classifier is successfully used for text classification when each feature is a word, although the words in the text are not independent. This can be explained by the fact that the Naive Bayes algorithm can still be correct if the features are dependent, but the dependencies have a certain structure and cancel each other out [Zhang, 2004]. By using the independence assumption, the classification problem can be rewritten as

$$\hat{y} = \underset{c}{\operatorname{argmax}} \, Pr(y = c) \prod_{i=1}^{m} Pr(x_i \mid y = c) \qquad (2.47)$$

The parameters of this model are the values $Pr(y = c)$ and $Pr(x_i \mid y = c)$. One possible approach to fit the model is to treat these values simply as unknown variables, rather than probabilities, and to maximize the log-likelihood that corresponds to equation 2.47. However, it can be easily shown that this leads to exactly the same results as if we treat the parameters as empirical probabilities. In other words, the maximum likelihood estimate of $\hat{y}$ in expression 2.47 can be obtained if $Pr(y = c)$ is estimated as the frequency of class c in the training data set and $Pr(x_i \mid y = c)$ is estimated as the frequency of samples that belong to class c and have the feature value x_i. This makes it easy to fit the Naive Bayes model in practice.

In the general case, the Naive Bayes classifier is not linear. However, it is linear under certain assumptions that are accurate in many applications, so it is often described as linear. For example, let us consider a case where the distribution $\Pr(\mathbf{x} \mid y = c)$ is assumed to be multinomial. This is a valid assumption, for example, for text classification when each element of the feature vector is a word counter. The probability of a feature vector follows a multinomial distribution with parameter vector $\mathbf{q}_c$

$$\Pr(\mathbf{x} \mid y = c) \propto \prod_{i=1}^{m} q_{ci}^{x_i} \tag{2.48}$$

in which q_{ci} is the probability of the feature value x_i occurring in class c. We can rewrite this expression in the vector form as follows:

$$\log \Pr(\mathbf{x} \mid y = c) = \mathbf{x}^\mathsf{T} \log \mathbf{q}_c + \text{constant} \tag{2.49}$$

We can now show that the decision boundary between the classes is linear by considering the ratio of class probabilities, similarly to the method we used for logistic regression. By assuming only two classes $y \in \{0, 1\}$ for the sake of simplicity, we can write

$$\log \frac{\Pr(y = 1 \mid \mathbf{x})}{\Pr(y = 0 \mid \mathbf{x})} = \log \Pr(y = 1 \mid \mathbf{x}) - \log \Pr(y = 0 \mid \mathbf{x}) \tag{2.50}$$

$$= \mathbf{x}^\mathsf{T} (\log \mathbf{q}_1 - \log \mathbf{q}_0) + \log \Pr(y = 1) - \log \Pr(y = 0)$$

This is a linear function of $\mathbf{x}$, which means that the decision boundary between the classes is linear.

2.4.4   Nonlinear Models

Linear methods can be an appropriate solution for many marketing applications and the power of these methods should not be underestimated, but they can perform poorly on data sets with nonlinear dependencies. We need to develop methods that are able to model more complex distributions. This problem can be approached from different perspectives, and we discuss here two major families of methods that are often used in practice. We will discuss a few more methods, such as neural networks, later in the book in the context of specific application areas.

2.4.4.1   Feature Mapping and Kernel Methods

The linearity or nonlinearity of the regression or classification problems that we are trying to solve reflects the nature of the process that we are modeling, but we should also realize that data representation can contribute to this. For example, two linearly dependent values would not be linearly dependent if one of them was measured on a logarithmic scale. The opposite is also true – data sets that are not tractable for linear methods can be become tractable if mapped to a different space. Consider the example in Figure 2.4: the one-dimensional data set on the left-hand side consists of two classes that are not linearly separable, but the two-dimensional data set constructed from the first one by using the mapping $(x) \rightarrow (x, x^2)$ is linearly separable.

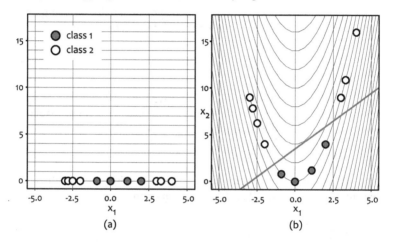

Figure 2.4: Feature mapping by using a quadratic function. (a) Original data points. (b) Mapped data points.

This transformation of the original feature space into another space, typically of higher dimensionality, is referred to as *feature mapping*. It is intuitively clear that the addition of more dimensions, specified as nonlinear functions of one or several existing features, provides more flexibility for a regression or classification algorithm that we are trying to improve. However, we need a method to define the mapping function $\phi(x)$ that produces a new feature vector of higher dimensionality.

The first thing we have to note is that many regression and classification methods can be expressed in terms of distances between the input vector and the training vectors. For example, we have shown that coefficients of linear regression can be calculated as

$$\mathbf{w} = (\mathbf{X}^T\mathbf{X})^{-1}\mathbf{X}^T\mathbf{y} \tag{2.51}$$

We can multiply this expression by the identity matrix $\mathbf{I}$, which can be expressed as

$$\mathbf{I} = \mathbf{X}^T\mathbf{X}(\mathbf{X}^T\mathbf{X})^{-1} \tag{2.52}$$

and, by doing some algebra, we get

$$w = X^T X (X^T X)^{-1} \cdot (X^T X)^{-1} X^T y$$
$$= X^T \cdot a = \sum_{i=1}^{n} a_i x_i \qquad (2.53)$$

in which the vector a is defined as

$$a = X(X^T X)^{-2} X^T y \qquad (2.54)$$

This means that we can estimate the response variable by using only dot products between the input x and training vectors x_i:

$$y(x) = w^T x = \sum_{i=1}^{n} a_i \cdot x^T x_i \qquad (2.55)$$

This is a very important result because we can now avoid the explicit feature mapping and replace it with a *kernel function* that encapsulates computation of the dot product in the mapped space:

$$k(x, z) = \phi(x)^T \phi(z) \qquad (2.56)$$

in which x and z are two feature vectors. Equation 2.55 can then be rewritten purely in terms of the kernel function:

$$y(x) = \sum_{i=1}^{n} a_i k(x, x_i) \qquad (2.57)$$

In other words, we simply modify the distance function between the feature vectors, as opposed to using the dot product in expression 2.55. Thus, the input vectors do not need to be mapped, but the algorithm should be modified to use the kernel function instead of the dot product. The relationship between the kernel function and the mapping function can be illustrated by using a quadratic kernel:

$$k(x, z) = (x^T z)^2 \qquad (2.58)$$

If the original feature space is two dimensional, the kernel expands it into a three-dimensional space that contains both derivatives of the individual features and cross-products of features that can make the data set tractable for linear methods:

$$\begin{aligned}
k(x, z) = (x^T z)^2 &= (x_1 z_1 + x_2 z_2)^2 \\
&= x_1^2 z_1^2 + x_2^2 z_2^2 + 2x_1 x_2 z_1 z_2 \\
&= (x_1^2, \sqrt{2}x_1 x_2, x_2^2)(z_1^2, \sqrt{2}z_1 z_2, z_2^2) \\
&= \phi(x)^T \phi(z)
\end{aligned} \qquad (2.59)$$

in which

$$\phi(\mathbf{x}) = \left\{ x_1^2, \ \sqrt{2}x_1 x_2, \ x_2^2 \right\} \tag{2.60}$$

Note that the kernel is simply a distance function between the original feature vectors, so the underlying expansion of dimensionality is totally hidden; therefore, we can devise kernels that correspond to $\phi(\mathbf{x})$ with a very high or infinite number of dimensions but remain computationally simple. This technique is known as the *kernel trick*, and a number of machine learning methods can be extended this way. Selection of the right kernel can be a challenge, but there are a few kernel functions that are known to be quite universal and are widely used in practice. The choice of the kernel function also depends on the application because it is essentially a measure of similarity between the feature vectors – kernels that work well for consumer profiles might not be the best choice for textual product descriptions, and so on.

Among the best known members of the kernel methods family are support vector machines (SVMs). The basic SVM algorithms are linear classification and regression methods, but they can be efficiently kernalized to learn nonlinear dependencies. Consider the example of an SVM classifier in Figure 2.5. It uses the same data that we used for the nearest neighbor and logistic regression examples earlier, but its decision boundary is clearly nonlinear.

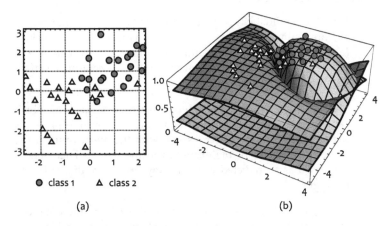

Figure 2.5: Classification of two-dimensional points by using support vector machines with a nonlinear kernel. (a) Training data set with two classes of points. (b) Class probabilities as a function of features.

2.4.4.2   *Adaptive Basis and Decision Trees*

The shortcoming of the kernel method is that the kernel function has to be specified as a parameter instead of being learned. The kernel function imposes limitations on the shape of the decision boundary, and, although we can try several kernels or kernel parameters to find a good fit in practice, we may sometimes be better off by choosing a different approach. We can state the problem of learning a set of q basic functions $\phi_i(x)$ so that the response can be predicted as their weighted composition:

$$y(x) = \sum_{i=1}^{q} w_i \phi_i(x) \tag{2.61}$$

Provided that the basis functions are highly adaptive and nonlinear, we can expect this solution to outperform linear methods in appropriate tasks. One of the most widely used realizations of the adaptive basis concept is classification and regression trees, a family of methods that generate the adaptive basis $\phi_i(x)$ by using a greedy heuristic algorithm. Let us consider the most basic version of this solution.

A classification or regression tree is created by recursive splitting of the feature space into two parts by using a linear decision boundary, as illustrated in Figure 2.6. In each step of the recursion, the decision boundary can be selected as follows:

- First, the candidate hyperplanes that can be chosen as the boundary are enumerated. One possible way is to try all dimensions (e. g., we can split by using either a horizontal or vertical line in Figure 2.6) and, for each dimension, to try the coordinates of all data points in the training set.

- The candidate boundary produces two regions, each of which can be labeled with the most frequent class of examples in this region or, in the case of regression, with the mean value of the response variables of the examples in the region. This label is then used as a predicted value for any data point that falls into the region.

- The region label is used to score the quality of the candidate split by the misclassification rate (the ratio between the number of incorrectly and correctly classified training examples in the region) or another metric. The boundary is selected as the candidate with the highest score.

Once the boundary is selected, the algorithm is recursively applied to the regions on both sides of the boundary. This algorithm produces

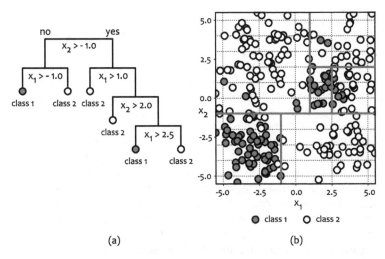

(a)   (b)

Figure 2.6: Example of a classification tree. (a) Classification tree model. (b) Training data and decision boundaries that correspond to the tree.

a set of labeled rectangular regions R_i that can be considered as an adaptive basis. To see this, we can rewrite equation 2.61 in terms of the regions as

$$y(\mathbf{x}) = \sum_{i=1}^{q} w_i \mathbb{I} (\mathbf{x} \in R_i) \tag{2.62}$$

in which w_i is the region label and $\mathbb{I}$ is either 1 or 0, depending on whether $\mathbf{x}$ falls into the corresponding region or not. Decision trees and more complex derivatives of this approach, such as *random forests*, provide a powerful and widely used regression and classification solution.

2.5 REPRESENTATION LEARNING

The supervised learning methods we have just discussed help to describe the dependency between the input independent variables and the response variable. The input variables, however, can have an entangled structure and redundancies that complicate data exploration and model training. We can attempt to find a different representation of the data that better suits the modeling purposes by removing redundancies and correlations, that is, by disentangling the original data.

Machine learning methods are typically categorized as *supervised* and *unsupervised*. Supervised methods are concerned with dependencies between the input variables and responses, that is, conditional probability densities $p(y \mid x)$. The goal of unsupervised methods is to learn the structure or patterns in the input data, that is, to model the unconditional density $p(x)$. Unsupervised learning makes no assumptions about response variables to guide the model training and analyzes only the design matrix to find the dependencies between the features or samples. A canonical example of unsupervised learning is clustering, which can be defined as the grouping of data samples into clusters such that the samples in one cluster are similar to each other and samples from different clusters are dissimilar – this task does not require response variables but relies on a sample similarity measure. Unsupervised learning is widely used in marketing applications for data exploration and analysis. Clustering of customer profiles and interpretation of the obtained results, for example, is one of the most important techniques in marketing analytics. In programmatic applications, however, we are more concerned with automation than with exploration and interactive analysis. Representation learning is one application of unsupervised learning methods that can be useful in this context, so we are focusing here specifically on representation learning aspects, rather than unsupervised learning in general.

2.5.1   Principal Component Analysis

Principal component analysis (PCA) is a powerful technique for finding a condensed uncorrelated data representation. PCA is a mathematical method that transforms the data into a new presentation that guarantees certain properties and also produces artifacts that describe the structure of the data. We may be interested in different properties of the PCA transformation, depending on the application, so we will discuss these properties sequentially in the next sections, although it is important to keep in mind that all of them are based on the same algorithm.

2.5.1.1   Decorrelation

In marketing applications, the data typically correspond to the observed inputs, properties, and outputs of some real-world marketing process. Examples of such processes include marketing campaigns, interactions between customers and products, and the interplay of price and demand, among many others. Each feature in the design matrix can be viewed as a signal that carries the information about the process. We do not have complete knowledge of the process and observe only certain *projections* of the process on the feature dimensions that are available in the input data, just as a physical object can be photographed by cameras from different perspectives. For example, one does not observe consumer tastes and thoughts directly but captures certain signals, like purchases, that partially reflect the tastes, thoughts, and decisions. Representations obtained this way are likely to have some redundancy, and dimensions are likely to be correlated, just as images of the same object from different perspectives are redundant and correlated. This idea is illustrated in Figure 2.7.

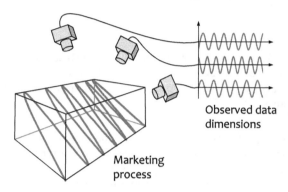

Figure 2.7: Different data dimensions can be correlated because they are projections of the same real-life process.

We can pose the problem of finding a new, potentially smaller, set of features that are statistically independent and, consequently, provide a less redundant and more structured data representation. PCA can be applied to this problem under the assumption that the statistical independence of features can be replaced by zero correlation, which may or may not be true, depending on the data distribution. This is a restrictive assumption because the feature values have to be jointly normally distributed to ensure statistical independence with zero correlation. If the distribution is different, the PCA may fail to achieve the decorrelation goal (but can still be useful because of other properties). Let us consider an $n \times m$ design matrix $\mathbf{X}$, in which n is the number of samples and m is the number of features. We also assume that the data are centered, that is, $\mathbb{E}[\mathbf{x}] = 0$. If this is not the case, we can subtract the mean from all data samples. The decorrelation problem can then be defined in terms of the covariance matrix $\mathbf{C}$:

$$\mathbf{C_X} = \text{Var}[\mathbf{x}] = \frac{1}{n-1}\mathbf{X}^\mathsf{T}\mathbf{X} \tag{2.63}$$

This is a square symmetric $m \times m$ matrix in which the diagonal elements are the variance of the corresponding features and the off-diagonal elements are the covariance between the features. The features are decorrelated if the covariance matrix is diagonal, that is, all off-diagonal elements in $\mathbf{C}$ are zeros. If the covariance matrix is not diagonal, the features are correlated, which makes it more difficult to understand the distribution of x because it cannot be described in terms of distributions of individual features. Our next step is to find the transformation of X that produces a different $n \times m$ design matrix Z in which the covariance matrix is diagonal. In the PCA approach, we make an assumption that this matrix can be obtained by using a linear transformation

$$Z = XT \tag{2.64}$$

in which T is the transformation matrix. To construct this matrix, let us first show how the design matrix can be factorized on the basis of vectors that correspond to the directions of maximum variance in the design matrix.

The first step of factorization is to find the directions of maximum variance in the data. These directions can be thought of as the main axes of the point cloud in a scatter plot, as illustrated in Figure 2.8. Each of these directions can be defined as a vector, so we start by finding an m-dimensional unit vector that satisfies the following condition:

$$v_1 = \operatorname*{argmax}_v \|Xv\|^2, \qquad \|v\| = 1 \tag{2.65}$$

This vector corresponds to the axis with maximum variance. Next, we find a second unit vector that is orthogonal to the first one to capture the remaining variance:

$$v_2 = \operatorname*{argmax}_v \|Xv\|^2, \qquad \|v\| = 1 \text{ and } v \cdot v_1 = 0 \tag{2.66}$$

We continue this process by requiring each vector to be orthogonal to all previous ones, and, assuming that the design matrix has rank r, we can create as many as r non-zero vectors v. By construction, each vector corresponds to the axis with maximum remaining variance in the design matrix. These vectors are referred to as the *principal components* of the design matrix.

Let us denote an $m \times r$ matrix assembled from column vectors v as V. As all of the unit vectors that we have constructed are orthogonal, this matrix is column-orthonormal, that is

$$V^T V = I \tag{2.67}$$

Unit vectors v capture the directions of the variance but not its magnitude. Let us calculate these values separately and denote them as

$$\sigma_i = \|Xv_i\| \tag{2.68}$$

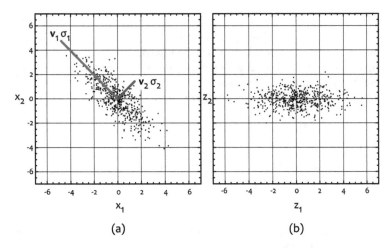

Figure 2.8: Example of principal component analysis. (a) A data set of 500 normally distributed points and the corresponding principal components. Features x_1 and x_2 are strongly correlated. (b) A decorrelated
representation obtained by using PCA. Features z_1 and z_2 are not
correlated.

Each principal component captures only the *remaining* variance, so the
value of σ is biggest for the first component and then decreases, in the
order

$$\sigma_1 \geqslant \sigma_2 \geqslant \ldots \geqslant \sigma_r \tag{2.69}$$

Let us denote an $r \times r$ diagonal matrix with the σ values on the main
diagonal as

$$\Sigma = \mathrm{diag}(\sigma_1, \ldots, \sigma_r) \tag{2.70}$$

At this point, we have an orthonormal basis of vectors $\mathbf{V}$ and the
corresponding scaling factors Σ. To complete the factorization of the
design matrix, we need a third factor that projects the design matrix
onto the principal component basis or, alternatively, mixes the basis
into the design matrix. By denoting this factor as $\mathbf{U}$, we can define the
decomposition as

$$\mathbf{X} = \mathbf{U}\Sigma\mathbf{V}^\top \tag{2.71}$$

for which $\mathbf{U}$ can be obtained by solving equation 2.71 with respect to
this factor:

$$\mathbf{U} = \mathbf{X}\mathbf{V}\Sigma^{-1} \tag{2.72}$$

The decomposition defined by equation 2.71 is known as the singular value decomposition (SVD). To summarize, the principal component, that is, the columns of matrix V, can be interpreted as orthogonal principal axes that are aligned with the directions of variance. The columns of $U\Sigma$ can be interpreted as coefficients that mix the principal vectors to produce X. It can also be shown that matrix U is column-orthonormal:

$$U^T U = I \qquad (2.73)$$

Once the SVD of the design matrix is obtained, we can use the factors to find the decorrelating linear transformation T. Let us consider the product

$$Z = XV \qquad (2.74)$$

and calculate its covariance matrix by using the fact that matrices V and U are orthogonal:

$$
\begin{aligned}
C_Z &= \frac{1}{n-1} Z^T Z \\
&= \frac{1}{n-1} V^T X^T X V \\
&= \frac{1}{n-1} V^T V \Sigma^2 V^T V \\
&= \frac{1}{n-1} \Sigma^2
\end{aligned}
\qquad (2.75)
$$

As Σ^2 is diagonal, the representation Z is uncorrelated. This means that the decorrelating transformation we were looking for is actually given by matrix V. This transformation is effectively a rotation because the matrix of principal components is orthonormal. Note that the assumption about the linearity of the transformation is quite restrictive. In the example provided in Figure 2.8, it works well because the data set has an elliptical shape, which is the result of the normal distribution; therefore, the correlation between features can be removed by simple rotation. This may not be the case for data sets with more complex shapes.

2.5.1.2 Dimensionality Reduction

The key property of PCA is that the principal vectors are sorted by the variance magnitude. This property is important because one can argue that high-variance dimensions in the data are typically more informative and carry a stronger signal than low-variance dimensions. For example, we can say that axes x_1 and x_2 in Figure 2.8 are equally important and the one-dimensional representations obtained by projecting the data points on x_1 or x_2 are not good approximations of the original two-dimensional representation. At the same time, dimensions z_1 and z_2 of the decorrelated data set obtained by using the PCA transformation are not equally important and dimension z_2 can be discarded with a relatively small loss of information.

This property can be used in several ways. The first application is dimensionality reduction, in which the m-dimensional data set X needs to be reduced to a k-dimensional data set and $k < m$. In the case of PCA, this reduction can be done by using a truncated matrix V_k that includes only the first k principal component vectors and calculating a new data representation as

$$Z_k = XV_k \tag{2.76}$$

Matrix Z_k has only k columns, which correspond to the first principal axes. This approach is often used for data visualization to project a multidimensional data set to a two- or three-dimensional space that can be shown on a plot.

The second important application is *low-rank approximation* of the design matrix. Consider the SVD given by expression 2.71. Similarly to dimensionality reduction, we can remove the least significant columns of matrix V to create the truncated version V_k. The factors U and Σ then also need to be cropped to remove the columns and rows that correspond to the least significant components, as shown in Figure 2.9. Let us denote these truncated versions as U_k and Σ_k, respectively. The design matrix X can then be approximated from the product of these truncated factors:

$$\hat{X}_k = U_k \Sigma_k V_k \tag{2.77}$$

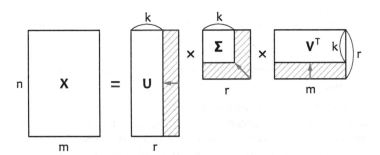

Figure 2.9: Dimensionality reduction by removing axes with low variance.

The reconstructed matrix $\hat{X}$ is of the same size as X, but, of course, has some approximation error because of the discarded dimensions.

This error is smallest if we discard only the least significant dimension and increases as we remove more columns from the SVD factors. In fact, it can be shown that this method of matrix approximation is optimal, in the sense that the reconstructed matrix has the smallest possible approximation error, given the constraint that the ranks of factors cannot exceed k. In other words, expression 2.77 is a solution of the following optimization problem:

$$\min_{\mathbf{A}} \quad \|\mathbf{X} - \mathbf{A}\|$$
$$\text{subject to} \quad \text{rank}(\mathbf{A}) \leqslant k \tag{2.78}$$

Low-rank approximation is useful in marketing applications, especially in searches and recommendations, because it can help to deal with sparse, noisy, and redundant data sets. This is often the case for data sets that describe the interactions between two entities. For example:

- The design matrix can capture the interactions between customers and products. Each row of the matrix corresponds to a customer, each column represents a product, and each element is some interaction metric, such as the number of purchases. In practice, this matrix is likely to be very sparse because each user purchases only a small fraction of the available products. The data is also highly correlated because many products are similar to each other and many customers have similar shopping habits.

- In search applications, texts such as product descriptions are often modeled as vectors with each element corresponding to a word; hence, the length of the vector is equal to the total number of distinct words in the vocabulary. A collection of texts can then be represented as a matrix in which each row corresponds to a text document and each column corresponds to a word. This matrix can be sparse, especially for short texts, and redundant because words with related semantic meaning frequently appear together.

In the examples above, each element x_{ij} of the design matrix is some measure of affinity between the entities, such as the affinity between a customer and product or between a word and document. However, the raw affinity values in the design matrix are often noisy and incomplete. How can we create a smoother affinity model that predicts the affinity for any pair of entities? One possible approach is to model the affinity as a dot product of two vectors

$$\widehat{x}_{ij} = \mathbf{p}_i \cdot \mathbf{q}_j^{\mathsf{T}} \tag{2.79}$$

in which the first entity (e. g., the customer) is somehow mapped to numerical vector $\mathbf{p}$ and the second entity (e. g., the product) to numerical vector $\mathbf{q}$. The length of vectors k is typically chosen to be much smaller than the size of the design matrix. By rewriting this expression in matrix form as

$$\hat{X} = \mathbf{P} \cdot \mathbf{Q}^{\mathsf{T}} \tag{2.80}$$

we can see that the vectors $\mathbf{p}$ and $\mathbf{q}$, which minimize the average affinity approximation error, can actually be obtained from the low-rank approximation expression 2.77 as

$$\begin{aligned} \mathbf{P} &= \mathbf{U}_k \mathbf{\Sigma}_k \\ \mathbf{Q} &= \mathbf{V}_k \end{aligned} \tag{2.81}$$

This result is very useful because it helps to convert sparse and redundant representations of entities into compact and dense numerical vectors. It is a very powerful and generic modeling technique, which will be extensively used in the following chapters.

2.5.2 Clustering

Clustering is a process of grouping similar items together. Alternatively, it can be thought of as splitting of the data set into *clusters* in such a way that data points inside one cluster have high similarity and points that belong to different clusters have low similarity.

In traditional marketing applications, the most important usage of clustering is exploratory data analysis. Clustering can partition a data set into a relatively small number of clusters, and each cluster can then be described, interpreted, and studied as one entity. A canonical example is customer *segmentation*, where a large number of customer profiles can be divided into a few clusters or segments based on a similarity metric that accounts for demographic properties, behavior, and shopping habits. Each segment can then be described based on its geometric center in the profile vector space (average profile) and the spread of feature values, so a typical cluster description may look like *price-sensitive customers under 30 who are engaged primarily through digital channels*. Thus, segmentation allows a large data set to be summarized into a few points that are tractable for manual analysis. Segmentation projects are among the largest and most strategic projects in marketing analytics because a large part of the corporate marketing strategy can be built around customer segments and their typical needs and properties.

Programmatic applications, which are more focused on execution than strategic analysis, often consume the outputs of segmentation as additional features. For example, a customer profile vector that contains values such as age, income, and average monthly spending can be extended with segment labels that describe the person as a *bargain-hunter, brand-loyal fashionista*, and so on. These additional features can then be used in predictive modeling, like any other features, to improve the prediction accuracy and interpretability of the results. From this standpoint, clustering can be viewed as a feature-engineering method.

Clustering can also be applied to entities that are used as features in modeling of other entities. In online advertising, for example, user profiles typically include the URLs visited by the user in the past, so the profile data may look like

$$\text{user 1}: \quad (\text{url}_1,\ \text{url}_2,\ \text{url}_3,\ \dots)$$
$$\text{user 2}: \quad (\text{url}_4,\ \text{url}_5,\ \text{url}_6,\ \dots)$$

This representation can be extremely sparse because the number of distinct URLs is extremely high. Consequently, it can easily be the case that user profiles have no or very few URLs in common, so a model that uses this profile representation as a feature cannot accurately fit on the data. Each URL, however, can also be associated with a vector of attributes, such as the domain name and related web sites, and a clustering algorithm can then be applied to group URLs into categories. The categories produced by the clustering algorithm can have some semantic meaning. For example, one cluster of URLs may mainly correspond to sport-related resources, whereas another cluster may correspond to technology-related resources. The URLs in the user profiles can then be mapped to the clusters, so the profiles can be expressed in terms of behavioral features:

$$\text{user 1}: \quad (\text{sport, fashion, technology}, \dots)$$
$$\text{user 2}: \quad (\text{news, fashion, sport}, \dots)$$

With the assumption that the number of clusters is much smaller than the number of URLs, this representation is much denser, and many profiles have common cluster labels. This usage of clustering is pure representation learning that aims to find a convenient set of features, and it is substantially different from the exploratory analysis applications.

Clustering is an inherently challenging problem because learning is unsupervised, and, consequently, the optimization objective cannot be unambiguously defined. There exist several families of clustering algorithms that take different perspectives on this issue. One of the approaches is to consider clustering as a model fitting problem: because our goal is to group similar items together, we can assume that each group is produced by some random but unknown process, and we can fit a *mixture* of distributions that is likely (in the sense of the maximum likelihood principle) to generate the observed data set. This approach is illustrated in Figure 2.10, where the clusters are determined by fitting the mixture of three normal distributions on the data.

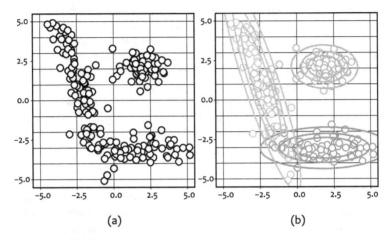

(a)   (b)

Figure 2.10: Example of clustering by using the mixture modeling approach. (a) Input data set. (b) Three clusters found by fitting a mixture of three normal distributions.

This model can be specified as follows:

$$p(\mathbf{x}) = \sum_{k=1}^{K} w_k \mathcal{N}(\mathbf{x} \mid \mu_k; \Sigma_k) \tag{2.82}$$

in which K is the number of clusters, w_k are the mixing weights, and μ_k and Σ_k are the means and covariance matrices of the distributions in the mixture, respectively (note that the normal distribution is just one possible option and one can use a mixture of other distributions as well). Given that the parameters of the distributions are estimated, we can easily assign each data point to the corresponding cluster based on the probability densities at this point. The opposite is also true – given that the cluster assignments are known, we can easily estimate the parameters of each distribution in the mixture. The challenge, however, is that we do not know either the cluster mappings or the parameters of the distributions; we only know the raw data points. This leads to complex likelihood functions that are much more difficult to compute than the likelihoods we have discussed in the previous sections. However, there exist a number of iterative methods that can find an approximate solution. The most widely used include the expectation-maximization (EM) and K-means algorithms.

2.6 MORE SPECIALIZED MODELS

Standard supervised and unsupervised learning methods address the most typical modeling needs that arise in marketing applications. Many marketing concerns can be translated into such standard predictive modeling problems in a relatively straightforward way. Other marketing problems, however, may need more specialized data analysis techniques or complex economic models that bridge the business objective and basic primitives of predictive modeling. Some of these methods were originally developed in economics, others in game theory, biology, and the social sciences. In this section, we describe several specialized models and methods that extend the toolkit of standard machine learning techniques.

2.6.1 *Consumer Choice Theory*

The understanding and prediction of consumer choice is one of the most fundamental problems in marketing, as well as economics in general, because many important questions related to product design, assortment planning, and distribution cannot be answered if the demand is not well understood. In this section, we consider the discrete choice problem, that is, the situation when a decision-maker faces a choice among a set of alternatives. For example, a consumer decides which of several competing products to buy, whether to cancel their subscription to a certain service or not, and so on. We can assume that the decision-maker compares the options in a consistent way (if option k is preferable to option m and option m is preferable to n, then k is preferable to n) and chooses the most preferable one, so it is valid to introduce a virtual numerical metric that is proportional to the *utility* of a given option to the decision-maker.

Let us denote the utility that decision-maker n obtains by choosing option j from the alternatives $(1, \ldots, J)$ as Y_{nj}. The decision-maker chooses option Y_{nj} among the other options if $Y_{nj} > Y_{ni}$ for all cases in which $i \neq j$. The utility of the same alternative j is not necessarily equal for all decision-makers because of differences in tastes, income, and other properties between individuals.

A model of consumer choice can be created by using the known properties of the individual and the alternatives. However, each decision-maker is likely to have additional considerations that influence their choice that cannot be observed by the model creator. More formally, we can state that utility Y_{nj} is a function of known factors x_{nj} and unobserved factors h_{nj}:

$$Y_{nj} = Y(x_{nj}, h_{nj}) \tag{2.83}$$

The hidden factors $\mathbf{h}_{nj}$ are known to the decision-maker but not to the model creator, so the utility model $V_{nj} = V(\mathbf{x}_{nj})$ approximates the true utility Y_{nj} with some error ε_{nj} that can be considered as a random variable:

$$Y_{nj} = V_{nj} + \varepsilon_{nj} \tag{2.84}$$

This approach to utility analysis is known as the *random utility model*. Definition 2.84 allows us to express the probability of choosing alternative j by decision-maker n as

$$\begin{aligned} P_{ni} &= \Pr\left(Y_{ni} > Y_{nj}, \forall j \neq i\right) \\ &= \Pr\left(V_{ni} + \varepsilon_{ni} > V_{nj} + \varepsilon_{nj}, \forall j \neq i\right) \end{aligned} \tag{2.85}$$

Let us denote the random vector of errors as

$$\varepsilon_n = (\varepsilon_{n1}, \dots, \varepsilon_{nJ}) \tag{2.86}$$

By assuming that the distribution of ε_n is known, we can evaluate the choice probability by integrating over the probability density $p(\varepsilon_n)$:

$$P_{nj} = \int_\varepsilon \mathbb{I}\left(V_{ni} + \varepsilon_{ni} > V_{nj} + \varepsilon_{nj}, \forall j \neq i\right) p(\varepsilon_n)\, d\varepsilon_n \tag{2.87}$$

in which $\mathbb{I}$ is the indicator function that equals 1 when the argument is true and 0 otherwise. We do not need to make any specific assumptions regarding model V to evaluate expression 2.87 – we are free to choose any linear or nonlinear function of known factors $\mathbf{x}_{nj}$ to estimate the utility. However, for practicality, we have to make certain assumptions regarding distribution $p(\varepsilon_n)$ in order to make the evaluation of P_{nj} tractable.

Different assumptions about residual errors ε_n lead to different choice models with distinct strengths and limitations. The ultimate goal is to find a computationally tractable formula that expresses P_{nj} as a function of V_{nj}, which, in turn, is a function of the observed properties $\mathbf{x}_{nj}$ and some parameters $\mathbf{w}$. For example, it can be a linear model:

$$V_{nj} = \mathbf{w}^\mathsf{T}\mathbf{x}_{nj} \tag{2.88}$$

As P_{nj} can typically be estimated from the known statistics for alternatives that were available in the past, the parameters $\mathbf{w}$ can also be estimated and a prediction model for P_{nj} can be built. This model can be used to evaluate new alternatives specified in terms of properties $\mathbf{x}$, and, consequently, economic metrics like demand for a new product can be predicted. In the next section, we discuss one of the most simple yet powerful and practical models, multinomial logit, to show how computationally tractable expressions for P_{nj} can be obtained. This model will be used in the subsequent chapters as a component of more complex models that are created for specific marketing problems.

2.6.1.1 *Multinomial Logit Model*

The multinomial logit model, commonly abbreviated as the MNL model, can be derived from the random utility model by assuming that the residual errors ε_{nj} are independent and follow a Gumbel distribution. The assumption about the Gumbel distribution leads to a convenient model and can also be considered as a practical approximation of the normal distribution [Train, 2003]. The assumption about independent distributions is much more restrictive and leads to limitations that will be discussed later in this section. In general, the Gumbel distribution is used to describe the distribution of the maximum or minimum value of a number of random samples drawn from some underlying distribution. For example, if one generates batches of random numbers by drawing them from the normal distribution and then takes the maximum value in each batch, the distribution of these maximums can be modeled by using the Gumbel distribution. It is useful in applications that deal with extreme events, such as earthquakes, manufacturing defects, and equipment failures. A drug manufacturer that produces oral drug tablets in batches, for instance, can use the Gumbel distribution to model the probability of producing a batch where the level of active chemical components is higher than the maximum acceptable level. The probability density for the Gumbel distribution is defined as

$$p(\varepsilon_{nj}) = e^{-\varepsilon_{nj}} \exp(-e^{-\varepsilon_{nj}}) \tag{2.89}$$

and the cumulative distribution is given by

$$F(\varepsilon_{nj}) = \exp(-e^{-\varepsilon_{nj}}) \tag{2.90}$$

To take advantage of the assumption that the residual errors follow the Gumbel distribution, let us first rewrite the choice probability given by equation 2.85 as follows:

$$\begin{aligned}
P_{ni} &= \Pr(V_{ni} + \varepsilon_{ni} > V_{nj} + \varepsilon_{nj}, \ \forall j \neq i) \\
&= \Pr(\varepsilon_{nj} < \varepsilon_{ni} + V_{ni} - V_{nj}, \ \forall j \neq i)
\end{aligned} \tag{2.91}$$

By assuming for a moment that ε_{ni} is given and by using the independence of errors, we can state that

$$P_{ni} \mid \varepsilon_{ni} = \prod_{j \neq i} \Pr(\varepsilon_{nj} < \varepsilon_{ni} + V_{ni} - V_{nj}) \tag{2.92}$$

The terms on the right-hand side are effectively cumulative distributions of ε_{nj}, so by inserting the definition of the Gumbel distribution given by equation 2.90, we get the following:

$$P_{ni} \mid \varepsilon_{ni} = \prod_{j \neq i} \exp\left(-e^{-(\varepsilon_{ni}+V_{ni}-V_{nj})}\right) \tag{2.93}$$

As ε_{ni} is not actually given, we need to integrate over its probability density to obtain a complete expression for P_{ni}:

$$P_{ni} = \int_{\varepsilon} (P_{ni} \mid \varepsilon_{ni}) \cdot e^{-\varepsilon_{ni}} \exp(-e^{-\varepsilon_{ni}}) d\varepsilon_{ni} \tag{2.94}$$

A concise closed-form expression for the choice probability can be obtained directly from the equation above by means of algebraic transformations that we skip here for the sake of brevity; the result is a canonical formula for the MNL model:

$$P_{ni} = \frac{e^{V_{ni}}}{\sum_j e^{V_{nj}}} \tag{2.95}$$

The model given by equation 2.95 has several important properties and implications:

INDEPENDENCE OF IRRELEVANT ALTERNATIVES One of the most important questions that should be answered by choice modeling is how changes in the utility of one alternative influence other alternatives. For example, a product manufacturer may be interested in estimating the share of consumers that can be drawn away from competitors by reducing the product price or launching a new product. The MNL model implies that an increase or decrease in the probability of one alternative will evenly affect all other alternatives. To see this, consider the ratio of any two probabilities:

$$\frac{P_{ni}}{P_{nj}} = \frac{e^{V_{ni}}/\sum_k e^{V_{nk}}}{e^{V_{nj}}/\sum_k e^{V_{nk}}} = \frac{e^{V_{ni}}}{e^{V_{nj}}} = e^{V_{ni}-V_{nj}} \tag{2.96}$$

The ratio of probabilities depends only on the ratio of the corresponding utilities, a property commonly referred to as *independence of irrelevant alternatives*; if the utility V_{ni} changes, the pairwise ratios for all other pairs P_{np}/P_{nq} remain constant. This property of MNL is somewhat restrictive because products within a group of interest are not always perfectly substitutable and more complex substitution patterns can take place. This limitation can be illustrated by the following paradox [Debreu, 1960].

Consider a transportation system where a consumer chooses between a car and a bus and where the initial choice probabilities are equal:

$$P_{car} = P_{bus} = 1/2 \qquad (2.97)$$

Suppose now that a second bus is introduced, and it is identical to the first bus. Let's say that the only difference is the color: the first one is red and the second one is blue. The MNL model will evenly redistribute the probabilities to produce

$$P_{car} = P_{red\,bus} = P_{blue\,bus} = 1/3 \qquad (2.98)$$

because the utilities are equal for both buses. A more realistic assumption, however, is that the ratio

$$P_{car}/(P_{red\,bus} + P_{blue\,bus} + \ldots) \qquad (2.99)$$

will remain constant no matter how many identical buses are offered, which produces the probabilities $P_{car} = 1/2$ and $P_{red\,bus} = P_{blue\,bus} = 1/4$.

COMPLETENESS OF THE UTILITY MODEL The independence of the residual errors ε_{ni} implies that the utility model V_{ni} should capture all factors that influence the choice. If model V_{ni} is not complete, some systematic biases start to leak into the error components and violate the independence assumption. For example, we can build a utility model for a washing machine by using the price p and energy consumption c as predictive variables, so $V_{ni} = w_1 p_i + w_2 s_i$. However, the choice is likely to depend on the consumer's income g, which might not be known, so the utility will actually be

$$Y_{ni} = w_1 p_i + w_2 s_i + w_3 g_n + \varepsilon_{ni} = V_{ni} + \varepsilon_{ni}^* \qquad (2.100)$$

in which $\varepsilon_{ni}^* = w_3 g_n + \varepsilon_{ni}$ and represents the errors that are not independent because of the random variable g_n.

MARGINAL CHOICE PROBABILITY The choice probability is a sigmoid function of utility V_{ni}, as shown in Figure 2.11. This means that small changes in the utility cause a substantial increase or decrease in the probability that the corresponding alternative will be chosen only if the probability is close to 0.5, that is, if the decision-maker is in a marginal state. If the probability of the choice of a certain alternative is low or high, then even major changes in the utility have limited impact on the probability.

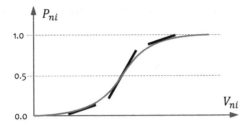

Figure 2.11: Probability of choice as a function of the utility and its derivatives at different points.

This S-shaped dependency between V_{ni} and P_{ni} suggests that investment should be focused on the development of alternatives with intermediate probability of selection by the majority of decision-makers. For example, an online retailer that is improving its order delivery network can expect the highest return on investments by improving the service in the areas where it already has average market share, whereas areas with very low or very high shares are likely to be less responsive to improved services.

2.6.1.2   Estimation of the Multinomial Logit Model

Let us now describe how the parameters of the utility model V_{ni} can be estimated from training data samples. Let us assume that we know features x_{ni} that are included in the utility model for some subset of decision-makers $n = 1, \ldots, N$ and each alternative $i = 1, \ldots, J$, as well as the actual choices made. Let $y_{ni} \in \{0, 1\}$ be the observed choice of decision-maker n with respect to alternative i; this equals 1 if the decision-maker has chosen this alternative and 0 otherwise. Under the assumption of independent residual errors, we can express the probability of the choice that was actually made by the decision-maker as

$$\prod_i (P_{ni})^{y_{ni}} \tag{2.101}$$

The probability that all decision-makers in the data set made their choices as we actually observe, that is, the likelihood of the data set, can then be expressed as

$$L(\mathbf{w}) = \prod_{n=1}^{N} \prod_i (P_{ni})^{y_{ni}} \tag{2.102}$$

under the assumption that all decisions are independent. Consequently, the log-likelihood will be

$$LL(\mathbf{w}) = \sum_{n=1}^{N} \sum_{i} y_{ni} \log(P_{ni})$$
$$= \sum_{n=1}^{N} \sum_{i} y_{ni} \log \frac{e^{V_{ni}}}{\sum_{k} e^{V_{nk}}}$$

(2.103)

in which V_{ni} is a function of $\mathbf{w}$ and $\mathbf{x}$, for example, a linear model $V_{ni} = \mathbf{w}^T \mathbf{x}_{ni}$. The log-likelihood described by equation 2.103 can further be estimated by taking the gradient with regard to $\mathbf{w}$ and applying numerical optimization methods.

2.6.2   Survival Analysis

Classification methods, even the most basic ones such as logistic regressions, provide a powerful toolkit for estimating the probabilities of consumer actions. For example, the response probability for a promotional email can be estimated by building a model that uses customer attributes, such as the number of purchases, as features and a binary variable that indicates whether a customer responded to the previous promotional email as a response label. Although this approach is widely used in practice, as we will discuss in detail in subsequent chapters, it has a few shortcomings. First, in many marketing applications, it is more convenient and efficient to estimate the time until an event, instead of the event probability. For example, it can be more useful for a marketing system to estimate the time until the next purchase or time until subscription cancellation, rather than the probabilities of these events. Second, marketing data very often include records with unknown or missed outcomes, which cannot be properly accounted for in classification models. Going back to the example with the subscription cancellation, it is often impossible to distinguish between customers who have not defected and those who have not defected *yet* because we build a predictive model at a certain point in time and cannot wait indefinitely until the final outcomes for all customers are observed. Consequently, we only know the outcomes for customers who have defected and can certainly label them as negative samples; the remaining records are incomplete but those customers will not necessarily not defect in the future, so one can argue that labeling these samples as positives or negatives is not really valid. This suggests that it is not accurate to use a classification model with a binary outcome variable determined on the basis of currently observed outcomes and we might need a different statistical framework to deal with this sort of problem.

A comprehensive framework for time-to-event modeling and incomplete data handling was originally developed for medical and biological studies. The main focus of the studies was the survival of individuals after medical treatment, so the framework became known as survival analysis. Let us describe the main methods of this framework by starting with the basic terminology. The main goal of survival analysis is to predict the time to an event of interest and quantitatively explain how this time depends on the properties of the treatment, individuals, and other independent variables. In marketing applications, the treatment is typically an incentive or trigger, such as a promotion. An event is typically a purchase, promotion redemption, subscription cancellation, or any other customer action that a marketer might be interested in influencing. Note that a positive outcome of the treatment can be either acceleration or deceleration of the event, depending on the application. Advertisements, for example, aim to stimulate earlier purchases; meanwhile, retention offers aim to suppress subscription cancellation events. By contrast, medical research typically measures the time from diagnosis to death, so the standard terminology of survival analysis assumes that the event corresponds to some negative outcome, which can be confusing when the opposite is the case.

As we discussed earlier, some events may be unknown, in the sense that the outcomes have not been observed at the time of study. These unknown outcomes can occur because the outcome is not known by the time of the analysis (the customer has not yet purchased but may still purchase in the future) or the customer record has been lost (for example, because of a browser cookie expiration). The records with unknown outcomes are referred to as *censored* records. By the time of the analysis, we initially have a set of observations, each of which has the time of the treatment and, optionally, the time of the event of interest, as shown in Figure 2.12.

The time between the treatment and event is referred to as the *survival time*. We can transform the original observations to align all of the treatment times, so the observed data for k individuals (customers) is a sequence of pairs

$$(t_1, \delta_1), \ldots, (t_k, \delta_k), \qquad t_1 \leqslant \ldots \leqslant t_k \qquad (2.104)$$

in which t stands for a timestamp of the event and δ is an indicator that equals 1 if the observation is not censored and 0 otherwise. We generally assume a continuous timescale, but two customers can have the same event time, so we can summarize the input data as

$$(t_1, d_1), \ldots, (t_n, d_n) \qquad (2.105)$$

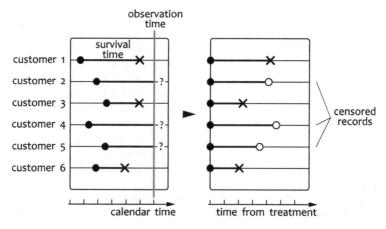

Figure 2.12: Data preparation for survival analysis. The filled circles correspond to treatments. The crosses correspond to events. The empty circles denote censored records.

in which n is the number of distinct event times; d_i is the total number of observed events at time t_i. We also assume that the events are non-repeatable, that is, that an individual cannot experience more than one event. This assumption is not literally true for many marketing events such as purchases, but we can typically work around it by creating separate models for first, second, and subsequent event occurrences, as we will discuss in later chapters. At this point, we are interested only in the distribution of the events and are not trying to explain the dependency between the survival time and the properties of the treatment or customers.

2.6.2.1   Survival Function

The distribution of survival times can be described in terms of the survival probability, also called the *survival function*, S(t), which is defined as the probability that an individual survives from the time origin to time t. The survival function is a fundamental characteristic that describes the dynamics of a customer group. If the survival function falls sharply, most customers are likely to experience the event relatively soon. If the function falls slowly, most customers are likely to experience the event at a relatively distant point in the future.

Let us denote the survival time of a customer as T and its probability density function as f(t). The cumulative distribution function of the survival time, which corresponds to the probability of the event by time t, will then be

$$F(t) = \Pr(T \leqslant t) = \int_0^t f(\tau)\,d\tau \tag{2.106}$$

and the survival function can then be defined as

$$S(t) = \Pr(T > t) = 1 - F(t) \tag{2.107}$$

The value of the survival function at time point t corresponds to the fraction of customers who have not yet experienced the event at that point. Note that the statistical properties of the survival time, such as the mean, median, and confidence intervals, can be estimated based on the cumulative distribution function. Consequently, these properties can be estimated if an estimate for the survival function is available.

The survival function can be estimated from the observed data, by taking into account both censored and uncensored records, based on the assumption that events are independent from each other. In this case, the cumulative survival probability can be obtained by multiplying the probabilities for survival from one interval to the next. More formally, the probability to survive to time t can be straightforwardly estimated as

$$S_t = \frac{n_t - d_t}{n_t} = 1 - \frac{d_t}{n_t} \tag{2.108}$$

in which n_t is the number of individuals who have not yet experienced the event at time t and d_t is the number of individuals who have experienced the event at time t. By multiplying the probabilities from the origin time until time t, we can estimate the cumulative probability to survive, that is, the survival function:

$$\hat{S}(t) = \prod_{i \leqslant t} \left(1 - \frac{d_i}{n_i} \right) \tag{2.109}$$

This estimator is known as the Kaplan–Meier estimator, which can be proved to be the maximum likelihood estimator [Kaplan and Meier, 1958]. The survival function equals 1 at time zero, and then each sample contributes to the estimate as we increase the time. Let us illustrate the estimation of the survival function with a small numerical example.

EXAMPLE 2.1

Let us assume that we are analyzing a group of 14 customers after each of them received a promotional email. All emails were sent at   ▼

different times and the time of the first purchase after an email has been recorded. The observed data set looks like this:

$$t = \{2, \ 3, \ 3, \ 3, \ 4, \ 6, \ 7, \ 8, \ 12, \ 12, \ 14, \ 15, \ 20, \ 23\}$$
$$\delta = \{1, \ 1, \ 0, \ 1, \ 1, \ 1, \ 1, \ 0, \ 1, \ \ 1, \ \ 0, \ \ 1, \ \ 1, \ \ 1\} \tag{2.110}$$

in which the i-th element of set t is the observed event time for the i-th customer measured in days since the email was sent. Set δ contains the indicators for whether each observation is censored (0) or not censored (1). For example, the first customer made a purchase on the second day after the email, and the third customer did not make a purchase by the time of the analysis although she got the email three days before the analysis date. In this context, the probability to survive means the probability of not having made a purchase at a given time. By repeatedly applying formula 2.109, we obtain the following sequence:

$$S(0) = 1 \qquad \text{(all customers are "alive" at the beginning)}$$
$$S(2) = 1 - \frac{1}{14} = 0.93$$
$$S(3) = S(2) \cdot \left(1 - \frac{2}{13}\right) = 0.79 \tag{2.111}$$
$$\cdots$$

This result corresponds to the stepwise *survival curve* plotted in Figure 2.13. The survival curve summarizes the dynamics of a customer group, and curves for different groups can be compared. For example, a survival curve for customers who were treated with a promotion can be plotted together with a curve for those who were not, and the efficiency of the promotion can thus be graphically assessed.

▲

2.6.2.2 Hazard Function

The second important concept in survival analysis is the *hazard function*. Whereas the survival function focuses on the probability of the event not happening, that is, *survival*, the hazard function describes the risk of the event. As we will see later, this perspective is convenient for analyzing how different factors, such as treatment parameters, influence the survival time.

The hazard function $h(t)$ is defined as the instantaneous hazard rate, that is, the probability of the event in an infinitesimally small time period between t and $t + dt$, given that the individual has survived up until time t:

$$h(t) = \lim_{dt \to 0} \frac{\Pr(t < T \leqslant t + dt \mid T > t)}{dt} \tag{2.112}$$

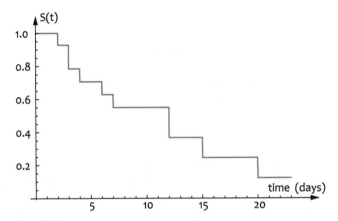

Figure 2.13: An estimate of the survival function for the data set given in definition 2.110.

The hazard function can be linked to the survival function. To
see this, let us first decompose the conditional probability in definition 2.112 into two factors; note that one of them corresponds to the
survival function:

$$
\begin{aligned}
h(t) &= \lim_{dt \to 0} \frac{\Pr(t < T \leqslant t + dt)}{dt \cdot \Pr(T > t)} \\
&= \lim_{dt \to 0} \frac{\Pr(t < T \leqslant t + dt)}{dt \cdot S(t)} \\
&= \lim_{dt \to 0} \frac{F(t + dt) - F(t)}{dt \cdot S(t)}
\end{aligned}
\tag{2.113}
$$

Next, recall that the probability density function is defined as

$$
f(t) = \lim_{dt \to 0} \frac{F(t + dt) - F(t)}{dt}
\tag{2.114}
$$

By using this definition, as well as the definition of the survival function 2.107, we obtain the following result:

$$
\begin{aligned}
h(t) &= \frac{f(t)}{S(t)} = \frac{f(t)}{1 - F(t)} \\
&= -\frac{d}{dt} \log(1 - F(t)) \\
&= -\frac{d}{dt} \log(S(t))
\end{aligned}
\tag{2.115}
$$

By solving this equation with respect to $S(t)$, we can express the
survival function as a function of $h(t)$:

$$
S(t) = \exp(-H(t))
\tag{2.116}
$$

in which

$$H(t) = \int_0^t h(\tau)\,d\tau = -\log(S(t)) \tag{2.117}$$

is called the cumulative hazard function. This straightforward relationship allows us to switch between the hazard and survival functions in the analysis.

2.6.2.3 *Survival Analysis Regression*

The basic survival and hazard functions can be used to describe the performance of a customer group or compare different groups to each other. This is not enough for applications where we need to understand and predict how survival and hazard are influenced by factors like marketing actions and customer properties. This problem is similar to the classification and regression problems, in the sense that the survival time has to be predicted as a function of the observed factors, that is, the independent variables.

Let us assume that each individual is associated with a vector $\mathbf{x}$ that consists of p independent variables, so that each individual is now represented by three values:

t   survival or censoring time

δ censoring indicator, taking the value 1 for observed

   events and 0 for censored cases

$\mathbf{x}$ vector of features

The input data set contains observations for k individuals:

$$(t_1, \delta_1, \mathbf{x}_1),\ldots,(t_k, \delta_k, \mathbf{x}_k), \qquad t_1 \leqslant \ldots \leqslant t_k \tag{2.118}$$

In marketing applications, the feature vector can include customer demographic and behavioral properties, marketing communications to that customer, and so on. The goal is to define and fit a model that expresses the survival and hazard functions as a function of $\mathbf{x}$. As both $S(t)$ and $h(t)$ are probabilities, we can construct different survival regression models by assuming different probability distributions and different functional dependencies between the features $\mathbf{x}$ and the parameters of the distribution.

Among the most commonly used choices for survival regression models are *proportional hazard* models. This model family is based on the assumption that a unit increase in observed factors is multiplicative with respect to the hazard rate, that is

$$h(t \mid \mathbf{w}, \mathbf{x}) = h_0(t) \cdot r(\mathbf{w}, \mathbf{x}) \tag{2.119}$$

in which $h_0(t)$ is the baseline hazard, r is the *risk ratio* that increases or decreases the baseline hazard depending on the factors, and $\mathbf{w}$ is the vector of model parameters. Note that the baseline hazard does not depend on the individual, but the risk ratio does. In other words, the risk ratio determines how the properties of an individual encoded in the feature vector influence the hazard rate. The risk ratio cannot be negative because the hazard rate is not negative, so it is typically modeled as an exponential function:

$$h(t \mid \mathbf{w}, \mathbf{x}) = h_0(t) \cdot \exp\left(\mathbf{w}^\mathsf{T}\mathbf{x}\right) \tag{2.120}$$

This model can be interpreted as a linear model for the log of the risk ratio for an individual to the baseline:

$$\log r(\mathbf{w}, \mathbf{x}) = \log \frac{h(t \mid \mathbf{x})}{h_0(t)} = \mathbf{w}^\mathsf{T}\mathbf{x} \tag{2.121}$$

In regards to the baseline hazard $h_0(t)$, we have two choices: nonparametric and parametric. The parametric approach assumes that the hazard follows a certain probability distribution. In this case, we obtain a fully parametric model that needs to be fitted to the data by finding the optimal values of parameters $\mathbf{w}$ and the parameters of the distribution. The disadvantage of this approach is that the baseline hazard is assumed to vary in a specific manner with time, so we need to be sure that the distribution we choose matches the data. On the other hand, the parametric approach smooths noisy data and provides a simple model for the baseline hazard.

The second option is to use a nonparametric baseline hazard model that can be estimated from the data by using the Kaplan–Meier estimator or other methods. This leads to a semiparametric model for the overall hazard where the parametric part is defined by expression 2.120 and the baseline hazard $h_0(t)$ is the nonparametric part. This solution is known as the Cox proportional hazard model [Cox, 1972]. The advantage of the Cox model, as we will see in a moment, is that it allows us to estimate the hazard ratios without having to estimate the baseline hazard function or making any assumptions about the structure of the baseline hazard. This makes it very convenient for applications that require only the risk factors to be estimated, not the absolute hazard values. The downside of the Cox model is that the baseline hazard needs to be estimated by using parametric methods. It is also important to keep in mind that the Cox model belongs to the proportional hazard models family and, consequently, is based on the proportional hazard assumption, which may or may not hold for the observed data. The Cox model is widely used in many domains including marketing, and we will use it as the main vehicle for survival analysis in the next chapter.

Our next step is to estimate the parameters of the Cox model from the data. The standard approach to this problem is to derive the likelihood of the model and then find the parameters that maximize it. The challenge, however, is that observations can be censored, which requires us to specify how such records will be accounted for in the likelihood. First, let us note that each observation contributes to the likelihood. If the i-th observation is censored, it contributes the probability of survival up until t_i:

$$L_i(\mathbf{w}) = S(t_i \mid \mathbf{w}, \mathbf{x}) \tag{2.122}$$

If the observation is not censored, it contributes the probability of the event at t_i, which is defined by using the survival time probability density function:

$$L_i(\mathbf{w}) = f(t_i) = h(t_i \mid \mathbf{w}, \mathbf{x}) S(t_i \mid \mathbf{w}, \mathbf{x}) \tag{2.123}$$

So the full likelihood can be expressed as follows:

$$L_i(\mathbf{w}) = \prod_{i=1}^{k} h(t_i \mid \mathbf{w}, \mathbf{x})^{\delta_i} S(t_i \mid \mathbf{w}, \mathbf{x}) \tag{2.124}$$

We cannot maximize this by using numerical methods without specifying the form of the baseline hazard. However, it is possible to approximate the full likelihood with a different measure called the partial likelihood. First, let us introduce the notion of the *risk set* at time t, which is defined as the set of individuals who are at risk of the event at time t, that is, those who have not yet experienced the event:

$$R(t) = \{i : t_i \geq t\} \tag{2.125}$$

For simplicity, let us also assume that there are no event ties, that is, all event times t_i are distinct[1]. In this case, the *partial likelihood* can be defined by using the conditional probability that a particular person i will fail at time t_i, given the risk set at that time, and that exactly one failure is going to happen [Cox, 1972, 1975]. This probability is given by the area under the hazard curve for a small time interval dt, so the likelihood contributed by individual i can be expressed as

$$L_i(\mathbf{w}) = \frac{h(t_i \mid \mathbf{w}, x_i) dt}{\sum_{j \in R(t_i)} h(t_j \mid \mathbf{w}, x_j) dt} \tag{2.126}$$

---

1 The case with ties is more complex, but there exist a number of generalizations that account for ties [Breslow, 1974; Efron, 1977]. In most marketing applications, we can avoid ties by spreading the conflicting observations by a small margin.

By inserting the specification of Cox model 2.120 into this partial likelihood, we can see that the baseline hazards cancel each other out and we get

$$L_i(\mathbf{w}) = \frac{\exp\left(\mathbf{w}^\mathsf{T}\mathbf{x}_i\right)}{\sum_{j \in R(t_i)} \exp\left(\mathbf{w}^\mathsf{T}\mathbf{x}_j\right)} \tag{2.127}$$

Finally, the partial likelihood for the entire training data set is a product of the individual partial likelihoods given by equation 2.127:

$$L(\mathbf{w}) = \prod_{i=1}^{k} \left[\frac{\exp\left(\mathbf{w}^\mathsf{T}\mathbf{x}_i\right)}{\sum_{j \in R(t_i)} \exp\left(\mathbf{w}^\mathsf{T}\mathbf{x}_j\right)} \right]^{\delta_i} \tag{2.128}$$

This likelihood does not depend on the hazard function, so we can fit it by using numerical methods with respect to the weights $\mathbf{w}$. This, in turn, enables us to estimate the risk ratios defined by equation 2.121. The ability to estimate the risk ratios without estimating the hazard function is one of the key advantages of the Cox model.

Thus far, we have been focused on the estimation of regression weights. Our last step is to specify how the baseline hazard and survival functions can be estimated. First, let us note that the expected number of events at time t_i can be approximated by the area under the hazard function for a small interval between t_i and $t_i + dt$:

$$\widehat{d}_i = \sum_{j \in R(t_i)} h_0(t_i) \exp\left(\mathbf{w}^\mathsf{T}\mathbf{x}_j\right) dt \tag{2.129}$$

We can rewrite this relationship as

$$\widehat{h}_0(t_i)dt = \frac{\widehat{d}_i}{\sum_{j \in R(t_i)} \exp\left(\mathbf{w}^\mathsf{T}\mathbf{x}_j\right)} \tag{2.130}$$

and then approximate the cumulative hazard function as follows:

$$\widehat{H}_0(t) = \sum_{i < t} \widehat{h}_0(t_i)dt \tag{2.131}$$

This result is known as the Breslow estimator [Breslow, 1972]. It enables us to estimate the baseline survival function by inserting the estimator into expression 2.116:

$$\widehat{S}_0(t) = \exp(-\widehat{H}_0(t)) \tag{2.132}$$

Finally, the complete survival function can be obtained directly from the specification of the Cox model in equation 2.120 and expression 2.116 as follows:

$$
\begin{aligned}
S(t \mid \mathbf{x}) &= \exp\left[-\int_0^t h_0(\tau) \exp\left(\mathbf{w}^\mathsf{T}\mathbf{x}\right) d\tau\right] \\
&= \exp\left[-\int_0^t h_0(\tau) d\tau\right]^{\exp(\mathbf{w}^\mathsf{T}\mathbf{x})} \\
&= S_0(t)^{\exp(\mathbf{w}^\mathsf{T}\mathbf{x})}
\end{aligned}
\tag{2.133}
$$

Survival functions for different values of features $\mathbf{x}$ can then be plotted together and compared to each other to quantify the impact of different features on the distribution of the survival time. We will continue to discuss this and other practical applications of survival analysis in advertising and marketing communications in the next chapter.

2.6.3 Auction Theory

As we discussed in Chapter 1, the algorithmic approach facilitates the development of marketing services that can be offered to clients by exchanges. An exchange or any other type of broker in between a service provider and service client adds an extra layer of complexity because both the provider and client should optimize their service buying and selling strategies, in addition to pursuit of the primary marketing objectives.

The basic goal of a service exchange is to enable competition between buyers for a limited resource, such as advertisement placements. The standard approach to this problem is an *auction* where each buyer places a *bid* and the resource is auctioned off to the bidder with the maximum bid. However, auction settings and rules can be set up differently, so we need to spend some time discussing auction types.

First, we have to acknowledge that the bidders participate in the auction because the auctioned resource has a certain value for each of them and they are aiming to make profits by buying the item below this valuation. Consequently, it is critically important for a bidder to estimate the value of the item correctly, and we can classify all auction settings by the following valuation types:

PRIVATE VALUE Each bidder evaluates the item independently from other bidders and the estimate does not depend on other bids, even if they are known.

INTERDEPENDENT VALUE The actual value is not known to the bidders, and, although each bidder has their own estimate of what the value is, information about other bids can help to improve the estimate. For example, a bidder who highly values the resource might reduce their bid if other participants bid lower, because this additional information can indicate the presence of negative factors that are unknown to the given bidder but are somehow recognized by the others.

COMMON VALUE This is a particular case of an interdependent value auction where the actual value is the same for all bidders. Examples of common value auctions include selling natural resources such as oil or timber, selling financial assets such as bonds, or selling a company. In all of these cases, the true value might not be precisely known at the auction time and bidders must estimate it based on the limited information that they have, but eventually the value becomes known (actual amount of recoverable oil, long-term company performance, etc.) and it is the same for all participants.

Although the value is often interdependent to some degree, a bidder's ability to take advantage of knowing other bids depends on the auctioning process. The four main types of auctions studied in theory and used in practice are as follows:

OPEN BID Every bidder observes the value of all other bids.

- Open ascending-price auction (English auction). The price starts at a low level and increases. At any point of time, a bidder can either stay or quit. The auction ends when only one bidder remains, and the winner pays the final price.

- Open descending-price auction (Dutch auction). The price starts at a high level and decreases. The auction ends when any bidder accepts the current price.

SEALED BID Bidders are unaware of what others have bid.

- First-price sealed-bid auction. All bidders submit their bids simultaneously, so that no bidder knows the bid of the other participants. The bidder with the highest bid wins and pays the winning bid.

- Second-price sealed-bid auction (Vickrey auction). Similarly to the first-price auction, all bidders submit their bids simultaneously and the bidder with the highest bid wins, but the winner pays the second highest bid.

Although the optimization problem for the open-bid auctions might seem dynamic, it is essentially static and equivalent to the sealed-bid auctions. The Dutch auction ends right after the first bid, so bidders do not receive any additional information during the process and can decide on a bid in advance. Consequently, a Dutch auction is equivalent to a first-price sealed-bid auction in the sense that,whatever strategy the bidder chooses, it uses the same inputs and leads to the same winners and prices, both for private and interdependent values. In an English auction with private values, the bidder can also evaluate the item in advance. As the auction progresses and the price goes up, the bidder should always compare the current highest bid with the estimated value and either make a new bid, calculated as the current highest plus some small increment, or quit the auction if the price has gone above his valuation. Hence, an English auction is equivalent to a second-price sealed bid auction for private values, although this is not true for interdependent values because the bidder can learn from the observed bids in the case of an English auction.

We now study the Vickrey auction in detail to obtain a toolkit for building optimization models that include auctions. We focus on the Vickrey auction because it is convenient for analysis and widely used in practical applications, although similar results can be obtained for other auction types by using more advanced analysis methods.

First, we can prove that the optimal strategy for bidders is to bid their true value. Consider Figure 2.14, in which the bidder evaluates the item at a price v but makes a lower bid $v - \delta$. If the second highest bid from another bidder is p, then the following three outcomes are possible:

1. $p > v$: the bidder loses; it does not matter if he bids v or $v - \delta$

2. $p < v - \delta$: the bidder wins and pays price p; it does not matter if he bids v or $v - \delta$

3. $v - \delta < p < v$: the bidder loses; a bid of v would have meant winning and making a margin of $v - p$

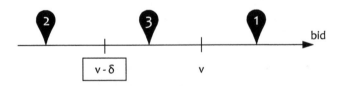

Figure 2.14: Vickrey auction – bidding below the true value.

So, a bid below the true value always gives the same or a worse result as a bid of the true value. Figure 2.15 depicts the opposite situation, when the bid is above the true value. We again have three possible outcomes:

1. $p > v + \delta$: the bidder loses; it does not matter if he bids v or $v + \delta$

2. $p < v$: the bidder wins and pays the price p; it does not matter if he bids v or $v + \delta$

3. $v < p < v + \delta$: the bidder wins and pays the price p with a loss of $p - v$, whereas a bid of v would mean losing the auction without any financial loss

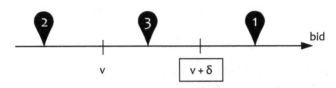

Figure 2.15: Vickrey auction – bidding above the true value.

We can conclude that bidding the true value is the optimal strategy. This simple result implies that we need to focus on estimation of the expected revenue for the bidder when discussing marketing settings with sealed-bid auctions.

Our next step will be to take the seller's perspective of the auction and estimate the revenue for the seller. Let us assume that there are n bidders participating in the auction and their bid prices $V_1, \ldots, V_n$ are independent and identically distributed random values drawn from some distribution $F(v)$ with the probability density $f(v)$. By recalling that k-th order statistic $V_{(k)}$ of a sample is equal to its k-th smallest value, we can express the expected revenue as the mean of the second-highest order statistic that corresponds to the second-highest bid:

$$\text{revenue} = \mathbb{E}\left[V_{(n-1)}\right] \tag{2.134}$$

Let us consider a slice of the probability density function for the order statistics:

$$\Pr\left(v < V_{(k)} < v + dv\right) \tag{2.135}$$

This is the probability that $k - 1$ bids in the sample of n bids are smaller than v, exactly one bid falls into the range $[v, v + dv]$, and the remaining $n - k$ bids are higher than v. These three conditions can be expressed by using the bid cumulative distribution $F(v)$ and probability density f(v), so we get the following expression for the order statistics probability density:

$$f\left(V_{(k)}\right) = \lim_{dv \to 0} \Pr\left(v < V_{(k)} < v + dv\right)$$

$$= \binom{n}{k-1} [F(v)]^{k-1} \cdot (n - k + 1)f(v) \cdot [1 - F(v)]^{n-k} \quad (2.136)$$

$$= \frac{n!}{(k-1)!(n-k)!} f(v) [F(v)]^{k-1} [1 - F(v)]^{n-k}$$

We can simplify this expression with certain assumptions regarding the bid distribution. For example, if bids are drawn from a uniform distribution between zero and one, the expression reduces to

$$f\left(V_{(k)}\right) = \frac{n!}{(k-1)!(n-k)!} v^{k-1}(1-v)^{n-k} \quad (2.137)$$

This is a beta distribution, so we can use a standard formula for its mean to get the expected revenue of the auctioneer:

$$\mathbb{E}\left[V_{(n-1)}\right] = \frac{n-1}{n+1} \quad (2.138)$$

This result is in alignment with the intuitive expectation that an increase in the number of bidders leads to an overall increase in the revenue. We use these results in subsequent chapters, mainly to optimize the bidding process for exchanges. It is worth noting, however, that other marketing processes, including such important ones as the selection of the best offers on the market by a consumer, can be modeled as auctions, which makes auction theory an important tool for building programmatic solutions.

2.7 SUMMARY

- Many marketing problems can be expressed as optimization problems in which the business outcome is the subject of optimization and the business actions are the variables.

- The dependency between the actions and business outcomes can often be learned from historical data. This problem can be solved by using supervised learning methods.

- The primary goal of supervised learning is to estimate the conditional distribution of the response given the input. In many practical applications, this problem can be reduced to finding the most probable outcome values. The main two types of supervised problems are classification and regression.

- The number of predictive model parameters can be fixed or can grow with the size of the training data set. The former type of model is referred to as a parametric model, and the latter is known as a nonparametric model.

- Model fitting can be viewed as an optimization problem where the model parameters need to be chosen to maximize the probability that the observed data follows the model distribution.

- A wide range of supervised learning problems can be addressed by linear models, that is, models that either express the dependency between the input and output as a linear function or express the boundary between the classes as a straight line. The most basic examples of linear models are linear regression and logistic regression.

- Nonlinear dependencies and decision boundaries can be captured by using nonlinear models. Examples of nonlinear modeling methods include kernel methods, decision trees, and neural networks.

- Marketing data may have a redundant structure because different features and metrics are projections of the same marketing process. This structure can be nonoptimal for analysis and modeling, and a better data representation can be found by removing correlations, reducing data dimensionality, and clustering data points and entities. Some of these tasks can be solved with unsupervised learning methods, such as principal component analysis and clustering.

- Some marketing tasks cannot be easily solved by using standard machine learning methods and require more specialized models and techniques. Examples of such models include consumer choice models, survival analysis methods, and auction theory.

3

PROMOTIONS AND ADVERTISEMENTS

Every product or service has its target market, the group of consumers at which the product or service is aimed. The distinction between the target and non-target groups is often fuzzy and ambiguous because consumers differ in their income, buying behavior, loyalty to a brand, and many other properties. The diversity of customers is often so high that an offering created for an average consumer, that is, for everyone, does not really fit anyone's needs. This makes it critically important for businesses to identify the most relevant consumers and tailor their offerings on the basis of consumer properties. This problem occurs in virtually all marketing applications, and it plays an especially important role in advertisements and promotions because the efficiency of these services directly depends on the ability to identify the right audience and convey the right message.

The problem of finding the optimal match between consumers and offerings can generally be viewed from two perspectives. First, it can be stated as finding the right offerings for a given customer. This is a *product discovery* problem, which we will discuss in the following chapters dedicated to search and recommendations. The second perspective is that of finding the right customers for a given offering. This problem is known as *targeting*, and it is the main subject of this chapter. It should be kept in mind, however, that we draw a line between product discovery and targeting services mainly based on the principal applications (interactive browsing versus advertising), and the methodologies used to implement the services can sometimes be viewed from both perspectives. Consider customer base segmentation as an example. One can argue that segmentation identifies the right groups of customers first and the offerings and experiences are then tailored for each segment. However, it is also true that segmentation can be viewed as a method for allocating different offerings and experiences to the most appropriate customers.

Although targeting is concerned with matching customers and offerings, it should not be viewed simply as a set of methods for drawing connecting lines between these two entities. Instead, it should be viewed as a problem of customer experience optimization that is driven by a mix of multiple business objectives and controls many different marketing activities. The goal of a programmatic system is to unroll these initial objectives into a detailed execution plan and specific rules that can be used to manage interactions with the clients.

We will open this chapter with an overview of the retail promotion environment that will help us to better understand the problem of targeting. We will then describe a promotion targeting framework that includes a more formal definition of business objectives, basic building blocks of behavioral modeling, and more complex constructs used in marketing campaigns. After that, we will discuss the online advertising environment and related targeting methods. Although the retail and online advertising environments complement each other and many targeting methods are universally applicable, we will study them separately because of major structural differences and variations in objectives. Finally, we will discuss how the efficiency of targeting methods and marketing campaigns can be measured. Measurement plays an extremely important role in all marketing applications, and the framework that we develop will also be used in other programmatic services, including search, recommendations, and pricing. In this chapter, we generally avoid discussing price optimization, although it is an important part of promotions. This topic will be covered in a dedicated chapter later on.

3.1   ENVIRONMENT

The first business environment we will consider is that of consumer sales promotions, which are widely used in retail and brand relationship management. The goal of promotions is to provide added value or incentives to consumers in order to improve sales or build better relationships. Promotions can be distributed by product manufacturers, service providers, or retailers. In some market verticals , such as *consumer packaged goods* (CPG), manufacturers and retailers often collaborate on promotional campaigns, with the manufacturer covering the direct costs of the campaign and the retailer providing its physical and digital channels to communicate the offerings to the audience. As we discussed in Chapter 1, such interactions between promoters and consumer-base owners can be favorable for the algorithmic approach, so we will use this as our primary environment for further discussion. However, most of the methods that we will develop are not limited to the CPG environment and can be applied in other domains such as telecoms or insurance.

The model of the sales promotion environment is depicted in Figure 3.1. The main entities of this environment, assumptions, and terminology can be described as follows:

- We use the term *consumer* to refer to any person who consumes goods. A *customer* is a person who has purchased from a firm. Finally, a prospect is a person who is not a customer yet but who is known, in the sense that a firm can communicate with them (for example, a person who has registered on the website and provided an email). We also refer to consumers who interact with online channels as users.

- *Manufacturers* (or *brands*) produce products that are associated with product categories. We assume that each category has a relatively narrow scope, such as *low-fat cottage cheese,* so products within a category are considered by the consumer as interchangeable. Consequently, several brands can compete within a category for customers.

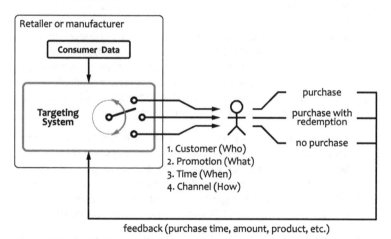

Figure 3.1: The sales promotion environment in the retail domain.

- A *retailer* purchases products from manufacturers and sells them to consumers with an added markup. A retailer can also produce its own branded products, referred to as *private-label products,* to compete with other manufacturers in the corresponding categories.

- We define a *targeted promotion* as an incentive that can be delivered to selected consumers through marketing channels. Promotions can be offered with some condition (e. g. *buy one, get one*) or without any condition, can provide a monetary value such as a discount, or can just advertise a product or brand. Promotions may or may not be *redeemable*, in the sense that a consumer might need to submit evidence of the promotion (scan a bar code on a printed coupon or enter a promotion code) to redeem its monetary value with a purchase. We also use the word *treatment* as a generic term that refers to promotions and other marketing communications.

- A retailer owns *marketing channels* such physical stores or eCommerce websites that can be used to communicate promotions to the consumers. The marketing channels of multiple retailers can be combined into a *promotion distribution network* that can be operated by retailers or a third-party agency. For example, an agency can install its coupon printers in stores that belong to multiple retail chains.

  It is critically important that the retailer or agency, as a marketing channel owner, can track consumers at the individual level and link together transactions made by the same consumer or household. This tracking is often based on *loyalty IDs* that are assigned to the customers by using loyalty cards or online accounts, credit card IDs, or other pieces of information that are available to a retailer. This process, however, is often imperfect, and a significant number of transactions can remain anonymous.

- Promotions can be distributed through the marketing channels on behalf of both manufacturers and retailers. Distribution can be done either in batch mode, when emails or printed catalogs are sent to a large number of customers, or in real-time mode, when promotions are generated in the scope of an individual transaction, such as an in-store purchase or website visit.

- The main decisions that a *targeting system* needs to make with respect to promotions are who are the right recipients for a promotion, what are the right promotional properties, what is the optimal time to offer it, and what is the right delivery channel.

- We assume that a retailer can identify consumers who have received a promotion, consumers who have purchased a promoted product, and, optionally, promotion redemption events. Note that purchases and redemptions are completely different events that should not be confused: consumers who have a promotion are not obligated to redeem it, and a product can typically be purchased by any consumer although the purchase may be on different conditions according to the granted promotions. Beyond these events, a targeting system can also access additional or external consumer data, such as demographic records or survey answers.

In the environment described above, the interactions with the consumer are often structured as marketing campaigns, which is a convenient unit of optimization. We define a *targeted campaign* as a marketing action constrained by a budget or duration that aims to achieve a certain business objective by distributing targeted offerings to existing customers or prospects. A targeted campaign generally includes the following activities:

PLANNING Planning of a campaign typically starts with setting business objectives that have to be achieved. The main properties of the campaign, such as budget, duration, or promotion types, should also be determined at the planning stage and can be derived from the objective.

EXECUTION The execution stage includes evaluation of potential recipients and making decisions about the right offerings, right messages, right communication time, and right delivery channels.

MEASUREMENT Measurement of the performance metrics is a critically important activity that can run in parallel with the execution to enable dynamic adjustments.

Let us note that the simple cycle depicted in Figure 3.1 does not fully reflect all important aspects of promotion management. First, the picture becomes much more complex for the management of multiple campaigns or campaigns with a complex structure, which is, of course, often the case in practice. Different marketing actions taken in the scope of one or multiple campaigns can interact with each other, which makes decisions and measurements more difficult. This means that it may not be sufficient to track only the immediate events associated with an action; instead, the entire *customer life cycle* should be taken into account. We discuss how a programmatic system can handle such effects later in this chapter. The second important consideration is that the customer's perspective of the targeting process is different from the perspective depicted in Figure 3.1. Each individual customer life cycle can include multiple interactions with a retailer or manufacturer and potentially involve multiple channels. The chain of such interactions, called the *customer journey*, should deliver a consistent experience across all touchpoints and throughout the life cycle. This aspect is a key consideration in campaign design that we will discuss in Section 3.6.1.

3.2 BUSINESS OBJECTIVES

Each marketing campaign is associated with certain costs and certain gains for each participant of the process, including the customers, retailers, manufacturers, and agencies. Conceptually, each campaign should have a positive *return on investment* (ROI), defined as the difference between gains and costs. The return on investment can be predicted before campaign execution or measured after the campaign is fully or partially executed. Predictive models typically estimate the ROI as a function of the campaign parameters, which enables economic optimization of the campaign.

The challenge is that campaign gains typically have a complex structure, which includes both monetary and non-monetary components, as well as immediate and long-term effects. These effects can be difficult to measure and even more difficult to predict. In this section, we will discuss some basic considerations regarding gains and losses, and we will then continue with a more formal framework that can be used for campaign modeling. This framework justifies the creation of targeting models, as described in the next section, and lays a foundation for campaign optimization.

3.2.1 *Manufacturers and Retailers*

A marketing campaign can be initiated and sponsored by either a manufacturer or a retailer. In many cases, they both benefit from harvesting more sales and more loyal customers. However, the way manufacturers and retailers collaborate heavily depends on the business domain and the marketing strategies for specific products or product categories. The details of these collaborations are important for our purposes because they influence how programmatic targeting services can be provided or used in the retail world.

The first important consideration is the customer relationship management strategy of the customer-base owner, which is typically a retailer. Mass market retailers, such as CPG retailers, typically welcome manufacturers to participate in the marketing process by requesting *manufacturer-sponsored campaigns*. Such campaigns help manufacturers to increase their share in a category and are also beneficial for a retailer. On the other hand, high-end retailers, such as fashion or cosmetics stores, position themselves as personal assistants and see a lot of added value in their merchandising services. This category of retailers cannot allow third parties to interact freely with their customer base. Instead, they purchase the inventory of products upfront and manage their marketing processes to sell it off over time and with maximum profits.

The second consideration is that many retailers offer private-label products, which leads to a conflict of interests with manufacturers. In the case of a promotion service, retailers and manufacturers can negotiate special rules to avoid destructive competition in such situations, for example, by excluding customers who are highly loyal to the private label from targeting.

Finally, retailers are interested in maximizing revenues in a category. Encouraging customers to switch from high-margin products to discounted ones can be harmful.

3.2.2 Costs

The costs of a promotional campaign can be borne by either a manufacturer or a retailer. In either case, the retailers and manufacturers are looking to compensate for the campaign costs by a higher volume of sales. In the CPG world, for example, manufacturer-sponsored campaigns are a very common practice. Such campaigns are initiated by the manufacturer, and the retailer tracks coupon redemptions during the campaign and then invoices the manufacturer for the total of the redemption costs, which is typically the sum of the following components:

DISTRIBUTION COSTS This includes coupon design and printing costs, marketing agency fees, and fixed costs associated with a campaign.

COUPON REDEMPTION COSTS This is a total nominal value of all promotions. This value can be estimated as a product of the total number of promotions to be distributed, the redemption cost of a single promotion, and the expected redemption rate.

CLEARING-HOUSE COSTS Store coupons have a life cycle that imposes additional post-redemption costs. When a consumer hands the cashier a coupon at the checkout counter, the cashier puts it into the cash drawer or a special envelope. At the end of the day, the coupons are added up as if they were cash and packed in bags. These bags are eventually shipped to a third-party clearing house. The clearing-house clerks sort these coupons, often by hand, invoice the manufacturer, and send a check to the retailer. This process results in substantial clearing-house costs because a major retailer can collect millions of coupons and the clearing-house fee per coupon can be comparable to the discount value. For instance, the clearing-house fee per coupon was around $0.10 in 2016, while the discount value for most CPG coupons was in the range of $0.50–2.00.

This structure can vary depending on the business domain and campaign type, but the estimation of monetary costs is typically straightforward. However, marketing actions are almost always associated with some non-monetary costs or losses that can be more challenging to estimate. One of the most basic examples is the so-called *email fatigue*, that is, a decline in email-opening rates and customer dissatisfaction caused by too frequent or irrelevant emails. Although such losses can be difficult to quantify directly, we will see later that it is possible to correlate monetary metrics such as revenues with the marketing actions in question and, thus, to quantify and predict the negative effects. These loss estimates can then be accounted for in the net profit equations.

3.2.3   Gains

The gains associated with a campaign can be viewed from several perspectives. The most straightforward element is the increase in sales volume. Both manufacturer-sponsored and retailer-sponsored campaigns incentivize consumers to make purchases, at the expense of the campaign costs, so the basic equation that describes the campaign gain will be as follows:

$$\text{profit} = Q\,(P - V) - C \tag{3.1}$$

in which Q is the quantity sold, P is the baseline unit price, V stands for variable campaign costs per unit (average redemption, distribution, and clearing-house cost), and C is the fixed cost of a campaign. Simplistically speaking, a campaign can be considered successful if the sales volume induced by the campaign Q_c exceeds the sales volume without the campaign Q_0 to an extent that is sufficient to cover the campaign costs:

$$Q_c\,(P - V) - C \;>\; Q_0 \cdot P \tag{3.2}$$

Manufacturer-sponsored campaigns aim to achieve this goal in the context of a given product and also to increase the market share of the manufacturer in the corresponding product category in the long run. At the same time, manufacturer-sponsored campaigns are typically beneficial for the retailer as well for the following reasons:

- Promotions stimulate return shopping trips. Manufacturers and retailers share the goal of stimulating more shopping trips, so promotional campaigns are often geared towards this mutually beneficial goal.

- Promotions increase basket size. Some promotions are explicitly designed to make people buy more of a given product. Other types of promotions can decrease the consumer's expenses and release money for additional purchases.

- Promotions improve loyalty to the retailer. It is natural for a consumer to perceive promotions as a result of a collaboration between the manufacturer and the retailer, so both are credited for their effort in adding value and improving the consumer experience.

Consequently, the retailer benefits from a collaboration with a manufacturer because of both improved revenues and loyalty effects. This is the reason why most CPG retailers provide promotions as a service to manufacturers. Retailer-sponsored campaigns typically aim to promote private labels, promote entire product categories, or stimulate the inventory turnover. From a promotional perspective, the gains of retailer-sponsored campaigns are similar to the gains of the manufacturer-sponsored campaigns described above. However, the inventory turnover perspective is different and we will discuss it in Chapter 6 in relation to price and assortment optimization.

The principle of sales volume maximization outlined in equation 3.2 is an important criterion for the campaign design, but it is, of course, a very simplistic view of customer relationship management. We need to do a more thorough analysis of campaign gains to better understand the objectives that we can use in the design of targeting models and campaigns. As a campaign aims to change the relationship with a consumer, its objectives can be better understood by studying a customer life cycle. We distinguish three main phases of interaction between a consumer and a brand (manufacturer or retailer) that follow one another, sometimes repeatedly:

- A consumer initially does not interact with the brand and prefers other brands or totally different product categories. The main goal of the brand at this phase is to acquire a new customer.

- Customers who interact with the brand can be incentivized to buy more products. Promotion campaigns for these customers typically follow up-sell or cross-sell methodologies. In the case of *up-selling*, the promotion offers a stretch in comparison to the normal quantities the customer purchases from the brand. In the case of *cross-selling*, the promotion incentivizes the customer to buy related products.

- Finally, a customer can stop interacting with the brand. This is typically referred to as *customer attrition, customer defection,* or *customer churn*. The cost of retaining an existing customer is typically much less than acquiring a new one, so a brand can offer special deals to customers who are about to churn.

These simple considerations provide a very important framework for customer relationship management and promotion targeting in particular. First, let us note that consumer behavior and business objectives are very different at each of the three stages of the life cycle, as depicted in Figure 3.2.

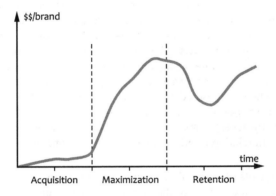

Figure 3.2: Phases of a consumer life cycle.

Consumers who are at the first stage need to be acquired and converted into customers by using marketing actions that are specifically designed for this purpose. Customers at the second stage need to be treated with incentives that are focused on maximization and growth of consumption. Finally, the customers who are about to churn need to be identified in a timely fashion and retained. These three objectives – *acquisition, maximization,* and *retention* – are a very popular coordinate system in marketing that can be used to orient individual campaigns and structure campaign portfolios. A brand should be able to distinguish consumers who belong to different phases, and this lays the foundation for the targeting process. As we will see later, each of these objectives can be mapped to a predictive model in a relatively straightforward way, so this set of targeting objectives is well suited for programmatics.

From the programmatic standpoint, a life-cycle-driven campaign design requires two fundamental problems to be solved. The first is the identification of consumers who have a high *propensity* to move along the life-cycle curve, as illustrated in Figure 3.3. If we assume that we can quantify this propensity, we can determine the right consumers to communicate with in order to achieve the objective and maximize the gains.

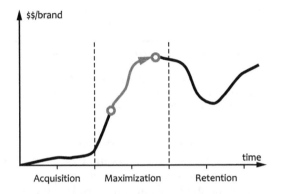

Figure 3.3: Moving customers along the life-cycle curve.

Although targeting of the right consumers can potentially improve the efficiency of marketing actions, it is not sufficient to quantify the expected gain. Estimation of the expected gain is the second major problem, and it requires not only prediction of the propensity of a consumer to move to a certain point of the life-cycle curve but also estimation of the total value that will be collected from a customer after this point. This value corresponds to the area under the life-cycle curve. The metric that we would ultimately like to measure is, however, not the total gain, but the incremental impact of the marketing action relative to the no-action alternative. This incremental gain corresponds to the shaded area in Figure 3.4. In other words, a campaign model needs to predict the incremental gain as a function of the expected value with a no-action strategy and the expected value delivered by the campaign, which, in turn, is defined in terms of propensity to respond and potential impact. We develop a more formal framework for this type of modeling and measurement in the next section.

3.3 TARGETING PIPELINE

Once the environment and business objectives are defined, we can discuss how a programmatic system can approach the problem of target-

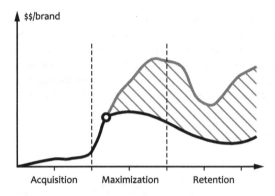

Figure 3.4: Incremental impact of a marketing action. The upper life-cycle curve corresponds to the aftermath of the action and the lower curve corresponds to the result with a no-action strategy.

ing and campaign management. This problem can be viewed as the creation of a process that takes a marketing budget and business objectives as parameters, breaks them down them into campaigns, and executes the corresponding marketing actions. This process can be designed differently depending on how exactly the targeting system is used, but a conceptual design of the process can often be represented as a pipeline similar to the one shown in Figure 3.5.

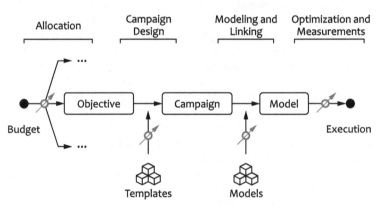

Figure 3.5: A conceptual view of the targeting pipeline.

The pipeline starts with the available marketing budget that can be allocated for different marketing activities. The first step of the process is to determine how the budget should be distributed across the possible activities: what are the main objectives and how are these objectives balanced? The output of this step is a set of objectives, such as acquisition of new customers for product A and retention of customers for product B, as well as budgeting parameters that should be followed by the subsequent stages of the process. The second step is the evolution of each objective into marketing campaigns, that is, campaign design. A programmatic system can use a repository of *campaign templates* that are selected and parametrized based on the objectives. Each campaign requires a number of decisions to be made to determine the customers to be targeted, optimal targeting time, message parameters, and so on. This generally requires the use of predictive models that need to be trained and linked to campaigns. The models produce relevance scores and other signals that can be used by the optimization process to determine the optimal parameters of the campaign, such as the list of customers to be targeted or maximum discount amount. Finally, the campaign is executed and the collected data are used for further optimization and measurement of the results. A programmatic system should be able to run the pipeline both in simulation mode to evaluate different strategies and in execution mode to do real targeting. To summarize, the targeting pipeline includes four major sets of controls: budget allocation, campaign design, modeling, and execution optimization. We discuss these controls in the next sections, starting with models that are used as the basic building blocks, moving on to campaign design and optimization, and finally considering the overall budgeting and budget allocation.

The targeting pipeline can be viewed not only from the engineering perspective outlined in Figure 3.5 but also from the end user (marketer) perspective. This perspective is very important because it describes the top-level functions and features of a programmatic system. The interface of the system heavily depends on particular applications and business environments, but we can consider a simple hypothetical example to illustrate the basic principles. This hypothetical campaign management flow is sketched in Figure 3.6.

This flow includes four principal steps. With the assumption that the budget allocation steps are done in advance, the entry point to the campaign creation workflow is the objective selection, which allows one to specify the promoted products and high-level marketing goals. The system uses historical data, best practices, and predictive models to identify opportunities and propose campaign strategies. The expected outcomes of the campaigns such as costs and gains are predicted, so the marketer can select the optimal option. Once the campaign template is selected and campaign parameters are estimated by the system, the customer experience and creative assets, such as marketing messages, fonts, and images, are created or customized. This step clearly

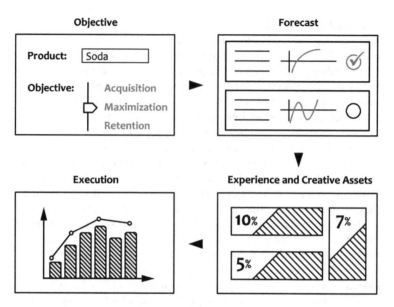

Figure 3.6: A conceptual view of the campaign management workflow.

requires human involvement. Finally, a completely specified campaign can be executed. Again, this is a hypothetical and oversimplified flow, but it demonstrates what are we trying to achieve, ideally, in designing a targeting system.

3.4   RESPONSE MODELING AND MEASUREMENT

Before we go deeply into modeling and campaign design, let us review some basic principles of campaign response modeling and measurements to get some idea of the role of modeling and optimization in the targeting system. In this overview, we introduce new concepts, such as response probability, but do not specify how exactly these values can be modeled and predicted; these details are left for a later discussion. Our goal here is to demonstrate how campaign costs, revenues, and the statistical properties of customers fit together in one model.

Promotions and advertisements aim to change consumer behavior and influence consumers' decisions by urging them to make more purchases, buy promoted products, and so on. Consequently, the success of a campaign can be defined in terms of the *response*, which can be measured with some simple metrics, such as the percentage of redeemed promotions, or with more complex measurements that include direct and indirect, tangible and intangible gains. These metrics can be predicted before the campaign execution for optimization and decision-making purposes or can be measured after the fact based on the collected response data. These two problems are equally important, and we discuss them separately in the subsequent sections by using the principles of life-cycle-based modeling.

3.4.1 Response Modeling Framework

The response modeling framework is a simple generic framework that helps to decompose the campaign modeling problem into several subroutines. This framework can be modified and extended to accommodate the complexity of real-life marketing campaigns. We assume a relatively abstract setting in which a brand needs to optimize the distribution of a promotion or some other treatment across a population of consumers by selecting the most promising candidates to receive the treatment in order to maximize the overall value of the campaign. We do not specify the exact meaning of the value at this point, deferring this discussion until the following sections, but we assume it to be some quantifiable measure that can be compared to costs. The acquisition, maximization, and retention tasks can be considered as variants of this problem.

Recall that the basic marketing optimization problem is defined as finding the strategy that maximizes the value function. In the case of campaign response, we model the overall value of the campaign in terms of the probability of response and the expected net value from a customer. Our subject of optimization will be the set of customers who receive the promotion, that is, the audience of the campaign:

$$U_{opt} = \underset{U \subseteq P}{\text{argmax}} \quad G(U) \tag{3.3}$$

in which P is the entire population of consumers, U is the subset of consumers reached in the scope of the campaign, and $G(U)$ is the expected profit of the campaign, which is a function of the targeting strategy that selects U from P. The expected profit of the campaign can then be modeled as follows:

$$G(U) = \sum_{u \in U} \Pr(R \mid u, T) \cdot (G(u \mid R) - C)$$
$$+ (1 - \Pr(R \mid u, T)) \cdot (-C) \tag{3.4}$$

in which $\Pr(R \mid u, T)$ is the probability of a response to the treatment (promotion) T from customer u, $G(u \mid R)$ is the response net value for customer u, and C is a cost of the promotion resource. The first term corresponds to the expected gain from a responding consumer, and the second term corresponds to the expected loss of sending a promotion to which there is no response. The objective is to maximize the expected profit by finding the subset of customers that are likely to respond in the most profitable way. Equation 3.4 can be reduced as follows

$$G(U) = \sum_{u \in U} \Pr(R \mid u, T) \cdot G(u \mid R) - C$$
$$= \sum_{u \in U} \mathbb{E}\,[G \mid u, T] - C \tag{3.5}$$

in which $\mathbb{E}\,[G \mid u, T]$ denotes the expected value for a given consumer on the assumption that the consumer will receive the promotion. Consequently, the customer selection criteria can be simplified to

$$\mathbb{E}\,[G \mid u, T] > C \tag{3.6}$$

because the expected net value is non-negative and all consumers are assumed to be independent. Next, the optimal subset of customers U can be determined as a subset that maximizes the value:

$$\operatorname*{argmax}_{U \subseteq P}\ G(U) = \operatorname*{argmax}_{U \subseteq P}\ \sum_{u \in U} \mathbb{E}\,[G \mid u, T] - C \tag{3.7}$$

Note that this approach can be interpreted as the maximization of the targeted net value relative to random resource distribution. To see this, let us compare these two options with the assumption that a fixed number of customers $|U|$ will be participating in a campaign. The incremental value of a targeted campaign relative to a campaign that distributes incentives among $|U|$ customers selected at random is given by

$$\operatorname*{argmax}_{U \subseteq P}\ \sum_{u \in U} \left(\mathbb{E}\,[G \mid u, T] - C \right) - |U| \left(\mathbb{E}\,[G \mid T] - C \right)$$
$$= \operatorname*{argmax}_{U \subseteq P}\ \sum_{u \in U} \left(\mathbb{E}\,[G \mid u, T] - \mathbb{E}\,[G \mid T] \right) \tag{3.8}$$
$$= \operatorname*{argmax}_{U \subseteq P}\ \sum_{u \in U} \mathbb{E}\,[G \mid u, T]$$

in which $\mathbb{E}\,[G \mid T]$ is the average net value per customer over the population. This average net value is constant; hence, it can be omitted if the fixed cardinality $|U|$ is assumed. On the other hand, we obtain exactly the same result by reducing equation 3.7 under the assumption that $|U|$ is fixed, and, consequently, the cost can be dropped:

$$\operatorname*{argmax}_{U \subseteq P}\ \sum_{u \in U} \mathbb{E}\,[G \mid u, T] - C = \operatorname*{argmax}_{U \subseteq P}\ \sum_{u \in U} \mathbb{E}\,[G \mid u, T] \tag{3.9}$$

In other words, the random selection of recipients represents the baseline, and the value maximization problem is equivalent to the redistribution of promotions from one group of consumers to another.

It can be argued that the model defined by equation 3.7 is imperfect because it favors consumers who are likely to respond to a promotion but does not take into account customers who are likely to respond anyway, thereby yielding the same profit even without the promotion [Radcliffe and Surry, 1999; Lo, 2002]. Consequently, the actual profit uplift of a promotion campaign in comparison to the no-action baseline can be very small or even negative. Another way to think about this problem is as an experiment in which we divide the set of customers identified by targeting equation 3.7 into two groups, send the promotion to one group but not the other, and then compare the outcome from the two groups. It may be the case that customers in the first group actively redeem the promotion and purchase the product but that customers in the second group purchase the product equally as much or even more. This campaign is clearly inefficient or even harmful. To understand this problem better, let us separately consider the following four possible strategies:

1. Select a set of customers $|U|$ according to equation 3.7 and send promotions to everyone in this group

2. Select a set of customers $|U|$ randomly and send promotions to everyone in this group

3. Select a set of customers $|U|$ according to equation 3.7 but do not actually send the promotions

4. Select a set of customers $|U|$ randomly but do not actually send the promotions

Each of these strategies yields a certain profit for the selected group of customers $|U|$, so let us denote the profit of the i-th strategy as G_i. Equation 3.7 maximizes the difference $G_1 - G_2$, that is, the lift from targeting compared to random distribution. The alternative approach, known as *differential response analysis* or *uplift modeling*, is to maximize the uplift metric, defined as follows

$$\text{uplift} = (G_1 - G_2) - (G_3 - G_4) \tag{3.10}$$

which measures not only the lift compared to random distribution but also the lift compared to the no-action baseline for the same set of customers [Berry, 2009]. In this case, equation 3.7 transforms into

$$\underset{U \subseteq P}{\text{argmax}} \sum_{u \in U} \mathbb{E}\left[G \mid u, T\right] - \mathbb{E}\left[G \mid u, N\right] - c \tag{3.11}$$

in which the second term corresponds to the expected net value for customers who were not provided with the promotion. The difference between equations 3.7 and 3.11 can be illustrated by the following problem: Should a retailer offer a discount coupon on potato chips to a person who buys potato chips every day? This question would most likely will be answered in the affirmative according to equation 3.7 because the person is likely to redeem the coupon. However, it is more probable that the customer would just buy the same amount of potato chips for a lower price, which basically decreases the retailer's profit. Equation 3.11 alleviates this problem by incorporating default customer behavior. By generalizing this example, we can categorize customers based on the difference between the probability to respond given the treatment and the probability to respond without the treatment, as shown in Figure 3.7.

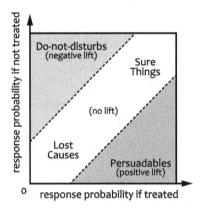

Figure 3.7: Customer categorization with respect to uplift.

Analysis of the probability differences suggests four customer types [Radcliffe and Simpson, 2007]. First, customers who have low probability of response, regardless of treatment, can be considered as Lost Causes, who are probably the wrong targets for communications. Customers who are likely to respond whether treated or not can be considered as Sure Things, who also seem to be the wrong targets. Customers who tend to be driven away by treatment, often referred to as Do-not-disturbs, should also be excluded from targeting. Finally, customers who are more likely to respond only if treated are the most valuable targets, the Persuadables. We will dive deeper into uplift modeling and profitability optimization in the following sections.

3.4.2   *Response Measurement*

The response modeling framework provides a basic tool for response prediction. The counterpart of this framework is a measurement framework that can be used to evaluate the results of a campaign – did it really help to acquire new customers, did it make existing customers spend more, or did it help to improve retention rates? We want to measure the effectiveness in terms of the ROI, which is defined as the incremental gain delivered by the campaign relative to the no-action strategy. This approach is consistent with the principles of life-cycle-based targeting and uplift modeling that we stated in the previous section.

The standard approach to measure the incremental gains is to compare the performance of two groups of consumers: ones who received the promotion (*test group*) and ones who did not receive it (*control group*). If we have a targeting model in place, both groups are typically selected from the high-propensity customers to make sure that the groups are statistically consistent and that the measured uplift reflects the impact of the promotion, regardless of the targeting strategy. This approach is typically implemented by excluding a small percentage of customers from the targeted audience at the very end of the targeting process, as illustrated in Figure 3.8.

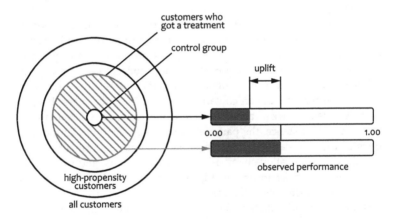

Figure 3.8: Measuring promotion effectiveness with test and control groups.

The performance of the groups is compared over some period of time that follows the campaign and is typically as long as several purchase cycles for a given product category to obtain stable results. Note that this approach does not require individual promotion redemptions to be tracked – we do not care about the redemption rate and simply need to compare the expenditures between the two groups. This can be a very convenient property if the redemption data is not available. We will return to the statistical details of measurements at the end of this chapter.

3.5 BUILDING BLOCKS: TARGETING AND LTV MODELS

Targeting models and lifetime value (LTV) models are the basic building blocks of the targeting process. The purpose of a targeting model is to quantify the fitness of a given consumer for a given business objective in a given context. For example, a model can score the fitness of a consumer for a potato chips promotional campaign given that the promotion will be sent tomorrow by SMS. Models can be created for different objectives and contexts, and a targeting system often maintains a repository of models attributed with the corresponding metadata, so that relevant models can be fetched according to the criteria. For example, one can have a model for acquisition campaigns in the potato chips category and another one for maximization campaigns in the soda drinks category. Models are the basic primitives that can be combined with each other, as well as with other building blocks, to create more complex programmatic flows. Marketing campaigns can be assembled from models, and marketing portfolios can be assembled from campaigns.

It should be stressed that a programmatic system can use models both in *predictive* and *prescriptive* ways. The most direct application is prediction of consumer properties, such as propensity to respond to an email or expected lifetime profit. Many models, however, express the dependency between inputs and outputs in a relatively transparent way, so the system can contain additional logic that uses this prescriptive insight or can at least make some recommendations to the marketer. For instance, the parameters of a regression model that predicts a response can indicate a positive or negative correlation with specific communication channels or other parameters, and this insight can be used to make additional adjustments, such as limiting the number of communications in the presence of a negative correlation. In this section, we consider three major categories of models that can be used separately or together:

PROPENSITY MODELS The idea of propensity models is to estimate the probability of a consumer to do a certain action, such a purchase of certain product. The output of such models is a score proportional to the probability that can be used to make targeting decisions.

TIME-TO-EVENT MODELS Propensity models can estimate the probability of the event, but they do not explicitly estimate when the event is most likely to happen. This type of estimate is more valuable in many marketing applications and requires a different statistical framework to be used.

LIFETIME VALUE MODELS LTV models are used to quantify the value of a customer and estimate the impact of marketing actions.

We start with a review of the data elements and data sources used in modeling and then discuss several traditional methods that can be viewed as heuristic propensity and LTV estimation models. These methods typically make the assumption that the probability of responding and the value of a customer are proportional to one or several basic characteristics, such as the frequency of purchases. The methods then group customers into segments so that an entire segment can be included or excluded from a certain campaign. These methods can be thought of as rule-based targeting. We then develop more advanced models with statistical methods.

3.5.1 Data Collection

Data collection and preparation is one of the most important and challenging phases of modeling. Although a detailed discussion of data preparation methodologies is beyond the scope of this book, it is worth reviewing a few principles that can help to streamline the process and avoid incorrect modeling. Targeting and LTV models generally aim to predict consumer behavior as a function of observed metrics and properties, so it is important to collect and use data in way that is consistent with causal dependencies. From this perspective, data elements can be arranged by tiers, with each tier depending on the previous ones [Grigsby, 2016]:

PRIMARY MOTIVATIONS Consumer behavior is driven by fundamental factors such as valuation of a product or service, tastes, needs, lifestyle, and preferences. Many such attributes cannot be observed directly, but some data such as demographics or marketing channel preferences can be collected through loyalty program registration forms and surveys or purchased from third-party data providers.

EXPERIENTIAL MOTIVATIONS The next tier of properties is created by the interaction between a customer and a brand. These properties characterize the overall customer experience, including customer satisfaction, loyalty, and usage patterns. Some of the ex-

periential properties can be directly or indirectly quantified by
using metrics like frequency of purchases.

BEHAVIORS The most important category of data is explicitly
observed behavioral data, such as purchases, website visits,
browsing history, and email clicks. These data often capture
interactions with individual products at specific points in time.
Behavioral data carry the most important signals needed for
modeling.

RESULTS Finally, customer actions result in directly observed financial
metrics, such as revenue or profits. It is important to keep in
mind that these metrics do not really explain the drivers of the
customer behavior and the ways it can be influenced; they merely
register the final outcomes.

The data described above should also be linked with additional dimensions, such as catalog data, seasonality, prices, discounts, and store
information. It is important to provide the ability to aggregate the data
at different levels of hierarchical dimensions to find the optimal level
of granularity. For example, a model can use data aggregated at the
product, category, or department levels.

The modeling process should generally be focused on revealing the
hidden properties and causality, not just analysis of the results. Although analysis of financial results is important, it is typically a good
idea to establish the link between marketing actions and these results
through behavioral concepts. For example, a solution that expresses the
revenue as a function of advertising intensity is not necessarily insightful and actionable enough. A solution that quantifies how advertising
influences customer loyalty and behavioral patterns (e. g., migration
from one customer segment to another) and then links customer properties to the revenue is likely to be more insightful and actionable.

3.5.2   Tiered Modeling

Targeting models score the relevance of a customer for a business objective and context, based on the features derived from a customer profile.
One of the most basic approaches is to use only one metric, such as the
monthly average dollar amount spent on a brand or category. This
metric can then be used in two ways. First, it is a measure of proximity between the customer and the promotion because promotions are
typically created for a specific brand and category. Consequently, the
most relevant promotions for a given customer can be selected based
on the brand and category with the highest monetary metrics. Second,
consumers can be sorted by the metric and the most valuable ones can

be selected for a given promotion. The classic example of this approach is tiered segmentation, whereby consumers are assigned to gold, silver, and bronze tiers depending on their score and heuristically selected threshold, as illustrated in Figure 3.9.

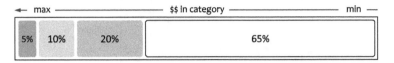

Figure 3.9: Example of segmentation by a monetary metric (gold–silver–bronze tiers). Customers are sorted by their spending in the category over some fixed time period, and the top 5% are assigned to the gold tier. The next 10% are assigned to the silver tier and the next 20% to the bronze tier. The remaining customers are not eligible for promotions.

Each tier is attributed with the metrics, such as the average expected response rate and average spending per customer, estimated based on the historical data. For each promotion, the optimal subset of tiers can be determined by running the promotion costs and tier metrics through the response modeling framework. For example, it can be determined that one campaign will be profitable if only the gold tier is targeted and another campaign has maximum profit when the gold and silver tiers are both targeted.

Single-metric segmentation can be elaborated by adding more metrics into the mix. As we discussed earlier, the consumer life cycle is an important consideration for the design of promotional campaigns, so the ability to target individual life-cycle phases is important. The life-cycle phases are characterized by both the total spending in a category and the loyalty to the brand, that is, the relative spending on a brand compared with that on other brands, so we can classify customers into segments by using these two metrics, as shown in Figure 3.10. This approach, known as *loyalty–monetary segmentation*, is used in traditional manufacturer-sponsored campaigns.

Customers who are highly loyal to the brand and spend a lot of money in the category are clearly the most valuable customers, who should be rewarded and retained. Customers who spend a lot in the category but are not loyal to the given brand are the best candidates for trial offers and so on. Similarly to the tiered segmentation, promotions can be assigned to the optimal subset of segments by starting from the upper left corner of the grid in Figure 3.10 and evaluating the potential outcome of including additional segments until the bottom right corner is reached. This approach can be considered as a simplistic targeting method that predicts consumer value based on two metrics – spending

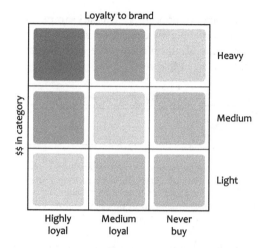

Figure 3.10: Example of loyalty–monetary segmentation.

in the category and brand share of wallet. These are very coarse criteria that can be improved by using predictive modeling methods.

3.5.3   RFM Modeling

Another popular segmentation heuristic is so-called *recency–frequency–monetary* (RFM) analysis. It is similar to the loyalty–monetary approach, but uses three metrics:

RECENCY The number of time units that have passed since the customer last purchased. This metric can be measured directly in time units (e. g., months) or can be mapped to some score. For example, customers can be sorted by the most recent purchase date and then those in the most recent 20% are assigned a score of 5, the next 20% a score of 4, and so on, until the last 20% get a score of 1.

FREQUENCY The average number of purchases per time unit. Again, the metric can be measured directly in units or scores.

MONETARY The total dollar amount spent per time unit. The monetary metric is typically measured by using intervals or scores.

It is quite typical to use the same discrete scoring scale, say from 1 to 5, for all three metrics. In this case, the RFM model can be considered as a three-dimensional cube made up of cells, each of which is determined by a triplet of metric values and corresponds to customer segments. The targeting decisions can be made by selecting a subset of segments from the RFM cube. One possible technique is to sum all three metrics into a single score and select customers whose score exceeds a threshold – this corresponds to cutting a corner away from the RFM cube.

RFM analysis is based on the empirical observation that recency, frequency, and monetary metrics are often correlated with the probability to respond and the lifetime value. Although this is a fair assumption, the RFM approach is shallow because it measures the final outcomes of the marketing processes and consumer actions, not the factors that impact consumer behavior. As we will see in a subsequent section, a more flexible solution can be obtained by using clustering.

3.5.4   *Propensity Modeling*

Simple segmentation models such as tiered segmentation and RFM analysis can be viewed as particular cases of regression analysis with a very limited number of features and heuristic assumptions about the relationships between the metrics and the expected outcomes. Our next step will be to build more formal scoring models.

The goal of propensity modeling is to find consumers who have a relatively high probability of behaving in a certain way or committing a certain action in the future. The number of actions that can be predicted and used in targeting is very high. Let us consider a few typical examples:

PROPENSITY TO TRY A NEW PRODUCT Consumers who currently do not buy a certain product but have a high propensity to buy it in the future are good targets for acquisition campaigns.

PROPENSITY FOR CATEGORY EXPANSION Consumers who have high propensity to switch from one category of products to another or to try a new category are good targets for up-selling or cross-selling campaigns. An example of such an audience are consumers who are likely to switch from casual to luxury products.

PROPENSITY TO BUY MORE Consumers who are likely to increase their average purchase quantity of a product are the right targets for maximization campaigns.

PROPENSITY TO CHURN Customers who are likely to unsubscribe from a service or stop buying a product can be targeted in retention campaigns.

PROPENSITY TO ENGAGE Propensity to engage is the probability of responding to a marketing action, for example, to click on an email link.

PROPENSITY TO CHANGE SHOPPING HABITS Each customer has shopping habits that eventually determine their customer value – how often the customer buys, which products, from which categories, and so on. These habits are generally stable over time, and once a brand manages to change a customer's level of engagement, this level tends to last. Consequently, brands are generally interested in finding customers who are open to changing their habits, for example, people who moved from one city to another, graduated a school or university, just married, and so on. The canonical example of such modeling is Target's attempt to predict customer pregnancies in the early stages because births obviously change the way customers shop [Duhigg, 2012].

Note that the major marketing objectives of acquisition, maximization, and retention can be expressed by using propensity language. The propensity-based approach is convenient from the response modeling perspective because the campaign ROI can be estimated by multiplying the expected gains and losses by the predicted outcome probabilities.

3.5.4.1 Look-alike Modeling

Look-alike modeling is one of the most important methods of propensity modeling. Look-alike modeling is based on the observation that propensity is essentially the probability of a customer moving from one point on the life-cycle curve to another, so one can train a predictive model by using profiles of consumers who exhibited this behavior in the past and then evaluate the model against the current profile of a given customer to estimate their propensity. For example, the profiles of customers who used not to buy a given product for a while and then started to buy it can be used to train a model that identifies customers with a high propensity to try this product for the first time.

Look-alike modeling is a classification problem, so it requires the profile features and response label to be specified. We assume that a customer profile can include individual attributes, such as income or household size, and a collection of behavioral events, each of which is attributed with a time stamp. For each profile, we put all of the events on a time line and specify three sequential time frames: the observation period, buffer, and outcome period. These frames are shown in Figure 3.11. The observation period is used to generate features, and the outcome period is used to generate the response label. These two intervals may or may not be separated by a buffer. The buffer can be used if one needs to predict events in the relatively distant future, instead of predicting immediate events. For example, a model that predicts customer churn should probably be trained with the outcome intervals shifted into the future – it would be impractical to predict customers who are likely to churn immediately because it gives no time to perform any mitigating marketing action.

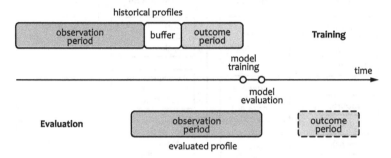

Figure 3.11: Look-alike modeling time frames.

The model is trained on a set of historical profiles that contain both the observation and outcome intervals. The model is then used to evaluate the current profiles, which, of course, contain only the observed part, and the expected outcome is predicted.

The design of features and response labels heavily depends on a particular domain. We focus on retail applications in this section, and feature engineering for the online advertising domain will be discussed in later sections. Look-alike modeling can generally use any customer data that is available including demographics, purchases, and marketing responses, such as email opens, clicks, and promotion redemptions. Profile features are typically specified as different combinations of time frames, metrics, and filters that can be applied to the profile data. This process is illustrated in Figure 3.12 for purchasing data. First, the features can be calculated for different time frames within the observation period. These subperiods are typically counted back from the end of the observation interval – last month, last three months, last six months, and so on. Within the subperiod, different metrics such as dollar amount or purchase frequency can be calculated, and different filters such as category, brand, product, payment type, or part of the week can be applied. Finally, the value can be expressed in units, such as dollars or days, percentages, per-basket averages, or binary yes/no variables. The curved line that connects the boxes in Figure 3.12, for example, corresponds to the share of the bakery category in consumer spending over the last 6 months relative to other categories. This approach allows the production of a relatively large number of features that can be used in predictive model training and evaluation. The same approach can be used for marketing response data and data from digital channels.

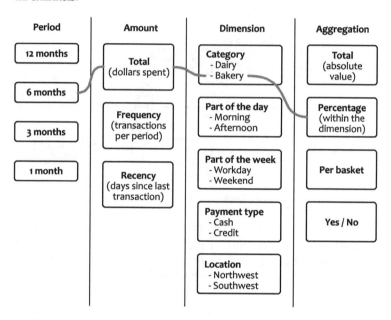

Figure 3.12: Example of profile feature engineering for purchasing data.

The response label is generated from the outcome period according to the objective. For example, if the model is created to target customers with a high propensity to try a given product, then the response label will indicate whether this product was purchased or not. Another example is a retention campaign where the response label indicates whether a customer defected or not. The set of training profiles can also be prefiltered according to the objective. In an example with a propensity to try a new product, the training set should include only customers who did not buy the product during the observation period (and then some of them started to buy it during the outcome period – such customers are called *natural triers*). The same rule is applied for model evaluation – a customer who already buys a promoted product is immediately excluded as a non-fit.

EXAMPLE 3.1

Let us run through a small example that illustrates look-alike modeling. Consider the following scenario: a CPG retailer with bakery and dairy departments started to work with a new brand of dairy desserts six months ago, and the brand has now asked to run a manufacturer-sponsored acquisition campaign. The targeting goal is to identify customers with a high propensity to try the dessert. Let us assume that a targeting system generated a training data set with 12 historical customers profiles and 5 features, as shown in table 3.1.

ID	Bakery Total	Bakery Weekend	Dairy Total	Dairy Weekend	Credit	Response
1	150	10	150	140	1	1
2	210	20	120	110	1	0
3	190	190	210	20	1	1
4	270	250	190	0	1	1
5	180	180	190	10	1	1
6	260	250	230	20	0	1
7	270	30	210	210	1	0
8	150	40	150	50	1	0
9	90	70	120	100	0	0
10	30	0	200	200	1	0
11	190	190	250	10	1	1
12	10	0	30	0	1	0

Table 3.1: Training data set for look-alike modeling.

The Bakery Total and Dairy Total features are the total spending in the corresponding categories during the observation period. The Bakery Weekend and Dairy Weekend features are the total spending on the weekend, so the amount spent on workdays equals the difference between the Total and Weekday values in each category. The Credit column is the payment method, credit or cash. Finally, the Response variable indicates whether the customer started to buy the dessert or not. By inspecting this tiny data set visually, we can conclude that the natural triers of the dessert are mainly the customers who buy a lot of bakery on the weekends and a lot of dairy on workdays. We choose here to use logistic regression to build a look-alike model, although other options including decision trees, random forests, and Naive Bayes are often used in practice as well. By fitting the logistic regression, we get the parameter estimates presented in table 3.2.

Note that bakery spending is positively correlated with the propensity to try the product, whereas dairy spending is negatively corre-

PARAMETER	ESTIMATE
BAKERY TOTAL	0.0012
BAKERY WEEKEND	0.0199
DAIRY TOTAL	− 0.0043
DAIRY WEEKEND	− 0.0089
CREDIT	− 0.4015

Table 3.2: Logistic function parameters for the training set in table 3.1.

lated[1]. By evaluating the model for six profiles with different proportions of bakery and dairy spending, we get the propensity score estimates shown in table 3.3. One can see that only customers with high spending on bakery and low spending on dairy have a high propensity to try the product, regardless of the payment method. In real life, one possible interpretation could be that dairy desserts are considered as substitutes for bakery desserts by customers who actively buy in both categories.

BAKERY TOTAL	BAKERY WEEKEND	DAIRY TOTAL	DAIRY WEEKEND	CREDIT	PROPENSITY TO TRY
10	0	50	50	1	0.26
20	20	200	200	1	0.07
150	20	100	30	1	0.37
250	20	190	30	1	0.31
250	200	190	30	1	0.94
250	200	190	30	0	0.96

Table 3.3: Predicted propensity to try the product.

Note that we do not use the historical response data as features in this example, that is, we do not take into account whether a customer used to respond to promotions in the past or not. In real life, this is an important signal for targeting accuracy, although it is valid to create models without response features if the data are not available.

▲

3.5.4.2 *Response and Uplift Modeling*

The most basic look-alike models, similar to those we just described in the previous section, estimate the unconditional probability of a certain action being done. By including marketing communications into the set of features, we can create a propensity model that estimates

---

1 See Chapter 2 for a detailed discussion of logistic regression. In this example, we skip typical steps, such as model validation and diagnostics, for the sake of simplicity.

the conditional probability of the response (action) given a marketing treatment. One possible methodology for creating such models is *pilot campaigns*. The idea of this approach is to distribute a promotion initially to a relatively small group of recipients, collect the responses, and create a classification model that maximizes the difference between treated responders and treated non-responders. This corresponds to a look-alike model trained on a population of treated profiles by using the response indicator as a training label. This model estimates the probability of the response given the treatment as

$$\Pr(R \mid T, \mathbf{x}) \tag{3.12}$$

in which R is the response indicator, T is the treatment indicator, and $\mathbf{x}$ is the profile feature vector. Once the model is created, it can be used to execute a full-blown campaign, that is, to target customers with a high propensity to respond when given the treatment. In certain cases, the model can be created by using historical data for similar campaigns without running a pilot. Thus, traditional propensity models are designed to identify customers who are likely to respond to a promotion or some other marketing communication. The downside of this approach is that such models can target customers who are likely to take an action anyway, even without the treatment. In other words, it can be the case that the propensity model predicts a high probability of responding, but once the campaign is executed, the observed difference between the test and control groups, that is, the uplift, is insignificant or the control group could even outperform the test group. We have already discussed this problem in the context of the response modeling framework, but we now need to dig deeper and specify how exactly this can be addressed in propensity modeling.

The problem with uplift arises from the fact that the basic propensity modeling process described above accounts only for treated customers and discards the information about the non-treated ones. This makes it structurally impossible to model the uplift. We can work around this problem by adding a control group to the pilot campaign. This group includes randomly selected profiles of customers targeted and not targeted in the pilot campaign. In this case, we can observe the results for four distinguishable groups: treated responders, treated non-responders, control responders, and control non-responders, as shown in Figure 3.13.

The four observed groups enable us to create a model that maximizes the uplift, that is, the difference between the response rates in the test and control groups:

$$\text{uplift}(\mathbf{x}) = \Pr(R \mid T, \mathbf{x}) - \Pr(R \mid C, \mathbf{x}) \tag{3.13}$$

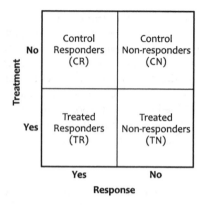

Figure 3.13: Measurement groups for propensity modeling with uplift [Kane et al., 2014].

in which the first term is the probability of a response after treatment and the second term is the probability of a response by an individual in the control group. These two probabilities can be estimated either by using two separate classification models trained on the test and control groups, respectively, or one model trained on a union of test and control profiles with the treatment indicator included as a feature [Lo, 2002]. The problem with the two-model approach is that separately created models may have incomparable score scales and may select features that are not actually predictive for the uplift, so this solution often fails to achieve better results than the baseline non-incremental propensity model [Radcliffe and Surry, 2011; Kane et al., 2014]. The single-model approach can achieve better results but may require more complex model design. For example, if logistic regression is used as the underlying modeling method, the feature vector should include both the profile features and profile–treatment interaction terms, so that the model has the functional form

$$f(\mathbf{x}, \mathbb{I}(T) \cdot \mathbf{x}, \mathbb{I}(T)) \tag{3.14}$$

in which $\mathbb{I}(T)$ is the indicator function and is equal to one if the customer $\mathbf{x}$ has been treated and zero otherwise [Lo, 2002]. Consequently, the uplift is estimated as

$$\text{uplift}(\mathbf{x}) = f(\mathbf{x}, \mathbf{x}, 1) - f(\mathbf{x}, \mathbf{0}, 0) \tag{3.15}$$

It can be argued that even more accurate results can be obtained by creating a multinomial model that predicts probabilities for each of the quadrants in Figure 3.13 [Kane et al., 2014]. We can create such a model to express the uplift as follows:

$$\begin{aligned}
\text{uplift}(\mathbf{x}) &= \Pr(R \mid T, \mathbf{x}) - \Pr(R \mid C, \mathbf{x}) \\
&= \Pr(R \mid T, \mathbf{x}) - (1 - \Pr(N \mid C, \mathbf{x})) \\
&= \Pr(R \mid T, \mathbf{x}) - \Pr(N \mid C, \mathbf{x}) - 1
\end{aligned} \tag{3.16}$$

in which N denotes a no-response outcome. By using the Bayes rule and the fact that $\Pr(T \mid \mathbf{x}) = \Pr(T)$ because the test and control groups are randomly selected, we get

$$\begin{aligned}
\text{uplift}(\mathbf{x}) &= \frac{\Pr(TR \mid \mathbf{x})}{\Pr(T \mid \mathbf{x})} + \frac{\Pr(CN \mid \mathbf{x})}{\Pr(C \mid \mathbf{x})} - 1 \\
&= \frac{\Pr(TR \mid \mathbf{x})}{\Pr(T)} + \frac{\Pr(CN \mid \mathbf{x})}{\Pr(C)} - 1
\end{aligned} \tag{3.17}$$

By repeating the same transformations for the response probability in the test group, we can also express the uplift as follows:

$$\begin{aligned}
\text{uplift}(\mathbf{x}) &= (1 - \Pr(N \mid T, \mathbf{x})) - \Pr(R \mid C, \mathbf{x}) \\
&= 1 - \frac{\Pr(TN \mid \mathbf{x})}{\Pr(T)} - \frac{\Pr(CR \mid \mathbf{x})}{\Pr(C)}
\end{aligned} \tag{3.18}$$

From the sum of equations 3.17 and 3.18, we obtain the final expression for the uplift estimation:

$$\begin{aligned}
2 \cdot \text{uplift}(\mathbf{x}) = \ &\frac{\Pr(TR \mid \mathbf{x})}{\Pr(T)} + \frac{\Pr(CN \mid \mathbf{x})}{\Pr(C)} \\
&- \frac{\Pr(TN \mid \mathbf{x})}{\Pr(T)} - \frac{\Pr(CR \mid \mathbf{x})}{\Pr(C)}
\end{aligned} \tag{3.19}$$

in which the probabilities in the numerators are estimated by using a single regression model. The uplift score can often be used as an alternative to the response probability estimated by basic propensity models – as we will see later, a targeting system can optimize the campaign ROI by selecting the recipients from those individuals with the highest uplift score as opposed to propensity scores.

3.5.5 Segmentation and Persona-based Modeling

Behavioral segmentation is the process of dividing customers into groups or *segments* in such a way that customers within a segment are similar to each other but dissimilar to customers in other segments. From the marketing analytics standpoint, segmentation is typically one of the most important, valuable, insightful, and complex projects.

It typically aims to define a small number of well-differentiated
segments with clear semantic meaning that can support strategic
decisions. The output of the segmentation process typically includes
segment profiles and segment models, also called clustering models.
A segment profile includes the distinctive properties and metrics
of the segment and some interpretation of what a typical customer
persona looks like. A simplistic example of segment profiles is shown
in table 3.4. The set with the most distinctive properties is usually
identified by running clustering algorithms on a set of historical
customer profiles, so each segment corresponds to a group of existing
customers and the segment profile is a set of statistical metrics for this
group. Although a segment is initially just a list of existing customers,
it can be converted into a clustering model that is essentially a
classification rule that maps any given customer profile to a persona.
The model-based representation of a segment is important because
it can dynamically assign customers to segments depending on their
profile features.

	SEGMENT 1	SEGMENT 2	SEGMENT 3
PERSONA	CONVENIENCE SEEKERS	CASUAL BUYERS	BARGAIN HUNTERS
% OF MARKET	20	50	30
% OF REVENUE	40	40	20
SHARE OF CLOTHING	40	60	60
SHARE OF ELECTRONICS	50	20	10
SHARE OF TOYS	10	20	30
REDEMPTION RATE	0.02	0.05	0.08

Table 3.4: Example of segments and segment metrics. Each segment can be interpreted in psychographic and behavioral terms. Convenience seekers,
for instance, seem to be less price sensitive and have fewer children
than consumers in other segments. This segment contains a relatively
small number of customers but makes a high contribution to the revenue.

Note that behavioral segmentation is very different from RFM analysis, although the RFM method can also be viewed as a segmentation
technique. RFM analysis segments customers based on the observed
financial results, whereas behavioral segmentation aims to identify the
traits that cause this result. In many cases, the resulting features, such
as spending, are deliberately excluded from the profile features before
clustering to make sure that segments are created based on the behavioral cause, not the financial outcome. The second important distinction is that RFM analysis and its variations use a fixed set of features,
whereas segmentation is a method to identify the most discriminative

features. These properties of behavioral segmentation are very important for strategic marketing analytics because they help us to understand the drivers of customer behavior (e. g., why one segment has more churners than another) and differentiate marketing strategies for each segment by using its distinctive characteristics. This differentiation can be taken to great lengths, such as the assignment of dedicated segment managers for each segment.

The programmatic perspective on segmentation is different from that we just discussed for marketing analytics because programmatics is more focused on execution and tactical aspects, rather than strategy. A programmatic targeting system is more often a user of the outputs produced by the behavioral segmentation process. First, persona tags are often used as features in look-alike modeling and other targeting rules and models; it does not matter how exactly these tags are created. Persona tags carry an important signal about consumer behavior and, hence, can have substantial predictive power for propensity modeling. The second important application of segmentation outputs is segment-level modeling. Propensity models created for an entire population of customers can have limited accuracy because propensities can be determined by different factors. For example, customers in one segment can churn because of low product quality, whereas customers in another segment churn because of high prices. Consequently, the model repository can maintain specialized models for different combinations of objective, product category, and customer segment.

3.5.6 *Targeting by using Survival Analysis*

Propensity modeling provides a powerful framework for estimating the probabilities of potential outcomes of marketing actions. This approach, however, has a number of shortcomings. The first issue is that the probability of the event does not straightforwardly translate into the time-until-event, which is usually a more actionable metric. For example, it can be more useful to know that a customer is likely to make a purchase in 10 days and that this time can be reduced by 5 days by offering a discount, rather than to know that the conditional probability of purchase by a customer given a discount is 0.8. Note the we cannot work around this problem by building multiple propensity models for adjacent time intervals because the intervals are interdependent. For example, we cannot build separate purchase probability models for January, February, and March because purchasing events in February depend on purchases in January and so on. The second challenge is that we do not always observe the outcomes needed to create the response labels for propensity modeling. For example, a look-alike model for a retention campaign can be trained to differentiate between the customers who have and have not churned. The training data set will include a number of profiles of customers who have churned during some time period in the past and also a number of profiles for customers who have not churned in the same period. This approach is not perfect because customers who have not yet churned may still churn in the future, so it is more accurate to say that their outcomes are unknown, rather than positive. This is a problem of the censored observations that we have already discussed.

These limitations of propensity modeling can be addressed by using survival analysis introduced in Section 2.6.2 . Survival models can properly handle censored data, predict the expected time-to-event (survival time), and specify how marketing actions and customer properties can accelerate or decelerate the events. Let us consider a numerical example that illustrates the basic usage of survival analysis in a targeting system.

EXAMPLE 3.2

▼ Consider the scenario of a retailer who sets up a promotional campaign in a programmatic system. To determine the optimal properties of the campaign, the system uses the data set for a previous similar campaign presented in table 3.5. This data set includes 12 customer profiles with 3 features: an indicator of whether a customer had made a purchase a week before the campaign announcement, the number of emails sent to the customer in the scope of the campaign, and the discount amount offered to the customer. The observed outcome is the time-of-purchase measured in days from the campaign announcement. The campaign ended after 20 days, so all three customers who did not purchase before the campaign had ended are considered censored.

We use this small data set to fit a Cox proportional hazard model, as described in Section 2.6.2.3. Recall that the Cox model is a semiparametric model with a nonparametric baseline survival function, which describes how the purchase times are distributed, and a parametric linear model for individual risk ratios. The risk ratio describes whether the "risk" of purchase for a given customer is higher or lower than the baseline. The risk ratio is also expressed as a function of profile features, so it is possible to quantify how different features impact the expected time-to-purchase. By fitting the Cox model, we get the following model for the risk ratios:

$$
\begin{aligned}
\log(\text{risk}) \quad = \quad & 1.957 \times \text{Previous Purchase} \\
& -0.510 \times \text{Number of Emails} \\
& +0.323 \times \text{Discount}
\end{aligned}
\tag{3.20}
$$

ID	PREVIOUS PURCHASE	NUMBER OF EMAILS	DISCOUNT, %	PURCHASE TIME
1	0	2	5	5
2	0	2	0	10
3	0	3	0	20 (censored)
4	1	1	0	6
5	1	2	10	2
6	1	3	0	15
7	1	4	0	20 (censored)
8	1	5	5	6
9	0	2	10	8
10	1	5	5	13
11	0	0	0	20 (censored)
12	1	2	5	8

Table 3.5: Training data set for survival analysis. The censored records correspond to customers who did not make a purchase during the first 20 days after the campaign announcement.

The interpretation of this model is that the previous purchase and discount are negatively correlated with the time-to-purchase and the number of emails is positively correlated. In other words, additional discounts decrease the time-to-purchase, but additional emails increase it. This indicates that sending more emails actually harms the campaign, so the emailing strategy and relevance of messages should assessed and fixed. This part of the model is useful but does not yet provide additional insights over standard propensity modeling. The more interesting part is survival functions. The Cox model can produce a survival function for any given value of the feature vector, and each function corresponds to the cumulative distribution of the purchasing times. In this example, the feature vector is a three-element vector with the previous purchase indicator, number of emails, and discount depth expressed as a percentage. Examples of the survival functions are shown in Figures 3.14 and 3.15. All of the curves have the same shape, but they are scaled according to the risk ratio estimated based on the feature vector x. One can see that the number of emails pushes the survival curve up, which justifies and quantifies the inefficiency of the communications. Meanwhile, the discount pushes the curve down, which indicates that discounts decrease the time-to-purchase.

It is important not only to obtain the survival curves but also to estimate the statistical properties of the time-to-purchase. Recall that the survival functions $S(t)$ are directly related to the cumulative distribution functions of the time-to-purchase $F(t)$:

$$S(t) = 1 - F(t) \tag{3.21}$$

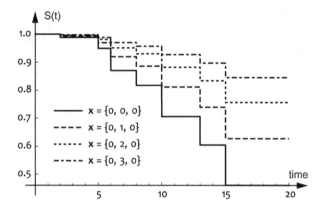

Figure 3.14: Survival curves for different numbers of emails. The purchase indicator and discount depth are equal to zero for all curves.

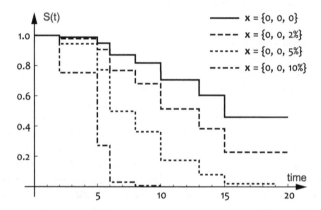

Figure 3.15: Survival curves for different discount depths. The purchase indicator and numbers of emails are equal to zero for all curves.

Consequently, we obtain the distribution functions from the Cox model as well. This enables us to estimate the average or median time-to-purchase, as well as confidence intervals and other statistical properties. As the survival function can be obtained for any combination of the independent variables, we can estimate the average or median time-to-purchase for each customer separately and then use these values in marketing rules (e.g., send a notification one day before the expected time-of-purchase) or targeting scores (e.g., target the ten percent of customers with the longest expected time to purchase). We can also quantify the impact of the independent variables in terms of the average or median time-to-purchase.

For example, it is possible to estimate how the average number of days until purchase decreases with every percent of discount.   ▲

Survival analysis can be applied to a number of marketing activities. The most typical applications include estimating the right timing for a message in replenishment campaigns, estimating time-until-churn in retention campaigns, and estimating the total number of purchases over some time interval for lifetime value modeling. Similarly to propensity models, survival models can be created for different products, categories, and customer segments. The expected times-to-purchase produced by these models can be compared with each other and then the most relevant products and offerings can be selected based on the ratio of times.

3.5.7   *Lifetime Value Modeling*

The last building block we will consider is estimation of the *customer lifetime value*, commonly abbreviated as LTV, CLV, or CLTV. The goal of LTV modeling is to estimate the total amount of money that a brand is likely to make from a given customer over the lifetime of their relationship. The exact structure of the LTV analysis heavily depends on the business model of a given brand, but it is possible to create basic LTV models that can be customized with brand-specific profit and loss terms.

The LTV is an important building block in campaign design and marketing mix management. Although targeting models can help to identify the right customers to be targeted, LTV analysis can help to quantify the expected outcome of targeting in terms of revenues and profits. The LTV is also important because other major metrics and decision thresholds can be derived from it. For example, the LTV is naturally an upper limit on the spending to acquire a customer, and the sum of the LTVs for all of the customers of a brand, known as the *customer equity*, is a major metric for business valuations. Similarly to many other problems of marketing analytics and algorithmic marketing, LTV modeling can be approached from descriptive, predictive, and prescriptive perspectives. We start with the basic descriptive approach and then develop more advanced models.

3.5.7.1   *Descriptive Analysis*

The LTV typically accounts for all revenues derived from a customer and variable costs associated with the relationship, and it can optionally include the cost of customer acquisition. One of the most basic ways to estimate the lifetime value of customer u is to sum the average expected profits for some time interval in the future:

$$LTV(u) = \sum_{t=1}^{T} (R - C) = T(R - C) \tag{3.22}$$

in which time t is measured in some units, typically months, R and C are the average expected revenues and costs, respectively, per customer per time unit, and T is the expected lifetime or projection horizon. The average expected revenues and costs are typically estimated based on historical data, such as transaction histories and campaign budgets. This estimate is not personalized (it is averaged over all customers) and is thus relatively straightforward. The revenues and costs can differ sharply for different customer segments, so it is very common to estimate R and C for each segment separately and then calculate segment-specific LTVs if the customer segment (persona) is known. The lifetime duration T can also be selected heuristically based on a typical relationship duration or planning horizon, often 24 or 36 months.

Basic LTV formula 3.22 does not account for several major effects. First, it does not explicitly account for customer retention. Although we can adjust the time horizon T according to the average customer lifetime, it can be more convenient to include the customer retention rate r into the formula as a parameter. For example, an annual retention rate of 0.8 means that 20% of the present customers will terminate the relationship within a year. Second, the LTV is typically measured for relatively long time intervals of 2–3 years, so we might need to account for the fact that money in the present is worth more than the same amount in the future, that is, for a discount rate d. The discount rate reflects the cost of tying up the capital for a period of time. For example, an annual discount rate of 0.15 means that the present value of $1 should be considered equivalent of $1.15 to be received in one year. Accounting for the discount rate gives the *net present value* of the LTV. By taking these two factors into account, we can estimate the customer net profit as $(R - C)$ for the first time period, $(R - C) \cdot r/(1 + d)$ for the second time period, and so on, which eventually adds up to the following definition of the LTV [Berger and Nasr, 1998] :

$$LTV(u) = \sum_{t=1}^{T} \frac{(R - C)r^{t-1}}{(1 + d)^{t-1}} \tag{3.23}$$

This formula is widely used and can be considered as a standard definition of the LTV. This expression, of course, does not include all of the effects that can be found in real life, and it can be extended to reflect other processes and parameters that influence the LTV. For example, we can model the net profit m not simply as a constant value $R - C$ but as a value that gradually increases over time as the relationship with the consumer matures:

$$m_t = m_0 + (m_M - m_0)\left(1 - e^{-kt}\right) \tag{3.24}$$

in which m_0 is the net profit at the beginning of the relationship, m_M is the potential maximum of the profit, and $k = \ln(2)/\tau$ is the profit growth rate specified in terms of the halfway time to maximum value. The halfway time τ determines how quickly the profit approaches the potential maximum – for every τ time unit, the difference between the current value of the profit and the maximum decreases by half. The net profit m_t can then be inserted into expression 3.23 instead of the constant $R - C$ value.

EXAMPLE 3.3
_____

We continue here by considering a numerical example of LTV calcula-   ▼
tions. We assume the following parameters of the model:

- The net profit at the beginning of the relationship, $m_0 = \$100$

- The potential maximum of the profit, $m_M = \$150$

- The halfway time to the maximum profit value, $\tau = 3$ years

- Retention rate, $r = 0.9$

- Discount rate, $d = 0.1$

By substituting these parameters into equations 3.23 and 3.24, we obtain the result shown in table 3.6. The nominal net profit in the first column grows in accordance with equation 3.24 and passes the halfway point of $\$125$ after the third year. The expected net profit is a product of the nominal net profit and total retention rate r^{t-1}. Finally, the discounted net profit is obtained by multiplying the expected net profit by the discount multiplier $(1 + d)^{t-1}$. The LTV is the sum of the annual discounted net profits.

Note that this analysis not only produces the total LTV but also shows the LTV dynamics over time. From the partial sums of the discounted net profit for one, two, and more years, we can draw an LTV curve against time. If the curve saturates quickly, it means that most of the value is extracted at the beginning of the relationship and long relationships do not bring a lot of additional value. If the curve grows steadily over a long time, it means that customer accounts remain profitable in the long run.   ▲

Year	Net Profit	Retention Rate	Expected Net Profit	Discount Multiplier	Discounted Net Profit
1	$100.00	1.00	$100.00	1.00	$100.00
2	$110.31	0.90	$99.28	0.91	$90.26
3	$118.50	0.81	$95.99	0.83	$79.33
4	$125.00	0.73	$91.13	0.75	$68.46
5	$130.16	0.66	$85.40	0.68	$58.33
LTV					$396.38

Table 3.6: Example of the LTV calculation for a horizon of five years.

The descriptive LTV model is similar to RFM analysis in the sense that it merely extrapolates the average revenues observed in the past into the future. It allows for some level of personalization if calculated for individual customer segments, but it does not predict how customer properties and marketing actions can influence the lifetime value.

3.5.7.2 *Markov Chain Models*

The descriptive LTV model does not provide us with much flexibility when it comes to complex customer journeys with multiple states of acquisition, maximization, and retention. At the same time, the presence of multiple states suggests that we can model a customer journey as a random process or, more specifically, a Markov chain. The idea of this approach is to define the set of customer states based on observed customer properties, such as recency of purchase, estimate the probabilities of transition between the different states and the corresponding profits and losses, and then estimate the LTV based on the expected customer path in the state graph [Pfeifer and Carraway, 2000].

A key part of the Markov chain approach is how the states and transitions are defined, so we choose to describe this method by using an example. Consider the case of a retailer who determined from its data that the recency of the last purchase is a good indicator for customer churn – customers who made a purchase last month make a purchase next month with a probability of $p_1 = 0.8$, customers who made their last purchase two months ago have a probability of $p_2 = 0.4$ to purchase again, three months corresponds to a probability of $p_3 = 0.1$, and, finally, customers who are inactive for four months are very unlikely to return. These sets can be modeled by using a Markov chain, as depicted in Figure 3.16. The chain has four states – one state for each value of recency and one for defected customers. Customer who do not make purchases move along the chain from left to right one step at a time until they reach the defunct state. A purchase resets the process and moves the customer back to the initial state.

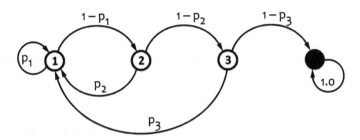

Figure 3.16: Example of a Markov chain for LTV modeling. The white circles correspond to three different values of recency. The black circle represents the defunct state.

This Markov chain corresponds to the following transition matrix:

$$\mathbf{P} = \begin{bmatrix} p_1 & 1-p_1 & 0 & 0 \\ p_2 & 0 & 1-p_2 & 0 \\ p_3 & 0 & 0 & 1-p_3 \\ 0 & 0 & 0 & 1 \end{bmatrix} \qquad (3.25)$$

Each row of the matrix corresponds to the current state and each column corresponds to the next state. Each element of the matrix is the probability of a customer moving from the current state to the next one. The probability that a customer who is currently in state s will end up in the state q after t months can then be calculated as the (s, q) element of the matrix $\mathbf{P}^t$, according to the standard properties of the Markov chain. This gives us a simple way to estimate the customer journey in probabilistic terms if the current state is known.

From an economic standpoint, each state of the chain corresponds to profits and costs. For example, the marketing strategy may be to spend some budget C on each active customer (e. g., send a printed catalog) and stop doing so after the customer moves into the defunct state. The first state is also associated with the revenue R of the purchase. Let us introduce a column vector $\mathbf{G}$ so that the net profit of the i-th state corresponds to its i-th element:

$$G = \begin{bmatrix} R-C \\ -C \\ -C \\ 0 \end{bmatrix} \quad (3.26)$$

It is easy to see that the matrix product $\mathbf{PG}$ produces a vector of expected net profits for each state after one time period. For example, the expected net profit for the first state will be

$$\mathbb{E}\left[\text{profit} \mid \text{state 1}\right] = p_1(R-C) - (1-p_1)C = p_1 \cdot R - C \quad (3.27)$$

because we are definitely spending the cost C and have p_1 chance to make a profit. Similarly, the expected profits for the second time period are given by $\mathbf{P}^2\mathbf{G}$, and so on. Consequently, the LTV can be estimated as a sum of such expected values over several time periods, and, if we also adjust each period by the discount rate d, we get the following expression:

$$V = \sum_{t=1}^{T} \frac{1}{(1+d)^{t-1}} \mathbf{P}^t \mathbf{G} \quad (3.28)$$

with column vector $\mathbf{V}$ containing the LTV estimates for each initial state. The LTV of a customer is also estimated as one of the elements of this vector based on the current customer states, that is, the recency value in this example. This result can be compared to the standard descriptive LTV model in equation 3.23 – we essentially replace the static net profit and retention rate parameters with a time-dependent probabilistic estimate.

Let us conclude the example by estimating the LTV for several different values of time horizon T. As before, we assume the transition probabilities of $p_1 = 0.8$, $p_2 = 0.4$, and $p_3 = 0.1$. Let us also assume that the expected revenue of one purchase is R = $100, monthly cost of marketing communications is C = $5, and monthly discount rate is d = 0.001. By evaluating expression 3.28 for these parameters and different values of the time horizon T, we get the following sequence of LTV vectors:

$$V_{T=1} = \begin{bmatrix} \$75.0 \\ \$35.0 \\ \$9.5 \\ \$0.0 \end{bmatrix} \quad V_{T=2} = \begin{bmatrix} \$135.5 \\ \$48.4 \\ \$10.4 \\ \$0.0 \end{bmatrix} \quad V_{T=3} = \begin{bmatrix} \$184.0 \\ \$53.4 \\ \$10.5 \\ \$0.0 \end{bmatrix} \quad (3.29)$$

We can see that the LTV heavily depends on the initial customer state. For a time horizon of three months, that is, $V_{T=3}$, the LTV of a customer who made a purchase a month ago is \$184.0. After two months, the expected LTV drops to \$53.4, and finally to \$10.5 after the third month.

We can extend the Markov chain method to accommodate more complex customer states and marketing strategies. For example, the probability of the next purchase is often correlated not only with the recency but also with the frequency of past purchases. In this case, each distinct pair of recency and frequency values can be modeled as a separate state in the chain. We can also replace the algebraic estimation of the LTV given by expression 3.28 with Monte Carlo simulations of the consumer journey, which can provide even more flexibility in how gains and loses are modeled. In this case, we randomly select the initial state according to the state frequencies estimated from the data; we then traverse the graph, flipping a coin in each state to decide in which direction to go and recording the profits and losses encountered on the way. By repeating this process many times, we obtain multiple samples of the expected lifetime value. The advantage of this approach is that the statistical properties of the LTV, such as mean, variance, or confidence intervals, can be straightforwardly assessed by analyzing the histogram of obtained samples. It also enables us to include additional business logic and parameters in each state, which can be difficult to encode with transition matrices.

3.5.7.3 Regression Models

The Markov chain model improves the descriptive LTV model by replacing the static retention rate and average expected profit with time-dependent and state-dependent estimates. The limitation of this approach is that the number of states grows exponentially with the number of customer properties that we include in the model. We can take one step back and note that, conceptually, both descriptive and Markov chain models estimate the LTV in terms of the customer's probability to stay with the brand and the expected net profit from the customer. This can be expressed as follows:

$$\text{LTV}(u) = \sum_{t=1}^{T} p(u, t) \cdot m(u, t) \tag{3.30}$$

in which $p(u, t)$ is the probability of customer u staying until time t and $m(u, t)$ is the net profit from the customer in time period t. The conventional descriptive model estimates both factors by using static retention rate and average profit, whereas the Markov chain model estimates the same factors with probabilistic analysis. A more flexible solution for problem 3.30 can be obtained by creating regression models for both factors. The advantage of this approach is that regression models can use a wide range of independent variables created from a customer profile and, thus, enable predictive and prescriptive capabilities.

One can see that survival analysis is a natural choice for the retention probability factor in equation 3.30. This probability directly corresponds to the customer's survival function $S_u(t)$, so the model can be rewritten as

$$LTV(u) = \sum_{t=1}^{T} S_u(t) \cdot m(u, t) \tag{3.31}$$

The survival model is trained to estimate the time to churn, and it requires the churn event to be defined. These events may be tracked directly (if a customer explicitly unsubscribes from a service) or heuristically by using some business rule (for example, all customers with five or more months without purchase activity are considered lapsed). Survival analysis efficiently solves the problem of the retention probability estimation by proper handling of censored data, and the ability to estimate personalizes survival functions parametrized by customer properties, such as recency and frequency of purchases.

The net profit values $m(u, t)$ can be estimated in several different ways with different accuracies. One of the most basic approximations is to estimate the average net profit value for each customer segment (persona) and use this static value for all customers within a segment. More elaborate regression models can be created by including seasonality and customer profile features.

3.6 DESIGNING AND RUNNING CAMPAIGNS

Targeting and LTV models, the basic building blocks of a targeting system, provide a solid foundation for efficient marketing decisions. A marketing campaign, however, is typically a flow with multiple actions and decisions geared to achieve a certain objective. This flow may require multiple models to be wired together and optimizations to be done with multiple signals and constraints taken into account. A targeting system often has some sort of repository for campaign templates, where each template describes a certain flow of actions and decisions. This flow is typically designed for a certain objective, but it can be parametrized with different targeting models, budgeting constraints, user experience properties, and so on. Forecasting of the campaign

ROI and optimization of the execution parameters and thresholds to balance the costs and profits is an important part of the campaign design process, and the corresponding routines and models can be considered as part of the template. In this section, we consider several types of campaigns and their relationship to the previously discussed basic models.

3.6.1   Customer Journeys

From an economic standpoint, interactions between a customer and brand can often be viewed as a collection of transactions that can be characterized in terms of total amounts, purchased items, margins, clicks on the website, and so on. The problem of marketing optimization can also be viewed in a transaction-centric way so that all components of the marketing mix become focused on the optimization of individual transactions, in terms of their probabilities and margins. The notion of the customer life cycle puts this optimization into a broader context but still focuses on the brand's concerns and objectives rather than the customer experience. This approach is incomplete in many marketing environments, including retail, where interactions with a customer are experience-centric and the success of a brand is determined by its ability to deliver a superior long-term customer experience, rather than optimizing individual transactions.

One popular approach to customer experience analysis and modeling is based on the notion of *customer journey maps*. A journey map tells the story of the relationship between a customer and the brand. The map can describe the entire arc of the engagement, similarly to the life-cycle curve, or can be focused on a specific scope, such a single purchase. The map is typically visualized as a diagram with the steps or stages of the engagement and the transitions between them. A very simplified example of a customer journey map is shown in Figure 3.17. This map depicts the flow of a single transaction but puts it in the context of the customer experience and long-term interactions with the brand.

The journey starts with triggers, which include browsing for a new idea and product, preparation for special events such as birthday parties, getting a promotional email, or the necessity to replenish a consumable product. The trigger is followed by researching product information and selecting the purchasing channel. The interaction then continues in the scope of the selected channel, including browsing of a specific product and checkout, and completes with post-purchase actions such as product return or writing a customer review. In real life, customer journey maps are typically much more complicated and in-

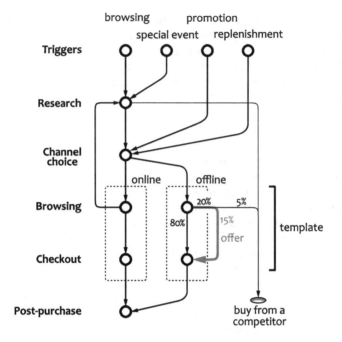

Figure 3.17: Example of a customer journey map.

clude a lot of details about the customer behavior and decision-making process, distribution of customers by different states and branches, and so on. In addition, customer journey maps are often created for each customer segment because the journeys can differ substantially across the segments.

A marketing campaign typically has a certain footprint on the journey map, in the sense that a campaign attempts to influence the path of a customer. In Figure 3.17, for example, customers who drop out of the offline purchasing funnel are provided with an offer to win them back. Each campaign can be viewed as a type of template that can be applied to a specific situation in the customer journey. A programmatic system can have a repository of *campaign templates*, where each template includes the rules that prescribe when the campaign actions should be triggered and how the situation should be handled, along with models to estimate the parameters of the required actions and forecast the outcomes. A template can describe a single action or a whole set of actions that can be executed at different points in time, by using different channels, and by taking the observed feedback into account.

Analysis of customer journeys and the creation of journey maps is usually a strategic project that often includes extensive analytical research, customer surveys, and marketing strategy development. Thus, the creation of customer journeys maps and campaign templates is not the responsibility of a programmatic system. We generally assume that these artifacts are created elsewhere and then entered into the system. The responsibilities of the system, however, include estimation and optimization of the template parameters and dynamic selection of the most optimal templates.

3.6.2 Product Promotion Campaigns

One of the most basic types of targeted campaign is a sales promotion for an individual product. Examples of such promotions include advertisements without monetary value, dollar-off coupons, buy-one–get-one (BOGO) coupons, and free product samples. In the CPG domain, this class of campaign is often referred to as *free-standing inserts* (FSI), named so because of coupon booklets that are inserted into local newspapers. In the most basic form, a standalone promotion corresponds to a simple customer journey with a trigger (promotion) and purchase (redemption). As we will see later, this approach is not necessarily the most efficient one, but it is applicable to all objectives:

- For acquisition, a brand can send BOGO or dollar-off coupons to customers who are heavy category buyers but do not buy this particular brand.

- For maximization, a brand can send conditional promotions like *Buy 3, Get $1 Off* to existing customers.

- For retention, a brand can send BOGO or dollar-off promotions to customers who have decreased their consumption relative to previous purchasing cycles.

The response modeling framework provides some guidance on how such promotions can be targeted by using predictive models that estimate the probability of response, but there are many additional aspects that need to be covered, including the targeting process, budgeting rules, and selection of promotion parameters.

3.6.2.1 Targeting Process

A targeting system can be used in both batch and real-time modes, depending on the environment and campaign nature. Some promotions can be distributed by sending millions of emails in one shot, so a targeting system can prepare a list of customers to be targeted in advance. Other promotions are targeted in near real time because of rapidly changing customer profiles or context. For example, a promotion may or may not be offered to customers depending on the content of their shopping baskets just before checkout. The real-time approach is generally more flexible, and a properly designed real-time targeting system can also simulate the batch mode by evaluating the targeting rules and models for the entire customer database. Consequently, we focus on the real-time targeting case and consider a process that receives a single customer profile and the corresponding context as the input and produces a list of promotions that should be offered to this customer.

We also assume that the system has a database of available promotions that can potentially be offered. This database includes promotions from all campaigns that are currently active. Each promotion needs to be attributed with properties such as business objective, promoted product, and category, so the targeting system can use this information to link the promotion with the proper targeting models and rules. This is the reason why promotion creation and targeting are closely related to each other, in the sense that each targeting step or feature requires a counterpart in the campaign configuration and promotion attributes. We will go though the targeting process and discuss both how promotions are selected from the set of available options and the methodology for creating and attributing promotions with the properties and conditions needed for targeting.

The targeting process can be thought of as a sequence of three steps. First, the system takes all available promotions and selects those that are valid for a given context and customer. Next, promotions are scored to produce a list sorted according to the fit to the objective. Finally, the optimal set to be offered to the customer is selected by applying budgeting limits and other constraints. This process is sketched in Figure 3.18. The initial filtering of promotions is typically based on business rules and conditions, so we refer to it as *hard targeting*. On the other hand, promotion scoring typically uses predictive models that produce a continuous score, so we call this stage *soft targeting*.

The goal of the hard-targeting stage is to select promotions that qualify for a given context. Promotions created in the targeting system are typically associated with conditions that must be met by a given context to activate the promotion. The purpose of these conditions is to encourage certain consumer behaviors and ensure the basic economic goals of the promotion. The hard-targeting conditions essentially define the campaign template, that is, the point in the customer journey

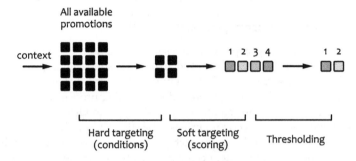

Figure 3.18: The promotion targeting process.

where the promotion should be applied. Consider the following typical examples:

- Quantity condition. Activates a promotion when the customer purchases a certain quantity of a certain product, brand, or category in a single transition or over a certain period of time. This condition is often used in maximization campaigns to *stretch* a consumer, that is, to give an incentive to buy more then usual. For example, a customer who typically buys two packs of yogurt can be offered a *Buy 4, Get 1 Free* promotion.

- Non-buyer condition. Activates a promotion for customers who have not bought a product or brand for a certain period of time. This condition can be used in retention and acquisition campaigns to separate active brand customers from inactive and prospecting consumers.

- Channel condition. Activates a promotion when a customer interacts with a brand or retailer via a certain channel. For example, a customer can be rewarded for visiting a store three times a week.

- Retargeting condition. Activates a promotion based on previously offered or redeemed promotions. For example, customers who have received but have not redeemed promotions via digital channels can be contacted by using in-store channels.

- Location condition. Activates a promotion based on the customer location as determined from mobile device data, store location, in-store beacons, or IP address.

- Availability condition. Some promotions can be temporarily de-activated if the corresponding products are out of stock or un-available through a given marketing channel.

The hard-targeting step produces a set of promotions that can poten-tially be offered to a consumer. The goal of the soft-targeting stage is to select the most relevant offers and filter out options that are likely to be inefficient. Soft targeting is often done by using propensity models. A targeting system can maintain a repository of models where each model is trained for a certain business objective and product category and is attributed accordingly. As each promotion is also attributed with similar properties, the system can dynamically link models to promo-tions. Scoring models can be combined with special conditions that complement the logic encapsulated in the model. For instance, the ba-sic look-alike acquisition model identifies customers who are similar to natural triers, but it does not ensure that a promotion will not be of-fered to those who already buy the product. In contrast, maximization and retention promotions typically should not be offered to customers who do not consume the promoted product. These additional checks can be implemented as a condition.

3.6.2.2 Budgeting and Capping

Once the set of candidate promotions is prepared and ranked, the sys-tem needs to select the final set of promotions that can be offered to the customer. This step can include several controls to manage differ-ent aspects of a campaign. First, the number of promotions received by a customer in the scope of a single campaign, as well as the total frequency of communications with the customer (number of messages per time unit), should be limited. These rules, often referred to as *pres-sure rules* or *frequency capping rules*, typically use thresholds selected heuristically or by means of experimentation. Next, the campaign bud-get or the total number of issued promotions is typically limited. The targeting system, however, often needs to determine the optimal num-ber of promotions to maximize the campaign ROI. It can be the case that this number is far below the limit specified by the marketer and consumption of the budget up to the limit can make losses. From the propensity modeling standpoint, the profitability optimization prob-lem can be viewed as finding the propensity scoring threshold that maximizes the profit if all customers with a higher score are targeted and all other customers are not. We have already shown how the trade-off between campaign costs and profits can be modeled by using the response modeling framework, and we now consider an example that provides more practical details.

EXAMPLE 3.4

Consider the case of a retailer who has 100,000 loyalty card holders. ▼
The retailer plans a targeted campaign where each promotion instance
costs $1 and the potential profit of one response is $40. The average response rate for this type of campaign and product category estimated
from historical data is 2%. On the basis that we have created a propensity model that estimates the response probability for each customer,
we can score all card holders and sort them by the scores. The result
can be summarized by splitting the customers into "buckets" of equal
size where the first bucket corresponds to the customers with the highest scores and the last bucket corresponds to those with the lowest
scores. The targeting problem can then be defined as finding the optimal number of top buckets to include in the targeting list, or, equivalently, finding the threshold score that separates these top bucket from
the bottom ones. We use bucketing for the sake of convenience in this
example and this approach is often used in practice as well, but there is
nothing to stop us from doing the same calculations for individual customers, that is, having as many buckets as customers. Let us assume
that we have 10 buckets or deciles, so that each bucket contains 10,000
customers; consequently, the average expected number of responders is
200 per bucket. In other words, we are likely to get 200 responses from
each bucket if we randomly assign customers to buckets. This number
is shown in the second column of table 3.7, and the third column contains the cumulative number of responders, which reaches 2,000 or 2%
of the customer base in the bottom row.

Decile	Responses, Random		Responses, Targeted			Lift
	Bucket	Total	Pr	Bucket	Total	
1	200	200	0.060	600	600	3.00
2	200	400	0.057	570	1,170	2.93
3	200	600	0.038	380	1,550	2.58
4	200	800	0.017	170	1,720	2.15
5	200	1,000	0.010	100	1,820	1.82
6	200	1,200	0.007	70	1,890	1.58
7	200	1,400	0.006	60	1,950	1.39
8	200	1,600	0.003	30	1,980	1.24
9	200	1,800	0.001	10	1,990	1.11
10	200	2,000	0.001	10	2,000	1.00

Table 3.7: Example of campaign lift calculations.

Next, let us assume that the lowest response probability scores generated by the propensity model in each bucket are those presented in the
fourth column. By multiplying the bucket size by this probability, we

get the expected number of responses in the case of the targeted distribution presented in the next two columns. The total number of responders still adds up to 2,000, of course. The ratio between the number of responders in the case of targeted and random distributions is called *lift*, and it is the key metric that describes the quality of the targeting model. The lift is typically visualized by using a *lift chart* similar to the one in Figure 3.19. This chart shows two lines that correspond to the cumulative number of responses: the straight line corresponds to the random distribution and the raised curve to the targeted distribution.

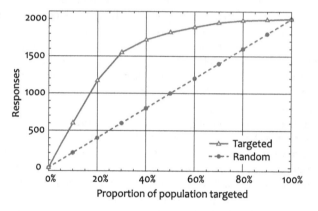

Figure 3.19: Lift chart for the targeting model.

To determine the number of buckets to be targeted, we need to estimate the campaign ROI. Each promotion costs $1, so the random distribution strategy is not profitable because each bucket causes a loss:

$40 response profit × 10,000 recipients × 0.02 response rate

−$1 per customer × 10,000 recipients

$= -\$2,000$

The targeted campaign, however, will be profitable for the first three buckets because of the high response rates, as summarized in table 3.8. One can see that including more buckets initially increases the campaign ROI but it then starts to decrease and eventually becomes negative.

The campaign ROI is maximized for outreach to three buckets, that is, the top 30% of the population. This corresponds to all customers with a propensity score above 0.038. The targeted campaign ROI is plotted in Figure 3.20. Note that the maximum possible budget, which

DECILE	COST	PROFIT		TARGETED ROI
		RANDOM	TARGETED	
1	10,000	-2,000	14,000	14,000
2	10,000	-2,000	12,800	26,800
3	10,000	-2,000	5,200	32,000
4	10,000	-2,000	-3,200	28,800
5	10,000	-2,000	-6,000	22,800
6	10,000	-2,000	-7,200	15,600
7	10,000	-2,000	-7,600	8,000
8	10,000	-2,000	-8,800	-800
9	10,000	-2,000	-9,600	-10,400
10	10,000	-2,000	-9,600	-20,000

Table 3.8: Example of campaign profitability calculations.

corresponds to sending a promotion to each and every customer, does not maximize the ROI. On the contrary, it causes a loss of $20,000.

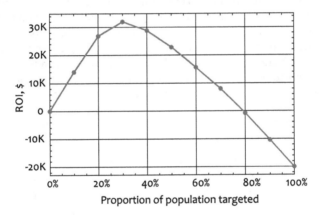

Figure 3.20: Targeted campaign ROI as a function of the outreach.

It is important to note that we used the basic response probability, instead of uplift modeling, in this example. In practice, this can result in poor campaign performance because high response rates do not guarantee uplift in customer spending or consumption. In other words, a control group in each bucket can perform equally well or even better than the targeted group in the same bucket. One can work around this problem by replacing the response probabilities in table 3.7 with the uplift scores discussed in Section 3.5.4.2.

The ROI maximization principle allows estimation of the optimal baseline parameters of a campaign, such as the total number of promotions to be distributed and the scoring threshold. In the real world, it can sometimes be beneficial to deviate from the baseline, especially for real-time applications when the set of customers who will actually interact with the system is not known in advance. Consider the following scenario. A system runs a promotional campaign with a fixed budget and spreads this budget evenly over the campaign's time frame. This suggests that we should use some fixed distribution rate, for example, 100 promotions per hour. However, what should we do if the campaign is running over this target rate (in our example, 100 promotions have already been issued during the last hour) but we encounter a consumer with a very high propensity score? It can be reasonable to go over the budget at this point and then slightly decrease the rate later to get back on track. This behavior can be implemented by dynamic adjustment of the scoring thresholds depending on the deviation from the target distribution rate. This idea is illustrated in Figure 3.21. We define the target distribution rate and and two margins, ε^- and ε^+, that determine the maximum acceptable deviation from the target line. Note that the target does not necessarily have to be a straight line, and one can use a more sophisticated curve that takes into account weekends, working hours, and so on. The actual distribution rate is constantly measured and controlled by the system to stay within the margins.

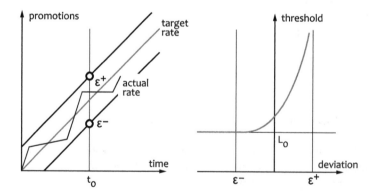

Figure 3.21: Dynamic scoring threshold for budget control.

The scoring threshold can then be expressed as a function of the deviation from the target line at the current moment of time t_0. If we are substantially under budget (under the ε^- line), the scoring threshold can be set to the minimum, which corresponds to the lowest affinity L_0 between the consumer and promotion that is sufficient to make the offer. If we are substantially over budget (above the ε^+ line), then the threshold should be set to the maximum possible scoring value to stop the distribution completely. These two extreme points can be connected by some growing function, as illustrated in Figure 3.21. Consequently, we become more and more demanding of consumers as we approach and cross our budgeting limits, and we lower the bar when we do not encounter enough high-quality prospects.

3.6.3 *Multistage Promotion Campaigns*

Standalone promotion campaigns, such as the distribution of trial or maximization coupons, are widely used in practice. However, it can be argued that this strategy can be inefficient because it has a very short and limited impact on the customer journey [Catalina Marketing, 2014]. It is sometimes possible to design more sophisticated campaigns with multiple phases that influence the customer journey over a longer period of time. Let us consider an example of a CPG maximization campaign with the following design:

- The first phase of the campaign is an announcement that aims to inform the customers about the offer. For example, a brand can distribute the following message via available marketing channels: *Buy Q or more units of product X and save on your next shopping trip. The more you buy, the more money you save.*

- The second phase is distribution. A targeting system tracks the transactions and issues dollar-off coupons to customers who qualify for the targeting condition, that is, the purchase of Q or more units in this example. The discount amount of the coupon is determined dynamically based on the purchased quantity – as announced, the more consumers buy, the more they save. At this stage, a consumer is incentivized to buy more units to get a coupon as a reward.

- The third and the last phase is redemption. On the second shopping trip, the consumer buys the promoted product to redeem the coupon issued in the previous stage. The consumer is incentivized to buy a product to redeem a coupon and get a discount.

This campaign template can be thought of as a customer journey with three steps: trigger, purchase, and redemption. It can be argued that this approach is more efficient than standalone promotions because it has a more durable impact on customer loyalty and lower costs per unit moved [Catalina Marketing, 2014]. The dynamically determined discount value in the second stage is an interesting detail because the targeting system needs to optimize this value and forecast how it will influence the campaign outcomes. This aspect is not addressed by the targeting and budgeting processes discussed in the previous sections. Let us consider an example that demonstrates how a targeting system can heuristically evaluate different promotion parameters and forecast the campaign outcomes by using just basic statistics. More formal discount optimization methods will be discussed later in Chapter 6 in the context of price optimization.

EXAMPLE 3.5

▼ Consider the case of a promotional campaign that follows the three-phase scenario described above. The goal of the targeting system is to choose a reasonable value for the quantity threshold Q and, in the second phase, to determine the discount amount based on the quantity that is actually purchased. We can start with a histogram of purchase quantities for the promoted product calculated for the time interval equal to the duration of the campaign. Let us denote the number of transactions with exactly q units of the promoted product purchased as $H(q)$, so the historical histogram is as follows:

$$H(1) = 4000 \ (32\%) \qquad H(4) = 1000 \ (8\%)$$
$$H(2) = 5000 \ (40\%) \qquad H(5) = 600 \ (5\%)$$
$$H(3) = 2000 \ (16\%) \qquad H(6) = 0$$

We want to stretch customers who buy relatively small quantities, so the system can select threshold Q to be above the majority of transactions. In this example, the value of 3 would be a reasonable choice because 72% of transactions are under this threshold. Consequently, the system will offer a discount coupon to customers who buy more than 3 units. The discount value depends on the quantity actually purchased. We will discuss this in more detail in Chapter 6, but we can assume for now that the discount values are static configuration parameters. For example, suppose that the minimal discount value is 15% and it increases by 5% at each level. This means that customers who buy 3 units get the discount of 15%, those who buy 4 units get 20%, and those who buy 5 units get 25%. Let us denote the number of units at level i as q_i and the corresponding discount value as d_i. Once all of these parameters are determined, the system can forecast the campaign outcomes. This can be done separately for each discount level. The expected number of coupons generated at level i can be estimated, based on the previously created histogram, as

$$coupons(i) = H(q_i) \tag{3.32}$$

The expected number of redemptions can then be estimated by using a response model that includes the discount depth as a feature:

$$\text{redemptions}(i) = \text{coupons}(i) \times r(d_i) \tag{3.33}$$

in which $r(d_i)$ is the average response rate predicted by the model. The cost of coupons at level i can then be estimated as

$$\text{cost}(i) = (\text{product price} \times d_i \times q_i + c) \times \text{redemptions}(i) \tag{3.34}$$

in which c stands for the additional costs associated with a coupon, such as distribution and clearing-house costs. The campaign efficiency can be predicted as the ratio between the total number of redemptions and the total costs summed over all levels (cost per redemption).

▲

3.6.4 *Retention Campaigns*

Retention campaigns aim to save customers who are likely to leave. This type of campaign is widely used in telecommunications, insurance, banking, and other subscription-based domains where the continuity of a relationship is critical. The problem of customer churn, however, is relevant for most non-subscription businesses as well, including retail. One of the key reasons why retention activities are important is that acquisition of new customers can be much more challenging and expensive than the retention of existing ones. According to some studies, the acquisition cost per consumer can be 10–20 times higher than the retention or reactivation cost because of lower response rates and other factors [Artun and Levin, 2015].

A retention campaign can be defined as a follow-up with customers who are at risk. The follow-up and risk, however, can be defined very differently depending on the campaign design. Examples of risk include the risk of subscription cancellation and the risk of switching to a different supermarket chain. The definition of risk depends on the business model, nature of the product or service, and usage patterns. A software service provider, for example, can be concerned about the risk of subscription cancellation but may also observe a significant number of customers who create an account but do not download the client application. Thus, the risk of not downloading the application can be recognized and addressed by a dedicated retention campaign. Examples of follow-up actions include reminder emails, distribution of educational materials, requests to review the recently purchased product, and special offers and discounts.

Compared to promotional campaigns, the design of retention campaigns puts more emphasis on the lifetime value and uplift. The incorporation of lifetime value projections is important because investments in the retention of customers with low value would be meaningless. Uplift modeling is important because targeting of the wrong customers can be counterproductive for several reasons [Radcliffe and Simpson, 2007]. First, many customers at risk are dissatisfied already, and additional communications, especially intrusive ones like phone calls, can catalyze the churn process. Second, some retention communications can remind customers that they have an opportunity to leave, which makes them reconsider their relationship with the brand and look around for alternative options. This makes it important for the communications to be focused and the outcomes to be constantly measured by using control groups.

Retention campaigns are typically assembled by using the standard building blocks, but there exist different design methods. One of the most basic approaches is to target based on the propensity to churn. This model can be created by using standard propensity modeling methods with a training data set assembled from active and churned customer profiles. This approach is seemingly simple, but it has pitfalls that should be discussed. As we have previously discussed, a marketing action can be described in terms of two conditional probabilities – the probability to respond if treated and the probability to respond without treatment. In the case of retention, the response event corresponds to churn. All customers can be categorized with respect to these two probabilities, as depicted in Figure 3.22.

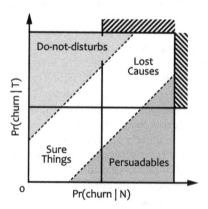

Figure 3.22: Categorization of customers from the perspective of a retention campaign.

If the overall retention strategy is focused, that is, the customers are not normally treated with retention offers, a propensity model trained to predict churn outcomes will actually predict the probability of churn given no treatment as

$$\text{score}(\mathbf{x}) = \Pr(\text{churn} \mid N, \mathbf{x}) \qquad (3.35)$$

in which $\mathbf{x}$ is the customer profile feature vector. A retention campaign driven by this probability focuses on the rightmost vertical slice of the square in Figure 3.22, which includes many Persuadables but also many Lost Causes. If the retention strategy is broad, that is, almost all customers are treated to some degree, the model will actually estimate the propensity to churn under treatment as

$$\text{score}(\mathbf{x}) = \Pr(\text{churn} \mid T, \mathbf{x}) \qquad (3.36)$$

which corresponds to the horizontal area at the top of the square in Figure 3.22, which contains many Do-not-disturbs and Lost Causes. This aspect of modeling should be taken into account when the population for model training is selected. The retention campaign can also use survival analysis to estimate the time-to-churn, which can be more convenient for choosing the right moment for treatment than the probability of churn.

Targeting customers based on their probability to churn does not take into account the long-term outcomes of the campaign. These outcomes can be quantified in terms of lifetime value because every retention saves the LTV of the corresponding customer and every churn is a loss of this LTV. If the probability to churn and LTV are estimated for a given customer, the product of these two values is the *expected loss*. We can expect that the ratio between the saved revenues and the campaign costs is maximized by treating those customers with the highest expected loss, so this measure can be used as a targeting score:

$$\text{score}(\mathbf{x}) = \Pr(\text{churn} \mid N, \mathbf{x}) \times \text{LTV}(\mathbf{x}) \qquad (3.37)$$

The LTV can be estimated based on the average customer spend or by using the more advanced LTV models described earlier. This model can be customized depending on the business model to account for the costs and profits associated with the different possible outcomes. For example, the expected retention gains, churn losses, and campaign costs can be separately estimated. The expected loss model specified by equation 3.37 is widely used in practice because of its simplicity and reasonably good efficiency.

The main shortcoming of the expected loss model is that it uses only the probability to churn and not the churn uplift, that is, the difference between the treated and non-treated churn probabilities:

$$uplift(\mathbf{x}) = Pr(churn \mid T, \mathbf{x}) - Pr(churn \mid N, \mathbf{x}) \qquad (3.38)$$

A positive churn uplift means that the treatment amplifies the churn, that is, the treatment has a negative effect. High uplift corresponds to the upper left corner of the square in Figure 3.22. A negative churn uplift means that the treatment decreases the churn, which corresponds to the lower right corner in Figure 3.22. Consequently, we want to target customers by using the inverse of the uplift as a score:

$$score(\mathbf{x}) = -uplift(\mathbf{x}) = savability(\mathbf{x}) \qquad (3.39)$$

This metric is also called *savability* because it estimates the propensity to react positively to the retention activity. Uplift/savability can be modeled by using the methods described in Section 3.5.4.2, including the two-model and single-model approaches. Similarly to other applications of uplift modeling, the savability-based approach helps to separate those customers who are likely to stay *only* if they are treated from other groups, thereby increasing the efficiency of the retention campaign. However, it is important to keep in mind that this approach also inherits the typical disadvantages of uplift modeling. It includes more complicated modeling and higher variance of estimates because the uplift is the difference of two random variables. The uplift can also be combined with the expected loss technique to take into account the long-term impact on the harvested LTVs:

$$score(\mathbf{x}) = savability(\mathbf{x}) \times LTV(\mathbf{x}) \qquad (3.40)$$

Once the targeted scores are calculated, the optimal targeting depth, that is, the percentage of the population to be targeted, can be determined by using the ROI maximization method described earlier in Section 3.6.2.2. The campaign can then be executed with the same targeting process as that used for product promotional campaigns.

3.6.5   Replenishment Campaigns

Retention campaigns are most relevant for subscription-based businesses, such as telecommunication services, insurance, software, and banking. In the retail domain, the subscription-based model is less frequently used, but many products are routinely replenished so the engagement model becomes similar to a subscription. Examples of replenishable products are numerous: food, cosmetics, office supplies, accessories like water filters, and many others. Replenishment campaigns aim to drive repeat purchases and decrease *purchasing cycles* by sending reminders, recommendations, and specialized promotions.

From the campaign design standpoint, the distinctive features of replenishment are the emphasis on communication timing and purchasing habits. The communication timing is important because the replenishment notifications should be aligned with the individual purchasing cycles – it is not efficient, for example, to send a notification immediately after a customer has purchased the product. Connection with the purchasing habits is also important because the notification message should be consistent with the products and categories typically purchased by the recipient.

Let us start with a very basic approach that can be implemented by a targeting system. First, the system estimates the average duration of a purchasing cycle for each replenishable product or product category. The replenishment campaign is then executed repeatedly, for example, on a daily basis. For each execution, the system goes through the customer profiles and determines the last purchasing date for replenishable products. This date is compared with the estimated duration of the purchasing cycle, and a notification is sent to customers who are apparently approaching the end of the cycle. The message can be personalized based on the most recently or most frequently purchased products found in the purchasing history.

One of the main limitations of the above approach is an estimate of replenishment cycles that is too rough. One possible improvement is to break down the estimate not only by product category but also by customer segment or persona, to account for the differences between customers. In other words, the cycle duration is estimated for each pair of a category and a persona. More accurate results can be obtained by using survival analysis to estimate the time-to-purchase, as we have already discussed. The survival model also allows the determination of the factors that positively or negatively contribute to the time-to-purchase, such as discounts or replenishment notifications themselves, so the message content and frequency can be adjusted accordingly.

3.7 RESOURCE ALLOCATION

The problem of optimal targeting can be viewed as a resource allocation problem where some limited resource, such as sales coupons, needs to be allocated across customers. So far, we have focused only on this type of allocation and have ignored the fact that marketing activities may be required to make many other allocation decisions. The corporate marketing resource allocation strategy generally includes allocation between marketing and non-marketing activities, products, product life-cycle stages, markets and territories, business objectives, marketing channels, and communication types [Carpenter and Shankar, 2013]. Many of these allocation decisions, such as allocation between marketing and research activities, are very strategic and thus cannot be addressed by a programmatic system. Some other decisions are more tactical, and the system can include modules that automate or at least facilitate the decision-making process. It should be kept in mind, however, that targeting is one of the most tactical and technical allocation problems, and the automation of other allocation decisions is increasingly more complex and challenging.

The modeling and optimization of how resources are allocated across marketing activities and capabilities is known as *marketing mix modeling* (MMM). It can be viewed as the statistical analysis of how the different components of the marketing mix, such as promotions and prices, impact business performance metrics, such as sales and revenues. In this section, we focus on two resource allocation problems, allocation by channel and allocation by business objective, and discuss how these problems can be addressed by using MMM methods.

3.7.1   *Allocation by Channel*

A targeting system often has multiple marketing channels at its disposal, and each channel has its own costs structure, audience, and efficiency. The direct mail channel, for example, may have a much higher cost per message than the email channel, but it may provide higher response rates for certain categories of customers. This requires marketing communications to be optimized with respect to channels. One possible approach to this problem is optimization at a customer level, where the channel is selected by using a response model that accounts for channel-specific response probabilities and costs. Another approach is to optimize the global budget allocation across channels to maximize the revenue. This is sometimes referred to as *channel mix modeling*. These two methodologies can be viewed as bottom-up and top-down solutions, respectively, and both are important.

Channel mix modeling is a set of statistical analysis methods that focuses on the following descriptive and predictive questions:

- What percentage of revenue (or other performance metric) is driven by each channel or communication type?

- How will an increase or decrease in a given channel spend affect the revenue?

- What is the optimal budget allocation across the channels?

Intuitively, we can expect these questions to be answered by a regression model that expresses the metric of interest as a function of the channel activity. The challenge is that the dependency between the activity and the observed metric can be complicated for several reasons. First, we can directly measure the channel activity only as the current number of emails or online advertising impressions, but the customer responses are typically delayed and spread over time. Second, multiple campaigns can overlap when they run in parallel, but we can only observe the cumulative effect. Finally, the dependency between the intensity of the channel activity and the magnitude of the response is often nonlinear because of saturation effects. One popular channel mix model that accounts for these effects is the *adstock model* [Broadbent, 1979].

The key assumption made by the adstock model is that each given sales period retains a fraction of the previous stock of advertising. By assuming, for now, that we have only one advertising channel, let us denote the intensity of the channel activity measured in dollars spent or the number of messages in time period t as x_t, the business metric of interest, often the sales volume or revenue, as y_t, and the current effect induced by the activity on the business metric as a_t. The effect variable a_t is called the adstock. The adstock model assumption can then be expressed as

$$a_t = x_t + \lambda \cdot a_{t-1} \tag{3.41}$$

in which λ is the decay parameter that corresponds to the fraction of the effect carried over the time period. For example, a parameter of 0.4 means that the treatment from one period ago has 40 percent of its effect during the current period. In other words, the adstock model assumes that each new marketing activity increases loyalty and awareness to the new level, but loyalty gradually fades until it is boosted again by the next portion of activity. By expanding recursive equation 3.41, we get

$$a_t = x_t + \lambda x_{t-1} + \lambda^2 x_{t-2} + \lambda^3 x_{t-3} + \dots \tag{3.42}$$

Note that this is essentially a smoothing filter applied to the input sequence. In practice, we can always assume that the treatment effect is finite and limited by n periods, so we rewrite the adstock transformation of the original sequence as

$$a_t = x_t + \sum_{j=1}^{n} \lambda^j \cdot x_{t-j} \tag{3.43}$$

The observed business metric is then estimated as a linear function of the adstock:

$$\hat{y}_t = w a_t + c \tag{3.44}$$

in which w is the weight and c is the baseline value given no adstock. In the case of multiple channels, we assume that the adstock is additive, so the full model specification is a linear regression over the adstocks:

$$\hat{y}_t = \sum_{i=1}^{n} w_i a_{it} + c \tag{3.45}$$

whereby each channel is modeled with its own decay parameter λ_i, so the full model requires estimation of the baseline parameter c, n decay parameters λ_i, and n channel weights w_i. We can fit the model by solving the following problem for the observed samples y_t:

$$\min_{c,\,w,\,\lambda} \quad \sum_t \left| y_t - \hat{y}_t \right|^2 \tag{3.46}$$

The fitted model allows us to estimate the impact of increasing or decreasing the channel budgets and to measure the relative contribution of each channel to the target metric as:

$$z_{it} = \frac{w_i a_{it}}{\sum_j w_j a_{jt}} \tag{3.47}$$

This value can be averaged over time to obtain the average relative *channel contribution*. The efficiency of the channel can be measured as the ratio between the absolute channel contribution and the channel budget, that is, the number of units sold generated by each dollar spent on marketing activities through this channel. The following example illustrates how the adstock model can be created and used.

EXAMPLE 3.6
_____

▼   Consider a retailer who uses two marketing channels: email and SMS. The retailer can measure and control the intensity of marketing communications through each of the channels by setting budgeting and capping rules. The retailer also observes the sales volume. A data sample with these metrics is plotted in Figure 3.23 for 20 sequential time intervals (we have omitted the table with numerical values for the sake of space).

The adstock model can be fitted by solving problem 3.46 with numerical optimization methods. By setting the length of the decay window n to 3, we get the following estimates for the model parameters:

baseline: $c = 28.028$

email: $\lambda_{email} = 0.790$ $w_{email} = 1.863$

SMS: $\lambda_{sms} = 0.482$ $w_{sms} = 4.884$

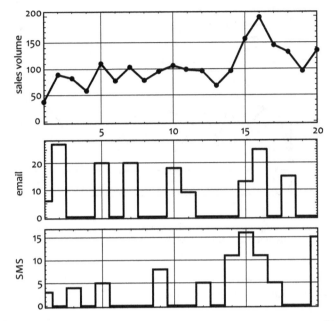

Figure 3.23: Data for adstock modeling: sales volume, email activity, and SMS activity.

We can use these parameters to calculate the adstock for each of the channels according to expression 3.43. The structure of the sales volume can then be visualized as three layers stacked one on top of the other: the baseline sales volume determined by constant c, the email contribution estimated as the email adstock scaled by w_{email}, and the SMS contribution estimated as the SMS adstock weighted by w_{sms}. This structure corresponds to expression 3.45, and the result is plotted in Figure 3.24. This decomposition enables us to estimate the efficiency of each channel and optimize budget allocation.

The basic adstock model accounts for overlapping marketing activities and decay effects but not for the advertising saturation that we mentioned earlier. In general, an increase in the treatment intensity increases the outreach of the campaign, which increases the demand. The dependency between the intensity and demand, however, is not linear. It typically follows the *law of diminishing returns*, so that spending more dollars on the marketing activity at some point yields a lower incremental demand. The adstock model can account for this saturation effect by nonlinear transformation of the intensity variable. One pos-

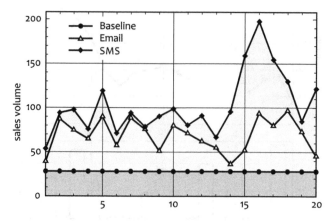

Figure 3.24: Decomposition of the sales volume into the layers contributed by different marketing channels.

sible choice is to use the sigmoid (logistic) function, so that recursive adstock equation 3.41 is redefined as follows:

$$a_t = \frac{1}{1 + \exp(-\mu \cdot x_t)} + \lambda \cdot a_{t-1} \tag{3.48}$$

in which μ is an additional model parameter that controls the steepness of the logistic curve. The adstock model can be extended or modified in many ways to account for additional effects that can be found in practice. For example, we typically need to account for the seasonality of demand, which can be done by extending the model with additional variables. At this point, channel mix modeling can take advantage of the demand modeling techniques discussed in detail in Chapter 6. Another example is that the geometric lag assumption made by the adstock model is somewhat restrictive because the time lag can have a more complex shape. In fact, the model described by equations 3.42 and 3.43 is known in econometrics as the Koyck distributed lag model, which, in turn, belongs to the family of distributed lag models [Koyck, 1954]. This family provides a number of more flexible alternatives, including a polynomial distributed lag model, which can be both more flexible and easier to estimate than the Koyck model [Almon, 1965; Hall, 1967].

3.7.2 Allocation by Objective

A programmatic system can use both LTV growth and acquire–maximize–retain goals as the input objectives for the targeting optimization. The ROI can be estimated in all of these cases by using the LTV uplift or immediate net profit uplift, in accordance with the response modeling framework. The choice between these objectives and global optimization of the ROI is a strategic question that does not necessarily need to be addressed by a programmatic system. However, the system can provide some guidance on how to allocate budgets across the objectives to maximize the overall ROI [Blattberg and Deighton, 1996].

We have discussed in Section 3.5.7 that the retention rate is a major factor that influences the LTV, so the LTV can be considered a function of the retention rate. We can make the assumption that the retention rate is, in turn, a function of the marketing budget spent on retention activities. For example, we can model the dependency between the budget and rate as follows:

$$r = r_{max}\left(1 - e^{-k_r R}\right) \tag{3.49}$$

in which R is the retention budget per customer, r_{max} is an estimate of the maximum retention rate (ceiling) that we can achieve given the unlimited budget, and k_r is a coefficient that determines how fast the rate approaches the ceiling. Similarly, we can model the acquisition rate a (response rate for an acquisition campaign) as a function of the acquisition budget:

$$a = a_{max}\left(1 - e^{-k_a A}\right) \tag{3.50}$$

in which A is the acquisition budget per customer, a_{max} is an estimate of the maximum response rate, and k_a is a parameter that controls the sensitivity of the rate to budget changes. Consequently, the acquisition net profit for a given customer can be defined as

$$a \cdot LTV(r) - c \tag{3.51}$$

in which c is the acquisition cost per prospect. The overall optimization problem for budgets A and R can then be defined as follows:

$$\max_{A,\,R} \quad N_p\left(a \cdot LTV(r) - c\right) + N_c \cdot LTV(r) \tag{3.52}$$

$$\text{subject to} \quad A + R \leqslant \text{total budget}$$

in which N_p is the total number of available prospects and N_c is the total number of current customers. The first term of equation 3.52 corresponds to the revenues from new customers and the second term corresponds to the revenues from existing customers, so it is effectively a revenue optimization problem. Equation 3.52 defines the optimization problem in terms of aggregated and averaged values, but it can be easily rewritten as a sum of individual LTVs over all customers to enable more accurate estimations with predictive models.

3.8   ONLINE ADVERTISEMENTS

The principles of promotion targeting discussed in the previous sections are geared towards consumer packaged goods and the traditional retail environment. It is clear that many of these principles hold for other marketing environments, but implementation heavily depends on the available data and exact definition of business objectives, which can vary across environments. We continue here by analyzing online advertising, which is perhaps the most important and well-developed application of algorithmic marketing and is an excellent example of an environment where the technical infrastructure and data flows are so complicated that the business objectives cannot be understood and achieved without careful examination of the technical capabilities and limitations.

3.8.1   *Environment*

The online advertising environment is very complex and diverse because it represents a marketplace where thousands of companies sell and buy ad inventory, offer and utilize technical systems that automate the buying process, and control and measure the quality and effectiveness of advertising campaigns. Additional complexity comes from the fact that, although most of the terminology and standard offers are generally accepted across the industry, there are many variations and cross-cutting solutions that appear as the industry evolves. The high complexity of the online advertising ecosystem makes it difficult to capture all important aspects of the environment in a single view, so we will start with a simplified model, shown in Figure 3.25, to support our discussion of business objectives and economic goals.

Figure 3.25 depicts the relationships between the following key entities that constitute the online advertising landscape:

- A *brand*, also commonly referred to as a *marketer*, is a seller of products or services. The brand invests money into advertising campaigns and expects to obtain a return on the investments by improving certain aspects of sales and customer relationships.

- An *advertiser* or agency runs advertising campaigns on behalf of the brand. The advertiser generally tries to achieve the same goals as the brand, but its exact strategy depends on the payment model established between the brand and the advertiser, as well as the methodology used to measure the performance of the campaign. The brand can work with multiple agencies that may compete against each other in the scope of one campaign.

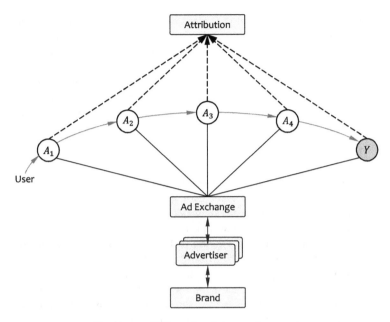

Figure 3.25: Online advertising environment.

- The advertisers can reach an internet user, who is a current or potential client of the brand, through different *channels*. Examples of channels include ad banners on a web page, paid results on a search-engine result page, and online video ads, among others. In a general case, the set of channels is not limited to internet channels and can include other media, like TV ads or printed catalogs.

- Each channel is represented by multiple *publishers*, for example, websites. Publishers sell their ad inventory, that is, the available slots that can contain the actual ads.

- The publishers and advertisers are connected by means of an ad exchange. The exchange receives ad requests from publishers when a piece of inventory becomes available (e. g., an internet user opens a web page) and distributes the requests across advertisers, who, in turn, can buy the available ad slot and show the ad to the user. The exchange is often organized as a Vickrey (second-price) auction that processes each ad request in real time, so the exchange is commonly referred to as a *real-time bidding* (RTB) process.

- A *user* is the recipient of the ads delivered via the channels. The user can interact with multiple channels and publishers over time, receiving ad realizations known as *impressions*. From the brand perspective, the user either eventually *converts* to produce some desired outcome, such a purchase on the brand's website, or does not convert. Consequently, there is a funnel of sequential impression events A_i for each user that ends with the outcome Y, as shown in Figure 3.25.

- Finally, the impressions and conversions are tracked by an *attribution system*. We consider the attribution system as an abstract entity that can trace the user identity across channels and publishers and can keep records of which user received which impression from which advertiser at which point in time. The purpose of the attribution system is to measure the effectiveness of the ad campaign and provide insights into the contributions of individual channels, advertisers, and user segments. The attribution system typically collects the information by using tracking *pixels* attached to ad banners and conversion web pages; users are identified with web browser cookies. However, the attribution process can consume additional data sources, such as purchases in brick-and-mortar stores, correlate this data with online profiles by using loyalty or credit card IDs, and measure causal effects across online and offline channels.

In the environment model above, the brand relies on the attribution system to measure the effectiveness of individual advertisers and ad campaigns as a whole. The metrics produced by the attribution system directly translate into the advertiser's fees and the brand's costs and revenues, so we will spend the next section examining attribution models and their impact on advertiser's strategies.

3.8.2   *Objectives and Attribution*

Similarly to the case with promotions, the business objectives of the brand are driven by a desire to shift the relationships with certain consumers from one level to another:

BRAND AWARENESS The marketer is generally interested in making its brand recognizable to potential customers and making it associated with a certain category of products, such as soft drinks or luxury cars, even if this does not immediately translate into conversions.

CUSTOMER ACQUISITION Acquisition aims to attract prospects who do not interact with the brand and drive them to conversion.

RETARGETING Retargeting, also known as remarketing, focuses on prospects who have already interacted with the brand, where there is potential to develop the relationship with them. A typical example is internet users who visited the brand's website one or more times but did not convert.

These primary objectives can be complemented by additional constraints that are important for the brand. For example, the brand might not be willing to advertise on websites with adult, violent, or hateful content. Ideally, the contract between the brand and the advertiser should be designed in such a way that the advertiser is paid for achieving the objectives above. More specifically, the desired properties of the contract can be described as follows:

- The targeting and bidding processes should be driven by the business objective of the campaign (e. g. , brand awareness, acquisition, or retargeting) and be restricted by additional rules such as *brand safety*.

- The effect of the campaign should be measurable, and the metrics should accurately reflect the value added by the advertiser. In other words, the metrics should answer the question "What will happen with the business objective if the advertiser is removed?" Note that this question directly relates to the uplift modeling discussed earlier in this chapter.

- It should be possible to answer the above question about advertiser removal for the case of multiple advertisers working for the same brand. Credits should be attributed to advertisers proportionally to their contribution to the total value increment.

Unfortunately, it is not straightforward to define a contract that fully meets the above criteria. The business objectives can be formalized in different ways, and the measurement of the incremental value also represents a non-trivial statistical and technical problem. Let us first describe several basic methods that are widely used in practice, and we will then discuss the outstanding questions and limitations that should be addressed in later sections.

From the brand perspective, the overall effectiveness of the campaign can be measured by using the *cost per acquisition* (CPA), which is defined as the total cost of the campaign C_{camp} divided by the total number of conversions N_{conv}:

$$CPA = \frac{C_{camp}}{N_{conv}} \tag{3.53}$$

Conversion, however, can be defined in different ways. One possible approach is to count *post-view actions*, that is, to count the users who visited the brand's site or made a purchase within a certain time interval (for example, within a week) after they received an impression. A more simple method is to count the immediate clicks on advertisements, which is referred to as the *cost per click* (CPC) model. From the advertiser perspective, it makes sense to split the cost of the campaign into a product of the number of impressions and the average cost of one impression, so the CPA metric can be expressed as follows:

$$CPA = \frac{N_{impr} \cdot \mathbb{E}\left[c_{impr}\right]}{N_{conv}} = \frac{1}{CR} \cdot \mathbb{E}\left[c_{impr}\right] \tag{3.54}$$

in which N_{impr} is the total number of impressions delivered by the campaign, $\mathbb{E}\left[c_{impr}\right]$ is the average price paid by the brand for one impression, and CR is the conversion rate. The advertiser's margin is the difference between the price paid by the brand and the bid value placed in the RTB, so we can define the advertiser's equivalent of the CPA as follows:

$$CPA_a = \frac{1}{CR} \cdot \mathbb{E}\left[c_{impr} - c_{bid}\right] \tag{3.55}$$

We need to specify contracts for c_{impr} and c_{bid} in order to evaluate the above expressions for CPA and CPA_a. The price c_{impr} paid by the brand is typically fixed, although there are two different types of contracts that are used in practice:

- *Cost per action* , also known as *cost per acquisition* (CPA) or *pay per acquisition* (PPA), contract. The brand pays a fixed fee for each conversion measured by the attribution system.

- *Cost per mile* (CPM) contract. The brand pays a fixed fee for each impression, but eventually measures the overall CPA by using the attribution system.

Both approaches are equivalent in the sense that the advertiser has to minimize the CPA metric to satisfy the client, even for CPM contacts. The fixed fee implies that the CPA metric in equation 3.54 can be optimized by maximization of the conversion rate CR. However, the bid value c_{bid} in equation 3.55 is not fixed and directly influences the conversion rate, so optimization of the CPA_a metric requires joint optimization of CR and c_{bid}.

The final area we need to cover is attribution in the case of multiple advertisers. The most basic approach is *last-touch attribution* (LT), which gives all the credit to the last impression that preceded the conversion. Consequently, the goal of the advertiser under the LT model is to identify customers who are likely to convert immediately after the impression.

The CPA and LT assumptions – we will refer to these settings as the CPA-LT model – provide a reasonably complete and formal problem definition that can be used for targeting process optimization. However, the CPA-LT model is overly simplistic and has a number of issues and limitations:

- There is no explicit relationship with the business objective. The model does not distinguish acquisition, awareness, or retargeting goals. In fact, CPA-LT principles are geared towards consumers with a high propensity to purchase, which implies a heavy bias towards retargeting and tactical acquisition rather than awareness and strategic acquisition.

- The model suggests optimization of the response, not uplift. This can lead to meaningless results under certain circumstances. For example, a targeting method that identifies only high-propensity users who are likely to convert without any impressions will have a very good performance under the CPA-LT model, although this is unlikely to be a good approach from the ROI standpoint.

- Last-touch attribution encourages advertisers to cheat and piggyback on each other's efforts. For example, an advertiser can buy a lot of low-quality inventory, such as ad slots at the bottom of web pages, to "touch" as many use users as possible (the so-called *carpet bombing*).

We will discuss how to optimize targeting and bidding strategies under the CPA-LT model in the next section, and we will then investigate how the shortcomings of this model can be addressed with more sophisticated attribution and controlled experiments.

3.8.3 *Targeting for the CPA-LT Model*

The basic goal of targeting under the CPA-LT model is to identify users who are likely to convert shortly after the impression. Similarly to the case of promotion targeting, we use a variant of look-alike modeling to solve this problem, but we want to explicitly account for the information about a user's response to advertisements as opposed to selecting natural buyers based on purchase histories. In particular, we want to account for the performance of the currently running advertisement, which means that we have to dynamically adjust our targeting method based on the observed results. In other words, we want to build a self-tuning targeting method.

We can assume that the advertiser has the following data for each consumer profile:

- Visited URLs. The advertiser listens to bid requests and other partner data sources that allow the user's browsing history to be captured. URLs can include both the domain, such as google.com, and the address of a particular page.

- User attributes. The advertiser can receive additional information about the user along with the URLs: for example, the properties of a browsing device and applications, geographical location, time spent on a page, and some others.

- Bids and impressions. The advertiser can track the bids it made for a given user and the impressions delivered to the user.

- Ad clicks. The advertiser can get information on how the user interacted with the delivered ads.

- Conversions. The brand can provide the advertiser with information about the conversions on its website.

- Additional brand data. The brand can provide additional data, such as products browsed by a user on the brand's website.

The features for predictive modeling can be engineered based on these data elements. Visited URLs and derived characteristics, such as recency and frequency, are known to carry a lot of predictive information about conversions. A major challenge, however, is a high number of observed URLs, in that a model that consumes a binary vector where each element, zero or one, indicates whether a user visited a URL or not, might have millions of dimensions.

The straightforward approach for the problem of self-tuning targeting is to start the campaign with random targeting, that is, to bid for random people, wait for a sufficient number of conversions, and then train the scoring model by using converted users as positive examples and non-converted users as negative examples, as shown in Figure 3.26. This approach, however, is not optimal because conversion events are very rare in the case of random targeting and the dimensionality of user profiles, as discussed above, is very high, so the creation of a sufficient training data set by using random bidding at the beginning of a campaign can be impractically expensive [Dalessandro et al., 2012a].

There are many different techniques that can help to improve the basic approach described above. In the rest of this section, we closely follow the staged targeting methodology described in the work of [Dalessandro et al., 2012a] and [Perlich et al., 2013], which provides a comprehensive practical solution for self-tuning targeting. The approach is to perform the targeting process in three sequential steps: calculate

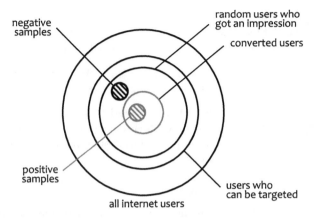

Figure 3.26: Desirable sampling for the targeting task. The shaded circles correspond to positive and negative examples.

the brand proximity, incorporate the ad response, and incorporate the inventory quality and calculate the bid amount.

3.8.3.1 *Brand Proximity*

The goal of this step is to estimate the probability of conversion Y regardless of the ad impact, that is, to calculate the unconditional *brand proximity* $\Pr(Y \mid u)$ for user u. If historical information about visitors to the brand site is available before the campaign begins, the advertiser can create models for a converting user by selecting converted profiles as positive examples and random profiles of internet users as negative examples. Note that this sampling is different from the desired sampling depicted in Figure 3.26. This step is essentially look-alike modeling that uses visited URLs as features and conversions as labels to model the unconditional brand proximity:

$$\begin{aligned}\varphi(u) &= \Pr(Y \mid u) \\ &= \Pr(Y \mid URL_1, \ldots, URL_n)\end{aligned} \tag{3.56}$$

in which URL_i are binary labels equal to one if the user visited the corresponding URL and zero otherwise. The advertiser can use different definitions of the URL and conversion to build multiple models $\varphi_{u1}, \ldots, \varphi_{uk}$ that capture different indicators of proximity:

- The URLs can be aggregated into clusters, and labels URL_i can be replaced by per-cluster binary labels that indicate whether the user visited some URL from a cluster or not. This reduces the dimensionality of the problem, which can be helpful if the number of available conversion events is relatively small. The distance between URLs needed for clustering can be calculated based on the inventory quality scores that are discussed later in this section.

- A conversion can be defined as a visit to the brand's site, a purchase after an impression, or any purchase.

The brand proximity model can be used to score users at the beginning of a campaign when the actual data about ad responses are not yet available. The next step will incorporate the new data when available and adjust the scores.

3.8.3.2 *Ad Response Modeling*

The goal of the response modeling step is to estimate the conditional probability of conversion $\Pr(Y \mid u, a)$ for an ad a. This step basically does the same thing as the baseline approach described at the beginning of this section – the advertiser uses the proximity model φ to target users at the beginning of the campaign, but, in addition to that, the ads are shown to a small number of random people to obtain the desired sampling shown in Figure 3.26. The difference from the baseline method is that we can now use the outputs of the previous step as features rather than high-dimensional raw URLs, which makes the learning process more efficient. Brand proximities can be supplemented with additional user information features $f_{u1}, \ldots, f_{ur}$, such as browser type and geographical location, so the model can be described as follows:

$$
\begin{aligned}
\psi_a(u) &= \Pr(Y \mid u, a) \\
&= \Pr(Y \mid \varphi_{u1}, \ldots, \varphi_{uk}, f_{u1}, \ldots, f_{ur})
\end{aligned}
\tag{3.57}
$$

The key difference between the models for unconditional proximity φ and conversion propensity ψ is sampling: the family of φ models is constructed to classify users as converted or non-converters regardless of the advertisements, whereas the ψ model classifies users as responders or non-responders and depends on the advertisement. The scores produced by models φ, however, have high predictive power for response, providing reasonable initial values for ψ and making re-estimation of ψ more effective as the actual response data arrives.

3.8.3.3 *Inventory Quality and Bidding*

The final step is to incorporate additional information that is not captured in the scores produced by the model ψ and to determine the actual bid price to be submitted to the ad exchange. With the assumption that the ad exchange is a second-price auction, the optimal bid price can be calculated as the expected value of conversion $v(Y)$:

$$b_{opt} = \mathbb{E}\left[v(Y)\right] = \Pr(Y \mid u, a) \cdot v(Y) \tag{3.58}$$

The value of conversion $v(Y)$ can typically be assumed to be constant for all users and is incorporated into some baseline bid price b_{base} set by the advertiser and depending on the contract with the brand and properties of the exchange. Consequently, propensity scores can be considered as multipliers to scale the baseline price.

Propensity scores produced by the model ψ are generally sufficient to make targeting and bidding decisions. The bid price for a given user can be calculated as

$$b(u) = b_{base} \cdot s_1(\psi_a(u)) \tag{3.59}$$

in which $s_1(\cdot)$ is some scaling function for the score ψ. In particular, $s_1(\cdot)$ can map all scores below a certain threshold to zero (no bidding), and the threshold can be determined based on the desired number of impressions and other considerations, as we discussed earlier in the context of promotions.

The targeting process we have described so far considers the user profiles and advertisements but not the context of the impression, that is, the inventory. The quality of the inventory is important for several reasons [Perlich et al., 2013]:

- The inventory carries information about the user's purchasing intent and the relevance of the ad for the user. For example, hotel advertisements will have higher conversion rates on travel websites than on news sites.

- The perception of an advertisement depends on the context. For example, users who are reading complex technical materials may pay less attention to ads than visitors to entertainment sites, some ad slots may be poorly positioned and require users to scroll down the page, etc.

Consequently, the advertiser can expect to get better results by using the probability $w_a(u, i) = \Pr(Y \mid u, a, i)$ in which i is the inventory. The ratio $w_a(u, i)$ and its expectation over all inventories $w_a(u) = \mathbb{E}_i\left[w_a(u, i)\right]$ can be used as a measure of inventory quality because it shows how much better or worse inventory i is in comparison to an average inventory. This metric can be used as an additional multiplier to scale the bid:

$$b(u) = b_{base} \cdot s_1\left(\psi_a(u)\right) \cdot s_2\left(\frac{w_a(u, i)}{w_a(u)}\right) \tag{3.60}$$

Note that although the notation we have used implies that $\omega_a(u)$ equals $\psi_a(u)$, the advertiser can use different data samples and models to estimate ω and ψ depending on the available data and other considerations. The steepness of the scaling functions $s_1(\cdot)$ and $s_2(\cdot)$ determines the trade-off between conversion rates and the advertiser's CPA. Steep scaling functions (e. g., zero if the argument is below the threshold and a very high value otherwise) generally maximize the conversion rate, but these can be suboptimal from the CPA standpoint. Scaling functions that are close to the identity function optimize the CPA as it follows from theoretical equation 3.58 but can be suboptimal in terms of conversion rates.

3.8.4   Multi-Touch Attribution

The obvious limitation of last-touch attribution is that the efforts that preceded the last impression are neglected. One can work around this by using more elaborate attribution methods that distribute the credit according to a position of the advertiser in the funnel. Several examples of such static models are shown in table 3.9. Static weight-based attribution, however, does not help to estimate the contribution of individual advertisers to the overall campaign effect. We need to create an *algorithmic attribution* method that measures the actual contributions and enables the brand to reward the best advertisers or channels and remove the worst ones.

Model	A_1	A_2	A_3	A_4	A_5
First impression	100%	–	–	–	–
First click	–	100%	–	–	–
Last touch	–	–	–	–	100%
Linear	20%	20%	20%	20%	20%
Position-based	35%	10%	10%	10%	35%
Time decay	10%	15%	20%	25%	30%

Table 3.9: Static attribution models. The table shows the percentage of credit assigned to each of five impressions $A_1, \ldots, A_5$.

Let us assume that the brand works with a network of advertisers or channels $C = \{C_1, \ldots, C_n\}$. We can think of this network as a set of states that can be traversed by a user before conversion, as illustrated in Figure 3.27. We can define the causal effect of channel C_k as the difference between the probability of conversion for the full set of channels and the probability of conversion if channel C_k is removed:

$$V_k = \Pr(Y \mid C) - \Pr(Y \mid C \backslash C_k) \tag{3.61}$$

To evaluate this expression, we can enumerate all possible subsets of the set $C \backslash C_k$ and estimate the causal effect for each subset separately [Dalessandro et al., 2012b]:

$$V_k = \sum_{S \subseteq C \backslash C_k} w_{S,k} \left(\Pr(Y \mid S \cup C_k) - \Pr(Y \mid S) \right) \tag{3.62}$$

Coefficients $w_{S,k}$ model the probability distribution of particular realizations of S, that is, the probability of a user traversing a certain sequence of channels. By assuming a uniform distribution of all sequences, we have

$$w_{S,k} = \binom{|C| - 1}{|S|}^{-1} \cdot \frac{1}{|C|} = \frac{|S|! \, (|C| - 1 - |S|)!}{|C|!} \tag{3.63}$$

because we draw sequences of length $|S|$ from the set $C \backslash C_k$ with cardinality $|C| - 1$. For example, the causal effect of channel C_3 in the network $C = \{C_1, C_2, C_3\}$ is given by the following equation:

$$
\begin{aligned}
V_3 = {} & \frac{1}{3} (\Pr(Y \mid C_1, C_2, C_3) - \Pr(Y \mid C_1, C_2)) \\
& + \frac{1}{6} \big[\, (\Pr(Y \mid C_1, C_3) - \Pr(Y \mid C_1)) \\
& \qquad + (\Pr(Y \mid C_2, C_3) - \Pr(Y \mid C_2)) \big] \\
& + \frac{1}{3} (\Pr(Y \mid C_3) - \Pr(Y \mid \varnothing))
\end{aligned}
\tag{3.64}
$$

The attribution formula 3.62 can be difficult to evaluate in practice because long sequences of channels have relatively low realization probabilities, which impacts the estimation stability [Dalessandro et al., 2012b; Shao and Li, 2011]. It can be reasonable to discard all sequences S longer than 2 channels to produce a more simple and stable model [Shao and Li, 2011]:

$$
\begin{aligned}
V_k^* = {} & \sum_{S \subseteq C \backslash C_k} w_{S,k} \left(\Pr(Y \mid S \cup C_k) - \Pr(Y \mid S) \right) \\
= {} & w_0 \big[\Pr(Y \mid C_k) - \Pr(Y \mid \varnothing) \big] + \\
& w_1 \sum_{j \neq k} \big[\Pr(Y \mid C_j, C_k) - \Pr(Y \mid C_j) \big]
\end{aligned}
\tag{3.65}
$$

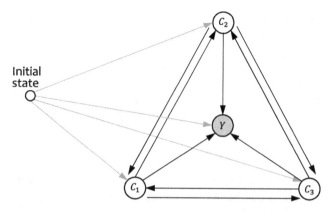

Figure 3.27: Example of a network with three channels.

The baseline probability of conversion $\Pr(Y \mid \varnothing)$ can also be discarded because it is equal for all channels, and the coefficients are defined as

$$w_0 = \binom{|C| - 1}{0}^{-1} \frac{1}{|C|} = \frac{1}{|C|}$$

$$w_1 = \binom{|C| - 1}{1}^{-1} \frac{1}{|C|} = \frac{1}{(|C| - 1)|C|}$$

$$(3.66)$$

We can therefore express the causal effect as

$$V_k^* = \frac{1}{|C|} \Pr(Y \mid C_k) +$$

$$+ \frac{1}{(|C| - 1)|C|} \sum_{j \neq k} [\Pr(Y \mid C_j, C_k) - \Pr(Y \mid C_j)]$$

$$(3.67)$$

The probability of conversion $\Pr(Y \mid C_k)$ can be estimated as the ratio of converted users who passed through channel C_k to the total number of users who passed through the channel. The second-order probabilities $\Pr(Y \mid C_j, C_k)$ can be estimated in the same way but for a pair of channels.

Equations 3.62 and 3.67 describe a practical solution for multi-touch attribution. However, it is worth noting that there are alternative ways to approach the same problem. For example, one can build a regression model that predicts conversions based on traversed channels and compare the magnitudes of the regression coefficients [Shao and Li, 2011].

3.9   MEASURING THE EFFECTIVENESS

The effectiveness of marketing campaigns is inherently challenging to measure because each consumer has unique properties, changes over time, and interacts with the brand and marketing media in their own way, so the attribution of any improvement or degradation to a particular marketing action can always be debated. Marketers typically cannot strictly prove the effectiveness of the action, but they can try to arrange an experiment or analyze the collected data in such a way that the actions in question and the outcomes are properly isolated, so that the causal effect cannot be attributed to external factors. This can be considered as proof of a statistically significant causal relationship between the actions and outcomes.

This problem statement enables us to leverage a huge statistical theory that was developed in other fields long before algorithmic marketing appeared. Importantly, experimentation frameworks developed in areas such as biology and healthcare are specifically adapted to deal with scenarios that are structurally similar to marketing campaigns.

3.9.1   *Randomized Experiments*

Consider a basic marketing campaign that distributes promotions or advertisements to prospects to make them convert. Although our ultimate goal is to estimate the causal relationship between the treatment and conversions, we can start with very basic questions and gradually build a statistical framework that estimates the causal effects.

3.9.1.1   *Conversion Rate*

One of the most basic questions that we can pose is the measurement of simple metrics, such as the *conversion rate*. Based on the assumption that the total number of individuals who received a treatment n is known and the number of converted individuals k among these n recipients is measured, we can estimate the conversion rate as

$$R = \frac{k}{n} \tag{3.68}$$

The obtained estimate may or may not be statistically reliable, depending on the number of individuals and conversions. If these numbers are small, we can expect the measured rate to have high variance and to change drastically if the same campaign is run multiple times. If the numbers are high, we can expect more consistent results. The reliability of the estimate can be measured in different ways by using different statistical frameworks. In this book, we generally advocate

Bayesian methods and Monte Carlo simulations because of their consistency and flexibility, so we use this approach for randomized experiments as well. Although it is not necessarily the most simple solution for the most basic problems, it helps us to establish a framework that can be efficiently extended for the more complex scenarios that we will consider later on.

Because the total number of promotions n is a non-random value chosen before the experiment, our goal is to understand the distribution of the conversion rate given the observed number of conversions $p(R \mid k)$. If this distribution is known, we will be able to estimate the probability that the results of hypothetical repeated experiments would deviate significantly from the observed value and thus measure the reliability of the estimated rate. According to Bayes rule, the distribution in question can be decomposed as follows:

$$p(R \mid k) = \frac{p(k \mid R)p(R)}{p(k)} \tag{3.69}$$

in which $p(k \mid R)$ is the likelihood, that is, the probability, of observing k conversions given that the conversion rate value is known to be R, and $p(R)$ is the prior distribution of conversion rates. The probability $p(k)$ can be viewed as a normalization factor because the data point k is given; hence, this term just ensures that the rate distribution is a probability distribution, that is, that the integral over the entire range is 1. So this value can be expressed as follows:

$$p(k) = \int p(k \mid R)p(R)\,dR \tag{3.70}$$

In words, we start with a prior belief about the rate distribution $p(R)$, and the observed data, that is, the number of conversions k, provide evidence for or against our belief. The posterior distribution $p(R \mid k)$ is obtained by updating our belief based on the evidence that we see.

As the posterior rate distribution includes two factors, $p(k \mid R)$ and $p(R)$, we need to specify these two distributions. Under the assumption that the conversion rate is fixed, the probability that exactly k individuals out of n will convert is given by a binomial distribution, with a probability mass function of the form

$$\begin{aligned} p(k \mid R) &= \binom{n}{k} \cdot R^k (1-R)^{n-k} \\ &= \frac{n!}{k!(n-k)!} \cdot R^k (1-R)^{n-k} \end{aligned} \tag{3.71}$$

The second factor, the prior distribution $p(R)$, can be assumed to be uniform or can be estimated from historical campaign data. Let us consider the case of uniform distribution first. If the prior distribution $p(R)$ is uniform in the range from 0 to 1, the posterior distribution $p(R \mid k)$ has the same form as the likelihood given by equation 3.71, but it is now a function of R, not k, so the normalizing constant will be different. We can denote this constant as $c(n, k)$ and obtain

$$p(R \mid k) = R^k (1 - R)^{n-k} \cdot c(n, k) \tag{3.72}$$

This distribution is known as a *beta distribution*, and there is a standard notation for it. In this notation, the posterior can be expressed as

$$p(R \mid k) = \text{beta}\,(k + 1, n - k + 1) \tag{3.73}$$

in which the beta distribution is defined as

$$\text{beta}\,(\alpha, \beta) = \frac{1}{B(\alpha, \beta)} \cdot x^{\alpha-1}(1 - x)^{\beta-1}$$
$$B(\alpha, \beta) = \int_0^1 x^{\alpha-1}(1 - x)^{\beta-1}\,dx \tag{3.74}$$

The distribution of the conversion rate given n treated individuals and k conversions is described by the beta distribution.

If the prior distribution is not uniform, it can also be modeled as the beta distribution:

$$p(R) = \text{beta}\,(x, y) \tag{3.75}$$

in which parameters x and y can be estimated, for example, based on historical data. In this case, the posterior distribution is still the beta distribution:

$$\begin{aligned}
p(R \mid k) &\propto p(k \mid R) \cdot p(R) \\
&\propto R^k (1 - R)^{n-k} \cdot \text{beta}\,(x, y) \\
&\propto R^{k+x-1}(1 - R)^{n-k+y-1} \\
&\propto \text{beta}\,(k + x, n - k + y)
\end{aligned} \tag{3.76}$$

It is said that the beta distribution is the *conjugate prior* to the binomial distribution: if the likelihood function is binomial, the choice of a beta prior will ensure that the posterior distribution is also beta. Note that beta $(1, 1)$ reduces to a uniform distribution, so result 3.73 obtained for the uniform prior is a particular case of expression 3.76.

We can now estimate the probability that the conversion rate R lies within some *credible interval* $[a, b]$ as

$$\Pr(a < R < b) = \int_a^b \text{beta}\,(k + 1, n - k + 1)\,dR \tag{3.77}$$

Equation 3.77 can be evaluated analytically, but we can also estimate the credible interval for a conversion rate by using Monte Carlo simulations. In this case, the estimation process can be described as follows:

1. The inputs are n, k, and the desirable confidence level $0 < q < 100\%$.

2. Generate a large number of random values with distribution beta $(k + 1, n - k + 1)$.

3. Estimate the $q/2$-th and $(100 - q/2)$-th percentiles of the generated values to obtain the desired credible interval. For example, we can be 95% confident that the estimate R lies in between the 2.5% and 97.5% percentiles.

Examples of beta distributions for different values of n and k, as well as the corresponding credible intervals, are shown in Figure 3.28. The simulation approach can look excessively complicated for the assessment of basic metrics such as the conversion rate, but its advantages will become more apparent as we move to more complex cases.

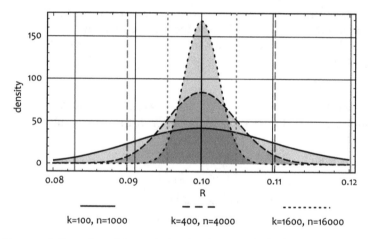

Figure 3.28: Examples of the posterior distribution $p(R \mid k)$ for the uniform prior and different sample sizes n. The mean $k/n = 0.1$ for all samples. The vertical lines are the 2.5% and 97.5% percentiles of the corresponding distributions. We start with the uniform prior, and the more samples we get, the narrower the posterior distribution becomes.

3.9.1.2 Uplift

The conversion rate by itself is not a sufficient measure of the quality of a targeting algorithm or the effectiveness of a marketing campaign. As we discussed earlier in this chapter, the effectiveness is typically measured as the uplift, which is the difference between conversion rates in the test and control groups. The conversion rate in the control group is considered as the baseline, and the uplift can be estimated as the conversion rate in the test group measured against the baseline rate:

$$L = \frac{R}{R_0} - 1 \tag{3.78}$$

in which R_0 is the baseline conversion rate and R is the conversion rate for the campaign in question. From a statistical standpoint, we also want to measure the reliability of this estimate, that is, the probability

$$\Pr(R > R_0 \mid data) \tag{3.79}$$

to ensure that the obtained results are attributed to the impact of the campaign in question relative to the baseline, not to some external uncontrolled factors. The standard way to tackle this problem is *randomized experiments*. The approach is to randomly split the consumers who can potentially be involved in the campaign into two groups (test and control), provide the test group with the treatment (send promotion, show ads, present a new website design, etc.), and provide the control group with the no-action or baseline treatment. Random selection of test and control individuals is important to ensure that the observed difference in outcomes is not caused by a systematic bias between the two groups, such as a difference in average income. Running the test and control in parallel is also important to ensure equality of the test conditions for the control groups, which might not be the case, for example, in a comparison of new data with historical data.

The design of randomized experiments for targeted campaigns is illustrated by Figure 3.29. The high-propensity customers identified by the targeting algorithm are divided into test and control groups, and the test group receives the treatment. The number of positive and negative outcomes is measured for both groups: n_T and n_C are the number of individuals and k_T and k_C are the number of conversions in the test and control groups, respectively. The uplift is measured by comparing the conversion rate of the test group k_T/n_T with that of the control group k_C/n_C.

We now want to assess the probability $\Pr(R_T > R_C)$ or, equivalently, to find a credible interval for uplift L. We can calculate this in a similar manner to that we used for the credible interval of the conversion rate in expression 3.77, but now we need to account for the joint distribution for R_T and R_C:

$$\Pr(a < L < b) = \iint\limits_{a<L<b} L(R_T, R_C) \cdot \Pr(R_T, R_C) dR_T dR_C \tag{3.80}$$

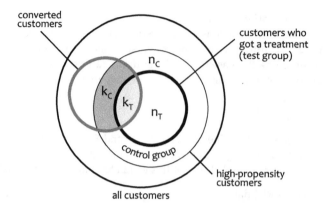

Figure 3.29: Sampling in randomized experiments.

If the randomized experiments are properly designed and executed to achieve independence between the test and control groups, we can assume that the joint probability above can be split into individual distributions of conversion rates:

$$\Pr(R_T, R_C) = \Pr(R_T \mid k_T, n_T) \cdot \Pr(R_C \mid k_C, n_C) \qquad (3.81)$$

At this point, we can apply the same simulation approach that we used for the individual conversion rate. Conversion rates R_T and R_C follow the beta distribution, so we can generate the uplift samples by drawing two conversion rates from the corresponding beta distributions and calculating the ratio. The process will be as follows:

1. The inputs are values k_T, n_T, k_C, and n_C, measured from the observed data, and the desirable confidence level is $0 < q < 100\%$

2. Generate a large number of values L by computing each sample as follows:

    a) Draw R_T from the distribution beta $(k_T + 1, n_T - k_T + 1)$

    b) Draw R_C from the distribution beta $(k_C + 1, n_C - k_C + 1)$

    c) Compute $L = R_T/R_C - 1$

3. Estimate the desired credible interval for L by taking the $q/2^{\text{th}}$ and $(100 - q/2)^{\text{th}}$ percentiles for the generated values.

The above approach works for many practical scenarios, for example, promotional campaigns, advertisements, and testing of arbitrary improvements, such as a new design of a website. Randomized experiments, however, impose certain limitations on how a campaign is executed, and this can be a problem in some cases. In particular, the requirement for a control group can incur additional expenses – we will study this issue in detail in the next section.

It is important to note that measurement of the revenue uplift does not necessarily require a conversion rate to be measured or even individual conversions to be tracked. We just need to know the total revenues generated by the test and control groups over a period of time after the campaign and estimate the uplift as a ratio between these two revenue values. This can be the only way to measure the uplift if the conversion information is not available.

3.9.2 Observational Studies

Randomized experiments can be used in the online advertising environment to measure the conversion uplift delivered by campaigns. Randomized methods, however, require one to be very careful with control group selection to make sure that there is no systematic bias between the test and control groups. The standard approach to achieve unbiased randomization is to leave picking of the control users until the very end of the ad delivery pipeline and to sample the users after the targeting and bidding stages, as shown in Figure 3.30. The test users are exposed to the actual ad impressions and the control users are exposed to some dummy ads, such as public service announcements (PSA), so the uplift between the groups is a measure of the ad impact.

The presence of an ad exchange, however, introduces a major challenge because impressions for the control group do not come for free and have to be purchased, just like the actual impressions. The question that arises is whether control group selection can be moved to before the bidding stage, as shown in Figure 3.31.

This approach effectively means that we do not do a controlled experiment anymore, because the bidding process – which bids are won and which are lost – is not controlled, and, consequently, it can induce an arbitrary bias in the test group compared to the control group. We can only observe bidding outcomes and conversions and measure the causal effect of the ad by doing statistical inference. This leads us to the large theory of observational studies and causal inference, which was under intensive development for decades and is driven by the necessity to analyze processes that are not under the control of researchers. Our problem with the bidding bias closely matches the problem of *treatment effect under non-compliance* in clinical trials. The causal effect of a treatment can be evaluated by using randomized experiments and comparing subjects from the test group who received the treatment

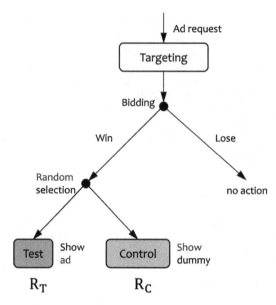

Figure 3.30: Uplift estimation in online advertising by using randomized experiments. R_T and R_C are the conversion rates in the test and control
groups, respectively.

with the control group. Although subjects can be assigned to the test
and control groups randomly, some people in the test group cannot
be exposed to the treatment because of compliance issues. The split
into compliant and non-compliant subgroups after randomization corresponds to the win–lose split in the bidding process when it follows
control group selection, so we can leverage the studies dedicated to
clinical trials with non-compliance.

The problem of uplift estimation with observational studies can
be approached by using different techniques. We start with a basic
method that illustrates how some concepts of causality theory can be
applied to the problem [Chalasani and Sriharsha, 2016; Rubin, 1974;
Jo, 2002].

We can see in Figure 3.31 that we have at least three conversion rates
that can be measured directly: R_C for the control group, R_T^L for the lost
bids in the test group, and R_T^W for the users who got actual impressions.
Our goal is to find the conversion rate R_C^W, which can be interpreted as
a *potential* conversion rate of the users who would have been won even
if they were not provided with impressions. This value is hypothetical
because we cannot go into the past, revoke the impressions we already
delivered, and see what would happen. However, it can be estimated

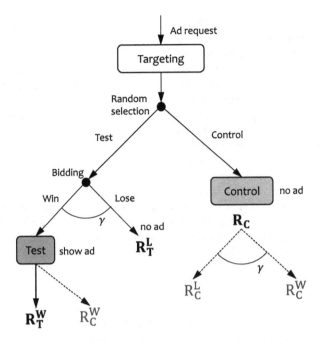

Figure 3.31: Uplift estimation by using observational studies.

from the known data under certain assumptions. First, we can note that the ratio γ between the number of users who were won and the number of users who were lost is directly observable. By assuming that the distribution of "winners" and "losers" is the same in both test and control groups, we can claim that

$$R_C = \gamma \cdot R_C^W + (1 - \gamma)R_C^L \tag{3.82}$$

in which R_C^W and R_C^L are the conversion rates that we can expect from the control users who could be won or lost, respectively, if reassigned to the test group. The second assumption we can make is that $R_C^L = R_T^L$ because both groups contain only "losers" who have not been exposed to the ad, so we do not expect any bias between them. Consequently, we can express R_C^W by using the known values as follows:

$$R_C^W = \frac{1}{\gamma} \cdot \left(R_C - (1 - \gamma)R_T^L\right) \tag{3.83}$$

Finally, the uplift can be estimated as the ratio between the observed R_T^W and inferred R_C^W.

The reliability of the uplift estimate can be evaluated by using the same simulation approach we used for randomized experiments. This requires us to generate samples according to the uplift distribution, which can be quite challenging to specify because it is a composition of several random processes: control group selection, bidding, and conversions. We observe only a few bits of information for each realization of this complex process (assigned group, bidding outcome, and conversion outcome), but we do not observe the intrinsic properties of the users and other *latent factors* that determine the joint probability distribution of the observed outcomes. In the rest of this section, we will discuss a statistical framework that combines the idea of potential outcomes discussed above with advanced simulation methods to infer distributions of different campaign properties, including, but not limited to, the uplift [Chickering and Pearl, 1996]. We describe the framework in two steps. First, we specify the model of the random processes of interest. Second, we discuss how the model can be evaluated by using simulations.

3.9.2.1   *Model Specification*

We can account for the latent factors and their impacts by using the graphical model presented in Figure 3.32. Each node represents a random variable, and the arrows indicate the dependencies between the nodes. Random variables Z, A, and Y correspond to randomization, bidding, and conversion. More specifically, binary variable $Z \in \{0, 1\}$ takes a value of one if the user is assigned to the control group and zero otherwise, variable $A \in \{0, 1\}$ takes a value of one if we won the bid and showed the ad and zero otherwise, and, finally, variable $Y \in \{0, 1\}$ equals one if the user converted and zero otherwise. The random variable S corresponds to the user state and, possibly, other latent factors that influence the advertiser's ability to win the bid and get a response after the impression.

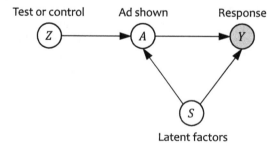

Figure 3.32: Graphical model for an observational study with latent factors.

At a very high level, we want to understand the joint distribution $\Pr(z, a, y, s)$ and integrate over it to obtain a credible interval for the uplift L. The question is how to decompose the distribution $\Pr(z, a, y, s)$ to make it computationally tractable. The graphical model in Figure 3.32 makes certain assumptions that can be used for decomposition : Z and S are considered independent because randomization must not be influenced by external factors, and Z and Y are conditionally independent given A and S because conversions can be influenced only through events A. This leads to the following decomposition of the probability density:

$$\Pr(z, a, y, s) = \Pr(z)\,\Pr(a)\,\Pr(a \mid z, s)\,\Pr(y \mid a, s) \qquad (3.84)$$

We now need to specify the state random variable S and its role in the densities $\Pr(a \mid z, s)$ and $\Pr(y \mid a, s)$. The idea behind the latent factors is to capture "the state of the world" that is not observed directly but can influence outcomes like the uplift. This concept can be considered as a counterpart of the potential outcomes that we discussed at the beginning of this section, because if we can infer the state from the observations then we can evaluate the potential outcomes for different preconditions. For example, if we know that a given user can never be won on the exchange, then we can predict the outcomes for assigning this user to both the test and control groups.

The latent state can be modeled differently depending on the available data, metrics of interest, and general understanding of the domain. We use a standard model that illustrates how the latent states can be defined as functions of the observed data and how metrics like uplift can be derived from the states [Heckerman and Shachter, 1995; Chickering and Pearl, 1996].

From a campaign efficiency standpoint, we are interested mainly in two properties of the user: compliance with the advertising method (ability or inability to win a bid) and response to the advertisement (converted or not). These properties correspond to the probabilities $\Pr(a \mid z, s)$ and $\Pr(y \mid a, s)$ discussed above and can be considered as the user's internal state that systematically influences the outcomes obtained for the user. We can enumerate the possible states separately for compliance and response and specify a condition for each state that indicates whether the state is possible for the observed tuple (z, a, y) or not.

The set of possible user states is a Cartesian product of the compliance and response behaviors, which gives us a 16-element

Compliance	Condition	Description
C_1	$a = 0$	User can never see the ad
C_2	$a = z$	User sees the ad every time we bid and only if we bid
C_3	$a \neq z$	User sees the ad if and only if we do not bid
C_4	$a = 1$	User always sees the ad

Table 3.10: User compliance states and conditions. States C_3 and C_4 should never be the case in the scenario that we consider, but they can occur in other environments such as omni-channel advertising.

Response	Condition	Description
R_1	$y = 0$	User never converts
R_2	$y = a$	User converts only after impression
R_3	$y \neq a$	User converts only without impression
R_4	$y = 1$	User always converts

Table 3.11: User response states and conditions.

set $\{s_1, \ldots, s_{16}\}$, in which s_i iterates through all pairs (C_p, R_q) of compliance and response behaviors listed in tables 3.10 and 3.11:

$$S \in \{s_1, \ldots, s_{16}\}$$
$$s_{p+4(q-1)} = (C_p, R_q), \quad 1 \leqslant p, q \leqslant 4 \tag{3.85}$$

Consequently, the random variable S is a 16-state random variable drawn from the set of 16 possible states.

We directly observe binary tuples (z^j, a^j, y^j) for each user j, but user states s^j are never observed directly. However, if we infer the state, it is possible to evaluate potential metrics of interest, such as uplift, based on the inferred states. More specifically, we are interested not in the individual user states but in a vector of state shares

$$\mu = (\mu_1, \ldots, \mu_{16}) \tag{3.86}$$

in which each share μ_i is the ratio between the number of users in the corresponding state s_i and the total number of observed users. The metrics can then be defined as functions of μ. For example, the uplift $L(\mu)$ can be defined as the ratio between the sum of the four μ_i values that correspond to states with the R_2 response component (and any compliance component) and the sum of another four μ_i values that correspond to the states with the R_3 response component. It is possible, however, to define different functions of μ to answer other questions.

3.9.2.2 *Simulation*

By assuming the model specified above, we can express the credible interval of the metric $L(\mu)$ via the posterior distribution of the random vector μ:

$$\Pr(a < L(\mu) < b) = \int_{a < L(\mu) < b} L(\mu) \cdot p(\mu \mid data) d\mu \qquad (3.87)$$

in which data represents all observed tuples (z^j, a^j, y^j). Let us denote the vector of user states as

$$s = \left(s^1, \ldots, s^m\right) \qquad (3.88)$$

in which m is the number of observed users. The distribution of the state shares μ can then be considered as a random function of user states s, which, in turn, are also random variables that are not observed but are probabilistically inferred from the data. Consequently, we have to consider the joint distribution of 16 variables in μ and m variables in s:

$$\Pr(a < L(\mu) < b) = \int_{a < L(\mu) < b} L(\mu) \cdot p(\mu, s \mid data) d\mu ds \qquad (3.89)$$

The simulation approach requires the distribution $p(\mu, s \mid data)$ to be estimated based on the observed data, so we will be able to draw vectors μ from this distribution. Once the vectors are generated, it is possible to calculate samples $L(\mu)$ and estimate their distribution. The question we have to answer now is how to draw samples from the distribution $p(\mu, s \mid data)$ for the sake of the simulation. We do not know the functional form of the distribution, but statistical methods do exist that can help us with generating samples from the distribution without specifying it explicitly.

Gibbs sampling is a widely used method of drawing samples from a multivariate distribution [Geman and Geman, 1984]. Let us assume that we need to draw samples from a multivariate distribution $p(x_1, \ldots, x_n)$. The Gibbs sampler exploits the fact that this multivariate distribution can be split into n conditional distributions

$$p(x_i \mid x_1, \ldots, x_{i-1}, x_{i+1}, \ldots, x_n), \qquad 1 \leqslant i \leqslant n \qquad (3.90)$$

It can be the case that we cannot sample points directly from the multivariate distribution, but sampling from the conditional distribution is possible. The idea in Gibbs sampling is that, rather than probabilistically picking all n variables at once, we can pick one variable at a time with the remaining variables fixed to their current values. In other words, each variable is sampled from its conditional distribution with the remaining variables fixed:

$$x_i \sim p(x_i \mid x_1, \ldots, x_{i-1}, x_{i+1}, \ldots, x_n), \qquad 1 \leqslant i \leqslant n \qquad (3.91)$$

This is an iterative algorithm that repeatedly draws samples from the conditional distributions by substituting previously generated samples into the conditions. For example, consider the basic case of two variables x_1 and x_2. The variables are first initialized to some values that can be sampled from the prior distribution and are then updated at each iteration i according to the following rules:

$$
\begin{aligned}
x_1^{(i)} &\sim p(x_1 \mid x_2^{(i-1)}) \\
x_2^{(i)} &\sim p(x_2 \mid x_1^{(i-1)})
\end{aligned}
\qquad (3.92)
$$

This process may need a certain number of iterations to converge, and then it starts to produce points that follow the distribution $p(x_1, x_2)$. This method is very powerful in practice because the conditional distributions are often much easier to specify than the joint distribution of interest. A generic version of the Gibbs sampler is provided in algorithm 3.1.

Initialize $\left(x_1^{(0)}, \ldots, x_n^{(0)} \right)$ from the prior distribution

for iteration $i = 1, 2, \ldots$ **do**

> draw $x_1^{(i)} \sim p\left(x_1 \mid x_2^{(i-1)}, x_3^{(i-1)}, \ldots, x_n^{(i-1)} \right)$
>
> draw $x_2^{(i)} \sim p\left(x_2 \mid x_1^{(i)}, x_3^{(i-1)}, \ldots, x_n^{(i-1)} \right)$
>
> ...
>
> draw $x_n^{(i)} \sim p\left(x_n \mid x_1^{(i)}, x_2^{(i)}, \ldots, x_{n-1}^{(i)} \right)$

end

Algorithm 3.1: Gibbs sampler.

Let us now come back to the distribution $p(\mu, s \mid \text{data})$ and investigate how the Gibbs sampler can be used to draw samples from it.

As the sampler draws each element of μ and s separately, we can separately specify the estimation routines for $p(s \mid \mu, \text{data})$ and $p(\mu \mid s, \text{data})$.

For the first probability, we can leverage the assumption that the users are independent, so the posterior probabilities of the user states are given by

$$p(s^j = s_i \mid \mu, s, \text{data}) \propto p(a^j, y^j \mid z^j, s_i) \cdot \mu_i \qquad (3.93)$$

in which $p(a^j, y^j \mid z^j, s_i)$ is the likelihood of observing the outcomes z^j, a^j, and y^j given the state s_i. We can assume that the likelihood is equal to one if the observed outcomes agree with the conditions of state s_i and zero otherwise. Consequently, the likelihood of state s_i for user j can be estimated based on the known values of a^j, y^j, and z^j and the state conditions from tables 3.10 and 3.11. For a model with 16 states, we estimate a vector of 16 probabilities for each user. This vector is then multiplied by the prior probability of the state μ_i, in accordance with the right-hand side of expression 3.93. The resulting vector of 16 numbers defines the multinomial distribution from which sample s^j can be drawn.

The second part is the conditional distribution $p(\mu \mid s, \text{data})$. Let us denote the number of times state s_i occurs in s as n_i. Because μ is the vector of state shares, that is, each element μ_i is the empirical probability of state s_i, the vector of counters n_i has a multinomial distribution with parameter μ. Consequently, the likelihood of observing vector s given the state shares μ is

$$\prod_i \mu_i^{n_i} \qquad (3.94)$$

and thus the posterior distribution of the state shares is

$$p(\mu \mid s, \text{data}) \propto \prod_i \mu_i^{n_i} \cdot \Pr(\mu) \qquad (3.95)$$

The last step is to specify the prior distribution $\Pr(\mu)$. Recall that we have used a beta distribution for the prior in randomized experiments because the likelihood had a binomial distribution and the beta distribution is a conjugate prior to the binomial. In a similar way, we now have a multinomial likelihood and its conjugate prior is the Dirichlet distribution (see Appendix A): if we choose $\Pr(\mu)$ to be the Dirichlet, the posterior distribution described in expression 3.96 will also be Dirichlet. More formally, we can express the prior belief as a set of counters n_i^0, which are used as parameters of the prior Dirichlet distribution, and the posterior can then be expressed as

$$p(\mu \mid s, \text{data}) \propto \prod_i \mu_i^{n_i} \cdot \text{Dir}(n_1^0, \ldots, n_{16}^0)$$

$$\propto \prod_i \mu_i^{n_i^0 + n_i - 1} \tag{3.96}$$

$$\propto \text{Dir}(n_1^0 + n_i, \ldots, n_{16}^0 + n_{16})$$

The above equations can be plugged directly into the Gibbs sampler: we generate the samples of μ by using expression 3.96, generate m samples of s by using equation 3.93, and then repeat this process iteratively until we have enough realizations of vector μ to evaluate the credible interval of $L(\mu)$.

3.10   ARCHITECTURE OF TARGETING SYSTEMS

Targeting systems can be implemented differently depending on the particular industry and applications. However, some logical components are common for the majority of targeting systems. In this section, we consider a canonical architecture that includes all of the major logical blocks needed to create targeted advertisements or promotions. This architecture assumes that the system functions in the request–response mode, that is, it receives real-time requests that contain some context information, such as consumer ID or channel ID, and returns one or more offers generated for this particular context. We consider this application and design to be the most universal and important; however, it can be adapted to other applications, such as batch email generation.

A high-level logical architecture for a targeting system is shown in Figure 3.33. This architecture assumes that there are three major subsystems, each of which contains multiple components.

3.10.1   *Targeting Server*

The targeting server encapsulates most of the logic related to processing of the incoming requests and crafting the response with advertisements or promotions. It can be thought of as a pipeline with the following typical stages:

CONDITIONS According to the targeting process that we previously described, one of the first steps is to validate explicit restrictions for all candidate advertisements or promotions. Examples

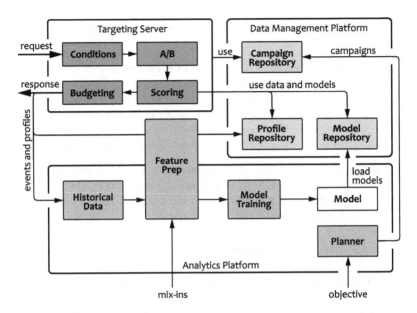

Figure 3.33: High-level architecture of a targeting system.

of such conditions are the presence of certain products in the current shopping basket, certain geographical locations, etc.

A/B TESTING Evaluation of multiple targeting strategies in parallel is a standard technique that helps to combat the inaccuracy of data and models, as well as to measure the performance of the campaigns. The targeting server is able to assign different advertising methods to different users and report performance metrics for each method separately, so the optimal strategy can be selected later on. A/B testing can be done for different aspects of the targeting process and consumer experience, such as different scoring methods, different text messages or images, etc.

Strategy selection is typically sticky with regards to consumers – once a certain strategy is selected, it is saved to the consumer profile and is consistently used for all requests related to this person. This helps to achieve a consistent user experience and create disjointed consumer segments for different strategies.

It is also typical to compare one or more experimental strategies with a control group, which is a group of consumers who receive an old or basic experience that can be considered as a baseline strategy or no strategy at all. The performance of the ex-

perimental strategies can then be measured as uplift relative to
the baseline.

SCORING The targeting server scores the incentives that have passed
the previous step by evaluating propensity models associated
with the incentive against the context, including the consumer's
historical profile. Propensity models can be dynamically selected
for an incentive based on metadata and business rules to avoid
manual binding of a model to each and every incentive.

BUDGETING RULES The final response is created based on a list of
valid scored candidate incentives by applying budgeting rules
and other constraints that limit the number of impressions for a
given consumer, channel, or campaign.

3.10.2 *Data Management Platform*

The data management platform can be viewed as an operational
database that stores customer profiles and other data required for
targeting, including campaign configurations. The following items
can be considered as the main components of the data management
platform:

PROFILE REPOSITORY The repository that stores historical data about
individual consumers. This can include both raw data, such as individual orders or website events, and aggregated statistics (features) that can be directly used in the evaluation of propensity
models. The repository can be populated by using context data
from the targeting server and external data sources.

MODEL REPOSITORY The model repository stores the pool of propensity models that are used by the targeting server for scoring.
These models are created and updated by the analytics platform
described below.

CAMPAIGN REPOSITORY The campaign repository contains configuration details of campaigns, including graphical assets, conditions, budgeting limits, etc.

3.10.3 *Analytics Platform*

The analytics platform collects, consolidates, and stores the customer
profile data, as well mix-ins needed for modeling, data preparation,
and reporting purposes. Examples of such mix-ins include product catalog information, sales data, and store data, among others. One of the

main outputs of the data preparation process is the *profile features* that can be used for training and evaluation of predictive models. The data consolidated and cleaned by the platform can be provided with different service level agreements for different consumers. For example, profile features can be created in batch mode for analytical purposes, but the same features are needed for real-time model evaluation in the targeting server. Thus, some data preparation modules can be designed to work in different modes. This aspect is illustrated by the feature preparation block in Figure 3.33, which is used for both modeling and real-time data aggregation for the data management platform.

One of the main functions of the platform is to produce propensity models by running machine learning algorithms over the data that come from the targeting server and external data sources. The platform can provide tools for manual model creation and automated model updates (re-training). In addition to that, the analytics system performs measurements and provides capabilities for reporting and exploratory data analysis.

Finally, the analytics platform can host a planner. This is a key component of a programmatic marketing system that designs and optimizes promotion and advertising campaigns. The planner uses historical data and statistics, business rules, best practices, and heuristics to determine the optimal strategies (duration and type of incentives, channels, propensity models, etc.) based on the input objective and additional constraints like budgeting limits. It can also forecast the performance of a campaign by using historical data. The planner might have several functional blocks including

INVESTMENT PLANNER The investment planner provides a high-level view of market opportunities derived from historical data. It helps the end user to set the right business objectives and distribute the budget amounts across different strategic directions and campaigns. It can be considered as a global optimization tool.

CAMPAIGN PLANNER The campaign planner optimizes the individual promotional and advertising campaigns that are suggested by the investment planner. It calculates optimal time frames, spending rates, etc.

3.11 SUMMARY

- Promotion and advertising services focus on the problem of targeting, that is, finding the optimal match between consumers and offerings. Depending on the application, the system may need to identify the offerings for a given consumer or the consumers for a given offering.

- Promotion and advertising services are typically driven by revenue optimization objectives, but it is important to focus on customer experience optimization as well.

- The main business environments for promotion and advertising services are sales promotion and online advertising. The main actors and entities in the sales environment are consumers, manufacturers, retailers, and marketing campaigns.

- The business objectives of manufacturers and retailers can be modeled in terms of campaign costs and gains. The immediate objectives include campaign profitability, and the strategic objectives can be described in terms of the customer life cycle. The key strategic objectives are the acquisition of new customers, maximization of existing customers, and retention of customers who may be lost.

- A targeting system can be designed as a pipeline that starts with resource allocation across the objectives, followed by fitting of campaign templates with the objective, linking targeting models, and, finally, executing the campaigns.

- The response modeling framework fits together the campaign costs, revenues, and statistical properties of the customers. The main principle of response modeling is to maximize the uplift, that is, the incremental profit gain. The uplift can be measured after the fact by using test and control groups.

- The main building blocks used in targeting systems are propensity models, time-to-event models, and lifetime value models. The most basic examples of targeting models are loyalty tiers and RFM analysis. These approaches focus on the financial outcomes and do not delve deeply into the drivers of the customer behavior.

- The goal of propensity modeling is to find consumers who have a relatively high probability to behave in a certain way, for example, to buy a new product. Look-alike modeling is one of the main methods of propensity modeling.

- It is often more convenient to measure the time-to-event than the probability of the event. This can be done by using survival analysis. Survival models, similarly to regression models, can express the time-to-event as a function of independent variables such as customer properties or discount depth.

- Lifetime value models estimate the total amount of money that a brand is likely to make from a given customer over the lifetime of their relationship. LTV modeling can be done with descriptive and predictive approaches.

- A marketing campaign can be assembled from multiple building blocks. A campaign template can include targeting conditions, scoring models, and budgeting and capping rules. A campaign typically corresponds to a certain point or set of points in a customer journey and aims to influence it. Examples of campaign templates include product promotional campaigns, multistage campaigns, and retention and replenishment campaigns.

- Targeting can be viewed as resource allocation to customers, but the resources can also be allocated to channels, objectives, territories, and other criteria.

- Many methods and principles of promotion targeting are applicable in other domains, such as online advertising, but each domain has its own business objectives and implementation challenges. The online advertising objectives are often defined in terms of cost-per-action and attribution across the competing advertisers.

- Online advertising uses a large number of targeting methods and techniques. Many of them are based on look-alike modeling, notions of brand proximity, response probability, and inventory quality.

- The effectiveness of promotion and advertising campaigns is typically measured by using randomized experiments involving test and control groups. In some environments, including online advertising, the control groups are associated with additional costs or missed gains, so the effectiveness can be measured with the more advanced methods of observational studies.

4

SEARCH

Targeted promotions and advertisements are focused on the problem of finding the right audience for a given product or service. An equally important counterpart of targeting is *product discovery*, that is, the task of providing customers with convenient services and interfaces for browsing the assortment and searching for the products they need. Targeting and discovery services are the two principal programmatic marketing tools that can be leveraged to improve different aspects of customer awareness of a product, service, or brand.

The product discovery problem revolves around the notion of *purchasing intent*. In some cases, customers can explicitly express their intent by entering a search query or specifying desired product attributes in a different way. In other cases, the intent is not explicitly expressed, and a programmatic service has to infer it from known customer attributes and behavior. These two scenarios are often distinguished and thought of as two different categories of services – search services help customers to find products that meet explicitly expressed requirements, whereas recommendation services do not require users to express their search intent in order to make suggestions. However, the boundary between search and recommendations is blurry. A basic search service can use only an explicitly entered query to find products. A more advanced solution can use additional pieces of information about a user to personalize search results. In certain applications, these implicit signals can become more important than the explicit ones and a search service structurally metamorphoses into recommendations. From this perspective, search and recommendation services can be compared to a store sales associate who can find a specific product upon request or can suggest options from only basic information about the customer and their needs.

Search and recommendations are important not only as functional services but also as a fundamental capability to combine multiple strong, weak, or noisy signals to correctly understand customer needs and determine products that match these needs. This capability is the key to building efficient customer-facing services and applications.

The first product discovery service that we will consider is the search. The purpose of a search service is to fetch offerings that are relevant to the customer's search intent expressed in a search query or with selected filters. This type of problem is addressed by information retrieval theory, so we have a wide range of theoretical frameworks and practical search methods at our disposal. The primary goal of this section is to put together, align, and adapt the frameworks and methods that are relevant to marketing applications. Some of these methods are borrowed from the toolkit of generic search methods developed in information retrieval theory, and others were developed specifically for marketing and merchandising. We will be taking a practical approach to search methods and will focus on industrial experience, techniques, and examples, rather than information theory. At the same time, we will try to avoid implementation details, such as data indexing, as much as possible and will stay focused on the business value delivered through relevant search results.

We will start this chapter with a review of the environment and economic objectives. We will then demonstrate that the problem of relevant search can be expressed in terms of features, signals, and controls, similarly to other programmatic services. We will review a number of methods for engineering, mixing, and tuning these signals and controls in manual mode, and we will then discuss how predictive analytics can be leveraged for automated optimization.

4.1 ENVIRONMENT

A search is one of the most natural and convenient interfaces between a human and a computer. This makes search an integral part in a wide range of services and applications that belong to different domains and use search functionality in very different ways. These environments can vary dramatically in both economic objectives and technical properties, such as data volume, which can dramatically influence the design and implementation of search services. Let us consider a few major examples:

WEB SEARCH The web is a collection of web pages that contain textual and media information, so it is not surprising that the web search has initially been approached as a text analysis problem. The scoring criteria of the first search engines were primarily based on the page content, which created a lot of opportunities for website owners to cheat the system by tampering with hidden fields and other relevance-boosting techniques. The search engines were forced to develop a totally new strategy that used cross-references between websites and their trustworthiness as the main scoring signal, so web domains and pages that are referenced by hyperlinks from trustworthy and popular sites are scored highly and the relevance of non-referenced resources is sharply discounted. This approach, pioneered by Google as a PageRank algorithm, became an important distinguishing feature of web search in comparison with most other search environments. The large scale of the web and necessity of indexing enormous amounts of data has also influenced web search methods to a very significant extent.

MERCHANDISING SEARCH In many search applications, organic relevance is complemented or overridden by business rules that ensure business objectives and constraints are met. A prominent example of such environments is the merchandising-oriented search, which can be found in eCommerce, retail, and other consumer applications, such as hotel booking or restaurant search services. These applications require search functions that can improve profits by boosting high-margin products, sell out expiring inventory, or promote sponsored offerings. Merchandising search should also take into account domain-specific terminology and usage patterns to recognize the user's intent and common idioms.

EXPERT SEARCH A large number of search services and applications in the law, medicine, research, and industry domains fall into the category of expert search. Used by professionals, an expert search requires deep understanding of the domain including jargon and latent relationships between the concepts. It also requires the accommodation of specialized usage patterns and relevance definitions that can be very different from typical consumer needs in web and merchandising search. For example, it can be critical for a lawyer or patent professional to find and examine every document relevant to the topic in question, whereas merchandising or web search users are typically interested in a few of the most relevant results. An expert search is also referred to as an *enterprise search* in certain contexts.

Despite all these dissimilarities, search solutions for different domains share many common principles and methods. We choose to focus on merchandising search in this chapter because these are best aligned with the agenda of this book, although most of the building blocks that we describe are perfectly applicable in other domains.

Let us start with a description of a minimal environment for a merchandising search, as depicted in Figure 4.1, that introduces the key entities and assumptions:

- The main purpose a merchandising search service is to provide customers with a simple interface that finds items such as products, services, or facilities through a free-text query and additional contextual information, which can include the customer profile, browsing device type, geographical location, and so on. In other words, the input of a search service is assumed to be made up of the pair of query and context, and the output is a list of entities in order from the most relevant to the least relevant. This basic functionality can be complemented by additional search tools and features that we will discuss in detail later on.

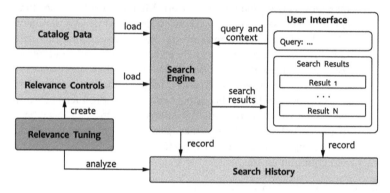

Figure 4.1: Example of a merchandising search environment.

- Each item that can be searched for typically represents a mix of structured or semi-structured data records that can be collected from multiple sources. For example, an online retailer can assemble its product items from the textual descriptions provided by manufacturers, user ratings and reviews, sales data, inventory data, store locations, prices, and in-house metadata, such as category hierarchies.

- A search engine produces the search results by matching query or context features with entity features. This process can be configured by using multiple relevance controls that determine how features are created from the original data, how they are matched, and how different signals are blended together to produce the final results.

• The search engine and interface application record the interactions with the users. The interaction history typically includes multiple metrics and parameters ranging from search queries to page scrolling timings. This information can be fed into the relevance tuning process that adjusts the relevance controls to meet the objectives.

The environment we defined above is focused exclusively on a free-text search where a user enters some free text into a form and gets back a ranked list of results. In a real-world search system such as an eCommerce website, this basic functionality is often extended with many additional tools and capabilities including facets, automatic query completion, and result sorting options. The core functionality of a search service almost completely depends upon the notion of relevance, that is, the differentiation between relevant and non-relevant items. We will spend most of this chapter discussing different and numerous aspects of this question. Our first step will be to explore how relevance can be related to economic objectives and measured.

4.2   BUSINESS OBJECTIVES

It is often said that the main objective of a search service is to understand the user's intent and deliver results that are relevant to this intent. Although this is generally true (and already very challenging to achieve), this view of the objective is limited and does not reflect many criteria that are important for a good search service. We can attempt to build a more comprehensive framework by using the basic profit equation as a starting point. Consider an online retailer who sells a certain assortment of products, so the total profit can be expressed as

$$G = \sum_j q_j \left(p_j - v_j \right) \tag{4.1}$$

in which j iterates over all products, q is the quantity sold, p is the price, and v stands for variable costs, which can include wholesale price and distribution costs. Although we cannot formally connect equation 4.1 to an intangible concept such as user intent, we can make a few heuristic assumptions that help to establish this link and work well in practice.

First, we can assume that all quantities sold q_j are roughly proportional to the organic relevance and overall ergonomics of a search service. That is, given that the number of search users is fixed, poor relevance leads to a relatively large fraction of users who cannot find products that match their purchasing intent, whereas good relevance leads to a relatively low fraction of users who are not able to find the right product. Consequently, relevance can be viewed as a plain multiplicative coefficient for the profit.

The second opportunity that becomes apparent from equation 4.1 is that we can try to redistribute quantities q_j to sell more high-margin products at the expense of the low-margin ones. We can exploit the fact that purchasing intents typically exhibit some flexibility: a customer might initially be looking to purchase one product but willing to substitute it with a different one, or they might simply browse available offerings with a broadly defined intent and accept the first suitable one. Given the fixed number of search users, we can promote high-margin products by boosting them in the search results to capture as many potential buyers as possible and, consequently, by pushing down those products with low margins, thereby negatively influencing their sale volumes. It is important to note that we can account not only for the margin (the difference between the cost of a product and its selling price) but also for the costs of alternatives associated with a product. For example, fashion retailers often practice clearance sales at the end of a season to free up space for the new collection, so the promotion of expiring products also becomes an objective.

We already stated that relevance is directly related to the total profit because it influences the number of conversions. We should, however, pay more attention to the negative effects associated with relevance and ergonomics defects. From the user viewpoint, the search process includes multiple steps, such as making an initial query, browsing and checking suggested results, query reformatting, and so on. Poor relevance or ergonomics can force users to repeat searches many times, which may or may not negatively impact conversion rates but is likely to create a negative user experience and, in the long run, to decrease the total number of users; this translates into a lower total quantity sold, according to equation 4.1.

The bottom line is that the objectives of a search service and its quality can be viewed, at least, from the following three standpoints:

1. Relevance

2. Merchandising controls

3. Ergonomics and customer satisfaction

We discuss each of these three aspects in the subsequent sections and then delve into the implementation details to see how a search service can achieve these goals.

4.2.1 *Relevance Metrics*

The *relevance* of search results can be defined as a measure of how well the results satisfy the user's search intent. The *search intent*, typically referred to as the *information need* in information retrieval texts, cannot be completely formalized in most applications, especially in merchandising, so the standard way to measure relevance is an expert assessment of the search results to classify each item as relevant or irrelevant. For example, relevant search results for the query *sore throat treatments* can be subjectively defined as remedies for this symptom ranging from hot tea to medications, not merely a set of items containing the words from the query. We will assume for now that the relevancy grades are set by experts from the search service team, but, as we will see later in this chapter, a search system can collect and analyze certain metrics about user behavior, such as click rates for items in the result set, to automatically estimate relevancy.

Let us consider an ideal case, when we are assessing a single pair of a search request and the result, and the total number of items is small enough to be manually classified. We can define the following three values: D is the total number of items relevant for a given intent indexed in the system, S is the number of items in the search result set, and R is the number of relevant items in the result set. The relationship between these three values is shown in Figure 4.2. The quality of search results can then be measured in terms of two metrics, *precision* and *recall*, defined as follows:

$$\text{precision} = \frac{R}{S} \tag{4.2}$$

$$\text{recall} = \frac{R}{D} \tag{4.3}$$

We typically need both of these metrics to describe the result set or search method. On the one hand, recall measures the completeness of the search results regardless of the result set size, so one can always achieve the maximum possible recall of 1.00 by returning the entire collection of items. On the other hand, precision measures the density of relevant items in the result set and tells us nothing about the relevant items that have not been fetched.

The difference between the two metrics, however, does not mean that they are independent. First, let us review Figure 4.2 again. It suggests that we can change the recall from 0 to 1 by stretching the search results rectangle in the vertical direction; meanwhile, the precision remains constant. This behavior is almost never the case for real data.

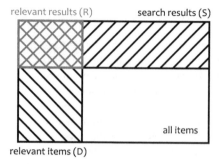

Figure 4.2: The relationship between relevant items, search results, and relevant results.

One of the main reasons is that we describe items and specify queries by using dimensions that are not necessarily aligned with the shape of the item set defined by the search intent. Let us consider the example depicted in Figure 4.3. A retailer has a large collection of shoes that are described by using properties such as price and category. A user who searches for *affordable quality shoes* might consider items scattered along the diagonal from inexpensive dress shoes to expensive sandals to be generally relevant. A search system, however, might not be able to repeat this shape. If it treats the terms *affordable* and *shoes* in a strict way, it can achieve high precision but relatively low recall by returning, for example, average running shoes. Loosening of the criteria increases the recall but also scoops irrelevant items, such as expensive dress shoes, which decreases the precision[1].

This pattern is almost constantly present in search applications, so we typically have to choose between high-precision, low-recall search methods and the low-precision, high-recall alternatives. Merchandising search is heavily biased towards high-precision search methods because the primary goal is to provide a user with a reasonable number of relevant results that can quickly be reviewed.

The basic precision and recall metrics provide a useful conceptual view of relevance but have many limitations as quantitative measures. First, precision and recall are set-based metrics that cannot be straightforwardly applied to ranked search results. This limitation is critical for merchandising search that strives to provide the user with a few valuable results sorted by relevance. One possible approach to account for ranking is to go through the items in the result set from top to bottom,

---

1 This problem is not specific for search and often comes up in machine learning, especially in deep-learning applications. For example, a set of photographic images is a very "curly" area in the space of all possible two-dimensional matrices. Such sets embedded into high-dimensional spaces are referenced as *manifolds*.

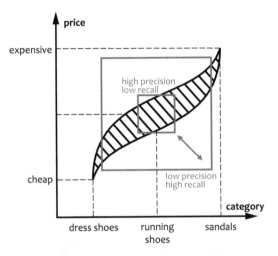

Figure 4.3: Precision–recall trade-off.

calculate the precision and recall at each point, and plot a *precision–recall curve*. This process is illustrated by the example in Figure 4.4. Let us assume that we have 20 items in total and 5 of them are relevant. The result set starts with a relevant item, so the precision is 1.00 and recall is $\frac{1}{5}$. The next two items are not relevant, so the recall remains constant but precision first drops to $\frac{1}{2}$ and then to $\frac{1}{3}$. Continuing this process, we get a precision of $\frac{1}{4}$ and recall of 1.00 at the twentieth item in the result set. The precision–recall curve is thus jagged but typically has a downward-sloping concave trend.

The precision–recall curve provides a convenient way to analyze search quality for a single query, but we often need a compact metric that expresses the overall performance of a search service as a single number. One standard way to do this is to determine the *mean average precision* (MAP), which first averages the precisions at each relevant item and then averages this value over all of the queries we use in the evaluation. If the number of queries is Q, the number of relevant items for query q is R_q, and the precision at the k-th relevant item is P_{qk}, then

$$\text{MAP} = \frac{1}{Q} \sum_{q=1}^{Q} \frac{1}{R_q} \sum_{k=1}^{R_q} P_{qk} \qquad (4.4)$$

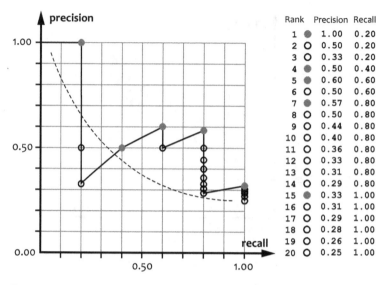

Rank		Precision	Recall
1	●	1.00	0.20
2	○	0.50	0.20
3	○	0.33	0.20
4	●	0.50	0.40
5	●	0.60	0.60
6	○	0.50	0.60
7	●	0.57	0.80
8	○	0.50	0.80
9	○	0.44	0.80
10	○	0.40	0.80
11	○	0.36	0.80
12	○	0.33	0.80
13	○	0.31	0.80
14	○	0.29	0.80
15	●	0.33	1.00
16	○	0.31	1.00
17	○	0.29	1.00
18	○	0.28	1.00
19	○	0.26	1.00
20	○	0.25	1.00

Figure 4.4: Precision–recall curve. The solid circles correspond to relevant items and the empty circles correspond to irrelevant items in the result set.

For example, the MAP for the single query illustrated in Figure 4.4 is the mean of the five precision numbers for each of the five relevant items:

$$\text{MAP} = \frac{1}{5}(1.00 + 0.50 + 0.60 + 0.57 + 0.33) = 0.6 \tag{4.5}$$

We typically cannot assess and enumerate all of the relevant results for a given query in web or merchandising search applications because the total number of relevant results is huge; even if we can do the assessment, it does not make sense because no user will be interested in reading all of the results. Consequently, the average precision above is often calculated not for *all* of the items relevant for a query but for the relevant items in the result set on the basis that the size of the result set is fixed [Manning et al., 2008].

A popular alternative to MAP is *discounted cumulative gain* (DCG), which abandons the notion of precision and recall completely and gives center stage to ranking [Järvelin and Kekäläinen, 2000]. Let us consider a search result that contains K items with each item graded with a relevance value R, so we have K relevance grades R_k. The relevance values can be binary (one for relevant and zero for nonrelevant items) or continuous or discrete with multiple levels. The *cumulative gain* of the result is defined as the sum of the relevance grades:

$$CG = \sum_{k=1}^{K} R_k \qquad (4.6)$$

Cumulative gain is similar to precision, given that K is fixed, but it allows the differentiation of documents based on their usefulness by setting multilevel grades R. This is the reason why the metric is called cumulative gain – it attempts to assess the usefulness of the search result. The shortcoming of cumulative gain is that it does not include the order of the items in the consideration, so changes in the ordering of search results do not affect the gain value. This can be fixed by penalizing for relevant results appearing low in a search results list, that is, relevance grades are discounted proportionally to their positions in the list. This leads to the notion of DCG, which uses a logarithm of the result position as a discounting weight:

$$DCG = R_1 + \sum_{k=2}^{K} \frac{R_k}{\log_2 (k)} \qquad (4.7)$$

It is more common, however, to use a slightly different definition of DCG that strongly emphasizes relevant items by assigning them exponentially high weights [Burges et al., 2005]:

$$DCG = \sum_{k=1}^{K} \frac{2^{R_k} - 1}{\log_2 (k + 1)} \qquad (4.8)$$

The magnitude of the DCG calculated according to formula 4.8 can vary depending on the number of results K. To compare DCG metrics obtained for different queries, we need to normalize them. This can be done by calculating the maximum possible DCG, called the Ideal DCG, and dividing the actual DCG by this value to obtain the normalized DCG (NDCG):

$$NDCG = \frac{DCG}{\text{Ideal DCG}} \qquad (4.9)$$

The ideal DCG can be estimated by sorting the items in a search results list by relevance grades and applying formula 4.8 to calculate the corresponding DCG. Consequently, the NCDG is equal to one for an ideal ranking. For example, let us consider a search results list with six items that are scored by an expert on a scale of 0 to 4, with 0 meaning nonrelevant and 4 meaning most relevant:

$$4, 3, 4, 2, 0, 1 \qquad (4.10)$$

The value of the DCG calculated for this search result in accordance
with formula 4.8 is 28.56. The ideal ordering for this search result is

$$4, 4, 3, 2, 1, 0 \qquad (4.11)$$

and the corresponding ideal DCG is 29.64. Consequently, the NDCG
for search results list 4.10 is 28.56/29.64 = 0.96.

4.2.2 *Merchandising Controls*

Merchandising controls are tools that enable merchandisers and other
business users to reshape search results in accordance with business
needs not covered by organic relevance. The boundary between
merchandising controls and relevance, however, is very blurry because
many business rules can be viewed as enhancements of content-based
relevance and, conversely, many relevance tuning methods can be
viewed as business rules that improve the search results by adding
some domain knowledge. For example, a merchandiser can create a
trigger that redirects all users who enter the query *insulated jackets*
to a manually curated category for seasonal jacket sales. On the one
hand, this aims to achieve the business goal of promoting products
that are on sale. On the other hand, it can be argued that this manually
curated content is a better match for the user's search intent than a
standard search result. Most search systems provide a rich toolkit of
merchandising controls that can include the following capabilities:

BOOST AND BURY As we will see in the next sections, organic relevance is typically calculated by matching different item and
query properties, mixing the resulting scores together, and ranking the items by the final score. A merchandiser can adjust or
override this logic by tweaking relevancy scores in a way that
promotes desirable items and demotes undesirable ones. This capability is often referred to in the merchandising world as *boost
and bury*. The boost and bury control can often be expressed as
a scoring formula that blends different item properties. This approach can be illustrated with an example that boosts new, discounted, or high-rated products and buries items that lack of
these properties:

$$\text{score} = 0.2 \times \text{newness} + 0.4 \times \text{discount} + 0.4 \times \text{rating} \quad (4.12)$$

given that each item is attributed with the corresponding newness, discount depth, and user rating grades measured on some
scale. The score calculated this way can override the relevance
score, or the two scores can be summed or multiplied.

FILTERING The primary purpose of filtering is to remove undesirable items from a search result set. Examples of filtering include removal of out-of-stock items and removal of irrelevant items that have cropped up in a search result because of data or scoring issues.

CANNED RESULTS It can be difficult to achieve a certain ordering of items by using boost and bury formulas, so a merchandiser might be willing to put a manually selected set of items at the top of the search results. The injection of such canned items is often triggered by certain keywords in a query.

REDIRECTION Redirection is a capability similar to canned results, but it completely replaces organic search results by redirecting the user to a manually curated category of products or some special content, such as an interactive fashion magazine.

PRODUCT GROUPING Efficient usage of the display space is an important goal for merchandising search. It is important not only to provide users with relevant search results but also to present the available assortment in the best possible way, given that display space is limited. For example, it might be beneficial to replace closely related products or product variants, such as different sizes and colors of the same model of jeans, by a single representative to free up more space for other models and avoid cluttering the search results with similar items.

From an economic standpoint, some merchandising controls can be viewed as market segmentation techniques. Consider the example of boosting high-margin or luxury products: it is essentially an attempt to segment customers by their price sensitivity, so price-insensitive customers spend little effort picking high-margin items at the top and price-sensitive customers have to spend more time going through pages of results to find a better value price.

4.2.3 Service Quality Metrics

The relevance of search results assessed by an expert and measured with metrics like the NDCG does not guarantee the acceptable performance of a search service. We need to define performance indicators that can be measured and monitored in real applications to ensure a high level of user experience and business efficiency. The quality of a search service can be related to relevancy algorithms, data quality, ergonomics of the user interface, and robustness of the technical implementation. Let us review a few key performance indicators that are often collected for search services:

CONVERSION RATE Conversion rate is by far the most important performance indicator for merchandising search. It can be defined as the ratio of user sessions that used the search service and converted to the total number of user sessions that used the search service. A user session is typically equivalent to a web session in this context. The conversion rate is a critically important metric because it is directly related to revenues and the user's ability to find the desired products.

CLICK-THROUGH RATE The ratio of users who clicked on specific search results to the total number of users who used the search is an important metric for the relevance of results.

TIME ON A PRODUCT DETAIL PAGE Although a high click-through rate is a generally positive indicator, a large number of users quickly glancing at the details page and then returning back may indicate poor relevance or problems with interface ergonomics, such that a user is not able to recognize relevant items by their summaries in the search results list.

QUERY MODIFICATION RATE There is a good chance that a user who modifies a query multiple times is unable to get satisfactory search results.

PAGING RATE Frequent usage of pagination and clicks on low-ranked search results may indicate relevance problems.

RETENTION RATE The fraction of users who continue to regularly use the search. Retention rate is typically calculated for some period of time, such as a week or month, as

$$\text{retention rate} = \frac{E - N}{S} \tag{4.13}$$

in which E is the number of regular users at the end of a period, N is the number of new users acquired during that period, and S is the number of users at the start of a period.

SEARCH LATENCY The time it takes to process a search query and return a result has a big impact on the user experience. Many retail and web search companies have reported impressive statistics on this matter. For instance, Amazon reported that every 100 millisecond increase in the page load time results in a 1% loss in sales, and Walmart showed that every second of latency improvement increases the conversion by 2% [Kohavi and Longbotham, 2007; Crocker et al., 2012].

These metrics can be broken down by dimensions, such as marketing channel (e.g., mobile, desktop, or tablet), for relevance fine tuning. We will return to the question of relevance tuning, including both manual and automatic tuning processes, in section 4.7, but we first need to delve into the details of relevance scoring.

4.3   BUILDING BLOCKS: MATCHING AND RANKING

The search relevance problem can be considered as a classification problem because it aims to distinguish relevant items from nonrelevant ones. At the same time, it is a very special case of classification because of its focus on textual data and ranking. These features enable very efficient heuristic methods that can achieve excellent relevance without training a classifier by using machine learning techniques. Although the machine learning approach is also possible (and we will discuss it in the next sections), the basic matching and ranking methods are sufficient for most merchandising search applications and also provide a solid methodology for feature engineering in cases when machine learning methods are applied. We will spend this section reviewing basic search methods that can later be assembled into more complicated and comprehensive relevance solutions that may or may not use machine learning for parameter tuning.

At a very high-level, we can describe a search as a calculation of some similarity metric between an item and a query, so all items can be ranked according to this metric or excluded from the search result set. Similarly to other classification problems, this requires the representation of an item, a query, and, optionally, other pieces of contextual information, such as user profile details, as features and then the calculation of one or more scores, which we will call *signals* hereafter, that indicate how well the item features match the query features. The signals are later combined together to make a final decision about whether an item should be included in the result list (*matching*) and about its position in the list (*ranking*). Figure 4.5 illustrates this flow.

Consequently, the designer of a search service has to address multiple controls at each of these stages: how to engineer features out of the raw data, how to match the features to produce signals, and how to mix signals together to achieve good relevance. Let us start to consider these controls with a few basic techniques and then gradually increase the complexity by chaining multiple blocks together and adding more variables into the equation.

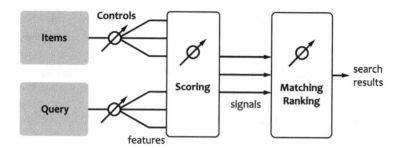

Figure 4.5: A high-level view of a search flow and its main controls.

4.3.1   *Token Matching*

In a merchandising search, items are typically quite complex entities with multiple textual and numerical attributes, such as name, description, price, and brand. The data can also contain a significant amount of structural information, such as a category hierarchy and different size/color product variants associated with one logical product. Let us put this complexity aside for a moment and consider the simple case of a retailer who represents each product as a document with a single description field that contains plain text, so an example with two products would be as follows:

```
Product 1
Description: Pleated black dress. Lightweight look
             for the office.

Product 2
Description: Fiery red dress. A black ribbon
             at the waist.
```

The most basic thing we can do to search over such documents is to break the descriptions up into words and allow only for single-word search queries, so a product will be included in a result set only if its description contains the same word as the query. The process of breaking up a text into words or other elements such as phrases is called *tokenization*, and the outputs – words in our cases – are called tokens. For English language, tokenization is usually done by using spaces and punctuation marks as delimiters, so the documents above will produce the following tokens:

$$
\begin{aligned}
&\text{Product 1: [Pleated], [black], [dress], [Lightweight],}\\
&\qquad\qquad\text{[look], [for], [the], [office]}\\
&\text{Product 2: [Fiery], [red], [dress], [A], [black]}\\
&\qquad\qquad\text{[ribbon], [at], [the], [waist]}
\end{aligned}
\tag{4.14}
$$

Consequently, the query *black* will match both products and the query *red* will only match the second product. Clearly, this method provides only a matching capability and the items in the result set are not ranked.

Although this token matching method is extremely simple and limited, it illustrates the main search controls that we discussed earlier. First, each token can be viewed as an individual feature that may or may not be present in a product. The tokenization process is then an example of feature engineering. Words are indeed reasonably good features because they carry a strong signal about a product type, such as shoes, and its properties, such as a black color. Second, token matching is a way to produce signals about correlations between product features and query features. Finally, the signals from all tokens are combined together to produce the final decision on match or mismatch. This flow is visualized in Figure 4.6.

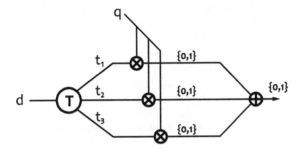

Figure 4.6: An illustration of a token matching flow that includes tokenization, scoring, and signal mixing. The product description and its tokens are denoted as d and t_i, respectively. The query is denoted as q.

4.3.2 Boolean Search and Phrase Search

The main shortcoming of basic token matching is an inability to process more meaningful queries than just a single term. The first enhancement that helps us to work around this limitation is the *Boolean query*, which enables chaining of multiple tokens by using Boolean operations, namely, AND, OR, and NOT. For example, the following Boolean query

```
dress AND red
```

will match only the second product from example 4.14, whereas the query

```
dress AND (red OR black)
```

will match both products. Boolean queries do not take into account positions of tokens in the text and, hence, can be thought of as several token matching queries combined together.

The second important capability that extends basic token matching is the *phrase query*. A phrase query is a query that searches for documents that contain a sequence of tokens that follow one another, as opposed to a Boolean query, which searches for documents that contain individual tokens irrespective of their order and positions in the text. We use square brackets to denote phrase queries and subqueries. For instance, the following query will match the first product from example 4.14 but not the second one:

```
[black dress]
```

This result has higher precision and lower recall than the result of the Boolean query *black AND dress*, which matches both products. Boolean and phrase queries together provide very powerful tools to control relevancy and manage the precision–recall trade-off. A query language that directly supports Boolean expressions is often a good solution for expert search where users are willing to learn and use advanced search functions, but its usage in merchandising search is limited because of the unintuitive user experience. We will discuss how free-text search can take advantage of complex Boolean and phrase queries in the later sections.

4.3.3   *Normalization and Stemming*

It is not difficult to see that chopping a text into tokens produces results that are not optimal from a matching standpoint. In natural language, words may have different forms and spellings that can be considered indistinguishable for almost all search intents. Some words do not carry any meaningful information at all and generate noise signals. This suggests that we need to perform a normalization of the raw tokens to create a cleaner token vocabulary. Such normalized tokens are typically referred to as *terms*.

Normalization is a complex process that usually includes multiple steps to address the different properties and phenomena of natural language. Let us go through an example that illustrates the key transformations by starting from the following original product description:

```
Maison Kitsuné Men's Slim Jeans. These premium
jeans come in a slim fit for a fashionable look.
```

The first step is to normalize the character set because a search query can be entered with or without diacritics and this difference typically does not mean different search intents. Tokenizing the text and converting it to a standard character set, we get the tokens

```
[Maison] [Kitsune] [Men's] [Slim] [Jeans] [These]
[premium] [jeans] [come] [in] [a] [slim] [fit]
[for] [a] [fashionable] [look]
```

The second issue that we face is the presence of lower- and uppercase characters that are also indistinguishable in most cases. The standard approach is to transform each token into its lowercase form, which gives the following result for our example:

```
[maison] [kitsune] [men's] [slim] [jeans] [these]
[premium] [jeans] [come] [in] [a] [slim] [fit]
[for] [a] [fashionable] [look]
```

The third possible step is to exclude high-frequency tokens such as *and, to, the,* and *will* because they are present in most texts and, hence, do not carry any specific information about an item. Such tokens are commonly known as *stop words*. Applying this transformation to the example, we get

```
[maison] [kitsune] [men's] [slim] [jeans] [premium]
[jeans] [come] [slim] [fit] [fashionable] [look]
```

The exclusion of stop words may have both positive and negative implications. On the one hand, it can positively influence some matching and ranking methods that we discuss later because meaningless high-frequency terms can skew some metrics used in relevancy calculations. On the other hand, the removal of stop words can result in losses of substantial information and reduce our ability to search for certain queries. For example, the removal of stop words prevents us from finding phrases like *to be, or not to be* or distinguishing *new* from *not new*. Stop words can also destroy the semantic relationships between the entities, so it becomes impossible to distinguish between an object *on the table* and *under the table*.

The fourth standard normalization technique is *stemming*. In most natural languages, words can change their form depending on number (*dress* and *dresses*), tense (*look* and *looked*), possession (*men* and *men's*), and other factors. Stemming is a process of reducing different word forms to the same root in order to eliminate differences that typically relate to the same search intent. The problem of stemming is challenging because of the multiple exceptions and special cases that can be found in natural languages. There exist multiple stemming methods, either rule based or dictionary based, with different strengths and weaknesses. One popular family of rule-based stemmers is based on the so-called Porter stemmer [Porter, 1980]. This represents a few groups of suffix transformation rules and conditions that check that a word is long enough to be reduced (see table 4.1 for an example). By applying stemming to our sample product description, we obtain the final set of regular terms, which looks more condensed and focused on the key features than the original text:

```
[maison] [kitsun] [men] [slim] [jean] [premium]
[jean] [com] [slim] [fit] [fashion] [look]
```

RULE	EXAMPLE
...ational ⟶ ate	relational ⟶ relate
...tional ⟶ tion	conditional ⟶ condition
	rational ⟶ rational
...ful ⟶ *none*	hopeful ⟶ hope
...ness ⟶ *none*	goodness ⟶ good
...izer ⟶ ize	digitizer ⟶ digitize

Table 4.1: An example of the rules used in the Porter stemmer. All rules in this example require at least one switch from vowel to consonant in front of the suffix, so the second rule applies to the word *conditional* but not to *rational*.

The same set of normalization algorithms is typically applied to both the query and documents to map all tokens into the same space of terms. For example, the query *Fashionable* will match a product that contains *fashioned* in the description because both words will be mapped to the term *fashion*.

4.3.4   *Ranking and the Vector Space Model*

Matching by using Boolean queries and phrase queries enables us to find a set of items that meet search criteria. However, the number of matching and potentially relevant items often exceeds the relatively small number of results that the average merchandising search user will look through, so the order in which items are presented to the user becomes critically important. We need to define a building block that can rank items according to their relevance.

Although ranking cannot improve the global precision–recall properties of the underlying matching, it can be considered a trick that improves precision–recall in the sense of local or perceived qualities. On the one hand, ranking increases the precision of the top results by boosting relevant items, but, at the same time, it does not remove items from the search results list, so it provides the same recall.

We can take a first step towards ranking by taking a closer look at Boolean queries and recognizing their scoring potential. First, we can notice that both item documents and queries can be represented as binary vectors, such that each element of a vector indicates whether a document or a query contains a certain term or not. In other words, an element that corresponds to a certain term is equal to one if a document or query contains the term and zero otherwise. If the total number of distinct terms in all documents in a collection is n, each document or query is a binary vector with n elements. It is easy to see that a Boolean query can be expressed by using a dot product between query vector $\mathbf{q}$ and document vector $\mathbf{d}$. Recall that a dot product between two vectors is given by

$$\mathbf{d} \cdot \mathbf{q} = \sum_{i=1}^{n} q_i d_i \qquad (4.15)$$

and the Euclidean norm of a vector is defined as

$$\|\mathbf{d}\| = \sqrt{d_1^2 + \cdots + d_n^2} \qquad (4.16)$$

Consequently, we can say that a Boolean query that contains multiple terms chained by using the *AND* operator is equivalent to the following condition:

$$\mathbf{d} \cdot \mathbf{q} \geqslant \|\mathbf{q}\|^2 \qquad (4.17)$$

because all terms in the query must match corresponding terms in the document, which results in a dot product that equals the number of one elements in the query vector. A Boolean query that chains its terms with *OR* is equivalent to the condition

$$\mathbf{d} \cdot \mathbf{q} \geqslant 1 \qquad (4.18)$$

because at least one term must match. This interpretation of Boolean queries reveals a kind of internal scoring that is converted into a matching decision by using a threshold. Equations 4.17 and 4.18 also suggest that the ratio between the dot product and query norm can be used as a continuous measure of similarity between the document and query. We can go even further and ask why we don't account for the norm of a document as well. One can argue that a short document that matches query terms is more relevant than a long document that matches the same number of terms. This can be justified from a probabilistic stand-point in the following way. Consider a person who talks about some topic – if that person uses a lot of relevant words in the first minute of the speech, it can be an indicator that the speech is really focused on the relevant topic, whereas the appearance of the same words in a one-hour speech can be attributed to a broadness of topics rather than focus. A metric that normalizes the dot product by norms of both vectors is a *cosine similarity*:

$$\cos(\mathbf{q}, \mathbf{d}) = \frac{\mathbf{q} \cdot \mathbf{d}}{\|\mathbf{q}\| \cdot \|\mathbf{d}\|} \tag{4.19}$$

The cosine similarity, that is, a cosine of the angle between the vectors, is a convenient metric that ranges from zero to one for positively defined vectors. A cosine similarity of zero means that a document vector is orthogonal to a query vector in the space of terms, and a similarity value of one means an exact match equivalent to a Boolean query. Unlike a Boolean query, the cosine similarity does not require operations to be specified in a query – it treats both query and document as an unordered collection of terms. Let us illustrate this *vector space model* by using an example.

EXAMPLE 4.1

▼

Consider two items that have the following descriptions (for simplicity, we assume that the descriptions have been tokenized and normalized):

```
Product 1: dark blue jeans blue denim fabric
Product 2: skinny jeans in bright blue
```

These two descriptions and the query *dark jeans* are represented as binary vectors in table 4.2.

	dark	blue	jeans	denim	fabric	skinny	in	bright	$\|\cdot\|$
d_1	1	1	1	1	1	0	0	0	$\sqrt{5}$
d_2	0	1	1	0	0	1	1	1	$\sqrt{5}$
q	1	0	1	0	0	0	0	0	$\sqrt{2}$

Table 4.2: An example of two documents and one query represented as binary vectors.

The similarity values between the query and each of the documents will be

$$\cos(\mathbf{q}, \mathbf{d}_1) = \frac{1+1}{\sqrt{2}\sqrt{5}} = 0.632$$

$$\cos(\mathbf{q}, \mathbf{d}_2) = \frac{1}{\sqrt{2}\sqrt{5}} = 0.316 \tag{4.20}$$

Figure 4.7 shows the relationship between the documents and query in a vector space. Note that the cosine similarity can be evaluated efficiently because only the non-zero dimensions of the query have to be considered.

▲

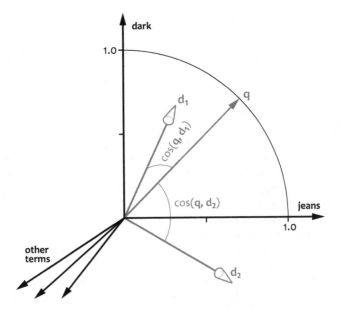

Figure 4.7: An example of the vector space model and cosine similarity for two documents and one query. The document and query vectors are depicted as normalized.

4.3.5 $TF \times IDF$ Scoring Model

The vector space model with binary vectors has two important shortcomings that negatively impact the relevance of results ranked by using this method. First, it does not take into account the term frequency in a document. We can expect that documents that have multiple occurrences of query terms are more relevant than documents where the same terms occur only once. Second, some terms can be more important than others: rarely used words are often more discriminative and informative than frequently used words. For example, an apparel retailer may have word *clothing* in most product descriptions so matching this term does not signal strong relevance. The stop words that we discussed earlier are an extreme case of this problem.

The first issue described above can be mitigated by replacing the zeros and ones in the document vectors with the corresponding term frequencies in the document. This variant of the vector space model is often called the *bag-of-words model. Term frequency* (TF) can be defined as the number of occurrences of term t in document d, which we denote as $n(t, d)$ or some non-linear function of this number. One popular choice is to use the square root of the number of occurrences:

$$tf(t, d) = \sqrt{n(t, d)} \tag{4.21}$$

For instance, a term that occurs in a document nine times will have a term frequency of three. The square root function is used to smooth down scores of documents that have a very high number of term occurrences.

The second issue can be addressed by calculating the term frequencies across the entire collection of documents to distinguish rare words from frequent ones. One possible way to estimate word rarity is to count the occurrences of a term in all of the documents, similarly to the method for term frequency but for the entire collection. This approach, however, is known to produce non-optimal results because a few documents with multitudinous occurrences of a rare term can skew the results. A more common method is to count the number of documents that contain a given term at least once. This metric is known as the *document frequency* of a term. The inverse of the document frequency can then be used as a measure of term rarity. The standard formula for the *inverse document frequency* (IDF) for term t is as follows:

$$idf(t) = 1 + \ln \frac{N}{df(t) + 1} \tag{4.22}$$

in which N is the total number of documents in the collection, and $df(t)$ is the document frequency of the term. Similarly to term frequency, a logarithm function is used to smooth down the magnitude of the coefficient for rare terms.

Term frequency and inverse document frequency are usually combined together so that the elements of a document vector are calculated as a product of values defined by equations 4.21 and 4.22 for the corresponding term:

$$\mathbf{d}(i) = tf(t_i, d) \times idf(t_i) \tag{4.23}$$

This is a widely used approach known as the TF×IDF model. Substituting expression 4.23 into the definitions of the dot product and Euclidean norm, we get the following formulas that can be used to calculate the cosine similarity score for query $\mathbf{q}$ and document $\mathbf{d}$ under the TF×IDF model:

$$\mathbf{q} \cdot \mathbf{d} = \sum_{t \text{ in } q} tf(t, d) \cdot idf(t) \times tf(t, q) \cdot idf(t) \tag{4.24}$$

$$\|\mathbf{q}\| = \sqrt{\sum_{t \text{ in } q} [tf(t, q) \cdot idf(t)]^2} \tag{4.25}$$

$$\|\mathbf{d}\| = \sqrt{\sum_{t \text{ in } d} [tf(t, d) \cdot idf(t)]^2} \tag{4.26}$$

The cosine similarity calculated by using formulas 4.24–4.26 is one of the most commonly used scoring methods. These formulas, however, are not a rock-solid standard, and many different variations can be found in real search engine implementations. Let us consider one particular example that makes the following three adjustments, which are known to work well in practice:

1. The document norm defined by equation 4.26 normalizes all document vectors to a unit length. In many practical applications, however, shorter documents are often more relevant if they contain the same number of term matches and equal term frequencies. This can be accounted for by replacing the standard document norm with a norm that is proportional to the total number of terms $n(d)$ in a document:

$$L_d(d) = \sqrt{\sum_{t \text{ in } d} 1} = \sqrt{n(d)} \tag{4.27}$$

2. All terms in a query can be considered equally significant and processed independently, even in the case of duplicates. Consequently, the term frequency $tf(t, q)$ is always equal to one. This allows us to redefine the query norm as follows:

$$L_q(q) = \sqrt{\sum_{t \text{ in } q} idf(t)^2} \tag{4.28}$$

3. The score of a document in the TF×IDF model depends on the number of words that match the query because missed words zero out the corresponding terms in the dot product. It can be argued that missed words should be penalized even more, so an additional coefficient called a coordination factor can be introduced. *Coordination factor* $c(q, d)$ is defined as the ratio of the number of common terms in a query and document to the total number of terms in the query. For example, the query *black skinny jeans* and the document *black jeans* will have a coordination factor of two thirds.

Collecting these adjustments together and substituting them into the definition of cosine similarity, we obtain the following final scoring formula:

$$score(q, d) = \frac{c(q, d)}{L_d(d) \cdot L_q(q)} \sum_{t \text{ in } q} tf(t, d) \cdot idf(t)^2 \tag{4.29}$$

The TF×IDF scoring model is a fundamental building block that we will use later to assemble more sophisticated scoring solutions. Nevertheless, it is worth noting that this method has been designed as a generic solution for the retrieval of relatively large texts, such as journal articles, and its usage in a merchandising search that deals with structured data can have pitfalls that sometimes require the use of alternative ranking methods, as we will see later.

EXAMPLE 4.2

▼

We will wrap up the discussion of ranking methods with an example of TF×IDF calculations. Let us take the following product descriptions:

    d_1: dark blue jeans blue denim fabric
    d_2: skinny jeans in bright blue

Applying formulas 4.21 and 4.22, we obtain the TF and IDF values summarized in table 4.3. Let us now score these products for the query *skinny jeans*. The query norm and document norms can then be calculated in accordance with formulas 4.27 and 4.28 by using the TF and IDF values that we just evaluated.

$$L_d(d_1) = \sqrt{6} = 2.449, \qquad L_d(d_2) = \sqrt{5} = 2.236 \qquad (4.30)$$

$$L_q(q) = \sqrt{idf(jeans)^2 + idf(skinny)^2} = 1.163 \qquad (4.31)$$

	dark	blue	jeans	denim	fabric	skinny	in	bright
idf($\cdot$)	1.00	0.59	0.59	1.00	1.00	1.00	1.00	1.00
tf($\cdot,1$)	1.00	1.41	1.00	1.00	1.00	0.00	0.00	0.00
tf($\cdot,2$)	0.00	1.00	1.00	0.00	0.00	1.00	1.00	1.00
d_1	1.00	0.83	0.59	1.00	1.00	0.00	0.00	0.00
d_2	0.00	0.59	0.59	0.00	0.00	1.00	1.00	1.00

Table 4.3: An example of TF and IDF calculations for two documents. The last two lines correspond to the TF×IDF vector representations of the documents.

The coordination factor is 0.50 for the first product and 1.00 for the second one. By substituting all norms and TF/IDF values into formula 4.29, we get a score of 0.062 for the first product and a much higher score of 0.520 for the second product, which is in agreement with the intuitive expectation that the second product is more relevant for the query that we used.

TF×IDF is also dependent on text normalization and stemming. For instance, it is not difficult to see that the following documents have equal TF×IDF scores for the query *dark* if no stemming is performed:

```
d₁: dark darker darkness
d₂: dark darker lightness
d₃: dark light lightness
```

The first document, however, looks much more relevant in this context. Stemming will map the words *dark, darker*, and *darkness* to the same root *dark*, which will result in higher scores for the first and second documents because of higher term frequency. Moreover, a user who searches for *darkish shoes* will get no results without stemming, which is unlikely to be a good user experience.

▲

4.3.6 Scoring with n-grams

We have shown that the vector space model is related to Boolean queries and TF×IDF scoring can be considered as a soft-output version of a Boolean query that fills the gap between OR-chained and AND-chained Boolean queries. This line of thinking can be continued, and a soft version of a phrase query can be created. From the ranking perspective, the drawback of standard Boolean phrase queries is that they are too restrictive and require all query terms to match. One possible relaxation is to match not the entire phrase but *shingles*, that is, sequences of several terms. Such sequences are also called *n-grams* and can include two terms (bigrams), three terms (trigrams), or more. Shingles can be viewed as a tokenization technique that is applied to both document and query, and the resulting n-grams are fed into a Boolean query or TF×IDF scorer. The following example shows how two products can be tokenized into bigrams:

```
black cotton polo shirt: [black cotton]
                         [cotton polo]
                         [polo shirt]

short sleeve black shirt: [short sleeve]
                          [sleeve black]
                          [black shirt]
```

The TF×IDF scorer treats n-grams just like single-word terms and calculates the cosine similarity in the vector space where each vector element corresponds to a shingle, and the TF×IDF metrics are also calculated for shingles. So these products produce equal TF×IDF scores for the query *black shirt* if tokenized into single words (unigrams), but the second product scores higher if bigrams are used because it explictly contains the *black shirt* subphrase. It can be argued that scoring using bigrams better captures semantic relationships in the text: the proximity of the words *polo* and *shirt* in the first product emphasizes that *polo shirt* is the primary property and *black* is just a refinment, but the proximity of *black* and *shirt* in the second product description indicates that *black* is the key property. This ability to capture semantic relationships is especially important to differeniate between compound terms such as *tuxedo coat* and *sports coat*. The use of shingles is a powerful method to increase search precision that is often combined with the standard single-word scoring, as we will discuss shortly.

4.4   MIXING RELEVANCE SIGNALS

Thus far, we have discussed how to search for items represented as plain textual descriptions. In merchandising search, as well as most other search applications, such a plain data format is rarely the case. We almost always deal with structured source data that characterize each item by multiple properties:

```
Name: Levi's Hooded Military Jacket
Description: Stand collar with drawstring hood
Brand: Levi Strauss
...
Price: 189.90
Category: Women's Jackets
```

Items can also have dynamic properties, such as sales data and user ratings, that also carry important information about their fitness and, ultimately, relevance. Item property values can be short strings such as product names, long text snippets such as descriptions or reviews, numbers, tokens from a discrete set such brand names, or even nested or hierarchical entities such as product variants or categories. This creates a diversity of features and signals that are measured on different scales and may not be directly comparable. We need to find a way to correlate all of these features with a query and mix the resulting signals together to produce a relevance score.

One naïve approach to this problem is to blend all of the property values into one large text and use basic scoring methods to search through this text. Although this approach is not totally meaningless, it results in a very smooth and blurry signal that unpredictably scores search results based on the interplay of term frequencies and text lengths. For instance, the seemingly simple query *black dress shoes* can result in a wild mix of dresses, shoes, black tuxedos, and other items that happen to have some of the query terms in the description. To manage this problem, we have to create a method that preserves the focused features and signals and provides enough controls to pick the strongest and most relevant results.

4.4.1   Searching Multiple Fields

A query can be considered as a description of a desired search result that specifies one or more properties an item should have to be relevant. For example, the query *black levi strauss jeans* clearly requests products of type *jeans*, color *black*, and brand *levi strauss*. On the other hand, each item is also represented as a set of properties, so we can expect to get a good result by creating documents with multiple *fields* where each field corresponds to an item property, running the query against each field in isolation to get multiple signals, and then blending the signals into the final score. This idea is illustrated in Figure 4.8.

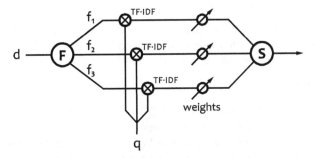

Figure 4.8: A basic schema of multifield scoring. F stands for splitting a document into fields $f_1, f_2, \ldots, f_n$. S is a signal mixing function that produces the final score.

This approach can produce reasonably good results, but it requires us to be careful about keeping signals focused and balanced. Problems with signal focusing can arise in connection with mismatches of the document fields and concepts in a user query, so the concept that a user searches for can be scattered across multiple fields. For example, a user can search for a person by using the first and last name, expecting that this pair will be interpreted as a single token, but the documents can store first and last names in different fields, thereby producing meaningless partial matches. The problem with signal balance appears because each field exists in its own universe and there is not a common scale for signal scores (e. g., 0.00 means nonrelevant and 1.00 means relevant).

EXAMPLE 4.3

▼

Let us illustrate the problem of signal disbalance by using the example of a fashion retailer catalog that contains a thousand products comprising jeans and shoes:

```
Product 1
  Name: Men's 514 Straight-Fit Jeans.
  Description: Dark blue jeans. Blue denim fabric.
  Brand: Levi Strauss
  ....
Product 1000
  Name: Leather Oxfords.
  Description: Elegant blue dress shoes.
  Brand: Out Of The Blue
```

We can expect that it is quite usual for jeans to have the term *blue* in the name or description, so its IDF value will be quite low. For instance, if we have 500 blue jeans out of a thousand products, we get

$$idf(\text{name:blue}) = 1 + \ln(1000/501) = 1.69 \tag{4.32}$$

At the same time, the brand *Out Of The Blue* that manufactures blue shoes may be very rare. Let us assume that we have only one product of this brand and there are no other brand names containing the word *blue*, so the IDF value for the term *blue* in the brand field is

$$idf(\text{brand:blue}) = 1 + \ln(1000/2) = 7.21 \tag{4.33}$$

Consider the query *blue jeans* now. The blue shoes will have a very high score for the brand field and a low score for the description field, whereas the blue jeans will have a relatively low score for the description field that matches both terms of the query but with low IDFs. Combining the signals by using a sum or maximum function, we are likely to get a search results list with the shoes at the top, which does not match the search intent. The reason is that IDFs depend on term distributions within a field; therefore, IDFs for different fields are not comparable.

▲

One possible solution for signal disbalance is to adjust signals by using manually set weights, as shown in Figure 4.8. In the example above, we can assign a low weight to the brand field to demote its signal and push the shoes down. This can help in cases of consistent differences in signal levels or importance (e. g., we know that name matching is more important than description matching), but this solution is very brittle. We need to approach the problem of signal equalization in a more systematic way.

4.4.2   *Signal Engineering and Equalization*

Multifield search has two aspects that complement each other and typically need to be solved in parallel – signal engineering and signal equalization. Signal engineering aims to create clear and focused signals; meanwhile, signal equalization aims to mix these signals together to produce the final results. The same relevance problem sometimes can be solved in different ways, either by tuning the mixing function or by constructing a better more accurate signal. When we are searching through multiple fields, the following types of relationship between the fields and the search intent can be distinguished [Gormley and Tong, 2015]:

- *One strong signal.* It can be the case that a user searches for a certain property that ideally should match with one of the fields and produce a single strong signal. Signals from different fields do not complement each other but rather compete. For instance, a user who searches for the brand *Out Of The Blue* is likely to be focused on the brand field and does not consider the color blue to be relevant.

- *Strong average signal.* We can be interested in taking the average signal rather than the strongest one if the individual signals are balanced and related to different aspects of the same search intent. For example, item size and color can be equally important.

- *Fragmented features and signals.* We can expect to get a clear signal by scoring individual fields only if a query and field are aligned and resonate in a meaningful way. It can be the case, however, that fields contain fragmented pieces of information, such that the resulting signals do not correlate with relevance. Such fragments can be merged together to obtain a better signal.

These three cases are, however, closely related. Let us go through the list and discuss signal engineering and equalization techniques for each case in detail.

4.4.2.1   *One Strong Signal*

The problem with the *Out Of The Blue* brand that we discussed in the previous section arises from inaccurate processing of the brand signal. We noted that one possible solution is to adjust the weight of the signal, but another alternative is to refine the brand signal to make it less ambiguous. We can argue that a brand name is a concept that cannot be broken down into separate words, so it makes sense to replace the TF×IDF scoring with bigram scoring. This will light up a signal only if a recognizable part of the brand name is present in a query. We can also choose to use a maximum function for signal mixing to select the strongest signal, so we end up with the scoring pipeline presented in Figure 4.9.

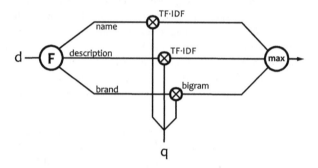

Figure 4.9: An example of a signal mixing pipeline that focuses on the strongest signal.

A search result produced by pipeline 4.9 is shown in Figure 4.10. The items marketed under the *Out Of The Blue* brand outstrip other items only if the brand name is clearly articulated in the query; otherwise, items with relevant descriptions and names will take precedence. Note that we might need to make more adjustments to make the bigram scoring work properly, for example, disable stop words.

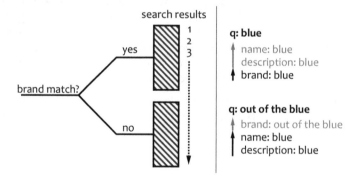

Figure 4.10: A search result structure for the strongest signal strategy.

The strategy of signal mixing with a maximum function is a powerful and popular approach to multifield search, and the use of n-grams is an efficient signal focusing technique. The creation of focused signals, however, is a complex process that is not limited to n-grams. It is not unusual to generate several signals from the same field, such as parallel unigram and bigram scores that can be mixed together, or to request merchandisers to attribute items with a completely new property that helps to produce a more focused signal than the available features.

The search result structure in Figure 4.10 is quite basic, and we can program more complex behavior by relaxing the signal mixing function. One possible solution is to mix weaker signals with the strongest one in a controllable way. This can be expressed by using the following signal mixing formula:

$$s = s_m + \alpha \sum_{i \neq m} s_i \tag{4.34}$$

in which s_m is the maximum (strongest) signal, $0 \leqslant \alpha \leqslant 1$ is a parameter that controls the weight of all other signals s_i in the mix, and s is the final score. It is easy to see that formula 4.34 provides a spectrum of scoring functions that starts with the strongest signal selection if α is zero and ends with signal averaging if α is set to one. This approach allows us to achieve result structures with more than two relevance tiers. For instance, we can prioritize products with a name that matches the query, but we can also keep brand matching as a second priority, as illustrated in Figure 4.11. This can be implemented by using the scoring function 4.34 and setting weights such that the product name signal is amplified and the matching items are elevated to the top tier of the search results list. Brand matching will be the second-strongest signal in the mix, so the items in the inner tiers created by name matching will be ranked based on the brand. A signal mixing pipeline that implements this strategy is shown in Figure 4.12.

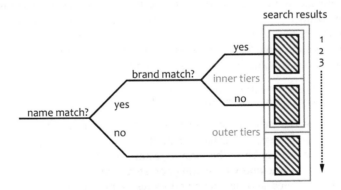

Figure 4.11: A search result structure for weighted signal mixing.

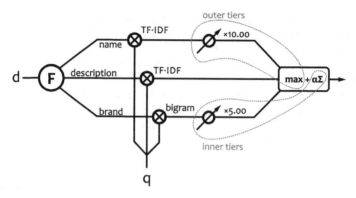

Figure 4.12: An example of a pipeline for weighted signal mixing.

4.4.2.2 *Strong Average Signal*

By increasing the magnitude of the secondary signals in formula 4.34, we arrive at a solution that ranks items based on the average signal. The sum of signals also produces a kind of tiered search results, although the tiers are based on the number of search criteria met by an item, rather than on individual fields. A search query can include several criteria that correspond to different item properties and, consequently, document fields. Summing the signals from different fields, we achieve a ranking behavior that places items with many resonating properties at the top of the search results list, followed by items with fewer properties that resonate with the query. We have already seen that this approach is vulnerable to signal disbalance, but it can be a suitable solution for mixing a group of equalized signals. A common use for this method is with signals obtained from different versions of the same property. For example, we can use stemming for a certain field to improve recall and, at the same time, use the original non-stemmed version of the same field to boost exact matches. The following product descriptions contain the words *fashion* and *fashionable*

d_1 : new popular fashion brand
d_2 : stylish and fashionable look

which are reduced to the term *fashion* by a Porter stemmer. Consequently, both descriptions have identical TF×IDF scores for the query *fashionable*. We can boost the second document that has a word that exactly matches the query by scoring non-stemmed versions and adding up the stemmed and non-stemmed scores. Summing of the signals is a feasible strategy here because the more matches we have, the better the result.

4.4.2.3 *Fragmented Features and Signals*

Finally, we have to discuss in detail the case of fragmented features, which requires its own signal engineering techniques. The problem of fragmented features and signals arises because the standard multifield search we discussed above scores each field independently. Although it may not be obvious at first glance, it can be the case that individual fields correlate reasonably well with a query to produce a strong average signal but the overall coverage of query conditions by all fields remains low. Let us consider the following basic example with two product documents [Turnbull and Berryman, 2016]:

```
Product 1
  Name: Polo
  Brand: Polo

Product 2
  Name: Polo
  Brand: Lacoste
```

It is quite intuitive that the second product is more relevant for the query *Lacoste Polo*, but TF×IDF calculations give a different result. Recall that the practical TF×IDF scoring formula 4.29 for one-term fields boils down to the following equation:

$$\frac{\text{query coordination factor}}{\text{query norm} \times \text{field norm}} \times \text{tf}(\text{term}, \text{field}) \times \text{idf}_{\text{field}}^2(\text{term}) \quad (4.35)$$

The query coordination factor is 0.50 for all four fields because only one of the query terms matches (*Polo* or *Lacoste*). The query norm, field norm, and TF value are also the same for all terms and fields. The IDF values for *Polo* and *Lacoste* are the same for the brand field, but different from the *Polo* IDF in the name field. Consequently, the name and brand fields (pairwise) have the same scores in both documents and the total document scores are equal as well; it does not matter which function we use to mix the query signals, sum or maximum. The fundamental reason is that each field matches exactly one query term (either *Polo* or *Lacoste*) to produce equally strong signals, but the fact that the second document as a whole covers two terms and the first document covers only one term is not taken into account. This issue can arise in many cases where different facets of the same logical property are modeled as different fields: a person name can be broken down into first and last names, a delivery address can be split into street name, city name, and country, and so on. Fragmented signals can lead to frustrating search results – a document that perfectly matches a query can be present in the search results list but may have a surprisingly low rank.

One possible way to address the problem is to merge several similar fields into one, thereby eliminating the problem with fragmented or imbalanced signals. This is a valid practical method that can improve relevance. The downside of this method is that the resulting signal can be too blurry, in the sense that secondary features become as important as the primary ones. For example, a dress can have the phrase *wear with any shoes* in the description, which can make the dress pop up in the search results for shoes if the product-type feature is not differentiated properly.

The second alternative for the fragmented feature problem is based on the observation that single-term queries are not vulnerable to the fragmentation described above. Moreover, each term in a query can be considered as a separate criterion added by the user to narrow down the search result, so it can be reasonable to score a document for each query term independently, producing a signal that indicates how well this particular criterion is satisfied, and then blend all the signals to produce the final score. This approach is called *term-centric scoring* to differentiate it from the field-centric approach that we used earlier. The term-centric signal pipeline can be thought of as multiple field-centric pipelines executed for every query term to produce signals that are finally mixed into the final output, as shown in Figure 4.13. The signals from different pipelines are summed up because the more terms that match, the better (the average signal strategy); meanwhile, the strongest signal strategy can be applied to signals from the different fields within a term pipeline.

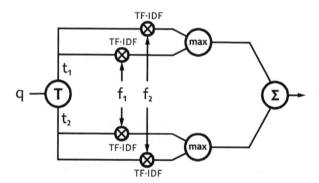

Figure 4.13: Term-centric scoring pipeline. t_1 and t_2 are query terms; f_1 and f_2 are document fields.

Returning to our example with the *Polo* and *Lacoste* brands, we can notice that the term-centric approach will produce more meaningful results for the query *Lacoste Polo*. The first document will get a high score for the query term *Polo* from both fields and zero scores for the term *Lacoste*, so the total score will be

$$\max\{\text{tf-idf}_{\text{name}}(\text{Polo}),\ \text{tf-idf}_{\text{brand}}(\text{Polo})\} + \max\{0,\ 0\} \qquad (4.36)$$

in which the TF×IDF score for *Polo* is 1.00 for the name field and 0.35 for the brand field due to the difference in IDF. At the same time, the second document will get a high score for both query terms:

$$\max\{\text{tf-idf}_{\text{name}}(\text{Polo}),\ 0\} + \max\{0,\ \text{tf-idf}_{\text{brand}}(\text{Lacoste})\} \qquad (4.37)$$

in which the TF×IDF score for *Lacoste* is 1.00 for the brand field. This result looks more relevant than the result we achieved by using the field-centric approach.

4.4.3   *Designing a Signal Mixing Pipeline*

We have seen that the structure of a search result can be derived from the design of the signal mixing pipeline. We can turn this process upside down and attempt to develop a pipeline from a known search result structure. This problem statement is of great practical value because it enables us to engineer features and scoring functions to a specification that describes a desired search result. This is closely related to both relevance engineering and merchandising controls because the specification can incorporate domain knowledge about relevance criteria and business objectives. A programmatic system can provide an interface that facilitates the specification of desired search results and design of the signal mixing pipelines, as well as experimental evaluation.

Let us go through an example of a relatively complex search result specification to demonstrate the end-to-end engineering of signals and scoring functions by using both textual and non-textual features. We will consider the case of a fashion retailer who builds an online search service. We will also assume that the user searches within a certain product category to keep the problem reasonably simple (we will discuss how to achieve good precision when searching across multiple categories in one of the next sections). Our starting point is the specification provided in Figure 4.14 that codifies the following business rules:

- If a user searches for a certain product by its name or ID, a matching product should be at the top of the search results.

- If a user searches for a certain brand, products of this brand should be given priority and additionally sorted by newness and customer rating in order to boost new or highly rated products.

- Otherwise, the results should be ranked according to average relevance of product descriptions and other fields.

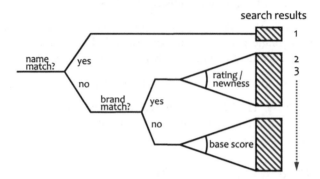

Figure 4.14: An example of a search result specification that can be used to design a signal mixing pipeline.

The specification mentions five different signals that should be taken into account: exact product name or ID match, exact brand match, product newness, product rating, and base average score. The exact match signals can be obtained by using n-gram scoring for the corresponding name and brand fields. A reasonably good precision can be implemented by using bigrams, and even stricter matching can be achieved with trigrams or Boolean phrase matching. Note that we can even turn off TF×IDF calculations for the n-grams and simply count the number of n-gram matches because we are interested in a binary outcome (does the product name match or not?), rather than continuous relevance grades. We can assume that newness and ratings are available as numerical product properties. Newness, for example, can be measured as the number of days since a product was introduced at the store, and the average customer rating can be a real number on a scale from 1 to 5. The base score can be calculated by using one of the signal engineering methods that we discussed earlier. One of the most straightforward methods would be to merge all product properties into one field and calculate a TF×IDF score for it.

We can start to build a signal mixing pipeline from the base score and put more relevance tiers on top of it in accordance with the search result specification. Each upper tier is created by amplifying the corresponding signal so that all products that exhibit a property required for this signal are elevated above the lower tiers in the search results list.

The first tier that we put on top of the base score is the exact brand match. We have to amplify the brand signal by assigning it a boosting factor, and we also have to mix it with the rating and newness features to achieve the desired secondary sorting, as shown in Figure 4.15. We clearly need to rescale the raw rating and newness values to convert them into meaningful scoring factors; this can be done in many different ways. A raw customer rating on a scale from 1 to 5 can be too aggressive as an amplification factor and can be tempered by using a square root or logarithm function to reduce the gap between low-rated and high-rated products. For instance, the magnitude of the brand signal amplified by a raw rating of 5.0 is two times higher than for a rating of 2.5; however, by taking the square root of the rating, we reduce the difference down to 1.41.

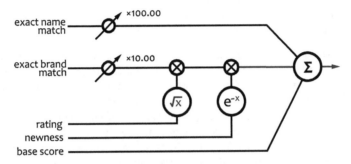

Figure 4.15: A signal mixing pipeline that corresponds to the specification in Figure 4.14.

The newness value should be transformed into a factor that gradually decreases with the age of a product. This can be done by using a linear function, exponential decay, or Gaussian decay. For example, it can be a reasonable choice to decrease the scoring factor by 10% every 30 days, which leads us to the exponential decay function

$$\text{newness factor} = \exp(-\alpha x) \tag{4.38}$$

in which x is the value of newness in days and parameter α is determined from the following equation (according to which, the ratio between any two factors separated by 30 days is 0.9):

$$\exp(-30 \cdot \alpha) = 0.9 \tag{4.39}$$

Combining the brand match signal with the rating and newness factors, we get a signal that corresponds to the second tier. Finally, the top tier is crafted from the name match signal mixed with a large constant factor that elevates the corresponding matching products to the very top of the search results list.

4.5   SEMANTIC ANALYSIS

The search methods that we have discussed so far are all based on token matching. Although we have used a few techniques, such as stemming, that deal with specific features of natural language, we have essentially reduced the search problem to a mechanical comparison of tokens. This approach, sometimes referred to as a *syntactic search*, works very well in practice and is used as a core method in most search engine implementations. Syntactic search, however, has limited ability for modeling the features of natural language that go beyond individual terms. The meaning of words in natural language is often dependent on the context created by the preceding and succeeding words and sentences, and several types of such dependencies exist. Most of them are related to one of the following two categories:

POLYSEMY Polysemy is the association of one word with multiple meanings. For instance, the word *wood* can refer to the material or an area of land filled with trees. Polysemy represents a serious problem for relevance because a user might have in mind one meaning of a word (e. g., products made of wood) but the search engine will return documents that use the same word with a different meaning (e. g., products that are related to woodlands, such as forestry equipment). We have already encountered the problem of complex concepts that are expressed with phrases that must be treated as a single token, for example, *dress shoes*. This issue can be viewed as a particular case of polysemy because the meaning of the individual words depends on the context, so the meaning of the word *dress* depends on whether it is followed by the word *shoes*. A particular case of polysemy that is very common in merchandising applications is the usage of vocabulary words in brand and product names. An example of this problem would be the brand name *Blue*, which is indistinguishable from the color *blue* in queries like *blue jeans*.

SYNONYMY Words are considered as synonyms if they can express nearly the same meaning in a given context, such as *candy* and *sweet*. Synonymy is also a major problem for search relevance because a basic syntactic search is not able to match relevant documents that do not contain the given query term but do contain synonyms. For example, items that contain the term *sweet* are likely to be relevant for the query *candy*, but all of the search methods we have discussed so far would fail to handle this dependency.

Some aspects of the polysemy problem can be handled by using n-grams and the more advanced phrase-matching methods that we discuss in the next sections, at least to a certain extent. In a similar way, stemming can be viewed as a technique that handles synonymy in a very basic form by reducing closely related terms to the same root. These methods, however, lack the insight into the words' meanings and relationships that is required to solve polysemy and synonymy problems. These issues require us to develop new techniques that are focused on contexts and meaning, rather than separate tokens. This approach is known as *semantic search*, named after the branch of linguistics that studies the meaning and relationships of words and phrases. Some methods of semantic searching are completely independent from syntactic searching and compete with it, but many semantics techniques can be used to extend syntactic search.

Polysemy and synonymy can be viewed as a problem of hidden relationships between words or, alternatively, as a problem of finding logical concepts that are materialized in words. From the latter standpoint, polysemy refers to the case of two distinct concepts mapped to one word, whereas synonymy refers to the opposite case of two distinct words mapped to one logical concept. The problem of semantic analysis and search can therefore be viewed as the problem of finding the right concepts and mappings between words and concepts. This way of thinking is often referred to as *concept search* [Giunchiglia et al., 2009; Hughes, 2015]. This term emphasizes the fact that concepts are not merely statistical relationships between words but logical entities that can be defined by using domain knowledge and other considerations.

We will spend the rest of this section discussing the methods of semantic search and analysis that can help with polysemy and synonymy problems; some of these methods are closely related to recommendations. We will also use examples from the grocery domain, instead of apparel, for a change.

4.5.1 *Synonyms and Hierarchies*

The most basic solution to the synonymy problem is a manually curated *thesaurus*, that is, a catalog of words and their synonyms. Once created, a thesaurus can be used to transform documents and queries in a way that closely resembles stemming. For example, we can define the following set of words as synonyms:

```
candy, sweet, confection
```

Our goal is to make these terms identical from the querying stand-point, so that documents containing the terms *sweet* and *confection* are retrieved for the query *candy*, and the other way around. This can be done in a few ways, and each method has advantages and disadvantages.

The first approach is *contraction*. One of the synonyms in the list is assigned to be the principal, and all occurrences of other synonyms are replaced by the principal. For example, we can choose to replace all occurrences of *sweet* and *confection* with *candy*, both in documents and queries. Note that a principal does not necessarily have to be a real word; it can be a special token that never appears in the input texts but is used as an internal representation of a synonym group. Thus, the contraction approach works exactly like stemming. Contraction clearly achieves the goal of making all synonyms identical from the query-ing standpoint, but the downside is that it collapses all synonyms into the principal, which makes frequently used synonym terms indistin-guishable from rarely used ones. This can negatively impact TF×IDF calculations.

The alternative to contraction is *expansion*. The expansion strategy replaces each synonym instance with a full list of synonyms:

```
best candy shop → [best] [candy] [sweet] [confection] [shop]
```

Expansion can be applied to either documents or queries, but not both. Document-side expansion may have the same negative impact on TF×IDF scoring as contraction and also increases the size of doc-uments. Query-side expansion preserves the correct IDF statistics but makes a query more complex from the computational standpoint.

The expansion technique has one very important application that goes far beyond basic synonym processing. Although synonyms are defined as words that have roughly the same meaning, it is often the case that one word represents a broader logical concept than another. The relationship between such synonyms becomes asymmetric in the sense that a broader concept can be considered as a synonym for a narrower one, but not the other way around. For example, *cake* can be used as a synonym for *cheesecake*, but it would be incorrect to replace *cake* with *cheesecake* in some contexts. Consequently, it can be beneficial to elaborate the expansion process and replace plain synonym lists with directed rules, such that occurrences of *cheesecake* are expanded into *cake* and *cheesecake* but occurrences of *cake* are not expanded. This type of expansion is called *genre expansion*.

Developing this idea further, we can construct a hierarchy of terms that describes nested classes of concepts, as illustrated in Figure 4.16. At every level of a hierarchy, terms are expanded from their prede-cessors and, thereby, become searchable for queries that contain more generic terms. For instance, an item that contains the term *fruitcake* will be included in a search results list for queries with the terms *cake* and *bakery*.

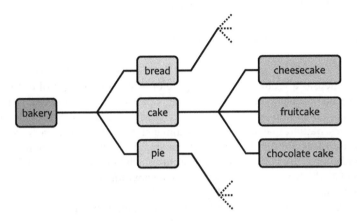

Figure 4.16: Example of a category hierarchy for grocery products.

Similarly to basic expansion, genre expansion can be applied to both documents and queries, but the methodology is quite different because of the asymmetry of expansion rules. By applying genre expansion to documents, we make queries for broad concepts match documents about specific concepts, but not vice versa. For example, a query for *cake* will return *cheesecakes* and *fruitcakes*. By applying expansion to queries, we make queries for specific concepts match documents about broad concepts, so a query for *cheesecake* returns *cakes*. In applying genre expansion to documents, we also artificially decrease the IDF of broad concepts because these terms are copied to more documents. This is not necessarily negative because specific concepts will be scored higher than broad ones, which is typically reasonable from a relevance standpoint.

Contraction and expansion are very powerful techniques for modeling semantic networks, and they give us some clues on how known semantic relationships can be utilized in query processing. At the same time, they provide no guidance on how these relationships can be inferred. One possible solution is to create lists of synonyms manually. This is the case in many merchandising search applications because it enables merchandisers to use synonyms as a control that can express certain business rules and domain knowledge. On the other hand, it can be a challenge to manually curate a thesaurus in search applications with dynamic content, such as marketplaces. Also, it can be difficult to reveal some types of semantic dependencies without machine learning methods. For example, the name of a famous athlete can connote to a certain sport, a type of sports equipment, or the brand that the athlete promotes. Our next goal will be to develop methods that are able to learn a thesaurus automatically.

4.5.2   *Word Embedding*

The vector space model states that a document or query can be represented as a vector in a linear space of terms. In the light of our discussion of the polysemy and synonymy problems, we know that terms can be ambiguous and redundant, so it can be the case that a document representation that uses terms as dimensions is not particularly good or is at least flawed. Indeed, we have already discussed that polysemy and synonymy can be viewed as a mismatch between words and concepts, which suggests that words are a convoluted representation that conceals semantic relationships.

We can attempt to find a better representation by changing the basis for the document space. Conceptually, we would like to map documents and queries to vectors of real numbers, so that the ranking scores can be calculated simply as a dot product between the query and document representations:

$$q \rightarrow \mathbf{p}$$
$$d \rightarrow \mathbf{v}$$
$$\text{score}(q, d) = \mathbf{p} \cdot \mathbf{v} = \sum_{i=1}^{k} p_i v_i \qquad (4.40)$$

in which $\mathbf{p}$ and $\mathbf{v}$ are the k-element vector representations of a query and a document and k is the dimensionality of the vector representation. Note that individual words can also be mapped to such vector representations because each word can be treated as a single-word document. This approach is generally known as *word embedding*. The term embedding is used because the number of dimensions k is typically small relative to the number of distinct words, so a high-dimensional vector space model representation where each word has its own dimension is *embedded* into a low-dimensionality space. Word embedding has many applications, which depend on how the vector representations are constructed and used. From the search services perspective, we are mainly interested in two possibilities. First, embedded representations can be used for actual query processing, so that document scores for a given query are calculated as dot products between the representations. Second, embedded representations of individual words can be analyzed to create a thesaurus, that is, to match words with their synonyms or related words.

The key problem of word embedding is, of course, how to construct the new vector representations. Conceptually, we want a vector space that preserves semantic relationships: words and documents with similar or related semantic meanings should be collocated or lie on the same line, whereas documents that have different semantic meanings should not be collocated or collinear, even if they contain the same (polysemic) words. If we could construct such a space, it would be possible to overcome the limitations of the vector space model. First, it would be possible to find relevant documents for a query even if a document and query did not have common terms, that is, to tackle the synonymy problem. Second, it would be possible to rule out semantically nonrelevent documents even if they nominally contained query terms. Intuitively, we can assume that the semantic space can be constructed by analyzing word co-occurrences, either globally in a document or locally in a sentence, and identifying groups of related words. The dimensions of the semantic space can then be defined based on these groups, and, consequently, the vector representations of individual documents and words will be defined in terms of affinities to the groups. It turns out that this simple idea is very challenging to implement, and there exist a large number of methods that use very different mathematical techniques. We continue this section with a detailed discussion of several important approaches and concrete models.

Finally, a note about terminology. Word embedding is a relatively new term, and many semantic analysis methods, including the latent semantic analysis and probabilistic topic modeling described later in this section, were not developed specifically for word embedding (in the sense of equation 4.40), but for different purposes and based on different considerations. Most of these methods are very generic and powerful statistical methods used in a wide range of applications from natural language processing to evolutionary biology. These methods, however, can also be viewed as word embedding techniques. In this section, we choose word embedding as the main theme because it is a convenient way to connect different semantic methods to each other, at least in the context of merchandising search. The reader, however, should keep in mind that it is just one possible perspective; semantic analysis methods are not limited to word embedding and search, and neither is word embedding limited to search applications. Even in the scope of algorithmic marketing, semantic analysis methods can be applied to many uses, including automated product attribution, recommendations, and image search.

4.5.3 *Latent Semantic Analysis*

One possible approach to semantic space construction is to analyze the bag-of-words representations of documents to figure out which terms frequently co-occur in one document. The intuitive expectation is that terms that frequently appear together can be synonyms that correspond to one logical *concept*. Thus, analysis of co-occurrences can reveal concepts that are not explicitly observed in the documents as terms but that exist at a semantic level. These concepts are referred to as *latent concepts*.

Let us start with a collection of single-field documents containing textual product descriptions. Our first step is to prepare a matrix that contains the term frequencies for each term t_i and document d_j:

$$\mathbf{X} = \begin{array}{c} \\ t_1 \\ t_2 \\ \\ \\ t_m \end{array} \begin{array}{cccc} d_1 & d_2 & & d_n \\ \left[\begin{array}{cccc} \text{tf}(t_1, d_1) & \text{tf}(t_1, d_2) & \cdots & \text{tf}(t_1, d_n) \\ \text{tf}(t_2, d_1) & \text{tf}(t_2, d_2) & \cdots & \text{tf}(t_2, d_n) \\ \vdots & \vdots & \ddots & \vdots \\ \text{tf}(t_m, d_1) & \text{tf}(t_m, d_2) & \cdots & \text{tf}(t_m, d_n) \end{array}\right] \end{array} \quad (4.41)$$

in which n is the number of documents and m is the total number of distinct terms in the collection. This matrix, known as a *term–document matrix*, is a representation of the documents in the term space. We can calculate the similarity between documents by calculating a dot product between the corresponding columns, and the similarity between terms can also be calculated by taking a dot product between the corresponding rows. The term similarity calculated this way already provides some hints about semantic relationships between terms, in the sense that terms that frequently appear together can be related to the same concept. This metric, however, can be too noisy, so we need to use a more robust statistical method.

Recall that the word embedding paradigm suggests the representation of each document as a k-dimensional vector. This representation can also be written as a matrix. Let us define it as the $n \times k$ matrix $\mathbf{V}_k$, in which each row corresponds to a document and each column corresponds to a semantic dimension. The latent semantic analysis method (LSA) creates this matrix based on the heuristic consideration that it should be possible to approximately reconstruct the term–document matrix $\mathbf{X}$ from $\mathbf{V}_k$ by using a linear transformation [Deerwester et al., 1990]. In other words, it should be possible to calculate the $m \times k$ matrix $\mathbf{L}_k$, such that

$$\mathbf{X} \approx \mathbf{L}_k \cdot \mathbf{V}_k^\mathsf{T} \quad (4.42)$$

More specifically, matrices $\mathbf{L}_k$ and $\mathbf{V}_k$ should be defined to minimize the reconstruction error. If the mean squared error is used as a measure, this principle leads to the following optimization problem:

$$\min_{\mathbf{L}_k, \mathbf{V}_k} \quad \left\| \mathbf{X} - \mathbf{L}_k \cdot \mathbf{V}_k^{\mathsf{T}} \right\| \tag{4.43}$$

Recall that the solution of this problem is given by the singular value decomposition (SVD) that we discussed in Chapter 2. It is also very important that the matrices produced by the SVD algorithm are column-orthonormal, which means that the k concept dimensions (the columns of matrix $\mathbf{V}_k$) will be orthogonal to each other. This essentially means that the original vector space model vectors (the rows of matrix $\mathbf{X}$) will be decorrelated by collapsing the strongly correlated vectors into a single principal vector. This follows our intuitive expectation – the frequently co-occurring terms correspond to highly correlated components of the original term vectors (the rows of matrix $\mathbf{X}$), so the decorrelation is likely to merge co-occurring terms (potentially synonyms) into one concept vector.

Let us now describe this process more formally. We first consider the case of full SVD, in which the number of concept dimensions k is not limited. The SVD algorithm breaks down the matrix into three factors:

$$\mathbf{X} = \mathbf{U} \mathbf{\Sigma} \mathbf{V}^{\mathsf{T}}$$

$$= \underbrace{\begin{bmatrix} | & & | \\ \mathbf{u}_1 & \cdots & \mathbf{u}_r \\ | & & | \end{bmatrix}}_{m \times r} \underbrace{\begin{bmatrix} \sigma_1 & \cdots & 0 \\ \vdots & \ddots & \vdots \\ 0 & \cdots & \sigma_r \end{bmatrix}}_{r \times r} \underbrace{\begin{bmatrix} - & \mathbf{v}_1 & - \\ & \vdots & \\ - & \mathbf{v}_n & - \end{bmatrix}^{\mathsf{T}}}_{n \times r} \tag{4.44}$$

in which r is the rank of the term–document matrix $\mathbf{X}$. Let us carefully examine this decomposition to understand how it can be helpful in semantic analysis and search.

The columns of matrix $\mathbf{U}$ can be interpreted as a new basis for a document space. Each column can be considered as a latent concept that can incorporate multiple correlated terms, that is, terms that frequently appear together in the same document. Each row of matrix $\mathbf{U}$ corresponds to a term, so the magnitude of the coefficient u_{ij} is the significance or contribution of term t_i to concept $\mathbf{u}_j$. It can be the case that certain terms in a concept have coefficients much higher than those of the remaining terms – such a pattern indicates that these terms frequently appear together in the same documents and are likely to have a semantic relationship. The space spanned on concept vectors is often referred to as the *latent semantic space*.

The rows of matrix $\mathbf{V}$ correspond to documents and the columns correspond to concepts. Consequently, each row can be interpreted as a vector of the coefficients that determine the significance of the corresponding concepts in a given document. This matrix is dual to the original term–document matrix in the sense that each element v_{ij} can be thought of as the *frequency* of a concept in a document, just like each element of the term–document matrix represents the frequency of a term.

The SVD representation enables us to calculate similarities between queries and documents by using the basis of concepts. First, we can calculate the cosine similarity between documents by using the rows of matrix $\mathbf{V}$. As each row is a vector representation of the corresponding document in the concept space, the similarity for a pair of documents can be straightforwardly calculated as

$$\cos\left(\mathbf{v_i}, \mathbf{v_j}\right) = \frac{\mathbf{v_i} \cdot \mathbf{v_j}}{\|\mathbf{v_i}\| \|\mathbf{v_j}\|} \tag{4.45}$$

Next, we need to convert the query into a vector in the basis of concepts in order to calculate the cosine similarity between the query and documents. This process is known as *query folding*. We can rearrange equation 4.44 to express the document vectors as a function of the term–document matrix:

$$\mathbf{V} = \mathbf{X}^T\mathbf{U}\mathbf{\Sigma}^{-1} \tag{4.46}$$

A user query can be considered as yet another document that corresponds to some vector $\mathbf{q}$ of term frequencies, so we can substitute it into equation 4.46 as a degenerate case of a term–document matrix with one column:

$$\mathbf{p} = \mathbf{q}^T\mathbf{U}\mathbf{\Sigma}^{-1} \tag{4.47}$$

in which $\mathbf{p}$ is the required representation of the query in the basis of concepts. Once this representation is obtained, we can score documents against the query by using the cosine similarity in the basis of concepts:

$$\text{score}\left(q, d_i\right) = \cos\left(\mathbf{p}, \mathbf{v_i}\right) = \frac{\mathbf{p} \cdot \mathbf{v_i}}{\|\mathbf{p}\| \|\mathbf{v_i}\|} \tag{4.48}$$

Equation 4.48 defines a new scoring method, latent semantic indexing (LSI) scoring, which can be used as an alternative to the standard vector space model and TF×IDF approach. The principal advantage of LSI scoring over term-based methods is the ability to fetch documents that do not explicitly contain query terms. For example, a concept vector can include the three key terms *candy*, *sweet*, and *confection*, which have strong semantic dependencies and are frequently used together. A document that contains only *candy* and *sweet* would still have a large coefficient for this concept in its vector representation. The same is true for the query *confection*. Consequently, the document and query would have high cosine similarity because of the intersection of this concept, although they do not have common terms.

The next step is to apply dimensionality reduction, that is, to limit the number of concept dimensions $k < r$. Although dimensionality reduction increases reconstruction error 4.43, it is generally beneficial in LSA applications because it decreases the noise and leaves only the concept dimensions with the highest energy. Recall that SVD guarantees that the columns of U are ordered by their significance[2]. This implies that concept u_1 corresponds to the most persistent and frequent combination of terms, whereas concept u_r corresponds to the least significant combination. Consequently, we keep only the strongest concepts and truncate the leftmost columns of matrices U and V, thereby reducing the dimensionality of the concept basis and document space. The number of concepts to preserve is an important parameter of the LSA method. It is often set empirically by evaluating the precision and recall for several possible values and selecting the best one. The optimal number of concepts is typically much lower than the number of distinct terms in the collection; 300–500 concepts is a good value, even for large collections [Bradford, 2008]. With the assumption that the number of concepts k is set, decomposition 4.44 is transformed as follows:

$$X_k = U_k \Sigma_k V_k^T$$

$$= \underbrace{\begin{bmatrix} | & & | \\ u_1 & \cdots & u_k \\ | & & | \end{bmatrix}}_{m \times k} \underbrace{\begin{bmatrix} \sigma_1 & \cdots & 0 \\ \vdots & \ddots & \vdots \\ 0 & \cdots & \sigma_k \end{bmatrix}}_{k \times k} \underbrace{\begin{bmatrix} - & v_1 & - \\ & \vdots & \\ - & v_n & - \end{bmatrix}}_{n \times k}^T$$

$$(4.49)$$

This truncated statement does not reconstruct the original term–document matrix exactly but produces the approximation X_k. The documents still correspond to the rows of matrix V, but each vector has only k elements. In other words, the documents and queries are mapped into a space with k dimensions, and the similarity metric is computed in the same space as well.

---

2 See Chapter 2 for a detailed discussion of the exact meaning of significance in the context of SVD.

EXAMPLE 4.4

▼

Latent semantic analysis can be quite difficult to understand without a numerical example, so we will provide one in the rest of this section. The example we use is fairly small, but it is composed to highlight the major features of LSA. It should be kept in mind, though, that LSA is a machine learning method that requires substantial amounts of data to work well in practice. We start with a collection of three small documents about candy stores:

d_1 : Chicago Chocolate. Retro candies made with love.
d_2 : Chocolate sweets and candies. Collection with mini love hearts.
d_3 : Retro sweets from Chicago for chocolate lovers.

Filtering out some stop words and applying basic normalization and stemming, we get the following term–document matrix:

$$X = \begin{array}{c} \\ \text{chicago} \\ \text{chocolate} \\ \text{retro} \\ \text{candy} \\ \text{made} \\ \text{love} \\ \text{sweet} \\ \text{collection} \\ \text{mini} \\ \text{heart} \end{array} \begin{array}{ccc} d_1 & d_2 & d_3 \\ \left[\begin{array}{ccc} 1 & 0 & 1 \\ 1 & 1 & 1 \\ 1 & 0 & 1 \\ 1 & 1 & 0 \\ 1 & 0 & 0 \\ 1 & 1 & 1 \\ 0 & 1 & 1 \\ 0 & 1 & 0 \\ 0 & 1 & 0 \\ 0 & 1 & 0 \end{array}\right] \end{array} \tag{4.50}$$

By applying SVD and reducing the dimensionality down to two concepts, we get the following factor matrices:

$$U_2 = \begin{array}{c} \\ \text{chicago} \\ \text{chocolate} \\ \text{retro} \\ \text{candy} \\ \text{made} \\ \text{love} \\ \text{sweet} \\ \text{collection} \\ \text{mini} \\ \text{heart} \end{array} \begin{array}{cc} \text{concept 1} & \text{concept 2} \\ \left[\begin{array}{cc} -0.318 & \mathbf{0.424} \\ \mathbf{-0.486} & 0.018 \\ -0.318 & \mathbf{0.424} \\ -0.333 & -0.148 \\ -0.166 & 0.257 \\ \mathbf{-0.488} & 0.018 \\ -0.320 & -0.239 \\ -0.168 & -0.406 \\ -0.168 & -0.406 \\ -0.168 & -0.406 \end{array}\right] \end{array} \tag{4.51}$$

$$\Sigma_2 = \begin{bmatrix} 3.562 & 0 \\ 0 & 1.966 \end{bmatrix} \tag{4.52}$$

$$\mathbf{V}_2 = \begin{array}{c} \\ d_1 \\ d_2 \\ d_3 \end{array} \begin{array}{cc} \text{concept 1} & \text{concept 2} \\ \left[\begin{array}{cc} -0.592 & 0.505 \\ -0.598 & -0.798 \\ -0.541 & 0.329 \end{array}\right] \end{array} \qquad (4.53)$$

The first observation we can make is that the columns of matrix $\mathbf{U}_2$ highlight some logical themes that we can find in the text. The two largest coefficients in the first column correspond to the terms *chocolate* and *love*, quite closely followed by the coefficients for *sweet* and *candy*. The largest coefficients in the second column correspond to the terms *Chicago* and *retro*. This is because we have two documents that consistently use the same set of words to talk about the Retro&Chicago theme, and all three documents consistently use the same words to talk about the Chocolate&Love theme.

A second insight can be gained from document matrix $\mathbf{V}_2$. The first column of the matrix corresponds to the Chocolate&Love concept. All coefficients in the column have the same sign, so all three documents are pointed in the same direction along this axis. The second column corresponds to the Retro&Chicago concept, and the documents are pointed in different directions because only the first and third documents mention this theme.

Let us now query the documents by using two queries, *Chicago* and *candy*. The queries correspond to the following term frequency vectors (the order of terms is the same as in matrix 4.50):

$$\begin{aligned} \mathbf{q}_{\text{chicago}} &= \left[\begin{array}{cccccccccc} 1 & 0 & 0 & 0 & 0 & 0 & 0 & 0 & 0 & 0 \end{array}\right] \\ \mathbf{q}_{\text{candy}} &= \left[\begin{array}{cccccccccc} 0 & 0 & 0 & 1 & 0 & 0 & 0 & 0 & 0 & 0 \end{array}\right] \end{aligned} \qquad (4.54)$$

Transforming these vectors with formula 4.47 and calculating the cosine similarities with the document vectors from matrix $\mathbf{V}_2$, we obtain the document scores presented in table 4.4. We can see that only the first and third documents have high scores for the query *Chicago*, which is expected. The second query, *candy*, is a more interesting case. All three documents score highly, although the third document has no occurrences of the term *candy*. This is because *candy* is a part of the Chocolate&Love concept that is clearly present in the third document. The LSA method was able to recognize the link between the query and the document through this concept and rank the document accordingly.

◆

LSA was designed as an alternative to the basic vector space model search methods, such as standard TF×IDF scoring. Empirical study

QUERY	d_1	d_2	d_3
Chicago	0.891	-0.510	0.806
Candy	0.183	0.969	0.338

Table 4.4: The final document scores for the example of LSA calculations.

shows that it can actually outperform the basic vector space model in many settings. In addition to that, LSA offers the following advantages:

SYNONYMS A low-dimensional representation is able to capture synonyms and semantic relationships. LSA can also estimate distances between words to generate a thesaurus that can be used for synonym expansions in the standard TF×IDF scoring, and there exist specialized LSA-based methods to compute semantic similarities, such as the correlated occurrence analogue to lexical semantic (COALS) method [Rohde et al., 2006].

NOISE REDUCTION Dimensionality reduction can efficiently remove noise and redundancy from the data.

HIGH RECALL LSA-based search works for queries and documents that have no common terms. This allows high recall to be achieved.

AUTOMATION LSA relies on unsupervised matrix factorization, and, thus, the process is completely automatic.

On the other hand, LSA has a number of shortcomings that stem mainly from its heuristic nature, which neglects the complex statistical properties of texts:

POLYSEMY LSA has a limited ability to capture polysemy. Although LSA is able to attach the same word to multiple concepts, thereby capturing the fact that a word may have different meanings depending on the context, LSA is not able to distinguish different meanings of the word within a document because all meanings are averaged into a term frequency in the term–document matrix. This limitation stems from the nature of the bag-of-words model and does not allow LSA to recognize more subtle semantic relationships between words.

COMPLETENESS The theoretical foundation of LSA is incomplete because it does not provide any model for documents and terms.

INTERPRETABILITY The concept dimensions created by LSA can be hard to interpret because of the negative values and absence of a formal document model.

GAUSSIAN ASSUMPTION One of the key advantages of the principal
component analysis leveraged by LSA is the ability to create uncorrelated concept vectors. The principle of decorrelation is based
on the assumption that the data have a Gaussian distribution, for
which zero correlation between the components implies independence. This assumption, however, is not true for count matrices,
such as the term–document matrix.

We will attempt to address some of the LSA limitations in the next
few sections. We first discuss how the heuristic factorization model can
be replaced by a solid probabilistic framework, and we then rethink
the bag-of-words approach to better capture the semantic relationships
between words.

4.5.4 *Probabilistic Topic Modeling*

Probabilistic topic modeling is a family of semantic analysis methods that captures the semantic relationships between documents and
words through latent variables called topics. One of the key assumptions made in topic modeling is that the documents are generated term
by term with some probabilistic process. This process models the the-
matic structure of a collection of documents by using latent (hidden)
variables that can be interpreted as topics. Each document is typically
represented as a mix of topics, and each topic determines the distribution of words in the document. The generative process is designed to
reflect only certain statistical properties of the documents, such as the
topic-specific distribution of words, but it does not necessarily generate a text that looks real or readable. Figure 4.17 illustrates the main
components of a topic model.

Next, the generative process model is fitted by inferring the values
of the latent variables from the data. The data are a collection of documents in which each document is merely a group of terms, and the
latent parameters, that is, the topics, topic distributions, and relations
between topics and terms, are just abstractions that are never observed
directly but can be estimated. The statistical inference process can be
thought of as the ascent from the bottom of Figure 4.17 to the top. The
fitted model describes the associations between terms and topics (what
are the most distinctive words for a given topic) and the relationships
between topics and documents (what the document is about). Documents can also be searched by fitting a query into the estimated topic
structure and computing the similarity between the query and the documents in the latent topic space.

The topic modeling approach is similar to LSA in the sense that it
also uses the notion of latent topics and maps documents to a vector

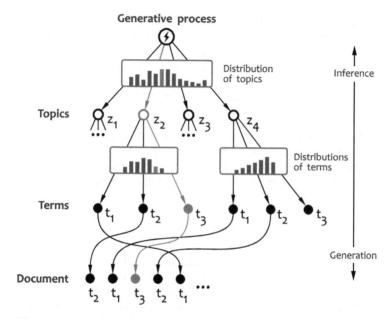

Figure 4.17: A conceptual view of probabilistic topic models. Document terms are generated sequentially, and each term corresponds to some path in the model graph.

representation in the topic space. At the same time, its mathematical foundation is very different from that of LSA. This foundation is very important because it enables not just a single model but a whole family of powerful methods and techniques. In the context of algorithmic marketing, this group of methods is important not only for search but also for recommendation services because it provides a generic framework for modeling the relationships between different entities, such as words and documents or users and products. In the next sections, we will discuss two popular topic models – probabilistic latent semantic analysis and latent Dirichlet allocation.

4.5.5 *Probabilistic Latent Semantic Analysis*

Probabilistic latent semantic analysis (pLSA) is one of the most basic methods of probabilistic topic modeling [Hofmann, 1999]. Although it approaches the semantic analysis problem from the probabilistic perspective, the resulting structure of the model can be viewed as matrix factorization, which makes pLSA directly comparable to SVD-based latent semantic analysis. pLSA can be viewed from two different perspectives. The first is the latent variable model, a probabilistic model that uses the notion of latent variables (topics) to explain the relationships between documents and terms. The second is matrix factorization, which bridges the probabilistic latent variable model with LSA. We discuss these two aspects separately in the next sections [Oneata, 1999].

4.5.5.1 Latent Variable Model

The pLSA model is one of the models from the probabilistic topic modeling family. To describe the pLSA model more formally, let us first define the following three main entities:

DOCUMENTS $D = \{d_1, \ldots, d_n\}$ is the set of n documents.

TERMS $T = \{t_1, \ldots, t_m\}$ is the set of m terms (words) that contains all distinct terms from all documents.

TOPICS $Z = \{z_1, \ldots, z_k\}$ is the set of k topics, and k is the model parameter. The notion of topics corresponds to the notion of latent concepts in LSA.

We explicitly observe pairs of documents and terms (d_j, t_i) but not topics. The latent factor model assumes that each document may correspond to multiple topics and the term probabilities within the document are determined by the topic. For example, let us imagine two topics that can be found in a grocery store catalog: *dairy* and *desserts*. Some product descriptions in the catalog will mainly relate to dairy, some will relate to desserts, and some will correspond to both topics mixed in a certain proportion. Although the topics are not observed directly, the distribution of terms in the document that corresponds to dairy will be determined by the corresponding topic. We can express this idea more formally by making the assumption that documents are created by the following generative process:

1. First, draw a document d_j from the probability distribution $Pr(d)$

2. For each term t_i in document d_j:

    2.1. Select a topic z_l by drawing it from the distribution $Pr(z \mid d_j)$

    2.2. Select a term t_i by drawing it from the distribution $Pr(t \mid z_l)$

This process corresponds to the probabilistic model shown in Figure 4.18. Each document is modeled as a mixture of topics, and the distribution of tokens within the document is determined by the topics. The same model is shown in Figure 4.19 in a more compact graphical notation.

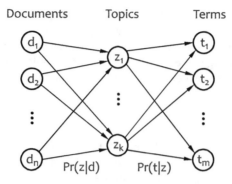

Figure 4.18: Detailed structure of the pLSA model.

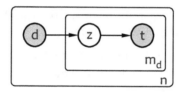

Figure 4.19: Graphical model representation of the pLSA model. The outer box represents the repeated choice of documents. The inner box represents the repeated choice of topics and terms within a document that contains m_d terms. The shaded circles correspond to the observed variables; the unshaded one denotes the latent variable.

Similarly to LSA, the pLSA model considers each document as a bag of words. From the probabilistic perspective, this means that the document–term pairs (d, t) are conditionally independent:

$$\Pr(D, T) = \prod_{d,t} \Pr(d, t) \tag{4.55}$$

In addition to that, the pLSA model assumes that terms and documents are conditionally independent given the topic, that is

$$\Pr(t \mid d, z) = \Pr(t \mid z) \tag{4.56}$$

A joint probability model over $D \times T$ can be expressed as

$$\Pr(d, t) = \Pr(d)\Pr(t \mid d) \tag{4.57}$$

for which the conditional probability of the term within the document can be expressed as a sum of the probabilities over all topics:

$$\Pr(t \mid d) = \sum_z \Pr(t, z \mid d) = \sum_z \Pr(t \mid d, z)\Pr(z \mid d)$$
$$= \sum_z \Pr(t \mid z)\Pr(z \mid d) \tag{4.58}$$

By inserting expression 4.58 into 4.57, we obtain the complete model specification:

$$Pr(d,t) = \sum_z Pr(d)Pr(t \mid z)Pr(z \mid d) = \sum_z Pr(d,z)Pr(t \mid z)$$
$$= \sum_z Pr(z)Pr(t \mid z)Pr(d \mid z) \tag{4.59}$$

The next step is to learn the unobserved probabilities and, thus, infer the latent topics. Given a set of training documents D, the likelihood function is defined as

$$L = Pr(D,T) = \prod_{d,t} Pr(d,t)^{n(d,t)} \tag{4.60}$$

in which $n(d,t)$ is the number of times term t occurs in document d, that is, the term frequency. Simplifying the likelihood function by taking the logarithm, we obtain the following equation:

$$\log L = \sum_{d,t} n(d,t) \cdot \log Pr(d,t)$$
$$= \sum_{d,t} n(d,t) \cdot \log \sum_z Pr(z)Pr(t \mid z)Pr(d \mid z) \tag{4.61}$$

The term probabilities $Pr(t \mid z)$, document probabilities $Pr(d \mid z)$, and topic probabilities $Pr(z)$ are parameters of the model that have to be fitted in a way that maximizes the likelihood. This is equivalent to solving the following optimization problem:

$$\begin{aligned} \max \quad & \log L \\ \text{subject to} \quad & \sum_t Pr(t \mid z) = 1 \\ & \sum_d Pr(d \mid z) = 1 \\ & \sum_z Pr(z) = 1 \end{aligned} \tag{4.62}$$

This problem can be tackled by using the expectation–maximization algorithm, which is the standard approach for maximum likelihood estimation in latent variable models [Hofmann, 1999]. The challenge, however, is that we have $k(m-1)$ parameters $Pr(t \mid z)$ for all possible pairs of terms and topics and $k(n-1)$ parameters $Pr(d \mid z)$ for all pairs of documents and topics. Note that we have $k(m-1)$ parameters, not km, because of the probability normalization constraints described by problem 4.62. Thus, the number of parameters is high, and it grows linearly with the size of the document collection. This issue is considered one of the major drawbacks of the pLSA model.

Given that the parameters are estimated, the relationships between the documents, terms, and topics, as well as the semantic meaning of the topics, can be analyzed by examining the magnitudes of the conditional probabilities. The same parameters can be indexed and stored to serve as search queries [Park and Ramamohanarao, 2009]. Similarly to LSA, the similarity between the query and the document can be calculated in the latent semantic space as the cosine distance or dot product between two vector representations. In the case of pLSA, the vector representations of query q and document d in the latent semantic space are given by the conditional probabilities $\Pr(q \mid z)$ and $\Pr(d \mid z)$, respectively. The similarity measure can then be defined as the following dot product:

$$\text{score}(q, d) = \sum_z \Pr(q \mid z) \cdot \Pr(d \mid z) \tag{4.63}$$

Values $\Pr(d \mid z)$ are known from the model, but the query representation $\Pr(q \mid z)$ needs to be learned for each query. This can be achieved by fixing parameters $\Pr(t \mid z)$ and $\Pr(z)$ and fitting model 4.62 with respect to $\Pr(q \mid z)$. The similarity metric can then be used to score and rank the documents in the search results list.

4.5.5.2   Matrix Factorization

Although the latent variable approach is very different from LSA (a probabilistic process instead of an algebraic matrix factorization), the two methods are closely related. This can be demonstrated by rewriting the latent variable model in matrix notion. First, recall that LSA approximates the term–frequency matrix defined by expression 4.41 as a product of three matrices:

$$\mathbf{X} = \mathbf{U} \cdot \mathbf{\Sigma} \cdot \mathbf{V}^\mathsf{T} \tag{4.64}$$

in which $\mathbf{X}$ is an $m \times n$ matrix of term frequencies for all pairs of terms and documents, $\mathbf{U}$ is an $m \times k$ matrix of term coordinates in the concept space, and $\mathbf{V}$ is an $n \times k$ matrix of document coordinates in the concept space. On the other hand, we have determined that the joint probability model in pLSA is given by a product of three factors:

$$\Pr(d, t) = \sum_z \Pr(z)\Pr(t \mid z)\Pr(d \mid z) \tag{4.65}$$

Rewriting this expression in matrix notation, we obtain the pLSA model in a form that can be directly compared to the LSA factorization:

$$\mathbf{P} = \mathbf{L} \cdot \mathbf{S} \cdot \mathbf{R}^\mathsf{T} \tag{4.66}$$

in which $\mathbf{L}$ is an $m \times k$ matrix of all term probabilities $\Pr(t \mid z)$, $\mathbf{R}$ is an $n \times k$ matrix of all document probabilities $\Pr(d \mid z)$, and $\mathbf{S}$ is a diagonal $k \times k$ matrix of the prior probabilities of the topics $\Pr(z)$. In other words, pLSA, similarly to LSA, can be viewed as a matrix factorization algorithm, but this factorization is driven by a different objective. Whereas LSA is driven by minimization of the approximation error, pLSA is driven by maximization of the likelihood function or, alternatively, minimization of the divergence between the observed distribution and the model.

4.5.5.3 pLSA Properties

The pLSA model offers several important advantages over LSA. First, the directions in the pLSA space are non-negative and interpretable as probabilities. The directions in the LSA space do not have formal interpretation and the values produced by the LSA factorization can be negative, which also complicates the interpretation.

The second important difference is the handling of the *polysemy* problem. LSA is able to map synonyms to the same location in the latent semantic space, but it is typically not able to distinguish different meanings of the same word depending on the context. By contrast, pLSA distributes the probability mass of a term over several different topics that can correspond to the different senses of a word [Hofmann, 1999]. More specifically, if the same term t is observed in two different documents d_i and d_j, the topic it has the strongest association with in the context of the first document

$$\underset{z}{\operatorname{argmax}} \Pr\left(z \mid d_i, t\right)$$

can be different from the topic that this term is associated with in the context of the second document

$$\underset{z}{\operatorname{argmax}} \Pr\left(z \mid d_j, t\right)$$

Despite these advantages, pLSA generally involves more complex implementation than LSA. Whereas LSA is based on the deterministic SVD factorization, pLSA requires the iterative expectation–maximization algorithm to estimate the parameters of the model. The pLSA model also has several structural issues, which we will discuss and address in the next section.

4.5.6 Latent Dirichlet Allocation

The pLSA model is a major step forward relative to LSA. It establishes a solid statistical framework that allows one to extend, simplify, or combine different models by using probabilistic techniques. The pLSA model, however, has several shortcomings:

- Each document is represented as a vector of probabilities, not a generative probabilistic model. These probabilities are the parameters that need to be estimated from the data. This results in a high number of parameters that grows linearly with the number of terms and documents and makes the learning process more prone to overfitting.

- pLSA does not impose constraints on how documents and terms are associated with topics. Intuitively, we would expect each document to be related to a small number of topics and each topic to be associated with a small number of terms, but pLSA does not provide explicit parameters to control this aspect of the model.

These issues can be addressed by creating a model with a more elaborate generative process than the pLSA process that we described earlier. In this section, we discuss one of the most prominent examples of such models, called the latent Dirichlet allocation (LDA). The LDA model can be viewed as a generalization of pLSA, and it is one of the most popular and widely used probabilistic topic models [Blei et al., 2003]. The LDA model is based on the notion of the Dirichlet distribution, so the reader can use Appendix A at the back of the book as a reference.

Similarly to pLSA, the LDA model uses the latent variable approach, which assumes that each document corresponds to a mixture of latent topics and the document terms are drawn from the distributions associated with the topics [Blei et al., 2003]. With the assumption that the number of latent topics k is predefined, the LDA model is described by using the following generative process for each document d from the collection of documents D:

1. Draw the number of terms in the document m_d from some random distribution. The choice of this distribution is not critical for the model design.

2. Draw a k-dimensional vector of probabilities $\mathbf{p}$ from the Dirichlet distribution $\mathrm{Dir}(\boldsymbol{\alpha})$, in which $\boldsymbol{\alpha}$ is the model parameter. Each element of $\mathbf{p}$ is interpreted as the probability of the corresponding topic, so that this vector defines the mixture of topics.

3. For each term in the document:

    3.1. Choose a topic z_t according to the probability vector $\mathbf{p}$, that is, $\Pr(z_t = i \mid \mathbf{p}) = p_i$

3.2. Choose a term t from the multinomial probability distribution $\Pr(t \mid z_t; \beta)$ conditioned on the topic z_t. This distribution is defined as the model parameter β for each pair of term and topic.

In comparison with the pLSA process described in section 4.5.5.1, the key difference is that the LDA model draws topics from a global parametric distribution, not from the distributions learned for each document. The parameters of this model are the k-dimensional Dirichlet parameter α and the $k \times m$ matrix of term probabilities β, in which m is the total number of distinct terms in all documents. Each row of the matrix β defines the multinomial distributions over the words for a corresponding topic. These parameters are sampled once for a collection of documents, and, consequently, the number of parameters is smaller than that with pLSA. The graphical model that corresponds to the generative process is shown in Figure 4.20.

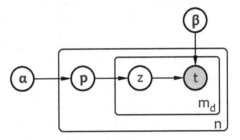

Figure 4.20: Graphical model representation of the LDA model.

In the context of a single document, the joint distribution of a topic mixture, all topics, and all terms is given by:

$$\Pr(p, z, t) = \Pr(p \mid \alpha) \prod_t \Pr(t \mid z_t; \beta) \Pr(z_t \mid p) \qquad (4.67)$$

in which the distribution $\Pr(p; \alpha)$ is defined as $\mathrm{Dir}(\alpha)$ and the parameters α and β are given. Note that $\Pr(z_t \mid p)$ is simply the probability value from p that corresponds to z_t. The marginal distribution of a document can be obtained by integrating over the topic probabilities and summing over all topics:

$$\Pr(d) = \int \Pr(p \mid \alpha) \prod_t \sum_z \Pr(t \mid z_t; \beta) \Pr(z_t \mid p) \; dp \qquad (4.68)$$

The likelihood function for a collection of documents can then be obtained by taking the product of the document probabilities:

$$\Pr(D) = \prod_d \int \Pr(p_d \mid \alpha) \prod_{t \in d} \sum_z \Pr(t \mid z_{dt}; \beta) \Pr(z_{dt} \mid p_d) \; dp_d \qquad (4.69)$$

The process of fitting this model is complicated because the parameters α and β are coupled in the internal sum of equation 4.69. This problem can be tackled with methods of approximate posterior inference, such as variational inference and Gibbs sampling [Blei et al., 2003; Asuncion et al., 2009].

The LDA model addresses the two issues with pLSA that we mentioned earlier. First, it reduces the number of parameters by defining a different generative process that does not use document-specific parameters. Second, the Dirichlet prior shapes the topic probabilities in a way that penalizes relationships between the topics and documents.

4.5.7 Word2Vec Model

Word2Vec is a group of models that attempt to overcome the limitations of the bag-of-words-based semantic analysis methods by taking into account the local context of a word, rather than the entire document [Mikolov et al., 2013a,b]. The two main types of Word2Vec models are the continuous bag-of-words and skip-gram models. The *continuous bag-of-words* approach is to build a predictive model that estimates the probability of a word based on one or more words in the surrounding context, as shown in Figure 4.21. The words in the sliding context are interpreted as a bag of words, that is, we account only for distinct terms and their frequencies, not for their order. The predictive model can be built in such a way that each word is associated with a vector of weights set by the model fitting process. These vectors can then be interpreted as word representations in some latent semantic space, similarly to the vectors produced by LSA or topic models, so this vector representation can be used for search and thesaurus creation. The skip-gram approach is somewhat opposite to the continuous bag-of-words model – it takes the target word as an input and predicts the context. The design of predictive models, however, is very similar for both the continuous bag-of-words and skip-gram models, and we choose to focus on the first approach in the rest of the section.

The Word2Vec model uses a shallow neural network to capture semantic relationships and predict a term based on its context. We first discuss the design of the network under the assumption that there is only one word in the context and later generalize the result for cases with multiple words. The neural network used in the Word2Vec model consists of the input layer, hidden layer, and output layer depicted in Figure 4.22.

The input of the network is a binary vector that represents a context. If the total number of terms in the collection is n, the input vector has n elements, and each element is equal to one if the corresponding term

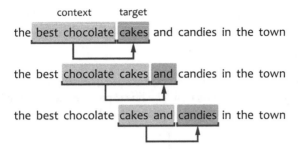

Figure 4.21: Example of the continuous bag-of-words model with a context of two words.

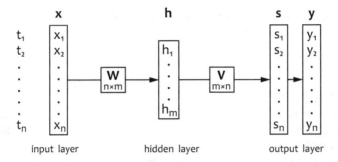

Figure 4.22: The design of a Word2Vec neural network for a single-word context.

is present in the context and zero otherwise. As we are considering the case of a single-word context, let us denote the only context term as t_k. The input vector has then only one non-zero element x_k:

$$x_i = \begin{cases} 1, & i = k \\ 0, & \text{otherwise} \end{cases} \qquad (4.70)$$

The input is transformed into m intermediate outputs by using the units of the hidden layer. This transformation is chosen to be linear (each intermediate output h_i is a weighted sum of the inputs x_i), so it is defined through the weight matrix $\mathbf{W}$:

$$\mathbf{W}_{n \times m} = \begin{bmatrix} - & \mathbf{w}_1 & - \\ & \vdots & \\ - & \mathbf{w}_n & - \end{bmatrix} \qquad (4.71)$$

The intermediate outputs can then be expressed as the product of the weight matrix and the input vector. According to our assumption, the input vector contains only one non-zero element, so the result will be identical to the corresponding row of the weight matrix:

$$\mathbf{h} = \mathbf{W}^\mathsf{T}\mathbf{x} = \mathbf{w}_k^\mathsf{T} \tag{4.72}$$

The output score is produced by the combination of a linear transformation and a softmax function. The linear part, similarly to the hidden layer, is defined by using the weight matrix $\mathbf{V}$:

$$\mathbf{V}_{m \times n} = \begin{bmatrix} | & & | \\ \mathbf{v}_1 & \cdots & \mathbf{v}_n \\ | & & | \end{bmatrix} \tag{4.73}$$

This matrix is multiplied with the intermediate outputs to produce scores for each of n terms:

$$s_i = \mathbf{v}_i^\mathsf{T}\mathbf{h}, \quad i = 1,\ldots,n \tag{4.74}$$

The signals s_i are arbitrary values, but we want to interpret them as predicted probabilities of the corresponding terms given the context. In other words, we are solving a multiclass classification problem where the context has to be assigned to one of n classes that corresponds to the predicted term. As we discussed in Chapter 2, the standard way to map a vector of arbitrary values to category probabilities is the softmax function, so the final outputs are defined as follows:

$$y_i = \Pr(t_i \mid t_k) = \frac{\exp(s_i)}{\sum_{j=1}^{n} \exp(s_j)} \tag{4.75}$$

The network defined above can be trained by using standard methods of training for artificial neural networks. We cannot go deeply into the details of training algorithms here, but it will be useful to briefly review the main steps to get the idea of how Word2Vec models can be fitted [Rong, 2014b]. We train the model iteratively by taking sample pairs of a context and a target word, evaluating the network for a context, comparing the network output with the target, and adjusting the weights in matrices $\mathbf{W}$ and $\mathbf{V}$. Let us assume that, for a given iteration, the actually observed target term for the context t_k is t_a. According to the principle of maximum likelihood, our objective to is to maximize the predicted probability of the actual term, given the context (because we ultimately want to maximize the mathematical expectation of this probability over all contexts):

$$\max \mathbb{E}_{t_k, t_a} \left[\Pr(t_a \mid t_k) \right] \tag{4.76}$$

Maximization of this probability is equivalent to minimization of the following loss function:

$$J = -\log \Pr(t_a \mid t_k) \tag{4.77}$$

Substituting definition 4.75 for the network output into definition 4.77 for the loss function, we find

$$J = -\log y_a = -s_a + \log \sum_{j=1}^{n} \exp(s_j) \tag{4.78}$$

Our goal is to minimize the loss function with respect to weights w and v. This can be done by updating the weights with the stochastic gradient descent based on the prediction errors. Our strategy is to start from the output side of the network and calculate the weight updates for matrix $\mathbf{V}$ based on the observed prediction errors. Next, we move one layer backward and calculate the weight updates for matrix $\mathbf{W}$. This approach is known as backward propagation of errors or simply *backpropagation*. At each layer, we need to calculate the gradient of the loss function with respect to the weights. We do this in two steps – we first calculate the gradient with respect to the scores, and we then use the result to calculate the gradient with respect to the weights. So, we start with the derivative with respect to the scores of the output layer:

$$\begin{aligned}
\frac{\partial J}{\partial s_j} &= -\mathbb{I}(j = k) + \frac{\partial}{\partial s_j} \log \sum_{i=1}^{n} \exp(s_i) \\
&= -\mathbb{I}(j = k) + \frac{\exp(s_j)}{\sum_{i=1}^{n} \exp(s_i)} \\
&= y_j - \mathbb{I}(j = k) \\
&= e_j
\end{aligned} \tag{4.79}$$

in which $\mathbb{I}(j = k)$ is the indicator function equal to one if $j = k$ and zero otherwise. We can see that this derivative is simply the prediction error, so we denote it as e_j. By taking the derivative with respect to the weights of the output layer, we find the gradient for weight optimization:

$$\frac{\partial J}{\partial v_{ij}} = \frac{\partial J}{\partial s_j} \cdot \frac{\partial s_j}{\partial v_{ij}} = e_j \cdot h_i \tag{4.80}$$

This result means that we should decrease weight v_{ij} if the product $e_j \cdot h_i$ is positive and increase the weight otherwise. The stochastic gradient descent equation for weights will thus be as follows:

$$v_j^{(new)} = v_j^{(old)} - \lambda \cdot e_j \cdot \mathbf{h}, \quad j = 1, \ldots, n \tag{4.81}$$

in which λ is a learning rate parameter. The next step is to repeat the process for the hidden layer. First, we take the derivative of the loss function with respect to the intermediate outputs:

$$\frac{\partial J}{\partial h_i} = \sum_{j=1}^{n} \frac{\partial J}{\partial s_j} \cdot \frac{\partial s_j}{\partial h_i} = \sum_{j=1}^{n} e_j \cdot v_{ij} = \varepsilon_i \qquad (4.82)$$

The result denoted as ε_i can be interpreted as a weighted sum of prediction errors. We calculate this value for each of m hidden units, so we obtain an m-dimensional vector of prediction errors:

$$\varepsilon = [\varepsilon_1, \dots, \varepsilon_m] \qquad (4.83)$$

Next, we calculate the gradient with respect to the weights of the hidden layer:

$$\frac{\partial J}{\partial w_{ji}} = \frac{\partial J}{\partial h_i} \cdot \frac{\partial h_i}{\partial w_{ji}} = \varepsilon_i \cdot x_j \qquad (4.84)$$

We use this result and the stochastic gradient descent to update the weights of the hidden layer, similarly to our method for equations 4.80 and 4.81 for the weights of the output layer. Taking into account the fact that all x_j values in equation 4.84 are zeros except for x_k, we find that only the k-th row of matrix $\mathbf{W}$ needs to be updated:

$$\mathbf{w}_k^{(new)} = \mathbf{w}_k^{(old)} - \lambda \cdot \varepsilon^{\mathsf{T}} \qquad (4.85)$$

The Word2Vec model can be trained by applying equations 4.81 and 4.85 iteratively for training pairs of context and target words. This process, however, is computationally intensive because, in accordance with equation 4.81, we need to update the weight vectors $\mathbf{v}$ for all terms for each training sample and the number of terms n can be large. This requires the use of optimization techniques, such as hierarchical softmax and negative sampling, in practical implementations of the Word2Vec model [Mikolov et al., 2013b; Rong, 2014b].

We can generalize the obtained results for the case of a context with multiple words in a straightforward way. The input vector for a context of q words, that is, q non-zero elements, can be thought of as a normalized sum (i.e. , average) of q single-word contexts. This is illustrated in Figure 4.23, although the actual network design does not change.

This allows us to rewrite the equation for the hidden layer in the following way:

$$\mathbf{h} = \frac{1}{q} \mathbf{W}^{\mathsf{T}} (x_1 + \cdots + x_q) = \frac{1}{q} \left(\mathbf{w}_{k_1} + \cdots + \mathbf{w}_{k_q} \right)^{\mathsf{T}} \qquad (4.86)$$

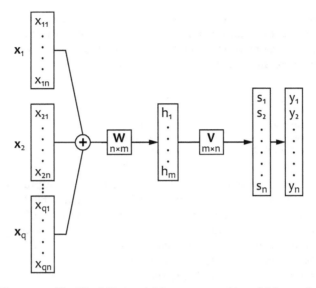

Figure 4.23: The Word2Vec model for a context with multiple words.

The equation for the loss function remains the same, although it represents a different conditional probability:

$$J = -\log \Pr\left(t_a \mid t_{k_1}, \ldots, t_{k_q}\right) = -s_a + \log \sum_{j=1}^{n} \exp\left(s_j\right) \quad (4.87)$$

Going through the gradient calculations, we find that all equations remain unchanged and result in the same pair of weight update formulas:

$$\mathbf{v}_j^{(\text{new})} = \mathbf{v}_j^{(\text{old})} - \lambda \cdot e_j \cdot \mathbf{h}, \quad j = 1, \ldots, n \quad (4.88)$$

$$\mathbf{w}_{k_j}^{(\text{new})} = \mathbf{w}_{k_j}^{(\text{old})} - \frac{\lambda}{q} \cdot \varepsilon^{\mathsf{T}}, \quad j = 1, \ldots, q \quad (4.89)$$

The only difference is that we update multiple weight vectors $\mathbf{w}$ because we have multiple terms in the context.

EXAMPLE 4.5

After the network is trained, each of n terms in the collection corresponds to a pair of m-dimensional vectors $\mathbf{w}$ and $\mathbf{v}$. The power of the Word2Vec model stems from the fact that these vectors provide

an insightful representation of words that preserves the semantic relationships. Let us illustrate this with an example of a Word2Vec model
trained on the following samples, where each sample is a pair of a
context word and a target word [Rong, 2014a]:

```
drink coffee          tea drink
drink juice           juice drink
drink tea             coffee drink
eat cake              pie coffee
eat pie               cookie juice
eat cookie            cake tea
pie tea               cake coffee
```

We choose to use a network with 8 hidden units to capture the semantic patterns in these samples, so each term is represented as two 8-
dimensional vectors after the model is trained. To visualize the weight
vectors, we can project them to a two-dimensional space by using principal component analysis. For instance, the weight vectors of a hidden
layer **w** are projected onto a plane in Figure 4.24. We can see that the
words are clustered according to their usage patterns and, ultimately,
meaning.

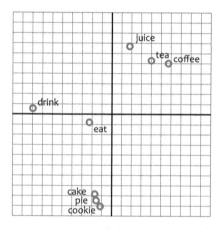

Figure 4.24: Example of word clustering with a Word2Vec model.

More surprisingly, a Word2Vec model trained on a large collection
of texts produces vectors that enable a sort of algebra in the latent
semantics space. Consider the following examples, in which $v(\cdot)$ stands
for a vector representation of a term produced by the Word2Vec model

and minus is used in the sense of a standard element-wise difference between the vectors:

$$v\,(\text{steak}) - v\,(\text{beef}) \approx v\,(\text{salad}) - v\,(\text{tomato})$$

$$v\,(\text{steak}) - v\,(\text{beef}) \approx v\,(\text{bread}) - v\,(\text{flour}) \qquad (4.90)$$

$$v\,(\text{france}) - v\,(\text{paris}) \approx v\,(\text{japan}) - v\,(\text{tokyo})$$

We can see that the vector difference captures the concept of cooking in the first two cases and the concept of country–capital relationship in the last case. In other words, by adding the difference between beef and steak (which can be interpreted as an act of cooking) to a tomato, we get a salad. This type of semantic relationship is called *word analogy*. Note that each concept, such as cooking or capital, that is, one of the vector differences in the examples above, is also a vector in the semantic space, so we can conclude that a certain direction in the space corresponds to cooking, another direction to zooming in from country to capital, and so on.

▲

One of the applications of the Word2Vec methods in merchandising search is thesaurus generation. For instance, it was used by Dice.com, a job search engine, to overcome the struggle with synonymy in job titles and descriptions [Hughes, 2015]. The benefit of this approach is that it can produce a thesaurus or word clusters that can be used by the standard syntactic search engine.

We conclude our discussion of Word2Vec with a brief comparison with the LDA, pLSA, and LSA methods. The key difference is that Word2Vec uses a local context window to learn semantic dependencies, whereas the topic modeling methods use global document statistics. Both approaches have strengths and weaknesses. For example, Word2Vec can generally capture word analogy better than topic modeling [Pennington et al., 2014]. On the other hand, the vector representations produced by the Word2Vec model are not sparse and may contain negative elements, which make them less interpretable relative, for example, to the results of LDA, which is able to create sparse vectors that are interpretable as probabilities. This makes Word2Vec less applicable in applications related to topic analysis.

4.6   SEARCH METHODS FOR MERCHANDISING

Thus far, we have discussed relatively generic search methods and their applications in merchandising search. The challenge of merchandising search, however, goes well beyond the tuning of standard methods and requires the creation of more specialized search techniques for domains like eCommerce. This is explained by a number of reasons [Khludnev, 2013]:

- *Structured entities.* Many standard search methods are designed for documents with a relatively simple structure that includes one or several textual fields. A merchandising search often deals with highly structured documents that resemble records in relational databases, rather than texts. For example, a typical product item can have hundreds of numerical and categorical attributes, so that the corresponding document looks like this:

  ```
  Brand: Tommy Hilfiger
  Type: Jeans
  Color: Black
  Weight: Super Skinny
  ...
  ```

  Moreover, it is often the case that the merchandise is grouped into nested entities or associated with category hierarchies. For example, a retailer can sell a dinnerware set as a single item, but this item includes multiple products, and each product, in turn, may have multiple variants of different colors or sizes. This requires a search service to operate with nested or interrelated entities that cannot be correctly represented as plain documents.

- *Diversity of merchandise.* Many search applications take advantage of ranking to improve the perceived precision of the search results. Unfortunately, it turns out that the power of ranking and its applicability is limited in merchandising search. One of the main reasons is that search results produced by standard scoring and signal mixing methods tend to be excessively diverse, which creates a poor user experience. For example, the query *red dress* can match a wide range of products that contain these two terms in their attributes, including dresses, shoes, and even watches. The advanced signal engineering and mixing techniques that we discussed earlier can help to improve the results, but they are unlikely to provide a robust solution for the problem. Another reason is that $TF \times IDF$ scoring and other popular scoring methods can perform poorly on highly structured documents with multitudinous categorical fields. This is not surprising because these methods are designed for natural texts.

- *Compound and polysemic terms.* Industrial experience demonstrates that the quality of a merchandising search significantly depends on proper handling of compound and polysemic terms. Search queries in merchandising applications often contain multiword brand names and concepts, such as *Calvin Klein* and *dress shoes*, that clearly communicate the search intent if processed as phrases but that can be misinterpreted if broken down into standalone words. Moreover, many brand names contain common words, which makes proper interpretation even more challenging. For example, the query *pink sweater* can match all products made by the brand *Pink Rose*, and, conversely, the query *pink rose sweater* can match all products of pink and rose colors although it clearly indiates an intent to find a certain brand.

The observations above suggest that we should develop search methods that are focused on precision, exact matching, and attribute structures, as opposed to scoring. In other words, we should consider search methods that treat documents more like database records that have to be queried, rather than free texts that have to be scored. A number of such techniques have been developed by Macy's, a leading US retailer, for their eCommerce search services [Kamotsky and Vargas, 2014; Peter and Eugene, 2015]. We will spend the rest of this section discussing these methods.

4.6.1 *Combinatorial Phrase Search*

Our first goal is to improve the precision of search results, given that documents have many categorical fields that often contain compound and polysemic terms. We can make the observation that making users write structured Boolean queries would be a great solution for this problem. For example, the free-text query *pink rose sweater* becomes much less ambiguous if the user explicitly articulates fields and compound terms:

```
brand:[pink rose] AND type:[sweater]
```

This approach can be used in certain applications of merchandising search if the user is provided with a convenient interface that helps to specify individual fields. For example, car selling sites often provide drop-down lists of car makers, car models, and other properties to enable the user to specify field-level search criteria. This can be a reasonable solution for business domains with a relatively cohesive assortment, such as automobiles or real estate, but free-text queries are arguably preferable for domains with diverse merchandise, such as department stores.

A free-text query does not contain document fields or demarcation of compound terms, which thereby creates ambiguity. The idea of a combinatorial phrase search is to recover some of this information by generating multiple Boolean queries with different combinations of fields and terms from the original free-text query and by searching for documents containing these artificial queries. A query generation algorithm is designed to produce relatively restrictive search criteria, so that documents must strongly correlate with a query to match. This increases the probability that documents are included in a search results list not because of accidental matching of separate terms but because the document attributes provide a really good coverage of query terms and phrases. This methodology can be considered as a generalization of shingling for multifield documents.

The first step of a combinatorial phrase search is to partition the query into sub-phrases. Let us assume that a query entered by a user is a sequence of n terms:

$$q = [t_1 \ t_2 \ \dots \ t_n] \tag{4.91}$$

There exist 2^{n-1} possible partitions of this query into sub-phrases because there are $n - 1$ gaps between the query terms, and we independently choose to split or not to split a query at any gap. For example, there are four possible partitions for a query with three terms (we use square brackets to denote sub-phrases):

$$
\begin{aligned}
&[t_1 \ t_2 \ t_3] \\
&[t_1] \, [t_2 \ t_3] \\
&[t_1 \ t_2] \, [t_3] \\
&[t_1] \, [t_2] \, [t_3]
\end{aligned}
\tag{4.92}
$$

The second step is to generate a Boolean query for each partition, such that each sub-phrase in a partition is required to match one of the fields in a document. If we have m sub-phrases $s_1, \dots, s_m$ in a given partition and a document has k fields $f_1, \dots, f_k$, the Boolean query will be as follows:

$$
\begin{aligned}
&(f_1 = s_1 \ \text{OR} \ f_2 = s_1 \ \text{OR} \ \dots \ \text{OR} \ f_k = s_1) \\
&\text{AND} \ (f_1 = s_2 \ \text{OR} \ f_2 = s_2 \ \text{OR} \ \dots \ \text{OR} \ f_k = s_2) \\
&\quad \dots \\
&\text{AND} \ (f_1 = s_m \ \text{OR} \ f_2 = s_m \ \text{OR} \ \dots \ \text{OR} \ f_k = s_m)
\end{aligned}
\tag{4.93}
$$

We use the equals sign in query 4.93 to denote an exact match between the query sub-phrase and the field value; both sides must be exactly the same, although we can apply normalization, stop words, or stemming to preprocess both the query and fields. Query 4.93 ensures that a document provides a reasonably high coverage of a given partition, in the sense that each sub-phrase must have an exact match with one of the fields.

Finally, the Boolean queries for all partitions are executed, and the final search result set is obtained as a union of the search results from all
Boolean queries. This is equivalent to combining all partition queries
into one big Boolean query with the OR operator. The overall structure of this query is visualized in Figure 4.25. Our partition generation
algorithm does not try to recognize compound terms in a query and
just mechanically splits it into sub-phrases. Consequently, sub-phrases
are likely to be misaligned with the compound term boundaries. For
example, the query *blue calvin klein jeans* can be partitioned into the
sub-phrases *blue calvin* and *klein jeans*. By combining all of the partitions together, we ensure that at least some of the splits capture the
compound terms correctly.

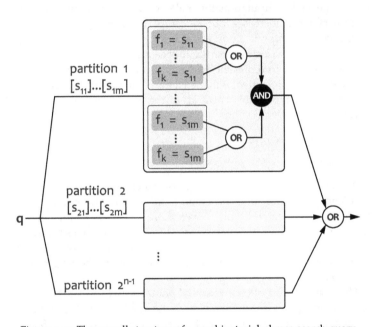

Figure 4.25: The overall structure of a combinatorial phrase search query.

EXAMPLE 4.6

▼

We will illustrate the logic of the combinatorial phrase search with an example. Let us take the query *pink rose sweater*, which can be partitioned in the following ways:

```
Partition 1 : [pink rose sweater]
Partition 2 : [pink rose] [sweater]
Partition 3 : [pink] [rose sweater]
Partition 4 : [pink] [rose] [sweater]
```

Let us assume that the products in the catalog are represented as documents with three fields: brand, product type, and color. A combinatorial phrase search query assembled for such fields and partitions will have the structure presented in Figure 4.26. The query can become very large and computationally challenging as the number of fields and query terms increases, but we can partially mitigate this by introducing certain simplifications. For example, we can limit the maximum length of sub-phrases in a partition because sub-phrases that are too long are unlikely to represent meaningful compound terms.

The following document will match the combinatorial query because the brand and type fields cover all of the sub-phrases in the second partition:

```
Brand: pink rose
Type: sweater
Color: black
```

At the same time, the query will not match a product of a sweater type and pink color until the brand name is *rose*. Moreover, a combinatorial phrase search becomes even more restrictive as the length of the query grows because all terms need to be covered. This behavior is different from the standard vector space model that appreciates every term match and, thereby, decreases in precision as the length of the query increases.

The disadvantage of combinatorial phrase search is that the number of partitions grows exponentially with the number of terms in the user query and so does the number of statements in the resulting Boolean query. In practice, the complexity of the Boolean query can often be reduced by excluding some statements based on the field type. For example, it can be the case that the field *color* has only a few valid possible values, so filters like

```
Color = [sweater]
Color = [pink rose]
```

can be eliminated by the query generator as meaningless.

▲

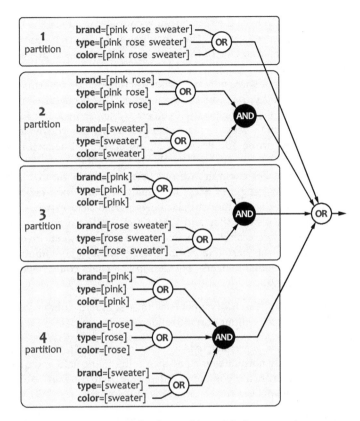

Figure 4.26: An example of a combinatorial phrase search query.

The combinatorial phrase search can be considered as a technique for finding documents that provide complete query coverage in terms of sub-phrases and fields. This method, however, can be connected to semantic search as well. Although the combinatorial search does not detect semantic relationships as explicitly as LSA or Word2Vec do, it attempts to identify and match compound terms that are likely to represent logical concepts. In other words, it can be viewed as an attempt to build a semantic search with syntactic search primitives [Giunchiglia et al., 2009; Khludnev, 2013].

4.6.2 Controlled Precision Reduction

The combinatorial phrase search achieves a high precision of search results by ruling out all documents that do not fully cover the search query. This helps to keep the search results consistent and use the available display space efficiently. The combinatorial approach, however, has its own downsides. One of the most significant issues is that strict matching can return an empty search results list if a query contains misspelled words or some other unfortunate combination of terms that cannot be covered by the available documents. This behavior is undesirable because it leaves the user with an empty screen instead of a list of products, which thereby decreases the probability of a conversion.

This problem can be addressed by taking additional actions if an empty search result is returned by the basic combinatorial phrase search algorithm. For example, we can first attempt to run a combinatorial search that requires exact field matching and then fall back to the basic vector space model that allows partial field matches. We can develop this idea further and create a chain of search methods with gradually decreasing precision, with each method invoked sequentially until at least one document (or some other minimum number of documents) matches. For example, a chain could have the following structure:

1. *Exact match.* Search documents with a standard combinatorial phrase search without normalization or stemming.

2. *Normalization, stemming, and spelling correction.* If there is no match, apply normalization and stemming to the field and query terms and run the combinatorial phrase search again. We can also apply spelling correction to the query terms.

3. *Shingling.* If there is no match, search by using shingling instead of seeking an exact match.

4. *Partial match.* If there is still no match, attempt to search with one or more words removed from the search query, so that a document does not need to provide full coverage of a query but only partial coverage.

Any search pass can terminate the process and return search results that have been found. For example, the misspelled query *Abibas sneakers* is likely to match no documents if the combinatorial phrase search is used, but the corrected query *Adidas sneakers* is likely to match enough documents to stop further relaxation of the search criteria. This technique, called controlled precision reduction, helps to manage the tradeoff between the high precision of combinatorial phrase search and the risk of frustrating the user with empty search results.

4.6.3   *Nested Entities and Dynamic Grouping*

From the merchandising standpoint, the problem of search can be viewed as the problem of efficient usage of display space. Although it is very important to present the user with a set of relevant products that meet the search intent, it is also important to demonstrate the available assortment in the best possible way, given that the user can browse only a limited amount of search results. Efficient utilization of the display space is a major challenge for merchandising search because product catalogs often contain closely related products that are likely to be perceived by the user as duplicates. For example, it can be more reasonable to present the user with a set of relevant but different dresses, rather than multiple variants of the same dress that comes in several colors and sizes.

The problem of duplicated products and inefficient usage of the display space arises from the hierarchical relationships between items in the product catalog. The nature and structure of these relationships heavily depend on the business domain. The following product hierarchy, for example, can often be found in department stores:

- The smallest unit of the merchandise is a product variant, commonly referred to as a *stock keeping unit* (SKU). An example of a product variant would be Levi's 511 jeans in a white color and size of 30W × 32L. All physical instances of the same variant are considered identical.

- A product is a logical entity that includes one or several product variants. For example, Levi's 511 jeans is a product that includes variants of different sizes and colors. A product typically has a price, with the implication that all of its variants are priced equally.

- Multiple products can be combined into a *product collection*. A collection can be sold as a single unit or a user can be allowed to select individual items from it. For example, multiple dinner plates, bowls, and mugs can be sold as a dinnerware set under one price tag. Alternatively, the user can choose to buy a subset of specific product variants.

All of the search methods that we have discussed so far assume that catalog items are modeled as plain documents, so we need to map a hierarchical structure with product collections, products, and product variants to a collection of documents. One possible way is to model each product variant as a separate document, so that each item in a search results list corresponds to one product variant. Although this

approach is generally valid and widely used in practice, it is vulnerable to the issue with duplicates and, consequently, inefficient usage
of the display space. Figure 4.27 illustrates this problem: variant-level
document modeling leads to a search result that is formally relevant
but not very efficient from the merchandising standpoint relative to
product-level modeling, which does a better job of demonstrating the
assortment.

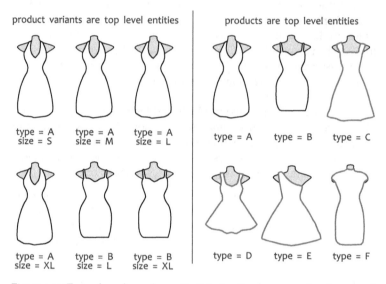

product variants are top level entities

products are top level entities

type = A   type = A   type = A
size = S   size = M   size = L

type = A   type = B   type = C

type = A   type = B   type = B
size = XL   size = L   size = XL

type = D   type = E   type = F

Figure 4.27: Examples of search results lists for the query *evening dresses* and
different approaches to data modeling.

Product-level document modeling can help to solve the problem
with duplicates, but it introduces its own challenges. A straightforward
approach to product-level modeling is to represent each product as a
single document. This requires all product attributes and product variant attributes to be merged into a plain list of fields; in other words, a
product has to inherit all of the attributes of its variants. For example,
consider the following two variants of a travel suitcase that belong to
one product:

```
Brand: Samsonite                      Brand: Samsonite
Name: Carry-on Hardside Suitcase      Name: Carry-on Hardside Suitcase
Color: red                            Color: black
Size: small                           Size: large
```

The two variants can be merged into one product-level document with the following structure:

```
Brand: Samsonite
Name: Carry-on Hardside Suitcase
Color: red black
Size: small large
```

The result looks reasonable because the document is scored well for queries like *red suitcase, small suitcase*, and so on. The major problem with this approach is that it loses the structural information about nested entities, which makes it impossible to distinguish valid attribute combinations from invalid ones. The document above is scored well for the query *small red suitcase*, and this is correct because one of the variants really is small and red. However, the same document is scored equally well for the query *small black suitcase*. This is not correct because none of the variants are small and black at the same time, which makes the product non-relevant for the user's search intent. This problem is quite challenging from the implementation standpoint because it cannot be solved purely in terms of plain documents and requires a search engine either to explicitly support nested entities or to operate with variant-level documents internally and then rework the results to group variants into products. If product filtering is implemented correctly, product-level results can substantially improve the merchandising efficiency of a search service.

We have found that collapsing product variants into products can be beneficial, so we can consider the possibility of collapsing products into product collections as the next step. This question is more complicated because a user can have different search intents and look for either products or product collections. For example, a user who searches for *dinnerware* is likely to expect collections, whereas a user who searches for a *cup* is more likely to expect individual products. This implies that we need to make a decision dynamically about grouping based on the query and matched results. This problem can be approached by introducing heuristic merchandising rules to analyze the structure of the results and matching attributes and make a grouping decision. For instance, we can choose to replace individual products by a collection only if a collection is generally consistent with the query, that is, all or almost all products in the collection and the collection-level attributes match the query. Consider the example in Figure 4.28. The query *white cup* is likely to match individual products or collections that include only white cups, but not dinnerware sets with plates, bowls, or cups of different colors. Consequently, we present a user with a search results list that contains mainly individual products. On the other hand, the query *white dinnerware* is likely to produce a different result. We can expect a significant number of dinnerware sets that mainly consist of white items that match the query term *white* and are attributed with the term *dinnerware* at the collection level. These dinnerware sets are generally consistent with the query, so we can include them into the search results list as collections, not as individual products.

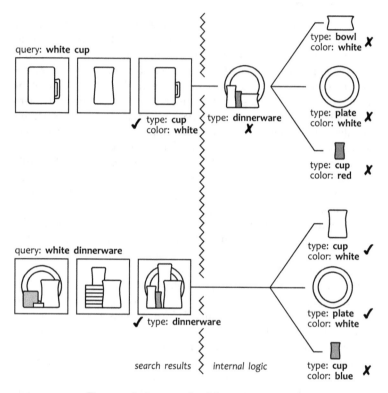

Figure 4.28: An example of dynamic grouping.

4.7 RELEVANCE TUNING

We have worked through a number of matching, ranking, and signal mixing methods that provide a wide range of controls for relevance tuning and merchandising adjustments. The fine-tuning of all of these controls to make them operate in concert can be a very challenging task that requires the development of a methodology and optimization methods. We have already made a step in this direction by introducing a few search quality metrics, such as precision, recall, and discounted cumulative gain. Our next step will be to develop relevance tuning methods with these metrics as optimization objectives.

Recall that the standard relevance metrics can be used to evaluate the quality of a single search results list or the average quality of search results over a set of queries. The optimization objective is to maximize the overall economic performance of a search service, so we should optimize the relevance metrics for a set of queries with the largest contribution to the total service profits. In other words, we can informally express the overall economic performance of a search service as the sum of contributions from individual search queries:

$$\text{Revenue} = \sum_{q \in Q} R(q) \cdot m(q) \tag{4.94}$$

in which q is a query, Q is a set of possible queries, $R(q)$ is the average revenue of conversions attributed to query q, and $m(q)$ is the quality metric of the search results, which is assumed to be proportional to the conversion rate. In practice, we are unlikely to be able to optimize all possible queries, but we can select the most popular and revenue-generating queries based on the historical data and use only this set for optimization. The relevance optimization process can then be organized as a continual review and improvement of the average performance over this set of queries; this process consists of the following steps:

1. Service usage statistics are collected and analyzed to determine the set of queries with the largest contribution to the service performance. We refer to this set as benchmark queries.

2. The relevance metrics are calculated for the benchmark queries to measure the overall performance of the search service.

3. The search results for each benchmark query are manually analyzed, and the search algorithms are tuned to improve the relevance metrics.

4. The new scoring configuration is first tested on a subset of real users and then applied permanently.

The processes above can be continually repeated to receive users' feedback on changes in scoring algorithms and to keep the set of benchmark queries up to date. The relevance metrics calculation and search algorithms tuning can be viewed as bottlenecks in the programmatic pipeline because both steps require substantial human involvement to make relevance judgments and rework scoring formulas. We can attempt to bridge this gap by developing methods that can automatically tune scoring formulas and assess the relevance of search results by analyzing user behavior and interactions with the search service. We will devote the next sections to a discussion of these two topics.

4.7.1   *Learning to Rank*

The primary goal of a search service is to rank documents according to their relevance to a given query and context. It is intuitively clear that this problem is closely related to classification or regression problems – given a certain query, one needs to accurately predict the *relevance grade* or *rank* of a document. A search results list can then be constructed by sorting all of the documents according to their predicted grades. This problem, commonly referred to as learning to rank, has been intensively researched by academics in the field of information retrieval and by web search companies such as Yahoo and Microsoft. This has resulted in a large number of research papers, industrial usage reports, and test data sets that are available for evaluation and comparison of learning to rank methods. Although the number of learning to rank algorithms is quite high, many of them use similar feature engineering techniques and objective functions that can be viewed as a common framework for learning to rank. Also, some benchmarks, such as the Learning to Rank Challenge organized by Yahoo in 2010, have demonstrated that the advantage of the most sophisticated learning to rank methods compared with the basic ones can be quite limited on real data [Chapelle and Chang, 2011]. Taking these considerations into account, we choose to focus on a common framework for learning to rank and consider one particular algorithm as an example. An extensive catalog of learning to rank algorithms can be found in [Liu, 2009].

We can formally define the problem of learning to rank as follows. There is a training set that contains Q samples, with each sample being a pair of a search query and the corresponding search results list. A results list for query q contains m_q documents, and each document d in the list is attributed with a relevance grade $y_{q,d}$. We assume that y is a categorical variable that takes one of K values. For example, the set of relevance grades can include five values: $1 - perfect$, $2 - excellent$, $3 - good$, $4 - fair$, and $5 - bad$. If we have defined a function that converts a pair of a query q and a document d into a feature vector $x_{q,d}$, the training set can be naturally represented as a collection of feature vectors and corresponding training labels:

$$\left(x_{q,d},\ y_{q,d}\right), \quad \begin{aligned} q &= 1,\ldots,Q \\ d &= 1,\ldots,m_q \end{aligned} \tag{4.95}$$

In practice, one can create a training data set by fetching the results lists for each query by using conventional search methods and setting relevance grades by using expert judgment. The goal is then to learn a ranking model that predicts the grade y from the input that consists of a query and a document.

Similarly to other supervised learning problems, learning to rank starts with feature engineering. As we have already mentioned, the relevance grade is predicted for a document in the context of a certain query, so a feature vector depends on both the document and the query. More specifically, the following groups of features are typically used in practice [Chapelle and Chang, 2011; Liu and Qin, 2010]:

DOCUMENT FEATURES This type of features contains the statistics and attributes for the document, including the following:

- The basic document statistics, such as the number of terms. These statistics can be calculated independently for each field and for the entire document to produce several groups of features.

- Product classification labels, such as product type, price category, and so on.

- Dynamic attributes and web statistics. Examples of such features include product sales data, user ratings, and newness.

- Web search implementation of learning to rank often includes web graphs and audience-related features, such as the number of inbound and outbound links for a web page. Although these may have limited applicability in merchandising search, such metrics can be valid candidates if available.

QUERY FEATURES These features include various statistics associated with a query. Similarly to the document features, this group can include several subcategories:

- The basic query statistics, such as the number of query terms.

- Query usage statistics, such as frequency of query and click-through rate.

- Attributes derived from the result set associated with the query. For example, a query can be attributed with a topic, such as *furniture*, if most of the results belong to this category.

DOCUMENT–QUERY FEATURES Features that depend on both the query and the document. This is the most important category of features and can include the following groups:

- Various statistics calculated for terms that the query and document have in common. For example, this can be a sum or variance of term frequencies or inverted document frequencies for common terms. These metrics can be calculated for each document field, as well as the entire document.

- Standard text matching and similarity metrics, such as the number of common terms and TF×IDF .

- Statistics related to user feedback. This includes different interaction probabilities, such as the probability of click (the share of users who clicked on a given document at least once among all users who entered a certain query), probability of the last click (the share of users who ended their search on a given document), probability to skip (the share of users who click on a document below the given one), and so on.

The structure of the feature vector is summarized in Figure 4.29. The total number of features in practical applications can reach several hundreds.

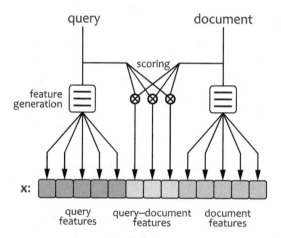

Figure 4.29: Feature engineering for learning to rank.

The next step in the creation of a ranking model is to define the loss function that will be used as a model training objective. Although learning to rank is closely related to classification and regression problems, setting the loss function is not trivial because we are concerned with the relative order of the documents in the results set, which is not the same as standard classification or regression errors. One possible approach is to define the loss function as a relevance measure, such as discounted cumulative gain (DCG). Unfortunately, DCG is a non-convex and non-smooth function, which can be a problem for many supervised learning algorithms that are based on a gradient approach. Although DCG is often used to evaluate the end quality of learning to rank algorithms, most methods use different loss functions for training. These functions typically fall into one of three categories:

POINTWISE The pointwise approach attempts to predict relevance grades for each document independently and thereby reduces ranking to a standard regression or classification problem. Consequently, the overall loss function L_0 is defined as a sum of the prediction errors for individual grades:

$$L_0 = \sum_{q,d} L\left(f\left(x_{q,d}\right), y_{q,d}\right) \tag{4.96}$$

in which $f\left(x_{q,d}\right)$ is a predicted relevance grade and $L(\cdot)$ is a classification or regression loss. For example, a classification loss can be defined by using an indicator function that equals zero if the prediction is correct and one otherwise:

$$L\left(f\left(x_{q,d}\right), y_{q,d}\right) = \mathbb{I}\left(f\left(x_{q,d}\right) \neq y_{q,d}\right) \tag{4.97}$$

The classification loss, however, is also non-convex and non-smooth, so we might need to approximate it with some different function. We will discuss the possible options later in this section in connection with concrete learning to rank algorithms. Another alternative is to use a regression loss, defined as

$$L\left(f\left(x_{q,d}\right), y_{q,d}\right) = \left(y_{q,d} - f\left(x_{q,d}\right)\right)^2 \tag{4.98}$$

It can be shown that the DCG error is upper bounded by the classification and regression losses, and minimization of the loss functions thus helps to optimize the DCG [Cossock and Zhang, 2006; Li et al., 2007]. However, the pointwise approach has a major downside, regardless of the choice of the loss function. The issue is that we are concerned with the relative order of items in the search results list, not in qualitative or quantitative estimates of individual grades. For example, the pointwise approach does not recognize that we will perfectly rank a results list of four items with relevance grades (1,2,3,4), even if the grades are predicted as (2,3,4,5). Consequently, we may take a different view on the loss function to account for the relative order of items.

The pointwise approach is used in a number of ranking algorithms, including McRank [Li et al., 2007] and PRank [Crammer and Singer, 2001].

PAIRWISE The pairwise approach attempts to overcome the limitations of the pointwise methods by penalizing for pairs of documents that are ranked in reverse order, instead of penalizing for incorrectly predicted relevancy grades. Consequently, the overall loss function is defined as a sum of the pairwise loss functions for all pairs of documents in the results list with different grades:

$$L_0 = \sum_q \sum_{i,j:y_{q,i} > y_{q,j}}^{m_q} L\left(f\left(x_{q,i}\right), f\left(x_{q,j}\right)\right) \tag{4.99}$$

The pairwise loss function is often defined based on the difference between the predicted grades, so that documents ranked in reverse order contribute to losses. For example, the function can be defined as exponential loss:

$$L\left(f\left(x_{q,i}\right), f\left(x_{q,j}\right)\right) = \exp\left(f\left(x_{q,j}\right) - f\left(x_{q,i}\right)\right) \tag{4.100}$$

The pairwise approach can also be considered as a classification problem, but, unlike pointwise classification, it aims to classify document pairs (pairs in which the first document is more relevant than the second document versus pairs in which the second document is more relevant).

Examples of pairwise ranking algorithms include RankNet [Burges et al., 2005], RankBoost [Freund et al., 2003], and RankSVM [Herbrich et al., 2000].

LISTWISE In the listwise approach, the loss function is defined based on the entire results list. In other words, the listwise approach uses document lists as "instances" in the learning, as opposed to the individual documents or document pairs that are used in the pointwise and pairwise approaches. The loss function has a fairly generic form that takes a list of pairs of predicted and actual relevance grades:

$$L_0 = \sum_q L\left(\left(f\left(x_{q,1}\right), y_{q,1}\right), \ldots, \left(f\left(x_{q,m_q}\right), y_{q,m_q}\right)\right) \tag{4.101}$$

The inner loss function L can be defined as a relevance measure, such as the DCG or its smooth approximations. Listwise ranking methods include AdaRank [Xu and Li, 2007] and ListRank [Cao et al., 2007].

Thus far, we have discussed how to prepare the training data and described possible options for the loss function. The last step is to choose a predictive model and train it to minimize the prediction loss. As learning to rank is closely related to classification, many standard supervised learning methods can be adapted for ranking. In particular, the industrial experience of Yahoo and Microsoft demonstrated that decision trees, neural networks, and their ensembles are especially efficient in practice [Chapelle and Chang, 2011; Burges, 2010]. We conclude this section with an overview of the McRank algorithm, which takes advantage of boosted decision trees to predict relevance grades [Li et al., 2007].

McRank is a pointwise learning to rank algorithm that reduces the ranking problem to a multiple classification. As we discussed earlier, the relevance grades are categorical variables with K classes:

$$y_{q,d} \in \{ 1, 2, \ldots, K \} \tag{4.102}$$

Our goal is to build a classification model that estimates the probability of each class based on a feature vector:

$$p_{q,d,k} = \Pr\left(y_{q,d} = k \mid x_{q,d}\right), \quad k = 1, \ldots, K \tag{4.103}$$

If these probabilities are estimated, the McRank algorithm sorts the documents according to their *expected relevance*:

$$r_{q,d} = \sum_{k=1}^{K} k \cdot p_{q,d,k} \tag{4.104}$$

The classification model is created in McRank by using a gradient boosting tree algorithm. As it is a gradient method, a smooth loss function is required. McRank chooses to use the following smooth version of the classification error described by expression 4.97 as a loss function:

$$\sum_{q,d} \sum_{k=1}^{K} -\log\left(p_{q,d,k}\right) \mathbb{I}\left(y_{q,d} = k\right) \tag{4.105}$$

McRank uses a standard gradient boosting tree algorithm that iteratively constructs an ensemble of decision trees to minimize loss function 4.105. The result is a model that estimates the probabilities described in equation 4.103, which can be used to rank documents in the search results list.

4.7.2 *Learning to Rank from Implicit Feedback*

Learning to rank provides powerful capability for automatic relevance tuning that helps to avoid or simplify manual signal mixing. This capability is essential for programmatic systems. Learning to rank, however, relies on expert judgment to set the relevance grades used in model training. This step often requires significant human effort and also limits the system's ability to self-tune dynamically. We can attempt to work around this problem by inferring relevance grades automatically based on user interactions with search results. For example, the results that nobody clicks on are likely to be irrelevant. One possible way to leverage this information is to incorporate it into feature vectors, as we already did in the previous section. We could take a step further and attempt to develop a method that learns the relevance grades from implicit feedback.

Although it is intuitively clear that users tend to click on relevant search results and skip irrelevant ones, user behavior can communicate more sophisticated relevance relationships. For example, a user can enter a search query, browse the results, click through some of them, reformulate the query, and click through some of the new results. All queries and documents in such a scenario are related to a single search intent, so relevance relationships can be established both within a single search results list and across the queries. In this section, we consider a feedback model that captures such relationships by using several heuristic rules [Radlinski and Joachims, 2005]. This particular model comes from academic research, although loosely similar methods for learning from implicit feedback have been reported by Yahoo [Zhang et al., 2015].

The model we will consider has two groups of relevance feedback rules. The first group, illustrated in Figure 4.30, includes two rules that are applied in the scope of a single search query. The first rule states that, if a user clicks on some document in the result list, this document is more relevant than all the documents above with regard to a given query. This is based on the assumption that a user typically reads the results from top to bottom. The second rule is based on empirical evidence (including eye-tracking studies) that a user typically considers at least the top two results in the list before taking an action. Consequently, if a user clicks on the first document in the list, it is considered more relevant than the second one (with regard to a given query).

The second group of rules is applied to *query chains*, that is, query sequences that represent different formulations of the same search intent. This first requires the detection of queries that belong to the same chain. This problem is not trivial because a user can make multiple queries with only one search intent but formulate it differently or can make multiple unrelated queries in a search for completely different products. The implicit feedback model that we consider approaches this problem by building an additional classifier that predicts whether a pair of queries belong to the same chain or not. The model is trained with manually classified query pairs and uses features, such as time

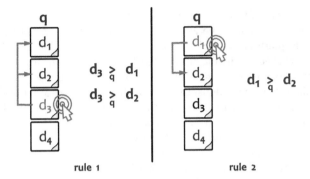

Figure 4.30: Implicit feedback rules for documents within one results list.

interval between queries, the number of common terms, and the number of common documents in the corresponding result lists. Once the queries are grouped into query chains, we can introduce four additional relevance rules that can be applied to pairs of search results lists. All of these rules are based on the assumption that queries in the chain express the same search intent and, hence, can be considered equivalent.

The first two rules in this group are presented in Figure 4.31. They repeat the two single-query rules that we considered earlier but with regard to adjacent queries in a query chain. Consider a chain in which query q_1 is followed by query q_2. Rule 3 mirrors rule 1 by stating that a clicked document in the result list for query q_2 is more relevant than the preceding skipped documents with regard to query q_1 because both queries are related to one search intent. Similarly, rule 4 mirrors rule 2.

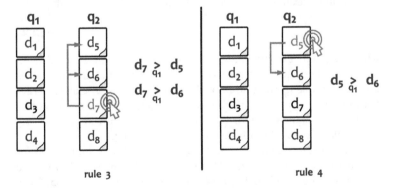

Figure 4.31: Implicit feedback rules for a chain of queries.

The last two rules are shown in Figure 4.32. These rules establish relevance relationships between the documents from different results lists in a query chain. Rule 5 states that documents that are viewed but not clicked on in the results list for query q_1 are less relevant than the documents that are clicked on in the results set for query q_2. This relevance relationship is established with regard to the earlier query. Consistently with rules 1 and 2, documents are considered to be viewed if they are above the clicked ones or right below the last clicked document, like document d_3 in Figure 4.32. Finally, rule 6 states that documents clicked on in the later results list are more relevant than the *first two* documents in the former list. This rule is based on the assumption that a user analyzes at least the first two results in the list before reformulating a query.

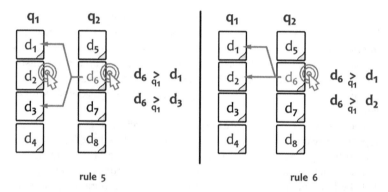

Figure 4.32: Implicit feedback rules for a chain of queries (continued).

All six rules are simultaneously evaluated against each query chain in the training data set to produce relevance relationships in the form

$$d_i \underset{q}{>} d_j \qquad (4.106)$$

which means that document d_i is more relevant that document d_j with regard to query q. These rules can be directly used as training labels for the pairwise learning to rank algorithms that we discussed earlier. For example, the authors of the feedback model that we just described used it in conjunction with the RankSVM algorithm to produce the final ranking model [Radlinski and Joachims, 2005].

Implicit feedback provides an important signal that can be used for automated relevance tuning. This signal can be mixed with organic relevance scores produced by other methods like TF×IDF so that flaws in organic ranking can be corrected by a ranking model learned from implicit feedback.

4.8   ARCHITECTURE OF MERCHANDISING SEARCH SERVICES

We conclude our journey through search methods with a review of the high-level logical architecture for a merchandising search service illustrated in Figure 4.33. The goal of this section is to summarize the key stages of data and query processing that we have discussed previously without going deeply into the technical and implementation details.

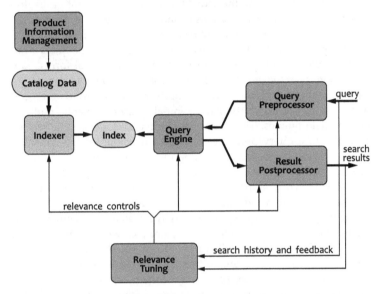

Figure 4.33: The main logical components of a merchandising search service.

A search service can be viewed as a database that contains the catalog data and provides search operations on top of it. As user queries are typically served in real time, a search engine needs to preprocess and index catalog data to enable efficient querying. This produces a set of indexes that are used by a query engine to match and score documents against a query. Consequently, the most basic search service consists of two components, an indexer and a query engine. The indexer typically includes two major data processing steps: mapping and indexing. The goal of the mapping step is to take various pieces of incoming data and create documents with well-defined fields, values, and hierarchical relationships. The mapping step typically includes a content analyzer, which performs tokenization, stemming, and other text normalization transformations. The documents created at the mapping step are then indexed to produce data structures that enable fast query processing. The query engine implements the basic search operations, such as token matching, Boolean querying, or TF×IDF scoring on top of the indexes.

Many search techniques, such as stemming, shingling, and synonym expansion, require certain transformations to be applied to both document fields and queries. On the document side, these transformations are often incorporated into the indexer and applied to the input data or documents before the index is build. This is necessary because indexes are constructed based on the actual tokens that are present in the documents, so many transformations cannot be efficiently applied at the query time if indexes are created based on raw non-transformed data. On the query side, the transformations are applied at the query time, so both indexes and queries are cast to the same normal forms. Normalization is not the only type of transformation applied to queries. As we discussed earlier, some search methods, such as controlled precision reduction, drastically transform the initial query or generate multiple intermediate queries. The query transformation logic is often encapsulated into a query preprocessor, which decomposes the incoming query into the basic primitives supported by the core query engine. The transformation logic on the indexer and query preprocessor sides must stay in synch so that the same stemming, shingling, or semantic expansion algorithms are applied on both sides.

The outputs of the query engine are the matching documents and their relevance scores calculated in accordance with the basic signal mixing methods. These results can be transformed by the result postprocessor to apply grouping and merchandising rules that extend or override the basic scoring. For example, the postprocessor can implement the boost-and-bury rules to elevate promoted products in the search results.

An efficient merchandising search requires at least two processes that work behind the scenes and complement the indexing–querying pipeline we just described. The first one is relevance tuning, which manages the relevance controls across all components of the indexing–querying pipeline and makes them operate in concert. This can be a manual process or a machine learning component that analyzes query history and user feedback to optimize relevance algorithms. The second process is product information management (PIM), which focuses on the cleaning, preparation, and enrichment of the catalog data loaded into the search engine. The quality and completeness of the input data are critical for the quality of the search because the range and accuracy of generated relevance signals directly depend on the range and accuracy of the product attributes. For example, basic product descriptions can be insufficient to properly serve queries such as *gluten-free soda* or *long sleeved dress*. To make a search engine understand such queries, products should be meticulously attributed with nutrition facts, sleeve types, and other specific properties. The total number of product fields indexed by a merchandising search engine can reach hundreds. It is a significant challenge to obtain and manage this metadata because different pieces of information can come from manufacturers or third-party data providers or may be created internally. A marketer can streamline this process by using a product information management system and specialized tools for metadata generation and quality checks. For example, some retailers use advanced image recognition tools to derive or validate certain product attributes, such as a dress type or color based on product images.

4.9 SUMMARY

- The purpose of search services is to fetch offerings that are relevant to the customer's search intent expressed in a search query or selected filters. Search services solve the problem of product discovery, which can be viewed as a particular case of targeting.

- The main components of the merchandising search environment include the user interface where search queries are entered and ranked catalog items are displayed, the search engine that processes the queries and ranks the items, and the relevancy tuning process that optimizes the relevance controls that determine how queries and items are matched.

- The main objectives of a search service include relevance, flexibility of merchandising controls, and service quality. Relevance and merchandising controls can be directly linked to the service profits.

- The main relevance metrics include the precision–recall and discounted cumulative gain in the ranked search results.

- Merchandising controls can be used to improve relevance and achieve additional business objectives, such as promotion of certain products. Merchandising controls include methods like boost and bury, filtering, canned results, page redirection, and product grouping.

- Search service quality metrics include conversion rate, click-through rate, time on a product detail page, query modification rate, paging rate, retention rate, and search latency. Some of these metrics can be used as objectives in automatic relevance tuning.

- A query processing flow can be viewed as a multistage process that breaks down documents and queries into features, correlates these two sets of features to produce relevance signals, and then uses the signals to make ranking decisions.

- The basic toolkit of search techniques includes text preprocessing methods (tokenization, stop words, stemming), token matching, and Boolean search. The most basic scoring techniques are based on the vector space model, which represents documents as vectors in a linear space where each dimension corresponds to an individual term. $TF \times IDF$, a popular scoring method, refines the basic vector space model and scores by using term frequency statistics.

- A real-life search service typically uses documents with multiple fields, which can be scored separately to produce multiple relevance signals. These signals can be mixed together with different signal engineering techniques.

- Term-matching methods are not able to capture semantic relationships, such as synonymy and polysemy. This limitation is addressed by semantic analysis methods. From a search perspective, most semantic analysis methods can be viewed as word embedding techniques that map words, documents, or queries to vectors of real numbers with certain semantic-related properties. The key semantic analysis methods include latent semantic analysis, probabilistic topic models, and contextual word embedding.

- Merchandising search often deals with structured entities and specific precision–recall requirements that cannot be properly addressed by generic search methods. Industrial experience shows that good results can be obtained by using high-precision and low-recall extensions of Boolean methods.

- Relevance tuning is a process of search quality metrics optimization with respect to relevance control parameters. This problem is closely related to classification and regression – given a query, one needs to predict the rank of a document. The problem, however, differs from standard classification; thus, specialized learning to rank algorithms exist. The typical features used by learning to rank methods are document statistics, query statistics, relevance signals, and implicit user feedback.

- The main components of a merchandising search service include the indexer, core query engine, query preprocessor, query postprocessor, and relevance tuning modules.

5

RECOMMENDATIONS

The variety of products and services offered to customers is limited by a number of factors including distribution and production costs. A grocery store can carry only a certain number of products that is limited by the available shelf space, a radio station can squeeze only a certain number of songs into its daily schedule, and a theater can put on only a limited number of performances. A seller can increase capacity and expand the assortment, but the additional revenues captured by this expansion start to diminish after a certain point because of the limited total demand. The marginal costs associated with the expansion, however, may not diminish as rapidly as the revenues or may not diminish at all, so the marginal costs eventually overrun the marginal revenue, which makes further assortment expansion uneconomical. Consequently, a seller usually has to focus on relatively popular products and offer only a limited variety of niche items.

The demand for niche products, however, does exist, which creates the *long tail* in the product popularity histogram shown in Figure 5.1. In practice, the total demand for such niche products can be comparable to the total demand for popular products [Anderson, 2008]. These two total demands correspond to areas D_1 and D_2 under the demand curve in Figure 5.1. Moreover, the long-tail items can often be high-end products with higher margins than the popular mainstream items, which makes the contribution of the long-tail products to the total profit even more significant.

As we already mentioned, many traditional distribution channels, such as brick-and-mortar stores, movie theaters, and radio stations, have limited ability to utilize the long-tail demand because of distribution costs. The advancement of digital channels, however, has changed the game dramatically. First, new media channels have almost eliminated the distribution costs for digital content and enabled the creation of online services with virtually infinite assortments. An online video service, for example, can offer an almost unlimited and con-

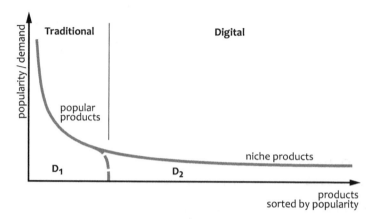

Figure 5.1: A typical product popularity histogram.

stantly growing variety of videos, including Hollywood movies, television series from all over the world, and amateur films. Second, digital channels have enabled retailers and manufacturers of non-digital goods to change the structure of their distribution costs and reach out to more consumers. The customer base of a brick-and-mortar store is limited to people who live in or visit that area, and so the variety of demand is similarly limited. An online retailer that operates nationwide or worldwide faces much more diverse demand. Therefore, sellers with enormous assortments, such as Amazon, have appeared and prospered. The impressive increase in the assortment with a strong emphasis on niche products challenges the old approaches to product discovery because an average customer can browse only a tiny fraction of available offerings that can be counted in millions. This need for powerful product discovery services was one of the main drivers behind the development of recommender systems.

Recommendation services, in contrast to search services, aim to provide the customer with relevant offerings when a search intent is not or cannot be clearly expressed. In some cases, the search intent cannot be explicitly expressed because the desired product properties are difficult to formalize or codify. For example, a customer who searches for music might have some sort of search intent determined by their tastes, but this intent can be difficult to translate into formal criteria. In other cases, a customer may be unaware of certain product types or categories or simply forget or doubt their own needs. An amateur photographer, for instance, might not realize that the type of photography they are interested in requires special lenses for the best results. Consequently, in contrast to search services that have a query to work with and can score products according to it, a recommender system needs to guess the purchasing intent based on indirect information such as product ratings and customer purchase histories. This information can then be used to calculate different similarity metrics that can be used as an alternative to the query–product similarity scores computed by search services. More specifically, a recommender system can leverage the following similarities:

USER SIMILARITIES The purchasing intent of a given customer can be inferred from the past behavior of similar customers. This approach resembles the look-alike modeling that we discussed previously.

PRODUCT SIMILARITIES Interactions with the merchandise and past purchases can be used to determine the most relevant product groups and categories for a given customer, so that more similar products can be recommended.

CONTEXT SIMILARITIES The accuracy of recommendations can be increased by using not only customer and product attributes but also contextual information that carries additional signals about the purchasing intent. For instance, a fashion retailer can recommend very different products for the same customer depending on the season.

Algorithmically, recommendation methods have a lot in common with search techniques and also take advantage of the predictive methods that we used earlier for targeted promotions. In the rest of this chapter, we will systematically describe recommender systems by starting with the environment and economic goals and then diving deeper into various recommendation methods.

5.1 ENVIRONMENT

The basic settings for recommendation services are similar to those for search services. Similarly to search services, the primary purpose of a recommender system is to provide a customer with a ranked list of recommended items. These recommendations can be delivered through different marketing channels. We will assume that the recommendations are requested by a channel in real time, which is typically the case for websites and mobile applications, although some channels such as email can have more relaxed requirements and allow recommendations to be calculated offline. The basic inputs of a recommender system, depicted in Figure 5.2, are, however, different from those of a search service and include the following:

- The vast majority of recommendation methods make the assumption that *customer ratings* are available for catalog items. The ratings can be explicitly provided by customers or derived from behavioral data, such as purchases and online browsing histories. Each rating value represents the feedback of a certain customer on a certain item measured on some scale. Note that a customer can rate any item in the catalog, not only the recommended ones. In other words, ratings capture customer feedback on catalog items, not recommendations. We will discuss ratings and their properties in greater detail in the next section.

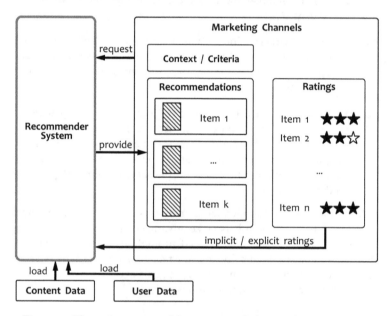

Figure 5.2: The main concepts of the recommendation service environment.

- Certain recommendation methods rely on content and catalog data to calculate similarities between the items based on their attributes. Similarly to search engines, this requires the integration of the recommender systems with the source of the catalog data, such as the product information management system.

- Some recommender systems can take advantage of additional user data, such as online order histories or store transactions. This information needs to be distinguished from the basic rating data: ratings describe individual user–item interactions, but external data such as order history can provide additional details on how interactions are grouped into orders and so on.

- Both recommendation requests and customer ratings can be complemented with contextual information, such as time, location, or marketing channel. A recommender system can use the contextual data to improve the relevance of recommendations. For example, rating time stamps can be used to account for seasonal and temporal trends in customer tastes. A recommendation request or context can also include explicit criteria or customer preferences that can be used to refine recommendations. For instance, skincare product recommendations can be adjusted based on the skin type (normal, dry, oily, etc.) specified in the customer's preferences.

Different families of recommendation methods can use different subsets of data, and their strengths and weaknesses are largely determined by the range of data that they can take advantage of.

5.1.1 *Properties of Customer Ratings*

Customer ratings are often considered the most important source of information for making recommendations, so we need to take a closer look at how ratings are defined and what the typical properties of rating data are.

Ratings are typically represented as a matrix where each row corresponds to a user and each column corresponds to an item. Let us denote the rating matrix as $\mathbf{R} = (r_{ij})$, so that r_{ij} is a rating given by user i for item j. In a recommender system that tracks m users and contains a catalog of n items, $\mathbf{R}$ is an $m \times n$ matrix. In practice, the rating matrix is almost always incomplete – ratings are known only for a subset of user–item pairs and the remaining elements are missing (unspecified). The known ratings are usually numerical values that can be defined differently depending on the business domain, marketing channel, and source of data. We will distinguish the following two cases:

ORDINAL The interface of a recommender system often allows the user to express their preferences by choosing ratings from a discrete set of numbers (e. g., 1, 2, or 3 stars) or a continuous range (e. g., from -5 to +5). It is also typical to capture ratings as categorical variables with two (e. g., like or dislike) or more (e. g., bad, good, or excellent) categories and then map them to discrete numerical values. Implicit feedback can also be expressed as ordinal values, but such values usually indicate *confidence* rather than *preferences*. For example, an implicit rating can indicate how frequently a user purchases a certain item or how much time a customer spent on a product details page on the website.

UNARY In many cases, a rating matrix does not capture the level of affinity between a user and item but merely registers the fact of an interaction. For example, many interfaces have only one Like button, so a user can either like an item or provide no feedback at all. Another typical example of unary ratings is implicit feedback that registers interactions between users and items but does not capture details, such as the number of purchases, although it can be argued that the simple quantitative properties of this feedback are important [Hu et al., 2008]. The elements of an unary rating matrix can take only two values – either one or unspecified.

The rating values in matrix $\mathbf{R}$ are often attributed with contextual information, such as the date and time that the rating was set, the marketing channel used by the customer to provide the rating, and so on. This information can be used by a recommender system to figure out which rating values are most relevant for a given context.

An important observation about rating values is that a matrix with explicit ordinal ratings also contains *implicit feedback*. The reason is that users typically tend to rate the items they like and avoid the items they find unattractive. For example, a user can totally avoid music of certain genres or products from certain categories. Consequently, which items are rated is important, in addition to how they are rated. In other words, the distribution of ratings for random items is likely to be different from the distribution of ratings for items selected by a user. This means that a recommender system, strictly speaking, should not rely on the assumption that the distribution of observed ratings is representative of the distribution of missing ones [Devooght et al., 2015]. As we will see later, some advanced recommendation methods take this consideration into account and infer the implicit feedback from the rating matrix. In a more general case, a recommender algorithm can involve two separate rating matrices for both explicit and implicit feedback.

The second important property of a rating matrix is *sparsity*. A rating matrix is inherently sparse because any single user interacts with only a tiny fraction of the available items, so that each row of the matrix contains only a few known ratings and all other values are missing. Moreover, the distribution of known ratings typically exhibits the long-tail property that we have discussed earlier. This means that a disproportionally large number of the known ratings correspond to a few of the most popular items, whereas niche product ratings are especially scarce. This property can be illustrated by a well-known data set published by Netflix, a video streaming service, which contains movie ratings for about 500,000 Netflix subscribers – it turns out that about 33% of ratings involve only the 1.7% of most popular items [Cremonesi et al., 2010]. The long-tail property is a challenge for the design and evaluation of recommender systems because both recommendation algorithms and recommendation quality metrics tend to have a bias toward popular items, which reduces the quality of recommendations for niche products.

5.2 BUSINESS OBJECTIVES

The key business objectives of recommendation services are closely related to the objectives of merchandising search. The main considerations that we discussed earlier in the context of merchandising search, such as relevance and merchandising controls, are generally applicable to recommender systems. The major difference, however, is that the search intent is not explicitly expressed and may not even exist. This requires an extension of the basic objective of providing relevant results because the notion of relevance becomes increasingly shaky as the search intent loses its sharpness. Consequently, the standard set of objectives for a recommender system is often defined as follows:

RELEVANCE The recommendations suggested to a user should be relevant, in the sense that a user has a high propensity to purchase the recommended items and rate them highly.

NOVELTY A recommender system does not fulfill an explicit search request but rather advises users on available options. Consequently, the recommender system should provide users with options that are not already known to them; otherwise, the recommendations can be perceived as trivial and useless. A typical example of this problem is the recommendation of popular similar items that the user is likely to be aware of. For instance, a user who bought one of the Harry Potter books might be provided with recommendations to buy more books from this series, instead of other books in the same genre.

SERENDIPITY Recommendations can help a user to discover products that are unexpected and surprising, as well as novel. For example, a user who buys books about machine learning might be provided with recommendations to buy more books on this topic – although some of the recommended items might be novel to the user, we probably cannot consider them as serendipitous. On the other hand, a recommender system can try to guess the business domain that the user is interested in and recommend a book on domain-specific analytical methods, such as customer analytics or trading models, which can be serendipitous. Even better examples of serendipitous recommendations are those for items from completely different categories. For example, a user who buys Harry Potter books can be recommended to visit an amusement park with a corresponding attraction or users who study European medieval epics such as Beowulf and The Song of Roland can be recommended to buy related opera tickets. Serendipitous recommendations not only increase usability and conversion rates but can also help to establish a new long lasting theme in the relationship with a client.

DIVERSITY Finally, a list of recommendations suggested to a user should be diverse to increase the chance of a conversion. A list of recommendations that consists of very similar items, even if they are relevant, novel, and serendipitous, might not be optimal.

Similarly to search services, the overall profit of a recommender system can be defined in terms of product margins and quantities sold:

$$\text{Profit} = \sum_{\text{products}} \text{Quantity sold}_{\text{product}} \times \text{Margin}_{\text{product}} \qquad (5.1)$$

The relevance, novelty, serendipity, and diversity objectives are focused on increasing conversion rates and, consequently, quantity sold. The recommendations produced in accordance with these objectives can be re-ranked in the pursuit of additional merchandising goals, such as the promotion of high-margin or seasonal products, with the aim of improving the margin part of the equation.

5.3 QUALITY EVALUATION

Our next step is to design quantitative metrics that can be used to evaluate the quality of recommender systems with regard to the objectives defined in the previous section.

The quality of search results can generally be evaluated by using expert judgement to score the relevance of items in the context of a given query, but this approach has limited applicability for recommendations because the context typically includes user profile data and, hence, is unique for each user. This makes it challenging or impossible to manually score the quality of recommendations for every possible context. On the other hand, the rating matrix already contains expert judgements provided by users in their own personalized contexts. Consequently, the recommendation problem can be viewed as a rating prediction problem (how to recommend items with the highest predicted ratings for a given user), and the quality of the recommendations can be measured by comparing the predicted ratings with the actual ratings known from the rating matrix. From this perspective, the recommendation problem is very close to classification or regression.

Recall that a classification/regression problem can be defined by using a matrix in which each row represents a data point and columns are either features or responses. A prediction model is trained on data with both features and responses, and it is then used to predict responses based on features. This is illustrated in example 5.2, where data points 1–3 are used for training and the actual prediction is done for points 4–6. Furthermore, in order to train and tune the model, data points with known responses are typically split into training, validation, and testing data sets. The model is initially built by using the training set. The responses of the validation set are then predicted and compared to the actual values, and the model quality is evaluated. Based on the evaluation results, the model can be re-built with different parameters by using the training data and evaluated again. The testing data set is used to finally assess the quality of the model at the very end of the process.

$$
\begin{array}{c}
\begin{array}{cccc}
\text{FEATURE 1} & \text{FEATURE 2} & \text{FEATURE 3} & \text{RESPONSE}
\end{array} \\
\begin{array}{c}
\text{DATA POINT 1} \\
\text{DATA POINT 2} \\
\text{DATA POINT 3} \\
\text{DATA POINT 4} \\
\text{DATA POINT 5} \\
\text{DATA POINT 6}
\end{array}
\left[
\begin{array}{cccc}
x_{11} & x_{12} & x_{13} & y_1 \\
x_{21} & x_{22} & x_{23} & y_2 \\
x_{31} & x_{32} & x_{33} & y_3 \\
x_{41} & x_{42} & x_{43} & - \\
x_{51} & x_{52} & x_{53} & - \\
x_{61} & x_{62} & x_{63} & -
\end{array}
\right]
\end{array}
\qquad (5.2)
$$

The key difference for the rating prediction problem is that there are no features and responses in the rating matrix. Known and unknown ratings are mixed together without any particular structure, as illustrated in example 5.3, and the goal is to train the model with known ratings to predict unknown ones. This task of filling in the missing entries of a partially observed matrix is known as the *matrix completion* problem.

$$
\begin{array}{c}
\begin{array}{cccc}
\text{ITEM 1} & \text{ITEM 2} & \text{ITEM 3} & \text{ITEM 4}
\end{array} \\
\begin{array}{c}
\text{USER 1} \\
\text{USER 2} \\
\text{USER 3} \\
\text{USER 4}
\end{array}
\left[
\begin{array}{cccc}
r_{11} & - & r_{13} & - \\
- & r_{22} & - & r_{24} \\
- & r_{32} & r_{33} & - \\
r_{41} & - & r_{43} & r_{44}
\end{array}
\right]
\end{array}
\qquad (5.3)
$$

As with the standard classification problem, we need to split the available data into training, validation, and testing sets in order to train the model and evaluate its quality. In the case of classification, this is done on a row-by-row basis. For example, the available data in matrix 5.2 can be split into three sets by assigning the first row to the training set, the second row to the validation set, and the third row to the test set. This approach does not work well for matrix completion because it implies that the model is trained on one set of users and evaluated on another, which is not really the case. Instead, the rating matrix is typically sampled on an element-by-element basis. This means that a certain fraction of known ratings is removed from the original rating matrix to leave a training matrix, and the removed ratings are placed into validation or testing sets, which are later used to evaluate the quality of prediction.

By interpreting the recommendation problem as a rating prediction problem, we can define several quality metrics that can be linked to the business objectives. We will spend the next sections developing these metrics.

5.3.1   Prediction Accuracy

The accuracy of rating predictions can be considered a measure of relevance because it quantifies how well a recommender system can predict the user utility as estimated by the users themselves. To measure the accuracy, we can choose from a wide range of metrics used in machine learning and information retrieval, including the search quality metrics that we discussed earlier.

The first family of metrics we will consider are prediction accuracy metrics that are widely used for the evaluation of classification and regression methods. Let us denote the set of observed ratings $r_{uj} \in \mathbf{R}$ as R and the test subset used for accuracy evaluation as $T \subset R$. For each rating in T, a recommendation algorithm produces an estimate $\hat{r}_{uj}$, so the prediction error can be defined as follows:

$$e_{uj} = \hat{r}_{uj} - r_{uj} \tag{5.4}$$

The overall quality of the rating predictions can then be obtained by averaging the pointwise prediction errors. There are several ways to define this average metric. The first option is the mean squared error (MSE) defined as

$$\text{MSE} = \frac{1}{|T|} \sum_{(u,j) \in T} e_{uj}^2 \tag{5.5}$$

The MSE metric is not always convenient because it operates with squared error values, which cannot be directly compared to the original rating values. We can fix this by defining the root mean squared error (RMSE), which is measured in the same units as the original ratings:

$$RMSE = \sqrt{MSE} \tag{5.6}$$

Furthermore, the RMSE can be normalized to the range $(0, 1)$ to obtain the normalized RMSE (NRMSE):

$$NRMSE = \frac{RMSE}{r_{max} - r_{min}} \tag{5.7}$$

The RMSE and its variations are widely used in practice for recommender system evaluation as a result of their simplicity. However, the RMSE and similar pointwise accuracy metrics have several important drawbacks:

- As we discussed earlier, ratings typically follow a long-tail distribution, which means that ratings are dense for the popular items and sparse for those items from the long tail. This makes rating prediction more challenging for the long-tail items relative to the popular items and results in different prediction accuracies for these two item groups. The RMSE does not differentiate between these two groups and simply takes the average, so poor accuracy for the long-tail items can be counterbalanced by high accuracy for the popular items. To measure and control this trade-off, we can calculate the RMSE separately for different item groups or add item-specific weights into equation 5.5 to account for item margins or other considerations.

- The goal of a recommender system is to predict how a user will rate an item in the future based on the historical data. User tastes and interests may change over time, so the system should be able to recognize such temporal trends to make accurate predictions about future behavior. The RMSE does not directly account for this aspect of recommendations. The problem, however, can be addressed with the proper design of a test set T. In order to test the ability to predict future ratings, we can select test set T from ratings R, not at random but in such a way that the training set contains the older ratings and test set T contains the most recent ones. This approach is somewhat inconsistent with the standard model evaluation methodology because training and test sets constructed this way have different distributions, but it is a valid practical technique that was used, for example, in the Netflix Prize, an open competition for the best collaborative filtering algorithm held by Netflix, an online video streaming service, in 2006–2009 [Aggarwal, 2016].

The consideration above is especially apparent in the case of ratings obtained from implicit feedback. For example, if ratings are defined based on purchasing events, the prediction of future ratings effectively means the prediction of future purchases.

- A recommender system provides a user with a ranked list of recommendations that is typically limited to the top K items. The RMSE does not account for ranking and equally penalizes prediction errors for items at both the top and bottom of the list. It can be argued that algorithms with a very small difference in RMSE can have a big difference in their lists of the top K items [Koren, 2007].

5.3.2 Ranking Accuracy

To measure the quality of the top K recommendations, we can leverage the large set of methods and metrics that we developed for search services. First, we should note that the concepts of precision and recall are directly applicable to the top K recommendations problem. If I_u is the subset of items in test set T that is positively rated (e. g., purchased) by user u and $Y_u(K)$ is the list of top K items recommended to that user, we can define the precision and recall metrics as functions of K:

$$\text{precision}(K) = \frac{|Y_u(K) \cap I_u|}{|Y_u(K)|} \tag{5.8}$$

$$\text{recall}(K) = \frac{|Y_u(K) \cap I_u|}{|I_u|} \tag{5.9}$$

For any given K, the quality of a recommender algorithm can be measured in terms of these two metrics – precision is the percentage of relevant recommendations in the list, and recall is the percentage of items consumed from the set of available relevant items. Two recommender algorithms can be compared in terms of precision and recall averaged by users, just like search methods can be compared in terms of these metrics. The number of recommendations in the list, however, is a critical parameter that influences the precision–recall trade-off achieved by an algorithm. Short recommendation lists tend to miss relevant items, whereas long lists tend to have a high percentage of irrelevant ones. This trade-off can be visualized by using a precision–recall curve, which we also discussed earlier in the context of search services. The curve depicts the precision and recall values for different values of K and makes it possible to see the range of precision–recall trade-offs that the recommendation algorithm can achieve.

The disadvantage of a precision–recall curve is that it does not provide a single numerical metric that summarizes the quality of a recommendation method. Fortunately, we have already introduced a range of ranking quality metrics that can be adapted to provide just such a summary view. For example, we can adapt the discounted cumulative gain (DCG) for recommendations by using known ratings as relevance grades. Recall that we defined the DCG for a list of K items as follows:

$$DCG = \sum_{i=1}^{K} \frac{2^{g_i} - 1}{\log_2 (i + 1)} \tag{5.10}$$

in which g_i is the relevance grade of the i-th item in the list. If test set T contains ratings provided by m users, we can define the overall DCG as the average of the DCGs for the recommendation lists for individual users:

$$DCG = \frac{1}{m} \sum_{u=1}^{m} \sum_{\substack{i \in I_u \\ R_{ui} \leqslant K}} \frac{2^{r_{ui}} - 1}{\log_2 (R_{ui} + 1)} \tag{5.11}$$

in which I_u is the subset of items in test set T positively rated by user u, R_{ui} is the rank of item i in the list of recommendations for user u, and r_{ui} is the rating from set T provided by user u for item i, which is used as an approximation of the relevance grade g_i from equation 5.10. Note that the inner sum in equation 5.11 simply iterates over the top K recommendations with known test ratings for a given user. The other standard information retrieval metrics, such as the normalized DCG (NDCG) and mean average precision (MAP), can be reformulated in a similar way.

5.3.3 Novelty

Recommendations are considered novel if the user is not aware of the recommended items at the moment that the recommendation is provided. This information is not directly available in the rating matrix, so it should either be gathered through real-life testing and user surveys or somehow inferred from the rating matrix. Since real-life testing and surveys are generally time and resource consuming, we can attempt to design a novelty metric based on the rating matrix, which requires certain assumptions to be made. One possible approach is to train a recommendation algorithm with older ratings and evaluate it by using more recent ratings, as illustrated in Figure 5.3.

The assumption is that a recommendation algorithm that tends to predict items ranked or purchased immediately after the time boundary t_T of the training set provides lower novelty than an algorithm

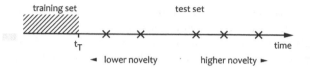

Figure 5.3: Evaluating the novelty of recommendations.

that tends to predict items ranked or purchased in the more distant future because the immediately purchased items are more likely to be known to the user. Consequently, the novelty metric can use time-weighted scores to boost farsighted accurate predictions and penalize shortsighted ones.

5.3.4 Serendipity

Serendipity is a measure of the extent to which recommendations are both attractive and surprising to the user [Herlocker et al., 2004]. The evaluation of serendipity is even more challenging than the evaluation of novelty because this property is highly subjective and feedback information typically provides no hint of the level of serendipity. It is, however, possible to develop heuristic serendipity measurement methodologies. One possible approach is to compare the recommendations produced by an algorithm under evaluation with the recommendations produced by some basic algorithm that is known to suggest trivial and non-serendipitous items [Ge et al., 2010]. If the set of items recommended to the user by the algorithm under evaluation is denoted as Y_u and the set recommended by the baseline algorithm is denoted as Y_u^0, the measure of serendipity can be defined as

$$\text{serendipity} = \frac{1}{m \cdot K} \sum_{u=1}^{m} \sum_{i \in I_u} \mathbb{I}\left(i \in \left(Y_u \setminus Y_u^0\right)\right) \qquad (5.12)$$

in which m is the number of users, I_u is the set of items in the test set positively rated by the user, K is the number of recommendations in the list, and $\mathbb{I}(\cdot)$ is the indicator function that equals true if the item belongs to the set Y_u but not to Y_u^0. In other words, this serendipity measure scores a recommender system based on the fraction of non-trivial and relevant items in the recommendation list.

5.3.5 Diversity

Diversity is the ability of a recommender system to produce a list of recommendations that consists of dissimilar items. High diversity is generally preferable because it increases the chance that at least some items in the list will be relevant for the user. High diversity can also be preferable from the merchandising perspective because it contributes towards cross-selling and wide catalog coverage.

We can leverage the similarity metrics developed earlier for search services to measure the diversity. For example, we can calculate cosine distances between item descriptions for all pairs of items in the list of recommendations and estimate the diversity as the reciprocal of the average distance.

5.3.6 Coverage

The goal of a recommender system is to predict the missing ratings in the rating matrix. As we will discuss later, many recommendation algorithms rely on item-to-item or user-to-user similarities computed on the basis of the rating matrix, so it can be a challenge to predict ratings for items or users who do not have many ratings in common with other items and users. This makes it important to measure the coverage provided by a recommender system, that is, the percentage of users or items over which the system can make recommendations. In certain cases, this percentage can be estimated based on the requirements imposed by a recommendation algorithm. For example, an algorithm might require a user to have at least five ratings to be eligible for recommendations. In a general case, a recommender system can always predict a rating for any pair of user and item by simply providing a default or random value. This means that we might be interested in tracking the reliability of predicted ratings (the probability that the estimated value is accurate) and assessing the trade-off between the coverage and accuracy by excluding users or items with the least reliable rating estimates from the accuracy evaluation.

An alternative view on coverage is the so-called *catalog coverage* [Ge et al., 2010]. Catalog coverage is defined as the percentage of items that are *actually* recommended to users. The problem is that a recommender system might be able to estimate ratings for a wide range of items but the top K recommendation lists presented to users might still include almost the same recommendations, which actually equates to poor coverage from the merchandising standpoint. We can define the catalog coverage metric as the percentage of items that appear in at least one recommendation list:

$$\text{catalog coverage} = \frac{1}{n} \left| \bigcup_{u=1}^{m} Y_u \right| \tag{5.13}$$

in which n is the total number of items in the catalog. Equation 5.13 uses the union of recommendation lists over all users in the system to estimate the number of covered items. An alternative approach is to count the number of distinct items recommended over a large number of real user sessions.

5.3.7   *The Role of Experimentation*

The metrics described above help to measure the quality of recommendations from several important standpoints. The ultimate goal of a recommender system, however, is to uplift the revenue and conversion rates. Although the discussed metrics provide a solid quality assessment framework, they do not have a strong link to financial performance indicators. This link can be established through practical experimentation, multivariate testing, and uplift measurements.

5.4   OVERVIEW OF RECOMMENDATION METHODS

Thus far, we have described the environment and data sources that a recommender system is integrated with, its business objectives, and the metrics that can be used to evaluate the quality of recommendations. This provides a reasonably solid foundation for the design of recommendation algorithms. This task can be approached from several different perspectives, and there are several families of recommendation methods that differ in the data sources leveraged to make recommendations (rating matrix, catalog data, or contextual information) and the type of rating prediction model. Although we will methodically go through all major categories of recommendation algorithms in the rest of this chapter, it will be worthwhile to briefly review the classification of recommendation methods and make a few general comments before we dive deeper into the details of individual methods.

Recommendation methods can be categorized in a number of ways, depending on the perspective taken. From the algorithmic and information retrieval perspectives, recommendation methods are categorized primarily by the type of predictive model and its inputs. The corresponding hierarchy is shown in Figure 5.4. Historically, the two main families of recommendation methods are content-based filtering and collaborative filtering. Content-based filtering primarily relies on content data, such as textual descriptions of items, and collaborative filtering primarily relies on patterns in the rating matrix. Both approaches can use either formal predictive models or heuristic algorithms that typically search for a neighborhood of similar users or items. In addition to these core methods, there is a wide range of solutions that can

combine the multiple core algorithms into hybrid models, extend them
to account for contextual data and secondary optimization objectives,
or make recommendations in settings where the core methods are not
optimal because, for example, of a lack of data for personalization. We
will thoroughly analyze each of these approaches in the following sections.

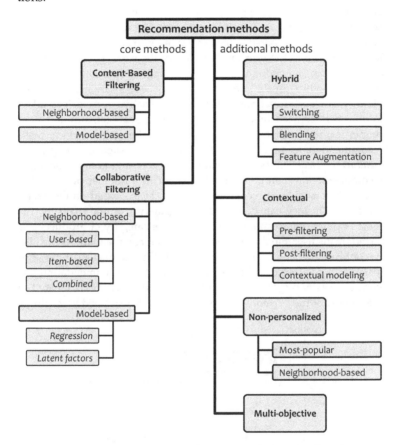

Figure 5.4: Classification of recommendation methods from the algorithmic perspective.

The hierarchy of recommendation methods will look different if we
focus on the usage scenarios rather than algorithmic and implementation details. One possible way to visualize this classification is shown
in Figure 5.5. We basically categorize all usage cases in two dimensions: level of personalization, from non-personalized to segmented to
one-to-one personalized, and usage of the contextual information, from

context unaware to context aware. The core recommendations methods that we mentioned earlier, content-based and collaborative filtering, are mainly focused on the personalized and context-unaware corner of the rectangle and make recommendations based on the interaction histories of individual users, that is, the items that the user rated, browsed, or purchased in the past. In the user interface, such recommendations are often displayed in sections such as *You might also like*, *Inspired by your browsing history*, or simply *Buy it again*. The recommendations can be made even more personalized by taking into account contextual information such as the user location, day of the week, or time of day. A restaurant recommendation system that suggests *Restaurants near your* based on both a user's interaction history and location is an example of this class of recommenders. An alternative approach is taken by non-personalized methods that rely on global statistics and item properties, rather than personal profiles. In the user interface, these recommendations are often presented in sections such as *Most popular*, *Trending*, or *New releases*. Note that personalized and non-personalized recommendations can be blended together in a number of ways. For example, personalized recommendations selected based on the user's interaction history can be sorted by popularity, or, alternatively, the most popular items can be selected within a category of products preferred by the user. Finally, non-personalized recommendations can also be contextualized by user location or marketing channel attributes. For instance, a product detail page can include the recommendation sections *Frequently bought together* and *More like this*, which are created in the context of the currently browsed item and constrained accordingly.

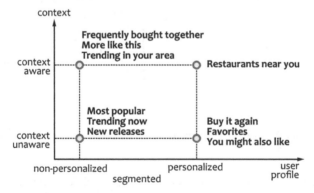

Figure 5.5: Some typical recommendation usage cases and the corresponding categories of recommendation methods.

5.5 CONTENT-BASED FILTERING

The first family of recommendation methods that we will consider relies mainly on the catalog data (content) and uses only a small fraction
of the information available in the rating matrix. This is the reason
why this group of methods is referred to as content filtering. The main
idea of content filtering is quite straightforward: take items that the
user positively rated in the past and recommend other items similar to
these examples, as shown in Figure 5.6. The important constraint, however, is that the measure of similarity is based on the item content [1] and
does not include behavioral data, such as information about items that
are frequently purchased or rated together by other users. This effectively means that a content-based recommender system uses only one
row of the rating matrix – the profile of the user for whom the recommendations are prepared. This limited usage of the rating information
is typically counterbalanced by a similarity function that uses a wide
range of carefully engineered item features. The recommendations are
then ranked according to their similarity scores and, optionally, the
rating values of corresponding items in the profile. For example, assuming that item 1 has the highest rating in the example shown in
Figure 5.6, that is, $r_{u1} > r_{u2}$ and $r_{u1} > r_{u3}$, a candidate item similar
to item 1 can be ranked higher than candidate items equally similar to
items 2 or 3.

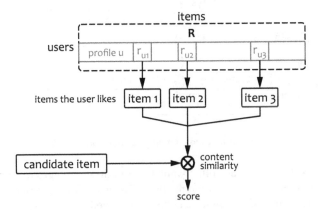

Figure 5.6: Similarity-based approach to content filtering.

The above approach to content filtering is, however, somewhat limited because it inherently relies on a nearest neighbor model for rating

---

1 See Chapter 4 for a detailed discussion of such measures. One of the most common examples would be the TF×IDF distance between textual descriptions discussed in Section 4.3.5.

predictions – a candidate item is scored based on the average pairwise similarity to the items in the user profile. A more generic and flexible interpretation of the content filtering problem is to consider it as a machine learning task in which each item should be rated by using a regression or classification model trained on the user profile. In other words, for each user, we create a dedicated *profile model* that can predict whether the user will like a given item or not. The model is trained by using items from the profile: each item rated by the user is converted into a feature vector by a content analyzer and the corresponding rating is used as a training label. Each candidate item is then also converted into a feature vector and evaluated by using the profile model, as illustrated in Figure 5.7. Finally, the list of recommendations is created by ranking the candidate items according to the predicted ratings and selecting the top ones. Note that the similarity-based approach depicted in Figure 5.6 is a particular case of the more generic schema presented in Figure 5.7 derived under the assumption that the profile model uses the nearest neighbor classifier.

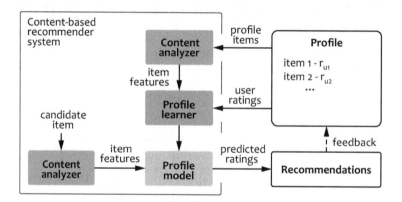

Figure 5.7: Rating prediction approach to content filtering.

Content filtering has both advantages and disadvantages in comparison to other recommendation methods. The main strengths of content-based recommender systems can be summarized as follows:

- *User independence.* Content filtering uses only the ratings provided by the user for whom recommendations are prepared. This can be a significant advantage when the total number of system users is small or the total number of collected ratings is small, as can be the case when a new recommender system is launched and the amount of historical data is limited. This problem is generally known as a *cold-start problem*. The second advantage of user independence is the ability to select recommendations for users with unusual tastes, which may not work well in systems that rely on user similarities and, hence, tend to follow average tastes.

- *New and rare items.* A particular case of the cold-start problem is the recommendation of new or rare items that have a few or no ratings. A recommendation algorithm that heavily relies on ratings may not be able to recommend such items, which negatively impacts the coverage of the catalog. Content filtering is not sensitive to this problem because it relies on content similarity. This capability is especially important in the context of the long-tail property that we discussed earlier – the catalog often contains many rare items that receive few ratings, even over a long period. The same issue appears in domains with a rapidly changing assortment, such as apparel stores, where it can be difficult to accumulate enough statistics about items.

- *Cross-category recommendations.* It can be difficult or impossible to do certain types of recommendations without taking the content into account. For example, it can be challenging to recommend furniture to people who bought clothes based only on purchasing patterns because the number of users who buy from both categories simultaneously is likely to be small [Ghani and Fano, 2002]. As we will see later, content filtering can be an appropriate solution for this kind of task if the content features are engineered properly.

- *Usage of catalog data.* Content filtering is able to leverage catalog data, which is an important source of information for recommendations. This contrasts with some other families of recommendation algorithms that ignore this data.

- *Interpretability.* Recommendations provided by content-based systems are often interpretable and explainable to the user because item scores are based on certain content features. For example, a movie recommender system can provide an explanation that an action movie is recommended because a user highly rated action movies in the past. Other families of recommendation methods can produce results that are much more difficult to explain or interpret.

On the other hand, content filtering has a number of disadvantages that are often the flip sides of its advantages:

- *Feature engineering.* It is clear that feature engineering plays a critically important role in content filtering, and the quality of rating predictions heavily depends on the quality and completeness of catalog data and feature design. Feature engineering for catalog items can be a challenging problem, even for textual product descriptions, because of polysemy, synonymy, and other issues that we have discussed previously in the context of search services. The problem can become far more challenging for images, movies, or music where one needs either to manually attribute each item with content tags, such as a music genre, or to leverage advanced deep learning methods. Content management and feature engineering are indeed the key challenges in practical applications of content filtering, and we will spend a significant amount of time later in this section discussing these aspects.

- *New users.* Although content filtering helps to solve the cold-start problem for new items, it is not able to provide recommendations for new users with empty profiles, which is the second variant of the cold-start problem.

- *Trivial recommendations.* One of the most important drawbacks of content filtering is the tendency to produce trivial recommendations, that is, recommendations that are neither novel nor serendipitous. This property is a direct result of content-based scoring, which favors closely related items, such as books from the same series.

We will continue this section with a more thorough analysis of content-based recommendation methods. We will first consider two specific examples of profile models and will then discuss a few advanced feature engineering methods developed for recommender systems in the retail domain.

5.5.1 Nearest Neighbor Approach

As we have already mentioned, one can build a content-based recommender system by using the k nearest neighbor (kNN) algorithm as a profile model. Let us flesh out the details of how this approach can be implemented. First, let us denote the set of items rated by user u as I_u. We can also assume that each item j is represented as a document d_j with one or more attributes or fields, similarly to the situation we had for search services. Consequently, the set of items I_u corresponds to the set of documents D_u. For each candidate item i, we can calculate similarity metrics between its document representation d_i and each of the documents in D_u. Let us denote k documents in D_u with the highest similarity to d_i as

$$\left\{ d_1^{ui}, \ldots, d_k^{ui} \right\} \subset D_u \tag{5.14}$$

These documents are the k nearest neighbors of d_i with regard to some similarity measure. The user rating for item i can then be predicted as the average rating of nearest neighbors:

$$\widehat{r}_{ui} = \frac{1}{k} \sum_{t=1}^{k} r_u \left(d_t^{ui} \right) \qquad (5.15)$$

in which $r_u(d)$ is the rating of an item that corresponds to document d. This estimate can be further refined by weighting the ratings according to the similarity score:

$$\widehat{r}_{ui} = \frac{1}{k} \sum_{t=1}^{k} r_u \left(d_t^{ui} \right) \cdot \mathrm{sim} \left(d_i, d_j^{ui} \right) \qquad (5.16)$$

The similarity measure is typically calculated by using the techniques that we developed for search services. One popular approach is to use the basic vector space model: the textual fields of the item documents are preprocessed by using stemming and stop words, each document field is represented as a vector of terms, the distance between the corresponding fields is calculated according to the TF×IDF model, and then the scores for different fields are combined into the final similarity score by using some signal mixing function. This is exactly the same as document scoring in search services; the only difference is that the TF×IDF similarity score is calculated for a pair of documents, rather than a document and query.

The second popular option is to use the latent topic model instead of the basic vector space model: each document field is represented as a vector in the space of latent topics by using latent semantic analysis (LSA) or latent Dirichlet allocation (LDA), the distance between the corresponding fields is calculated as a cosine distance between the corresponding vectors in the latent topics space, and the scores for different fields are combined together into the final score. Once again, this approach is almost identical to the LSA and LDA search methods that we discussed earlier. LDA-based scoring is sometimes considered to be superior to LSA and basic TF×IDF models [Falk, 2017]. It has been successfully used in some major industrial systems, such as The New York Times's article recommendation engine [Spangher, 2015]. On the other hand, some reports show that LSA can outperform LDA in certain applications, such as movie recommender systems [Bergamaschi et al., 2014]. Clearly, these results strongly depend on the used data sets and quality evaluation methodologies.

5.5.2 *Naive Bayes Classifier*

The second approach to content filtering that we will consider was developed for book recommendations [Mooney and Roy, 1999]. In contrast to the nearest neighbor regression, this method does not rely on heuristic similarity metrics but uses the Naive Bayes classifier, a standard algorithm for text classification, as a profile model to predict the ratings.

First, let us assume that each item in the catalog has multiple textual attributes. For example, a book may have attributes such as title, authors, synopsis, published reviews, customer comments, related titles, and related authors. We choose to apply tokenization, stemming, and stop words to the attributes and then model each attribute as a bag of words, that is, a vector in which each element corresponds to a word and the value is the number of word occurrences in the attribute text. Consequently, each item is represented as a document with multiple fields, and each field is a bag-of-words model of the corresponding attribute.

Next, we need to create a profile model. Recall that the ultimate goal of a content-based recommender is to rank catalog items for each user in order of preference. We can approach this problem by building a binary classifier that estimates two probabilities: the probability that an item would be rated positively by a user and the probability that it would be rated negatively. The ratio between these two probabilities indicates whether an item would be rated positively rather than negatively, and, consequently, we can use it as a ranking score for the recommended items. Let us assume that a user rates items on a discrete scale from 1 to r_{max}, and all ratings below $r_{max}/2$ are interpreted as negative, whereas ratings above $r_{max}/2$ are interpreted as positive. For example, with a rating scale from 1 to 10 stars, ratings of 1–5 are considered negative (dislike) and ratings of 6–10 are positive (like).

Recall that the main idea of the Naive Bayes text classifier is to estimate the probability of a document d being in a certain class c by using conditional probabilities of document words w occurring in a document of class c, under the assumption that these conditional probabilities are independent. This approach can be expressed by using the following formula:

$$Pr\left(c_j \mid d\right) = \frac{Pr\left(c_j\right)}{Pr\left(d\right)} \prod_{w_i \in d} Pr\left(w_i \mid c_j\right) \tag{5.17}$$

in which c_j is the document class, which in our case is either negative c_0 or positive c_1, $Pr\left(c_j\right)$ is the empirical probability of class c_j in the training data (the fraction of documents that belong to the class), and $\Pr(w_i \mid c_j)$ is the empirical conditional probability of word w_i (the fraction of documents of class c_j that contain this word). This basic Bayes rule needs to be extended to accommodate the multiple fields that we have in each item document. By assuming that each item document has F fields and each field f_{qm} is a text snippet that contains $|f_{qm}|$ words, we can rewrite formula 5.17 for the posterior class probability as follows:

$$\Pr(c_j, d) = \frac{\Pr(c_j)}{\Pr(d)} \prod_{m=1}^{F} \prod_{w_i \in f_m} \Pr(w_i \mid c_j, f_m) \qquad (5.18)$$

The ranking score of the item can then be estimated as

$$\text{score}(d) = \frac{\Pr(c_1 \mid d)}{\Pr(c_0 \mid d)} \qquad (5.19)$$

and items in the recommendation list can be sorted accordingly, from the highest to lowest scores.

Our next step is to estimate the probabilities in formula 5.18 based on the user profile, that is, items rated by the user. As we discussed earlier, user ratings are set on a scale from 1 to r_{max}. If a user has rated Q items, let us map each rating to two auxillary variables, for the positive and negative classes, respectively:

$$\alpha_{q1} = \frac{r_q - 1}{r_{max} - 1}, \quad q = 1, \dots, Q \qquad (5.20)$$

$$\alpha_{q0} = 1 - \alpha_{q1}, \quad q = 1, \dots, Q \qquad (5.21)$$

in which r_q is the original rating in the user profile. Note that we consistently omit the user subscript u in all equations because the algorithm uses only the profile of the active user. The class probability can then be estimated as follows:

$$\Pr(c_j) = \frac{1}{Q} \sum_{q=1}^{Q} \alpha_{qj}, \quad j = 0, 1 \qquad (5.22)$$

The conditional probabilities of words should be estimated for each field of an item document separately. If the number of times word w_i occurs in the field m of document q is denoted as $n_{qm}(w_i)$, we can estimate the conditional probability of the word as

$$\Pr(w_i \mid c_j, \text{field} = m) = \sum_{q=1}^{Q} \alpha_{qj} \cdot \frac{n_{qm}(w_i)}{L_{jm}}, \quad m = 1, \dots, F \quad (5.23)$$

in which L_{jm} is the total weighted length of the texts in field m for class j:

$$L_{jm} = \sum_{q=1}^{Q} \alpha_{qj} \cdot \left| f_{qm} \right|, \quad m = 1, \ldots, F \qquad (5.24)$$

The length of a field is defined as the number of words in its bag-of-words representation. These estimates enable us to evaluate the posterior document class probabilities from equation 5.18 and, finally, to score the items. Note that the probabilities $\Pr(d)$ can be ignored because they cancel each other out in scoring formula 5.19.

EXAMPLE 5.1

▼

Let us consider a numerical example to better understand how the Naive Bayes classifier can produce recommendations and what the limitations of this approach are. Consider an online bookstore where each book in the catalog is represented by a document with two fields: title and synopsis. Let us take a user profile with two books rated on a scale from 1 to 10 and create a profile model from it. The original profile is as follows:

```
Book 1
Title: Machine learning for predictive data analytics
Synopsis: Detailed treatment of data analytics applications
          including price prediction and customer behavior
Rating: 8

Book 2
Title: Machine learning for healthcare and life science
Synopsis: Case studies specific to the challenges of
          working with healthcare data
Rating: 3
```

We first convert the textual fields into bags of words and remove stop words to obtain the following:

```
title₁ :     (machine, learning, predictive, data, analytics)
synopsis₁ :  (detailed, treatment, data, analytics, applications,
             including, price, prediction, customer, behavior)
title₂ :     (machine, learning, healthcare, life, science)
synopsis₂ :  (case, studies, specific, challenges, working,
             healthcare, data)
```

$title_1 :$ (machine, learning, predictive, data, analytics)
$synopsis_1 :$ (detailed, treatment, data, analytics, applications, including, price, prediction, customer, behavior)
$title_2 :$ (machine, learning, healthcare, life, science)
$synopsis_2 :$ (case, studies, specific, challenges, working, healthcare, data)

Next, we calculate the class proximity values according to formulas 5.20 and 5.21.

$$\alpha_{11} = \frac{8-1}{9} = \frac{7}{9} \qquad (5.25)$$

$$\alpha_{10} = 1 - \alpha_{11} = \frac{2}{9} \tag{5.26}$$

$$\alpha_{21} = \frac{3-1}{9} = \frac{2}{9} \tag{5.27}$$

$$\alpha_{20} = 1 - \alpha_{21} = \frac{7}{9} \tag{5.28}$$

We use these values to estimate the class probabilities according to expression 5.22. As the user liked the first book (the rating is 8 out of 10) and disliked the second one (the rating is 3 out of 10), the probabilities are equal:

$$\Pr(c_0) = \frac{1}{2}(\alpha_{10} + \alpha_{20}) = \frac{1}{2}$$
$$\Pr(c_1) = \frac{1}{2}(\alpha_{11} + \alpha_{21}) = \frac{1}{2} \tag{5.29}$$

Calculating the weighted lengths of fields according to formula 5.24, we get

$$L_{0,\,\text{title}} = \alpha_{10}\,|\,\text{title}_1\,| + \alpha_{20}\,|\,\text{title}_2\,| = \frac{2}{9} \cdot 5 + \frac{7}{9} \cdot 5 = 5$$

$$L_{1,\,\text{title}} = \alpha_{11}\,|\,\text{title}_1\,| + \alpha_{21}\,|\,\text{title}_2\,| = 5$$

$$L_{0,\,\text{synopsis}} = \alpha_{10}\,\big|\,\text{synopsis}_1\,\big| + \alpha_{20}\,\big|\,\text{synopsis}_2\,\big| = \frac{23}{3}$$

$$L_{1,\,\text{synopsis}} = \alpha_{11}\,\big|\,\text{synopsis}_1\,\big| + \alpha_{21}\,\big|\,\text{synopsis}_2\,\big| = \frac{28}{3}$$

$$\tag{5.30}$$

Finally, we can estimate the conditional probabilities of words by using expression 5.23. As an illustration, let us estimate the conditional probability of the word *price* in the field *synopsis*, given the negative class:

$$\Pr(\text{price}\,|\,c = 0,\ \text{field} = \text{synopsis})$$

$$= \alpha_{10}\frac{n_{1,\,\text{synopsis}}(\text{price})}{L_{0,\,\text{synopsis}}} + \alpha_{20}\frac{n_{2,\,\text{synopsis}}(\text{price})}{L_{0,\,\text{synopsis}}} \tag{5.31}$$

$$= \frac{2}{9} \cdot \frac{1}{23/3} + \frac{7}{9} \cdot \frac{0}{23/3} = \frac{2}{69}$$

By estimating the probabilities for all combinations of words, classes, and fields, we obtain the results shown in table 5.1. This table is effectively the profile model that would be calculated by a recommender system in advance, stored, and then used to rank recommendations in accordance with formulas 5.18 and 5.19.

	TITLE		SYNOPSIS	
	$c = 0$	$c = 1$	$c = 0$	$c = 1$
ANALYTICS	0.044	0.160	0.029	0.083
APPLICATIONS	0.000	0.000	0.029	0.083
BEHAVIOR	0.000	0.000	▶ 0.029	▶ 0.083
CASE	0.000	0.000	0.100	0.024
CHALLENGES	0.000	0.000	0.100	0.024
CUSTOMER	0.000	0.000	0.029	0.083
DATA	0.044	0.160	0.130	0.110
DETAILED	0.000	0.000	0.029	0.083
HEALTHCARE	▶ 0.160	▶ 0.044	0.100	0.024
INCLUDING	0.000	0.000	0.029	0.083
LEARNING	▶ 0.200	▶ 0.200	0.000	0.000
LIFE	0.160	0.044	0.000	0.000
MACHINE	▶ 0.200	▶ 0.200	0.000	0.000
PREDICTION	0.000	0.000	0.029	0.083
PREDICTIVE	0.044	0.160	0.000	0.000
PRICE	0.000	0.000	0.029	0.083
SCIENCE	0.160	0.044	0.000	0.000
SPECIFIC	0.000	0.000	0.100	0.024
STUDIES	0.000	0.000	0.100	0.024
TREATMENT	0.000	0.000	0.029	0.083
WORKING	0.000	0.000	0.100	0.024

Table 5.1: Example of a Naive Bayes profile model.

Table 5.1 provides a few useful insights into the logic of the Naive Bayes recommender. First, we can see that the words that occur in both positively and negatively rated items cancel each other out. For example, both books have the words *machine learning* in their titles, so each of these words has an equal probability value for the positive and negative classes, and these values will cancel each other out in ratio 5.19 used for scoring. Second, we can see that words present in the attributes of the negatively scored book (e. g., *healthcare*) are interpreted as negative signals, in the sense that their probability values for the negative class are higher than those for the positive class. Similarly, some other words (e. g., *behavior*) are interpreted as positive signals. In practice, this interpretation may or may not be correct. In our example, the user has disliked the second book about machine learning for healthcare. We do not really know the reason – it may be that this particular book is not well written or the healthcare domain is not relevant for the user. If it is assumed that the user has rated the book after purchasing and reading it, the first explanation is probably more likely than the second one because the user was almost certainly aware that the book was about the healthcare domain and chose it deliberately. The Naive Bayes model, however, interprets the word *healthcare* as a negative signal, so all books with this word in the title will be scored lower. This limited ability to differentiate between the quality and relevance of content is one of the major shortcomings of content-based filtering. As we will see later, collaborative filtering takes a different approach to the problem and places more emphasis on item quality signals.

▲

5.5.3 *Feature Engineering for Content Filtering*

The main idea of content filtering is to create a regression or classification model that scores the item content. It is clear that this approach requires careful feature engineering because the quality of classification heavily depends on the available item attributes and the quality of their modeling. Trivial attributes often lead to trivial or meaningless recommendations, whereas thoughtfully designed features can enable a recommender system to accurately predict user decisions. Let us illustrate this problem with an example from the apparel domain [Ghani and Fano, 2002; Ghani et al., 2006]. Consider a user who purchased and rated several garments, such as dresses, blouses, or coats. We can expect that an average product information system can provide some basic information about each of these items, such as a product category, price, and color. A basic recommender system that calculates similarities between items by using such attributes is likely to recommend items from the same categories, in the same price range, and of the same color. Although this approach does not necessarily produce bad recommendations, it is flawed in at least two ways. First, customer choice is heavily influenced and driven by personality, attitudes, and lifestyle. Customers are likely to think about garments in terms of style and functionality, choosing between casual and formal, sporty and businesslike, conservative and flamboyant. Both users and garments can be described in terms of such *psychographic features*, and recommendations can be made based on a user's affinity to certain styles and attitudes. A recommender system that uses only the basic attributes, such as product category and price, is typically not able to recognize these latent affinities. Second, certain types of recommendations, such as cross-category recommendations, are fundamentally difficult to do if nothing but basic features are available. One of the reasons is that the layout of product attributes can be different in different categories, so it can even be difficult to define the similarity metric of a profile model that can compare and score items across categories. For example, a large department store may sell apparel, kitchenware, and furniture. It can, however, be challenging to recommend furniture based on purchases in the clothing department because garments and furniture have different attributes and different attribute semantics. For example, the size attribute has a totally different meaning for a dress relative to that for a bed. Again, psychographic features can be a solution because users who buy conservative garments can be recommended to consider furniture of a conservative style and so on.

One observation that we can make is that textual product attributes, such as product name, description, and customer reviews, often carry an implicit signal about the psychographic characteristics of a product. Merchandisers who create product names and descriptions, for example, deliberately choose certain words such as *stylish*, *sexy*, or *luxury* to make a product appealing to certain audiences. This fact can be leveraged to measure product affinity to certain psychographic properties and to define the corresponding product features. These features can then be used to train and evaluate a profile model. More specifically, we can use the following method to extract implicit psychographic features [Ghani and Fano, 2002]:

- We first define the set of product features to be extracted by using domain knowledge. Table 5.2 provides examples of such features for the apparel domain.

FEATURE NAME	FEATURE VALUES
AGE GROUP	The most appropriate age group for the product: juniors, teens, mature, etc.
FUNCTIONALITY	A typical product usage scenario: evening wear, sportswear, business casual, business formal, etc.
DEGREE OF FORMALITY	From informal to very formal
DEGREE OF CONSERVATIVENESS	From very conservative clothes, such as gray suits, to flashy clothes
DEGREE OF SPORTINESS	From sloppy or formal to athletic
DEGREE OF TRENDINESS	From timeless classic to fast fashion
DEGREE OF BRAND APPEAL	From unknown or unappealing brands to highly appealing brands

Table 5.2: Example of psychographic features for the apparel domain.

- Next, a subset of items is manually labeled by domain experts according to the features defined in the previous step. This set is used to train classification models that predict psychographic labels based on textual product descriptions and other standard attributes, such as brand name and size. For example, one can use a Naive Bayes classifier to identify words in product descriptions that indicate a high degree of formality or trendiness.

- The classification models are used to label the remaining items. This enables merchandisers to tag even very large and frequently changing catalogs with a limited amount of manual effort.

It is worth noting that some recommender systems completely rely on manually created item attributes. One of the best known examples is Pandora Internet Radio, a music streaming and recommendation service. Pandora uses professional music analysts to manually attribute each song in their catalog with 450 features, such as *Child or Child-like Vocal* and *Melodic Articulation Clean-to-Dirty*. This analysis, known as the Music Genome Project, requires significant effort because the catalog contains hundreds of thousands of songs and the classification of a single song takes about 20 minutes [Walker, 2009]. This metadata, however, is Pandora's core asset and a major competitive advantage in a market of music discovery services.

5.6   INTRODUCTION TO COLLABORATIVE FILTERING

Content-based filtering attempts to approximate user tastes and judgements by a similarity measure between the contents of catalog items. The fundamental shortcoming of this approach is that human tastes cannot be easily expressed in terms of basic product attributes, so manual product tagging and advanced feature engineering is often needed to achieve good results. On the other hand, the rating matrix captures a lot of information about user tastes and judgements. Indeed, each known rating can be interpreted as a manually set product attribute, and, consequently, the collection of ratings and other feedback data from users can be viewed as a crowdsourcing approach to product tagging with psychographic features. Content filtering does not fully leverage this valuable information because recommendations are created by using a single profile model. This line of thinking leads us to a different family of recommendation methods known as collaborative filtering.

The term *collaborative filtering* was coined by developers of Tapestry, a recommender system for news and articles created at Xerox PARC in 1992 [Goldberg et al., 1992; Terry, 1993]. In the context of Tapestry, collaborative filtering meant that users were able to provide feedback on news emails and prioritize incoming emails based on the feedback provided by other users. It was essentially a functional feature for email filtering, not a recommendation algorithm. The idea of prioritizing recommendations based on the feedback provided by other users, however, had a lot of traction and resulted in the development of new recommendation methods that leveraged this approach and the wide adoption of these methods in industrial recommender systems, including the major ones developed by Amazon and Netflix. The meaning of collaborative filtering has also transformed and become more focused on making rating predictions based on information available in the rating matrix. Collaborative filtering in this newer, narrower sense is a pure matrix completion problem. Consequently, collaborative filtering methods are essentially matrix completion algorithms that use the rating matrix as the only input. Under the hood, collaborative filtering uses a predictive model to capture interactions between users and items known from the rating matrix and to predict a rating for a given pair of user and item based on how similar users rated similar items in the past.

The key advantage of collaborative methods is that they are capable of making recommendations based only on the patterns and similarities available in the rating matrix, without any additional information about catalog items. This makes these methods much more universal than content-based filtering, which requires domain-specific knowledge, data, and feature engineering effort. Even more importantly, collaborative filtering implicitly accounts for the psychographic profiles of users and items because the ratings capture human tastes and judgements. This helps to produce non-trivial recommendations. On the other hand, collaborative filtering has a number of weaknesses:

- *Rating sparsity.* A collaborative recommender system requires a sufficient number of known and trustworthy ratings. If the rating matrix is too sparse, it can be difficult or impossible to build a reliable rating prediction model.

- *New users and items.* Collaborative filtering predicts ratings for a given user or item based on the known ratings for this user or item. This means that collaborative filtering does not work well for new users and items or for users and items with very few known ratings. Collaborative filtering is, therefore, more vulnerable to the cold-start problem than content-based filtering, which leverages content information in addition to the rating data.

- *Popularity bias.* Content filtering makes recommendations based on typical patterns in the rating matrix, so it is inherently biased towards popular items and standard choices. This limits the ability to produce non-trivial recommendations and recommendations for users with unusual tastes.

- *Product standardization.* Although collaborative filtering is able to recognize that some items are frequently bought together, it essentially treats each item as an opaque independent entity. This can create certain modeling challenges for products with a complex internal structure, such as garment variants in different sizes, customizable products, or products that are upgraded over time.

- *Domain knowledge.* As we mentioned earlier, one of the key advantages of collaborative filtering is its ability to work with an abstract rating matrix without any assumption about the nature of items and their attributes. Although this is generally true, collaborative filtering methods may need to make certain domain-specific assumptions. For example, a collaborative recommender system may or may not assume that customer tastes change over time and, consequently, may or may not account for rating recency.

Collaborative filtering algorithms are usually categorized into two subgroups: neighborhood-based and model-based methods. Neighborhood-based (also known as memory-based) methods predict unknown ratings for a given user or item by using the nearest neighbor approach, that is, by finding the most similar users or items and averaging known ratings from their records. Model-based methods go beyond the nearest neighbor approach and use other, usually more sophisticated, predictive models. Although the nearest neighbor algorithm can also be considered as a sort of predictive model and, hence, the boundary between the two categories is a bit blurry, it makes sense to separate them because of the high practical importance of neighborhood-based methods. We will analyze both approaches in detail in later sections.

5.6.1 Baseline Estimates

Most practically used collaborative filtering models are able to capture relatively complex interactions between users and items by recognizing sophisticated patterns in the rating matrix. Before discussing these models, it is important to note that observed ratings typically follow a few simple but strong patterns that can be captured by using a relatively simple model. This basic model can produce baseline rating estimates that can be used as building blocks in more advanced collaborative filtering methods.

A typical rating matrix exhibits strong user and item *biases* – some users systematically give higher (or lower) ratings than other users, and some items systematically receive higher ratings than other items [Koren, 2009; Ekstrand et al., 2011]. This can be explained by the fact that some users can be more or less critical than others, and items, of course, differ in their quality. We can account for these systematic user and item effects by defining the baseline estimate for an unknown user rating r_{ui} as

$$b_{ui} = \mu + b_u + b_i \qquad (5.32)$$

in which μ is the overall average rating in the rating matrix R, b_u is the observed deviation of user u from the average, and b_i is the observed deviation of item i from the average. In practice, the user and item biases have strong effects, and, consequently, the baseline estimate defined by equation 5.32 has substantial predictive power. Although this model captures only the average user and item effects, it can help to absorb the biases and isolate the signal that represents user–item interactions that can be captured by more specialized models.

The biases μ, b_u, and b_i can be estimated one after the other as the average residual errors of the previous estimate. This means that we first compute μ, and then estimate item biases b_i as follows:

$$b_i = \frac{1}{|U_i|} \sum_{i \in U_i} (r_{ui} - \mu) \qquad (5.33)$$

in which U_i is the set of users who rated item i. Then, the user biases are estimated as

$$b_u = \frac{1}{|I_u|} \sum_{u \in I_u} (r_{ui} - \mu - b_i) \qquad (5.34)$$

in which I_u are items rated by user u. The estimates calculated with formulas 5.33 and 5.34 can be unstable in the case of a sparse rating matrix where only a few known ratings are available for a user or item. The stability of the estimates can be improved by adding regularization parameters λ_1 and λ_2 as follows:

$$b_i = \frac{1}{|U_i| + \lambda_1} \sum_{i \in U_i} (r_{ui} - \mu)$$

$$b_u = \frac{1}{|I_u| + \lambda_2} \sum_{u \in I_u} (r_{ui} - \mu - b_i) \qquad (5.35)$$

The regularization parameters decrease the magnitudes of biases b_i and b_u when the user or item has few ratings, so the baseline estimate described by equation 5.32 becomes closer to the global mean and less dependent on the unreliable bias estimates.

The bias parameters can be estimated more accurately by solving the following least squares problem [Koren, 2009]:

$$\min_{b_i,\, b_u} \sum_{i,u \in R} (r_{ui} - \mu - b_i - b_u) + \lambda \cdot \left(\sum_u b_u^2 + \sum_i b_i^2 \right) \quad (5.36)$$

in which R is the training set of known ratings and λ is a regularization parameter. This is a straightforward optimization problem that can be solved by using standard methods, such as stochastic gradient descent. The advantage of this approach is that expression 5.36 can be easily modified and extended to include additional constraints and variables, such as temporal effects.

EXAMPLE 5.2

To illustrate the baseline estimates, as well as other collaborative filtering methods, we will need a sample rating matrix. We have chosen to use an example with movie ratings that became very popular after the Netflix Prize. It is worth noting, however, that all of the collaborative filtering methods considered in this chapter are domain agnostic, in the sense that they do not have any dependency on the nature of items, so the movie names are provided solely for the purpose of convenient reading and can be replaced by products from other domains like groceries or apparel.

Our example is a rating matrix with six movies and six users, as shown in table 5.3. The ratings are given on a 5-star scale where 1 is the lowest possible rating and 5 is the highest. The matrix contains 28 known and 8 missing ratings, so it is very dense in comparison with real-life rating matrices, where more than 99% of possible ratings can be missing. One can easily notice a few patterns in the example matrix. First, we can see that the first three users apparently like drama movies (*Forrest Gump*, *Titanic*, and *The Godfather*) more than action movies (*Batman*, *The Matrix*, and *Alien*). The last three users, in contrast, apparently prefer action to drama. Next, we note that user 3 generously gives high ratings to most movies, whereas user 2 seems to be more critical. We would expect that a good collaborative filtering model would be able to recognize such patterns and make adequate predictions.

	FORREST GUMP	TITANIC	THE GODFATHER	BATMAN	THE MATRIX	ALIEN
USER 1	5	4	—	1	2	1
USER 2	4	—	3	1	1	2
USER 3	—	5	5	—	3	3
USER 4	2	—	1	4	5	4
USER 5	2	2	2	—	4	—
USER 6	1	2	1	—	5	4

Table 5.3: Example of a rating matrix for a movie recommendation service.

Let us now calculate the baseline estimates for the missing ratings. Calculating the global average and bias values by using formulas 5.33 and 5.34, we get

$$\mu = 2.82$$
$$b_i = (-0.02 \quad +0.42 \quad -0.42 \quad -0.82 \quad +0.51 \quad -0.02) \quad (5.37)$$
$$b_u = (-0.23 \quad -0.46 \quad +1.05 \quad +0.53 \quad -0.44 \quad -0.31)$$

Although quite trivial, we should note that these coefficients correctly capture the fact that user 3 tends to give high ratings (bias +1.05) and the *Batman* movie has generally low ratings (bias –0.82). Substituting this result into baseline estimation formula 5.32, we obtain the final rating predictions shown in the table 5.4. Note that this result generally does not match our intuitive expectations about affinities between users and movie genres.

	FORREST GUMP	TITANIC	THE GODFATHER	BATMAN	THE MATRIX	ALIEN
USER 1	5	4	[2.16]	1	2	1
USER 2	4	[2.78]	3	1	1	2
USER 3	[3.85]	5	5	[3.05]	3	3
USER 4	2	[3.78]	1	4	5	4
USER 5	2	2	2	[1.55]	4	[2.35]
USER 6	1	2	1	[1.68]	5	4

Table 5.4: Example of baseline rating estimates.

▲

5.7   NEIGHBORHOOD-BASED COLLABORATIVE FILTERING

The neighborhood-based approach to collaborative filtering relies on a similarity measure between users or items defined in terms of the ratings that two users or two items have in common. These two cases, user-based and item-based similarity, are distinct but have a lot in common.

Let us first consider the user-based approach illustrated in Figure 5.8. Recall that the goal of a recommender system is to predict the ratings that a certain user would give to different catalog items and then to create a list of recommendations by selecting and ranking items with the highest predicted ratings. If we assume that the user has already rated some items in the catalog, so that the corresponding row of the rating matrix contains some known values, we can try to find more users who rated the same items and did it with a similar sentiment, in the sense that these users mainly like the items positively rated by the given user and dislike the negatively rated ones. The key idea of neighborhood-based collaborative filtering is that such users are likely to have the same tastes and preferences as the given user, so their past ratings can be used to predict the given user's future ratings. Consequently, the system can recommend items that have not been rated by the given user but have been positively rated by at least some neighborhood users. The predicted ratings for these items can be obtained by averaging the ratings provided by the neighborhood users.

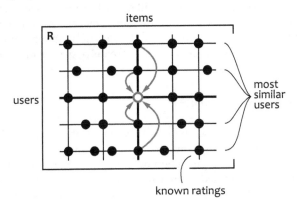

Figure 5.8: User-based collaborative filtering.

The item-based approach shown in Figure 5.9 is structurally similar to what we just described, but users (rows) are replaced with items (columns). In order to predict ratings for a given item, we first find items that are similar to the given one, in the sense that they are similarly rated by the same users. Next, the rating that a given user will give to this item is estimated based on the ratings that the user gave to other items in the neighborhood. Once again, the key assumption is that a user who positively rated a few items in the past will probably like items that are rated similarly to these past choices by many other users.

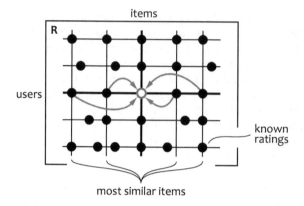

Figure 5.9: Item-based collaborative filtering.

Both user-based and item-based collaborative filtering require the definition of a similarity measure, between either users or items, and some rating averaging method. Although the user-based and item-based approaches are structurally similar, they can use different measures and there are many different variants of similarity and rating averaging formulas for each approach. We delve deeper into these details in the next sections.

5.7.1 User-based Collaborative Filtering

The two main steps of neighborhood-based collaborative filtering are the selection of users or items that should be included in the neighborhood and the rating prediction by averaging neighbors' ratings. In the case of the user-based approach, this means that we need to define two key functions: a similarity measure for users and a rating averaging formula. There are many different variants of these functions described in the academic literature and industrial reports, so we will first describe one the most basic and well-known options and will then discuss possible variations and improvements.

To define the similarity measure, let us consider two users u and v who have rated items I_u and I_v, respectively. The set of items rated by both users is

$$I_{uv} = I_u \cap I_v \qquad (5.38)$$

The similarity measure can then be defined based on this itemset. The most common way is to use the Pearson correlation coefficient, defined as follows [Herlocker et al., 1999]:

$$\text{sim}(u, v) = \frac{\sum_{i \in I_{uv}} (r_{ui} - \mu_u)(r_{vi} - \mu_v)}{\sqrt{\sum_{i \in I_{uv}} (r_{ui} - \mu_u)^2} \sqrt{\sum_{i \in I_{uv}} (r_{vi} - \mu_v)^2}} \qquad (5.39)$$

in which μ_u and μ_v are the average user ratings:

$$\mu_u = \frac{1}{|I_{uv}|} \sum_{i \in I_{uv}} r_{ui} \qquad (5.40)$$

Note that formula 5.40 computes the average user rating over the set of common items I_{uv}, as required by the definition of the Pearson correlation coefficient. Hence, this value is not constant for a given user u but is unique for each pair of users. In practice, however, it is quite common to use the global average rating for user u computed over all items I_u rated by this user [Aggarwal, 2016].

The similarity measure allows us to identify k users who are most similar to the target user u. The size of the neighborhood k is a parameter of the recommendation algorithm. As our goal is to predict the rating for user u and item i by averaging the ratings given for this item by other users, we select not simply the top k most similar users but the top k most similar users who have rated item i. Let us denote this set of peers as S_{ui}^k. This set can include less than k users if the rating matrix does not contain enough ratings for item i or enough peers of user u with commonly rated items. The rating can then be estimated as a similarity-weighted average of the peer ratings:

$$\hat{r}_{ui} = \mu_u + \frac{\sum_{v \in S_{ui}^k} \text{sim}(u, v) \cdot (r_{vi} - \mu_v)}{\sum_{v \in S_{ui}^k} |\text{sim}(u, v)|} \qquad (5.41)$$

Formula 5.41 exploits the idea of separating the user biases from the interaction signal, which we discussed earlier in the section devoted to baseline estimates. The global user averages μ_u and μ_v are considered biases and are initially subtracted from the raw ratings, then the interaction signal is estimated as a product of similarity measures and mean-centered ratings, and finally the user bias μ_u is added back to account for the preferences of the target user.

Let us now discuss several alternatives of formulas 5.39 and 5.41. Most of these variations are heuristic adjustments that can help to improve the accuracy of estimates and computational stability in practical applications [Su and Khoshgoftaar, 2009; Breese et al., 1998]. First, we consider several choices for the similarity measure:

BASIC SIMILARITY FUNCTIONS. The Pearson correlation coefficient is known to be a good option for the similarity measure, but one can choose to use other metrics including cosine similarity, Spearman rank correlation coefficient, and mean-squared difference. For example, the cosine similarity between two users can be defined as follows:

$$\text{sim}(u, v) = \frac{\sum_{i \in I_{uv}} r_{ui} \cdot r_{vi}}{\sqrt{\sum_{i \in I_{uv}} r_{ui}^2} \sqrt{\sum_{i \in I_{uv}} r_{vi}^2}} \qquad (5.42)$$

These alternatives are generally considered inferior to the Pearson correlation and, as we will see shortly, it can be more efficient to calculate similarity coefficients by using regression analysis, rather than heuristically selecting and tuning similarity functions.

DISCOUNTED SIMILARITY. The similarity measure is calculated based only on the items rated by both users. The reliability of this estimate depends on the number of items the users have in common, so it is often beneficial to adjust the similarity measure according to the item support (the number of ratings that two items have in common) [Koren, 2008]:

$$\text{sim}'(u, v) = \frac{|I_{uv}|}{|I_{uv}| + \lambda} \cdot \text{sim}(u, v) \qquad (5.43)$$

By increasing the regularization parameter λ, we can shrink the unreliable similarity coefficients with low support.

INVERSE USER FREQUENCY. The Pearson correlation coefficient, as well as many other standard similarity metrics, treats all items in the set I_{uv} equally. One can argue that this approach is not optimal because some items can be more indicative than others. For example, if two users positively rate some rare or niche item, it is probably a stronger indicator of their similarity than if they both like a very popular commodity item. This idea is inspired by the TF×IDF text similarity metric, in which each word is weighted proportionally to its inverse frequency. More formally, we can define the inverse user frequency (IUF) for item i as

$$w_i = \log\left(\frac{m}{|U_i|}\right) \qquad (5.44)$$

in which m is the total number of users and $| U_i |$ is the number of users who rated item i. This weight can then be inserted into the Pearson correlation formula as follows:

$$\frac{\sum_{i \in I_{uv}} w_i \left(r_{ui} - \mu_u\right) \left(r_{vi} - \mu_v\right)}{\sqrt{\sum_{i \in I_{uv}} w_i \left(r_{ui} - \mu_u\right)^2} \sqrt{\sum_{i \in I_{uv}} w_i \left(r_{vi} - \mu_v\right)^2}} \qquad (5.45)$$

DEFAULT RATINGS. The similarity measure for users u and v is typically calculated over the intersection of rated items $I_u \cap I_v$. Given a sparse rating matrix, this intersection is typically small, which decreases the reliability of the estimates. An alternative is to calculate the similarity over the union of rated items $I_u \cup I_v$, rather than the intersection, by inserting some default (neutral) rating for items that have only been rated by one of the users.

Rating prediction function 5.41 mixes together known mean-centered ratings by using the similarity scores as weights. There exist several alternative options for this function that differ in rating centering and weighting logic:

STANDARD SCORE (Z-SCORE). In statistics, the standard score (also known as the z-score) of a data point x is the deviation of this point from the mean measured in standard deviations:

$$z(x) = \frac{x - \mu}{\sigma} \qquad (5.46)$$

The standard score can be viewed as a normalization of the mean-centered values by standard deviation. We can use standard scores as an alternative to mean-centering in the rating prediction formula. First, we calculate the standard score of a rating in the context of a given user as

$$z\left(r_{ui}\right) = \frac{r_{ui} - \mu_u}{\sigma_u} \qquad (5.47)$$

in which σ_u is the standard deviation of the known user ratings:

$$\sigma_u = \sqrt{\frac{\sum_{i \in I_u} \left(r_{ui} - \mu_u\right)^2}{| I_u | - 1}} \qquad (5.48)$$

The rating prediction function can then be redefined with the standard scores instead of mean-centered ratings:

$$\hat{r}_{ui} = \mu_u + \sigma_u \cdot \frac{\sum_{v \in S_{ui}^k} \text{sim}(u, v) \cdot z\left(r_{vi}\right)}{\sum_{v \in S_{ui}^k} | \text{sim}(u, v) |} \qquad (5.49)$$

Similarly to mean-centering, we first transform the original ratings by applying formula 5.47 and then perform an inverse transformation by multiplying the result with the standard deviation of user ratings σ_u and adding back the mean μ_u. The standard score approach boosts ratings from users with low rating variance and decreases the weight of ratings from users with high variance.

BASELINE-CENTERING. Another alternative to mean-centering is baseline-centering, which uses the baselines estimates given by formula 5.32, instead of the average user ratings [Koren, 2008]. The baseline-centered prediction formula can be defined as follows:

$$\hat{r}_{ui} = b_{ui} + \frac{\sum_{v \in S_{ui}^k} sim(u, v) \cdot (r_{vi} - b_{ui})}{\sum_{v \in S_{ui}^k} |sim(u, v)|} \qquad (5.50)$$

AMPLIFICATION. The standard rating prediction function uses similarity scores as weights. We can choose to apply some nonlinear transformation to these raw scores to amplify certain ratings. For example, the following transformation boosts high similarity scores for the amplification parameter $\rho > 1$:

$$sim'(u, v) = sim(u, v) \cdot \left| sim^{\rho - 1}(u, v) \right| \qquad (5.51)$$

NEIGHBORHOOD SELECTION. The quality of recommendations generally depends on the number of users k included in the neighborhood. Some studies show that the accuracy of rating predictions can monotonically increase as the size of the neighborhood increases, given an advanced, properly designed, and well-tuned rating prediction model [Koren, 2008]. The incremental improvement delivered by the neighborhood expansion gradually diminishes, of course, and becomes negligible after a certain point. Some other studies, however, show that neighborhoods that are too large can negatively impact the accuracy of recommendations made by basic neighborhood-based methods because of noise added by neighbors with low similarity [Herlocker et al., 1999; Bellogín et al., 2014]. The size of the neighborhood k can be limited by either an empirically determined constant value or a similarity threshold that causes neighbors with small similarity scores to be filtered out.

EXAMPLE 5.3

Let us briefly illustrate the user-based approach with a numerical example by using the data in table 5.3. The first step is to estimate the pairwise similarities between the users according to formula 5.39. This generates the following similarity matrix:

$$
\begin{array}{c}
\\
\text{User 1} \\
\text{User 2} \\
\text{User 3} \\
\text{User 4} \\
\text{User 5} \\
\text{User 6}
\end{array}
\begin{array}{cccccc}
\text{User 1} & \text{User 2} & \text{User 3} & \text{User 4} & \text{User 5} & \text{User 6} \\
\left[\begin{array}{cccccc}
1.00 & 0.87 & 0.94 & -0.79 & -0.59 & -0.78 \\
0.87 & 1.00 & 0.87 & -0.84 & -0.81 & -0.88 \\
0.94 & 0.87 & 1.00 & -0.93 & -0.87 & -0.91 \\
-0.79 & -0.84 & -0.93 & 1.00 & 0.85 & 0.95 \\
-0.59 & -0.81 & -0.87 & 0.85 & 1.00 & 0.94 \\
-0.78 & -0.88 & -0.91 & 0.95 & 0.94 & 1.00
\end{array}\right]
\end{array}
\quad (5.52)
$$

We can see that the first three users are positively correlated to each other and negatively correlated with the last three. The similarity matrix allows one to look up a neighborhood of the top k most similar users for a given target user and mix their ratings to make a prediction. For example, let us predict the missing rating for user 1 and *The Godfather* movie by assuming the neighborhood size $k = 2$. The most similar neighbors are users 3 and 2 who rated *The Godfather* as 5 and 3, respectively. Applying rating prediction formula 5.41, we get the following estimate:

$$
\begin{aligned}
\hat{r}_{13} &= \mu_1 + \frac{\text{sim}(1,3) \cdot (r_{33} - \mu_3) + \text{sim}(1,2) \cdot (r_{23} - \mu_2)}{|\text{sim}(1,3)| + |\text{sim}(1,2)|} \\
&= 2.60 + \frac{0.94 \cdot (5 - 4.00) + 0.87 \cdot (3 - 2.20)}{0.94 + 0.87} = 3.50
\end{aligned}
\quad (5.53)
$$

By repeating this process for all missing ratings, we obtain the results shown in table 5.5. Note that these estimates look more intuitive and accurate than the baseline estimates in table 5.4.

In practice, user-based recommendation methods can face scalability challenges as the number of system users approaches tens and hundreds of millions. If the neighborhood for the target user is determined at the time that the recommendations are requested, similarity metrics need to be calculated between the target user and all other users in the system online. If the neighborhoods are computed in advance, the amount of computations will be a quadratic function of the number of users. In addition, the target user profile might not be available in advance (e. g., the browsing history within the current web session). One possible way to work around this limitation is to switch from user similarities to item similarities, as we will discuss in next section.

	FORREST GUMP	TITANIC	THE GODFATHER	BATMAN	THE MATRIX	ALIEN
USER 1	5	4	[3.50]	1	2	1
USER 2	4	[3.40]	3	1	1	2
USER 3	[6.11]	5	5	[2.59]	3	3
USER 4	2	[2.64]	1	4	5	4
USER 5	2	2	2	[3.62]	4	[3.61]
USER 6	1	2	1	[3.76]	5	4

Table 5.5: Example of ratings predicted with the user-based collaborative filtering algorithm.

5.7.2   Item-based Collaborative Filtering

The main idea of the item-based approach is to recommend items that are similar to items that have been positively rated by the target user by computing a similarity measure between the items based on the known ratings from other users. This approach is similar to content-based recommendations in the sense that recommendations are made based on the similarity between items, although the nature of the similarity measure is totally different. At the same time, this approach is structurally similar to user-based collaborative filtering because both methods are based on the notion of neighborhoods and, consequently, use the same algorithmic framework [Linden et al., 2003; Sarwar et al., 2001].

In order to predict the rating that user u would give to item i, the item-based recommender system first determines the neighborhood of item i, that is, the set of k most similar items. To calculate the similarity measure between two items i and j, let us denote the set of users who rated item i as U_i, the set of users who rated item j as U_j, and the users who rated both items as

$$U_{ij} = U_i \cap U_j \tag{5.54}$$

The similarity can then be measured as the Pearson correlation coefficient between the vectors of common ratings:

$$\text{sim}(i,j) = \frac{\sum_{u \in U_{ij}} (r_{ui} - \mu_i)(r_{uj} - \mu_j)}{\sqrt{\sum_{u \in U_{ij}} (r_{ui} - \mu_i)^2}\sqrt{\sum_{u \in U_{ij}} (r_{uj} - \mu_j)^2}} \tag{5.55}$$

in which μ_i and μ_j are the average ratings for items i and j, respectively. This formula is the same as the Pearson correlation for users in equation 5.39; the only difference is that users (rows) are replaced by items (columns). All items rated by user u can then be sorted by their similarity to given item i, and the top k most similar items can be selected from this list. Let us denote this neighborhood of item i as Q_{ui}^k. Note that the neighborhood includes only the items rated by the target user u and not the most similar items in the catalog in general, so set Q_{ui}^k converges to I_u as k increases. The rating can then be predicted as a weighted average of ratings of the top k most similar items by using mean-centered ratings as inputs:

$$\hat{r}_{ui} = \mu_i + \frac{\sum_{j \in Q_{ui}^k} sim(i,j) \cdot (r_{uj} - \mu_j)}{\sum_{j \in Q_{ui}^k} |\, sim(i,j)\,|} \tag{5.56}$$

Similarly to the user-based approach, formulas 5.55 and 5.56 are just the basic options, which can be adjusted and improved with the various techniques we discussed earlier, such as discounted similarity and weight amplification. Most of these techniques are applicable both to user-based and item-based methods. For example, one can use baseline-centered input ratings instead of mean-centered ones to improve the accuracy of predictions [Koren, 2008]:

$$\hat{r}_{ui} = b_{ui} + \frac{\sum_{j \in Q_{ui}^k} sim(i,j) \cdot (r_{uj} - b_{uj})}{\sum_{j \in Q_{ui}^k} |\, sim(i,j)\,|} \tag{5.57}$$

5.7.3 Comparison of User-based and Item-based Methods

The item-based approach was proposed years after the first user-based methods appeared, but it has quickly gained popularity because of better scalability and computational efficiency [Linden et al., 2003; Koren and Bell, 2011]. One of the key advantages is that the total number of items m in the system is often small enough to precalculate and store the m × m item similarity matrix, so the top k recommendations can be quickly looked up for a given user profile. This enables a more scalable architecture for the recommender system: the heavy computations required to create the similarity matrix are done in the background, and the recommendation service uses this matrix to make recommendations in real time. Although the same strategy can be applied to user-based methods, it can be very expensive or completely impractical in recommender systems with a high number of users. Finally, some studies found that item-based methods consistently outperform user-based approaches in terms of prediction accuracy for certain important data sets, such as Netflix data [Bell and Koren, 2007].

At the same time, it should be noted that user-based approaches are able to capture certain relationships that might not be recognized by item-based methods [Koren and Bell, 2011]. Recall that the item-based approach predicts rating r_{ui} based on the ratings that user u gave to the items similar to i. This prediction is unlikely to be accurate if none of the items rated by the user is similar to i. On the other hand, it may still be the case that the user-based approach will identify users similar to u who rated i, so the rating can be reliably predicted. As we will see later, some advanced recommendation methods combine item-based and user-based models to take advantage of both methods.

The ratio between the number of users and items is one of the key considerations in the choice of approach. In many retail applications, the item-based approach is preferable because the number of items is smaller than the number of users. The number of items, however, can exceed the number of users in some other domains. For example, an article recommender system for researchers can benefit from the user-based solution because the total number of all research articles ever published reaches many hundreds of millions, whereas the research community that uses the system is relatively smaller [Jack et al., 2016].

5.7.4 *Neighborhood Methods as a Regression Problem*

The neighborhood methods that we considered in the previous sections rely on a heuristic rating prediction function that estimates unknown ratings as weighted averages of known ones. To make the statement about weighted averages more explicit, let us note that the user-based and item-based rating prediction functions 5.41 and 5.56 essentially have the following forms:

$$\hat{r}_{ui} = \sum_{v \in S_{ui}^k} w_{uv} \cdot r_{vi} \quad \text{(user-based)} \tag{5.58}$$

$$\hat{r}_{ui} = \sum_{j \in Q_{ui}^k} w_{ij} \cdot r_{uj} \quad \text{(item-based)} \tag{5.59}$$

in which w_{uv} and w_{ij} are the weights proportional to the user-based and item-based similarities, respectively. In other words, weights w are interpolation weights. This consideration quite naturally leads to the question of how the optimal weights can be determined by means of regression analysis instead of the heuristic similarity-based weights. The regression analysis can be applied to both user-based and item-based models, as well as hybrid methods that combine these two models, so we will start with the arguably more practical item-based approach and then discuss alternative options [Bell and Koren, 2007].

5.7.4.1 *Item-based Regression*

The item-based methods predict the ratings for item i by averaging ratings from similar items according to expression 5.59. Input ratings r_{uj} can be taken directly from the original rating matrix or the matrix can be preprocessed to center the ratings by subtracting the global average, item average, or baseline predictions. In the case of centered input ratings, the output rating $\hat{r}_{ui}$ is also centered, so the global average, item average, or baseline prediction needs to be added back in at the end.

In order to solve a regression problem for the rating interpolation weights, let us first consider a hypothetical case in which the rating matrix is so dense that all users except u have rated both item i and all its neighbors Q_{ui}^k, as shown in Figure 5.10.

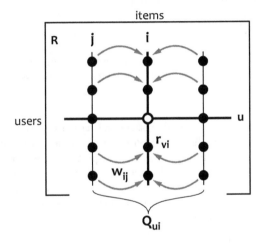

Figure 5.10: Item-based nearest neighbor regression.

The optimal interpolation weights for item i can then be determined by solving the following least squares problem (for each item separately):

$$\min_w \sum_{v \neq u} \left(r_{vi} - \hat{r}_{vi} \right)^2 \tag{5.60}$$

Inserting the rating prediction function 5.59 into this, we get

$$\min_w \sum_{v \neq u} \left(r_{vi} - \sum_{j \in Q_{vi}^k} w_{ij} \cdot r_{vj} \right)^2 \tag{5.61}$$

Rearranging the terms, we can rewrite this problem in vector form as

$$\min_{\mathbf{w}} \quad \mathbf{r}^T \mathbf{r} - 2\mathbf{b}^T \mathbf{w} + \mathbf{w}^T \mathbf{A} \mathbf{w} \tag{5.62}$$

in which $\mathbf{A}$ is a $k \times k$ matrix defined as

$$A_{jh} = \sum_{v \neq u} r_{vj} r_{vh} \tag{5.63}$$

$\mathbf{b}$ is a k-dimensional vector defined as

$$b_j = \sum_{v \neq u} r_{vj} r_{vi} \tag{5.64}$$

and $\mathbf{r}^T \mathbf{r}$ is a constant term with respect to $\mathbf{w}$:

$$\mathbf{r}^T \mathbf{r} = \sum_{v \neq u} r_{vi}^2 \tag{5.65}$$

If we take the gradient of quadratic form 5.62 with respect to $\mathbf{w}$ and equate it to zero, we get the following linear system of equations:

$$\mathbf{A}\mathbf{w} = \mathbf{b} \tag{5.66}$$

In a more realistic case with a sparse rating matrix, we would expect that only a few users had rated both item i and all its neighbors Q_{ui}^k. Consequently, the estimates of the corresponding elements of $\mathbf{A}$ and $\mathbf{b}$ can be more or less reliable, depending on the number of known ratings. We can account for this by using the discounted similarity technique that we discussed earlier and shrinking the estimates by the corresponding support:

$$A_{jh} = \frac{1}{|U_{jh}|} \sum_{v \in U_{jh}} r_{vj} r_{vh}$$
$$b_j = \frac{1}{|U_{ij}|} \sum_{v \in U_{ij}} r_{vj} r_{vi} \tag{5.67}$$

in which U_{ij} is the set of users who rated both item i and item j. It is worth noting that one can compute and store all possible elements of matrix $\mathbf{A}$ in advance, that is, compute the $m \times m$ item correlation matrix according to expression 5.63 for all values of $1 \leqslant j, k \leqslant m$ and then use those values to quickly assemble the $k \times k$ matrix $\mathbf{A}$ and vector $\mathbf{b}$ for a given item and target user.

One possible way to compute the optimal weights is to solve equation 5.66 numerically by inverting matrix $\mathbf{A}$, but this is not the only possible option. An alternative approach is to directly solve problem 5.62 by using the gradient descent or some other generic optimization method. The advantage of this approach is the ability to add additional constraints and variables. For example, it has been reported that prediction accuracy can be slightly improved when weights w are constrained to be non-negative [Bell and Koren, 2007]:

$$\min_{\mathbf{w}} \quad \mathbf{w}^T \mathbf{A} \mathbf{w} - 2\mathbf{b}^T \mathbf{w}$$

$$\text{subject to} \quad \mathbf{w} \geqslant 0 \tag{5.68}$$

Even better results can be obtained by adding more variables into basic rating prediction formula 5.59 and jointly optimizing them. For example, it has been shown that the following extension of the rating prediction formula is a good practical choice for baseline estimates [Koren and Bell, 2011]:

$$\hat{r}_{ui} = \mu + b_u + b_i + \sum_{j \in Q_{ui}^k} \left(w_{ij} \left(r_{uj} - b_{uj} \right) + c_{ij} \right) \tag{5.69}$$

in which μ is the global rating average, b_{uj} are the baseline estimates, and b_u, b_i, w_{ij}, and c_{ij} are the variables to be optimized. This expression can be inserted into least squares problem 5.60 and optimized with respect to b_u, b_i, w_{ij}, and c_{ij} by using the gradient descent method. In this case, one does not necessarily need to restrict the neighborhood to the top k items and can use the entire I_u set, instead of Q_{ui}^k.

EXAMPLE 5.4

We conclude the discussion of item-based regression with a numerical example that uses the movie rating matrix from table 5.3. We choose to work with mean-centered ratings, so we first preprocess the input matrix by subtracting the column average (i. e. , the average item rating) from each element, which gives the result presented in table 5.6.

	FORREST GUMP	TITANIC	THE GODFATHER	BATMAN	THE MATRIX	ALIEN
MEAN	2.80	3.25	2.40	2.00	3.33	2.80
USER 1	2.20	0.75	—	-1.00	-1.33	-1.80
USER 2	1.20	—	0.60	-1.00	-2.33	-0.80
USER 3	—	1.75	2.60	—	-0.33	0.20
USER 4	-0.80	—	-1.40	2.00	1.66	1.20
USER 5	-0.80	-1.25	-0.40	—	0.66	—
USER 6	-1.80	-1.25	-1.40	—	1.66	1.20

Table 5.6: Example of ratings centered by using item averages.

Next, we precompute the item correlation matrix $\mathbf{A}$ according to expression 5.63 for all values of $1 \leqslant j, k \leqslant m$ by using the ratings from table 5.6 as inputs:

$$
\mathbf{A} = \begin{bmatrix}
\mathbf{10.80} & 4.90 & 4.68 & -5.00 & -10.60 & -8.04 \\
4.90 & \mathbf{6.75} & \mathbf{6.80} & -0.75 & -4.50 & -2.50 \\
\mathbf{4.68} & \mathbf{6.80} & 11.20 & -3.40 & -7.20 & -3.32 \\
-5.00 & -0.75 & -3.40 & 6.00 & 7.00 & 5.00 \\
-10.6 & -4.50 & -7.20 & 7.00 & 13.33 & 8.20 \\
-8.04 & -2.50 & -3.32 & 5.00 & 8.20 & 6.80
\end{bmatrix} \tag{5.70}
$$

This precomputed matrix can be used to quickly assemble the system of equations described by expression 5.66 for a given target user and item. For example, with a neighborhood size of $k = 2$, we predict the rating that user 1 would give to *The Godfather* by averaging the ratings from *Titanic* and *Forrest Gump*, which are the two closest neighbors of *The Godfather* in terms of Pearson similarity. Consequently, we use the correlation values for these three movies (highlighted in bold in matrix 5.70) to construct the following equation for the interpolation weights:

$$
\begin{bmatrix} 6.75 & 4.90 \\ 4.90 & 10.80 \end{bmatrix} \begin{bmatrix} w_{32} \\ w_{31} \end{bmatrix} = \begin{bmatrix} 6.80 \\ 4.68 \end{bmatrix} \tag{5.71}
$$

By solving this equation, we get the weights $w_{32} = 1.033$ for *Titanic* and $w_{31} = -0.035$ for *Forrest Gump*. The rating can then be predicted as

$$
\begin{aligned}
\hat{r}_{13} &= \mu_3 + w_{32}r_{12} + w_{31}r_{11} \\
&= 2.40 + 1.033 \cdot 0.75 - 0.035 \cdot 2.20 = 3.09
\end{aligned} \tag{5.72}
$$

in which μ_3 is the average rating for *The Godfather* movie and the input ratings r_{12} and r_{11} are taken from table 5.6. Repeating this process for all unknown ratings, we get the final results presented in table 5.7.

5.7.4.2   User-based Regression

The regression analysis framework we have just developed for item-based methods can be applied to user-based models quite straightforwardly. The input to the process is the rating matrix centered by user averages (row average is subtracted from each element in the row) or baseline predictions. The user-based variant of the least squares problem 5.60 can then be defined as

$$
\min_{w} \sum_{j \neq i} \left(r_{uj} - \hat{r}_{uj} \right)^2 \tag{5.73}
$$

	FORREST GUMP	TITANIC	THE GODFATHER	BATMAN	THE MATRIX	ALIEN
USER 1	5	4	[3.09]	1	2	1
USER 2	4	[3.83]	3	1	1	2
USER 3	[4.02]	5	5	[1.98]	3	3
USER 4	2	[2.34]	1	4	5	4
USER 5	2	2	2	[2.28]	4	[3.15]
USER 6	1	2	1	[2.94]	5	4

Table 5.7: Example of ratings predicted by using item-based nearest neighbor regression.

This problem needs to be solved for each target user u. Inserting the rating prediction formula 5.58 into the previous equation, we get

$$\min_{w} \quad \sum_{j \neq i} \left(r_{uj} - \sum_{v \in S_{uj}^k} w_{uv} \cdot r_{vj} \right)^2 \tag{5.74}$$

Optimal weights w_{uv} can be determined by using the same methods as those used for the item-based approach – one can either solve a linear system of equations or use generic optimization methods to optimize weights based on cost function 5.74. In comparison to the item-based approach, user-based regression inherits all of the advantages and disadvantages of user-based methods that we discussed earlier. In particular, user-based methods are more challenging from a computational standpoint if there are many more users than items because one needs to precompute the $n \times n$ user correlation matrix, instead of the $m \times m$ item correlation matrix.

5.7.4.3 Fusing Item-based and User-based Models

One of the key advantages of the regression approach is the ability to extend the rating prediction function with new terms and variables that can be jointly optimized. We have already seen an example of such an extension in expression 5.69 where we added new variables to the basic item-based model to capture user and item biases. We can extend this solution even further and combine the item-based and user-based models into one rating prediction function:

$$\hat{r}_{ui} = \mu + b_u + b_i + \sum_{j \in Q_{ui}^k} \left(w_{ij}^{(item)} \left(r_{uj} - b_{uj} \right) + c_{ij} \right) \\ + \sum_{v \in S_{ui}^k} w_{uv}^{(user)} \left(r_{vi} - b_{vi} \right) \tag{5.75}$$

in which $w_{ij}^{(item)}$ and $w_{uv}^{(user)}$ are two different sets of weights to be learned. This model essentially sums a centered version of user-based function 5.58 with item-based function 5.69 [Aggarwal, 2016; Koren and Bell, 2011]. The rating function can then be inserted into the least squares problem for the prediction error and optimized with respect to all bias variables and weights. As the weights are learned from the data, the user and item neighborhoods do not necessarily need to be limited by the top k items, and sets I_u and U_i can be used instead of Q_{ui}^k and S_{ui}^k, respectively. However, if the sets are limited by a finite value of k, the computational complexity can be reduced, at the expense of model accuracy.

The combined model is able to learn both item–item and user–user relationships (see section 5.7.3 for details) and, consequently, to combine the strengths of the two approaches. It has been shown that combined models can outperform individual user-based and item-based models on industrial data sets [Koren and Bell, 2011]. It is important to note that the regression framework can be used not only to combine user-based and item-based solutions but also to integrate neighborhood-based methods with completely different models, including some that we will discuss in the next section.

5.8   MODEL-BASED COLLABORATIVE FILTERING

From the machine learning perspective, the neighborhood-based approach to collaborative filtering is a very narrow view of the problem because it focuses on the k nearest neighbor estimates and does not leverage other machine learning methods. Consequently, a neighborhood-based recommender system inherits some fundamental limitations of the k nearest neighbors approach. First, the performance of neighborhood methods can decrease on sparse data where items or users have very few common ratings, so that the recommendations can be made based on neighbors that are not really similar to the target user or item. Next, the k nearest neighbors algorithm relies on pairwise instance comparison and defers the computation of the recommendations until it is requested, which makes it challenging to split the computation into offline and online phases.

An alternative approach is to build a rating prediction model by using more advanced methods of supervised and unsupervised machine learning. Collaborative filtering is essentially a matrix completion task, so many standard classification and regression methods can be adopted to it. This approach, known as model-based collaborative filtering, generally offers a few advantages over the neighborhood-based methods:

ACCURACY. Some machine learning methods, such as the Naive Bayes classifier, are based on a solid theoretical framework that enables more accurate rating predictions than the heuristic similarity measures used by neighborhood-based recommender systems.

STABILITY. Dimensionality reduction methods can transform a sparse rating matrix into a more condensed representation, which improves the stability of rating predictions on the incomplete data.

SCALABILITY. Machine learning methods often consist of model training and model evaluation phases that help to separate offline computations from online recommendation requests, thereby improving system scalability.

Some model-based methods can deliver all of these improvements, whereas others achieve only some of these goals. In the rest of this section, we will consider several important methods that can outperform neighborhood-based systems or can be combined with neighborhood-based algorithms to create hybrid solutions.

5.8.1 *Adapting Regression Models to Rating Prediction*

In a general case, classification and regression models can be adapted to the rating prediction problem by treating known ratings as features and missing ratings as response variables. Let us first consider a hypothetical case where only one rating in the matrix is missing and all other ratings are known. Similarly to the neighborhood approach, we have two symmetrical alternatives, depending on how the columns and rows of the rating matrix are interpreted. The first option is to treat the columns of the rating matrix as features and the rows as data samples. A classification model is trained for each item i by separately considering the i-th column as the response and other columns as features, so that the rating for a given item is predicted based on the other item ratings, as illustrated in Figure 5.11. This approach is structurally similar to the item-based neighborhood methods. The second alternative is to treat the rows of the rating matrix as features and the columns as data samples, so that a classification model is created for each user and the ratings for the target user are predicted based on the ratings from their peers. This can be viewed as a user-oriented approach to the problem.

In practice, however, the rating matrix is often very sparse, so one cannot assume that all ratings in the training instances are known. This is a serious issue that can substantially impact the quality of rating predictions, depending on how the missing values are handled. There are several possible ways to address this challenge:

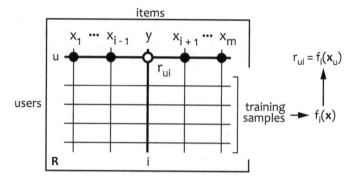

Figure 5.11: Adapting a regression or classification model to rating prediction in an item-oriented way. Known ratings of the target user u are interpreted as features $x_1, \ldots, x_m$, and the rating to be predicted is interpreted as response variable y. Regression or classification model $f_i(x)$ is trained for a given item i with other users as training instances, and it is evaluated on feature vector x_u, which corresponds to the target user.

- Some classification methods can be directly adapted to handle the missing values. The Naive Bayes classifier described in the next section is an example of such a solution.

- In certain cases, missing ratings can be filled with zeros. This primarily applies to unary rating matrices where each element indicates whether a user interacted with a given item or not [Aggarwal, 2016]. This approach, however, cannot be universally used for every rating type because the insertion of default (zero) rating values results in prediction bias.

- One of the most generic approaches to the problem is the iterative one [Xia et al., 2006; Su et al., 2008]. The missing values can be initialized with some basic estimates, such as row or column averages. This gives a complete rating matrix that can be used to train classification models. The originally missing ratings can then be estimated by using the obtained classifiers, and the corresponding elements in the rating matrix can be updated with these new values. This gives a second complete rating matrix that can used to retrain the models, so the process can be repeated iteratively until convergence.

Finally, it is worth noting that the techniques described above can be mixed with each other, as well as with neighborhood-based and content-based recommendation methods. For example, one can use the

Naive Bayes collaborative filtering algorithm described in the next section to initialize the missing ratings and then compute Pearson similarities between users or items based on this complete rating matrix to make the actual recommendations [Su et al., 2008].

5.8.2 Naive Bayes Collaborative Filtering

The Naive Bayes collaborative filtering algorithm attempts to predict a missing rating by estimating the probabilities of all possible rating values (e. g., 1, 2, 3, 4 and 5 stars) and selecting the most probable option [Miyahara and Pazzani, 2000; Su and Khoshgoftaar, 2006]. As we mentioned in the previous section, the Naive Bayes classifier can be constructed in either user-centric or item-centric ways. We choose to focus on the item-centric approach because it is arguably more important for practical usage, for the reasons we discussed in section 5.7.3. The user-centric solution can be constructed in almost exactly the same way by interchanging users and items, that is, the rows and columns of the rating matrix.

According to the item-centric approach, we build a Naive Bayes classifier for a given item i in order to predict rating r_{ui}. The rating estimate is then obtained by evaluating the model with the set of known ratings for user u, which we denote as I_u, as the input. If the ratings are categorical variables that take values from K possible classes $c_1, \ldots, c_K$, the prediction problem is to find the most probable rating class given the observed ratings:

$$r_{ui} = \underset{c_k}{\operatorname{argmax}} \quad \Pr\left(r_{ui} = c_k \mid I_u\right) \tag{5.76}$$

To evaluate the probability of a certain rating class, given the observed ratings, we first apply the Bayes rule to decompose this probability:

$$\Pr\left(r_{ui} = c_k \mid I_u\right) = \frac{\Pr\left(c_k\right) \cdot \Pr\left(I_u \mid r_{ui} = c_k\right)}{\Pr\left(I_u\right)} \tag{5.77}$$

in which $\Pr\left(c_k\right)$ is the prior probability of rating class c_k and $\Pr\left(I_u \mid r_{ui} = c_k\right)$ is the likelihood of observing the known rating of user u given that this user rated item i as c_k. The probability of the observed ratings $\Pr\left(I_u\right)$ in the denominator can be ignored because it is constant for all classes and, consequently, does not influence the choice of the most probable class. The next step is to apply the Naive Bayes assumption to estimate the likelihood of the observed ratings. According to this assumption, all observed ratings are considered conditionally independent, so the likelihood can be broken down into the product of individual rating probabilities:

$$\Pr\left(I_u \mid r_{ui} = c_k\right) = \prod_{j \in I_u} \Pr\left(r_{uj} \mid r_{ui} = c_k\right) \tag{5.78}$$

Gathering all of these intermediate results together, we obtain the final expression for the rating prediction:

$$r_{ui} = \underset{c_k}{\text{argmax}} \;\; \Pr\left(c_k\right) \cdot \prod_{j \in I_u} \Pr\left(r_{uj} \mid r_{ui} = c_k\right) \tag{5.79}$$

The last task is to estimate the probabilities in equation 5.79 from the data. In the context of item i, the prior probability of rating class c_k is estimated as the fraction of the ratings for item i that are equal to c_k:

$$\Pr\left(c_k\right) = \frac{\sum_{v \in U_i} \mathbb{I}(r_{vi} = c_k)}{|U_i|} \tag{5.80}$$

in which U_i is the set of users who rated item i, and $\mathbb{I}(x)$ is the indicator function that equals one if the argument is true and zero otherwise. The conditional probability that user u rates item j as r_{uj}, given that this user had previously rated item i as c_k, can be estimated as follows:

$$\Pr\left(r_{uj} \mid r_{ui} = c_k\right) = \frac{\sum_{v \in U_i} \mathbb{I}(r_{vj} = r_{uj} \text{ AND } r_{vi} = c_k)}{\sum_{v \in U_i} \mathbb{I}(r_{vi} = c_k)} \tag{5.81}$$

The numerator in expression 5.81 is equal to the number of users who have rated item j similarly to user u and, at the same time, rated item i as c_k. The denominator is simply the number of users who rated item i as c_k. Consider Figure 5.12 as an illustration. Assuming that we are assessing the probability of the hypothesis that r_{ui} is 3 stars, that we have three users who rated item i as 3 stars, and that there is one user among them who rated item j in the same way as user u (a rating of 5 stars), the likelihood of observing the known ratings for item j, given that the hypothesis is correct, is

$$\Pr\left(r_{uj} \mid r_{ui} = 3\right) = \frac{2}{3} \tag{5.82}$$

In practice, formula 5.81 is often adjusted by using the Laplace estimator technique to avoid zero counters and to smooth the estimates. If $|C|$ is the total number of rating classes, the smoothed version of the likelihood estimator is as follows:

$$\Pr\left(r_{uj} \mid r_{ui} = c_k\right) = \frac{\sum_{v \in U_i} \mathbb{I}(r_{vj} = r_{uj} \text{ AND } r_{vi} = c_k) + 1}{\sum_{v \in U_i} \mathbb{I}(r_{vi} = c_k) + |C|} \tag{5.83}$$

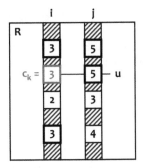

Figure 5.12: Example of likelihood estimation in the Naive Bayes recommender.

EXAMPLE 5.5

Let us now consider a complete numerical example by using the standard movie rating matrix from table 5.3. We have five rating classes, from 1 to 5 stars, and the input rating matrix is as follows:

$$
R = \begin{bmatrix}
5 & 4 & — & 1 & 2 & 1 \\
4 & — & 3 & 1 & 1 & 2 \\
— & 5 & 5 & — & 3 & 3 \\
2 & — & 1 & 4 & 5 & 4 \\
2 & 2 & 2 & — & 4 & — \\
1 & 2 & 1 & — & 5 & 4
\end{bmatrix}
\tag{5.84}
$$

Let us take the missing rating r_{13} as an example and go through the calculation needed to predict it with the item-oriented Naive Bayes algorithm. The first step is to estimate the prior class probabilities according to expression 5.80. This gives the following vector of probabilities for the classes from 1 to 5, based on their frequencies in the third column of the rating matrix:

$$
\begin{array}{cccccc}
 & c_1 & c_2 & c_3 & c_4 & c_5 \\
\Pr(c_k) & \begin{bmatrix} 2/5 & 1/5 & 1/5 & 0 & 1/5 \end{bmatrix}
\end{array}
\tag{5.85}
$$

Next, we estimate the conditional probabilities according to expression 5.83 with respect to the target item $i = 3$ for all classes c_k and all items $j \neq 3$. This results in the following matrix of probabilities:

$$
\begin{array}{c}
\begin{array}{cccccc}
 & c_1 & c_2 & c_3 & c_4 & c_5
\end{array} \\
\begin{array}{c}
j=1 \\
j=2 \\
j=3 \\
j=4 \\
j=5 \\
j=6
\end{array}
\begin{bmatrix}
1/7 & 1/6 & 1/6 & 1/5 & 1/6 \\
1/7 & 1/6 & 1/6 & 1/5 & 1/6 \\
— & — & — & — & — \\
1/7 & 1/6 & 1/3 & 1/5 & 1/6 \\
1/7 & 1/6 & 1/6 & 1/5 & 1/6 \\
1/7 & 1/6 & 1/6 & 1/5 & 1/6
\end{bmatrix}
\end{array}
\tag{5.86}
$$

The above matrix can be calculated on demand for a given target item, or we can precompute all $m \times m \times |C|$ values for all possible combinations of target items i, peer items j, and classes c_k. By multiplying the values in matrices 5.85 and 5.86 column-wise in accordance with expression 5.79, we obtain the following class probabilities:

$$
\Pr(r_{13}=c_k \mid I_1) \quad \begin{array}{ccccc} c_1 & c_2 & c_3 & c_4 & c_5 \\ [\ 2/84035 & 1/38880 & 1/19440 & 0 & 1/38880\ ] \end{array}
$$

(5.87)

This means that a rating of 3 is the best estimate for r_{13}. If we repeat the process for all missing ratings, we get the results presented in table 5.8.

	FORREST GUMP	TITANIC	THE GODFATHER	BATMAN	THE MATRIX	ALIEN
USER 1	5	4	[3]	1	2	1
USER 2	4	[4]	3	1	1	2
USER 3	[2]	5	5	[1]	3	3
USER 4	2	[2]	1	4	5	4
USER 5	2	2	2	[4]	4	[4]
USER 6	1	2	1	[4]	5	4

Table 5.8: Example of ratings predicted by using the item-based Naive Bayes collaborative filtering algorithm.

As a side note, let us also show how the Naive Bayes approach can be connected to neighborhood-based collaborative filtering. We can make their structural similarity more apparent by replacing the product in equation 5.78 by a sum of logarithms and inserting it into class probability formula 5.77:

$$
\Pr\left(r_{ui} = c_k \mid I_u\right) = \frac{\Pr\left(c_k\right)}{\Pr\left(I_u\right)} \cdot \sum_{j \in I_u} s_k(i,j)
$$

(5.88)

in which

$$
s_k(i,j) = \log \Pr\left(r_{uj} \mid r_{ui} = c_k\right)
$$

(5.89)

Note that $s_k(i,j)$ is estimated by a pairwise comparison of ratings for items i and j, so this value can be interpreted as a kind of similarity measure between the two items. This result can be compared to the item-based nearest neighbor formula 5.56 from which ratings are predicted with a heuristic item similarity metric. This more accurate foundation gives some advantage to the Naive Bayes approach relative to the basic neighborhood methods, and it can substantially outperform them on some data sets [Miyahara and Pazzani, 2000].

5.8.3 *Latent Factor Models*

The collaborative filtering algorithms that we have discussed so far do most of their calculations by using individual elements of the rating matrix as inputs. Neighborhood methods estimate the missing ratings directly from the known values in the rating matrix. Model-based methods add an abstraction layer on top of the rating matrix by creating a predictive model that captures certain patterns of user–item interactions, but model training still heavily depends on the rating matrix properties. Consequently, these collaborative filtering methods generally face the following challenges:

- The rating matrix may contain many millions of users, millions of items, and billions of known ratings, thereby creating major computational and scalability challenges.

- The rating matrix is typically very sparse (in practice, about 99% of ratings can be missing). This impacts the computational stability of the recommendation algorithms and leads to unreliable estimates in cases when a user or item has no really similar neighbors. This problem is often aggravated by the fact that most of the basic algorithms are either user-oriented or item-oriented, which limits their ability to capture all types of similarities and interactions available in the rating matrix.

- The data in the rating matrix are usually highly correlated because of similarities between users and items. This means that the signals available in the rating matrix are not only sparse but also redundant, which contributes to the scalability problem.

The above considerations indicate that a raw rating matrix can be a non-optimal representation of the rating signals and we should consider some alternative representations that are more suitable for collaborative filtering purposes. To explore this idea, let us go back to square one and reflect a little bit on the nature of recommender services. Fundamentally, a recommender service can be viewed as an algorithm that predicts ratings based on some measure of affinity between a user and item:

$$\hat{r}_{ui} \sim \text{affinity}\,(u, i) \tag{5.90}$$

One possible way to define this affinity measure is to take the latent factors approach and map both users and items to points in some k-dimensional space, so that each user and each item is represented as a k-dimensional vector:

$$
\begin{aligned}
u &\mapsto \mathbf{p}_u = (p_{u1}, \ldots, p_{uk}) \\
i &\mapsto \mathbf{q}_i = (q_{i1}, \ldots, q_{ik})
\end{aligned}
\tag{5.91}
$$

The vectors should be constructed in such a way that the corresponding dimensions of $\mathbf{p}$ and $\mathbf{q}$ are comparable to each other in a consistent way. In other words, each dimension can be viewed as a feature or concept, so that p_{uj} is the measure of proximity between user u and concept j, and q_{ij} is, symmetrically, the measure of proximity between item i and concept j. In practice, these dimensions are often interpretable as genres, styles, or other attributes that are applicable to both users and items. The affinity between the user and item and, consequently, the rating can then be defined as a product of the corresponding vectors:

$$
\hat{r}_{ui} = \mathbf{p}_u \cdot \mathbf{q}_i^{\mathsf{T}} = \sum_{s=1}^{k} p_{us} q_{is}
\tag{5.92}
$$

As each rating is decomposed into a product of two vectors that belong to the concept space that is not directly observed in the original rating matrix, $\mathbf{p}$ and $\mathbf{q}$ are called *latent factors*. The success of this abstract approach, of course, totally depends on exactly how the latent factors are defined and constructed. To answer this question, let us first note that expression 5.92 can be rewritten in matrix form as follows[2]

$$
\hat{\mathbf{R}} = \mathbf{P} \cdot \mathbf{Q}^{\mathsf{T}}
\tag{5.93}
$$

in which $\mathbf{P}$ is an $n \times k$ matrix assembled from vectors $\mathbf{p}$, and $\mathbf{Q}$ is an $m \times k$ matrix assembled from vectors $\mathbf{q}$, as illustrated in Figure 5.13. The main objective of a collaborative filtering system is usually set as minimization of the rating prediction error, and this allows us to straightforwardly define the optimization problem with respect to the latent factor matrices:

$$
\min_{\mathbf{P}, \mathbf{Q}} \left\| \mathbf{R} - \hat{\mathbf{R}} \right\|^2 = \left\| \mathbf{R} - \mathbf{P} \cdot \mathbf{Q}^{\mathsf{T}} \right\|^2
\tag{5.94}
$$

With the assumption that the number of latent dimensions k is fixed and $k \leqslant n$ and $k \leqslant m$, optimization problem 5.94 is an instance of the

---

2 In mathematics literature, it is very common to denote such factors as $\mathbf{U}$ and $\mathbf{V}$. We use $\mathbf{P}$ and $\mathbf{Q}$ notation here to avoid clashes with the user index u commonly used throughout the book.

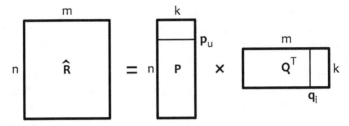

Figure 5.13: The latent factor approach to collaborative filtering.

low-rank approximation problem that we discussed in Chapter 2. To demonstrate an approach to the solution, let us ignore for a moment the sparsity of the rating matrix and assume it to be complete. In this case, the optimization problem has an analytic solution in terms of the singular value decomposition (SVD) of the rating matrix. More specifically, the rating matrix can be broken down into a product of three matrices by using the standard SVD algorithm:

$$\mathbf{R} = \mathbf{U}\mathbf{\Sigma}\mathbf{V}^{\mathsf{T}} \tag{5.95}$$

in which $\mathbf{U}$ is an $n \times n$ column-orthonormal matrix, $\mathbf{\Sigma}$ is an $n \times m$ diagonal matrix, and $\mathbf{V}$ is an $m \times m$ column-orthonormal matrix. The optimal solution of problem 5.94 can then be obtained in terms of these factors truncated to the k most significant dimensions:

$$\hat{\mathbf{R}} = \mathbf{U}_k \mathbf{\Sigma}_k \mathbf{V}_k^{\mathsf{T}} \tag{5.96}$$

Consequently, the latent factors that are optimal from the prediction accuracy standpoint can be obtained by means of the SVD as follows:

$$\begin{aligned} \mathbf{P} &= \mathbf{U}_k \mathbf{\Sigma}_k \\ \mathbf{Q} &= \mathbf{V}_k \end{aligned} \tag{5.97}$$

This SVD-based latent factor model helps to solve the collaborative filtering challenges outlined at the beginning of this section. First, it replaces a large $n \times m$ rating matrix with $n \times k$ and $m \times k$ factor matrices, which are typically much smaller because the optimal number of latent dimensions k is typically quite low in practice. For example, it has been reported that a rating matrix with 500,000 users and 17,000 items can be approximated reasonably well by using just 40 dimensions [Funk, 2016]. Next, the SVD decorrelates the rating matrix: the latent factor matrices defined by expression 5.97 are column-orthogonal, which means that the latent dimensions are decorrelated. If $k \ll n, m$, which is typically true in practice, the SVD also addresses the sparsity problem because the signal present in the original rating matrix is efficiently condensed (recall that we select the top k dimensions with the highest signal energy) and the latent factor matrices are not sparse. Figure 5.14 illustrates this property. The user-based neighborhood algorithm (5.14a) convolves the sparse rating vector for a given item with the sparse similarity vector for a given user to produce the rating estimate. In contrast, the latent factor model (5.14b) estimates the rating by convolving the two vectors of reduced dimensionality and higher energy density.

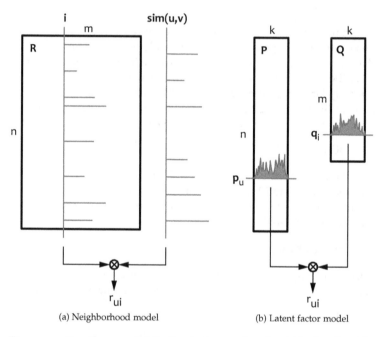

        (a) Neighborhood model   (b) Latent factor model

Figure 5.14: Signal energy distribution in the user-based neighborhood and latent factor models

Although the approach we just described looks like a neat solution for the latent factor problem, it actually has a major flaw because of the assumption that the rating matrix is complete. If the rating matrix is sparse, which is almost always the case, the standard SVD algorithm cannot be straightforwardly applied because it cannot handle the missing (undefined) elements. The simplest solution to this problem is to fill the missing ratings with some default value, but this can cause a major prediction bias. It is also inefficient from the computational standpoint because the computational complexity of this solution is equal to the complexity of the SVD for a full $n \times m$ matrix, although it is desirable to have a method with a complexity proportional to the number of known ratings. These issues can be addressed by the alternative factorization methods described in the following sections.

5.8.3.1 Unconstrained Factorization

The standard SVD algorithm is an analytic solution of the low-rank approximation problem. This problem, however, can be viewed as an optimization task, and generic optimization methods can be applied to it as well. One of the most basic approaches is to use the gradient descent method to iteratively refine the latent factor values. The starting point is to define the cost function J as the residual prediction error:

$$\min_{P, Q} \quad J = \left\| R - PQ^T \right\|^2 \tag{5.98}$$

Note that we do not impose any constraints, such as orthogonality, on the latent factor matrices at this point. Calculating the gradient of the cost function with respect to the latent factors, we get the following result:

$$\frac{\partial J}{\partial P} = -2 \left(R - PQ^T \right) Q = -2EQ$$

$$\frac{\partial J}{\partial Q^T} = -2P^T \left(R - PQ^T \right) = -2P^T E \tag{5.99}$$

in which E is the residual error matrix:

$$E = R - PQ^T \tag{5.100}$$

The gradient descent algorithm minimizes the cost function by moving in the negative gradient direction at each step. Consequently, we can find the latent factors that minimize the squared rating prediction error by updating matrices P and Q iteratively in accordance with the following expressions until convergence:

$$P \leftarrow P + \alpha \cdot EQ$$

$$Q^T \leftarrow Q^T + \alpha \cdot P^T E \tag{5.101}$$

in which α is the *learning rate*. The disadvantage of the gradient descent approach is that each iteration requires the computation of the entire residual error matrix and the updating of all latent factor values at once. An alternative approach that is arguably more suitable for large matrices is stochastic gradient descent [Funk, 2016]. The stochastic gradient descent algorithm exploits the fact that the total prediction error J is the sum of the prediction errors for individual elements of the rating matrix, so it is possible to approximate the overall gradient of J by a gradient at a single data point and update the latent factors element by element. A complete implementation of this idea is shown in algorithm 5.1.

input   training set $\mathbf{R}$ (sampled from the original rating matrix)

output   matrices $\mathbf{P}$ and $\mathbf{Q}$

initialize $p_{ud}^{(0)} \sim$ random with mean μ_0 $1 \leqslant u \leqslant n,\ \ 1 \leqslant d \leqslant k$

initialize $q_{id}^{(0)} \sim$ random with mean μ_0 $1 \leqslant i \leqslant m,\ \ 1 \leqslant d \leqslant k$

for concept dimension $d = 1, 2, \ldots, k$ **do**

    repeat

        for each rating r_{ui} in the training set **do**

$$\hat{r}_{ui} = \sum_{s=1}^{d} p_{us} \cdot q_{is}$$

$$e = r_{ui} - \hat{r}_{ui}$$

$$p_{ud} \leftarrow p_{ud} + \alpha \cdot e \cdot q_{id}$$

$$q_{id} \leftarrow q_{id} + \alpha \cdot e \cdot p_{ud}$$

$$SSE^{(t+1)} \leftarrow SSE^{(t+1)} + e^2 \quad \text{(sum of squared errors)}$$

        end

    until $\left| SSE^{(t+1)} - SSE^{(t)} \right| < \varepsilon$ (convergence condition)

end

Algorithm 5.1: Unconstrained matrix factorization with the stochastic gradient descent algorithm. t is the iteration counter for the middle loop, ε is the convergence threshold, μ is the mean known rating, and $\mu_0 = \mu/\sqrt{k|\mu|}$.

The first stage of the algorithm is to initialize the latent factor matrices. Selection of these initial values is not really important, but we choose to evenly distribute the energy of known ratings among the randomly generated latent factors. The algorithm then optimizes the concept dimensions one by one. For each dimension, it repeatedly goes through all ratings in the training set, predicts each rating by using the current latent factor values, estimates the prediction error, and adjusts the factor values in accordance with expressions 5.101. A given dimension is considered done once the convergence condition is met and the algorithm switches to the next dimension.

Algorithm 5.1 helps to overcome the limitations of the standard SVD. It optimizes the latent factors by cycling through the individual data points and, consequently, avoids the issues with the missing ratings and algebraic operations over ginormous matrices. The iterative element-by-element approach also makes the stochastic gradient descent more convenient for practical applications than the gradient descent, which updates entire matrices by using expressions 5.101.

EXAMPLE 5.6

The latent factor approach is essentially a group of representation learning methods that is able to reveal the patterns that are implicitly present in the rating matrix and render them explicitly as concepts. It is sometimes possible to interpret certain concepts, especially high-energy ones, in a meaningful and insightful way, although this does not mean that all concepts always have a clear semantic meaning. For example, the matrix factorization algorithm applied to the movie ratings database can produce factors that roughly correspond to psychographic dimensions, such as romance, comedy, horror, and so on. We illustrate this phenomenon with a small numerical example that uses the rating matrix from table 5.3 as an input:

$$
R = \begin{bmatrix}
5 & 4 & — & 1 & 2 & 1 \\
4 & — & 3 & 1 & 1 & 2 \\
— & 5 & 5 & — & 3 & 3 \\
2 & — & 1 & 4 & 5 & 4 \\
2 & 2 & 2 & — & 4 & — \\
1 & 2 & 1 & — & 5 & 4
\end{bmatrix}
\tag{5.102}
$$

We first subtract the global mean of $\mu = 2.82$ from all elements to center the matrix and then execute algorithm 5.1 with $k = 3$ latent dimensions and the learning rate $\alpha = 0.01$, to obtain the following two factors:

$$
P = \begin{bmatrix}
-1.40 & 0.30 & 0.95 \\
-1.03 & -0.90 & 0.34 \\
-0.94 & 1.53 & -0.12 \\
1.26 & 0.34 & 0.66 \\
0.80 & 0.16 & 0.07 \\
1.47 & 0.38 & 0.05
\end{bmatrix}
\quad
Q = \begin{bmatrix}
-1.16 & 0.31 & 0.60 \\
-0.96 & 0.82 & -0.43 \\
-1.26 & 0.71 & -0.83 \\
1.29 & 0.30 & -0.37 \\
1.18 & 0.90 & 0.60 \\
0.83 & 0.37 & -0.44
\end{bmatrix}
\tag{5.103}
$$

Each row in these matrices corresponds to either a user or a movie, and all 12 row vectors are visualized in Figure 5.15. Note that the elements in the first column (first concept vector) have the largest magnitudes, and the magnitudes in the subsequent columns gradually decrease. This is because the first concept vector captures as much signal energy as it is possible to capture with a single dimension, the second concept vector captures only a part of the residual energy, and so on. Next, note that the first concept can be semantically interpreted as the drama–action axis, where the positive direction corresponds to the action genre and the negative direction corresponds to the drama genre. The rating data in this example are highly correlated, so one can clearly see that the first three users and first three movies have large negative values in the first concept vector (drama movies and users who like such movies), whereas the last three users and movies have large positive values in the same column (action movies and users who prefer this genre). The second dimension in this particular case corresponds mainly to the user or item bias, which can also be interpreted as a psychographic attribute (Is the user generous or critical? Is the movie popular or not?). The remaining concepts can be considered as noise.

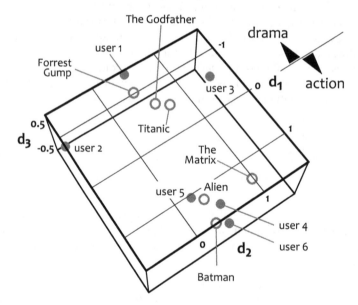

Figure 5.15: Visualization of latent factors 5.103. Dimensions d_1, d_2, and d_3 correspond to the first, second, and third columns of the matrices, respectively. Users and movies are shown as filled and empty circles, respectively.

The obtained factor matrices are not perfectly column-orthogonal, but they are leaning toward orthogonality because it follows from the optimality of the SVD solution. We can see this by examining products $P^T P$ and $Q^T Q$, which are close to diagonal matrices:

$$P^T P = \begin{bmatrix} \mathbf{8.28} & 0.19 & -0.62 \\ 0.19 & \mathbf{3.54} & 0.05 \\ -0.62 & 0.05 & \mathbf{1.47} \end{bmatrix}$$

$$Q^T Q = \begin{bmatrix} \mathbf{7.60} & -0.28 & 0.63 \\ -0.28 & \mathbf{2.31} & -0.49 \\ 0.63 & -0.49 & \mathbf{1.92} \end{bmatrix} \tag{5.104}$$

Matrices 5.103 are essentially a predictive model that can be used to estimate both known and missing ratings. The estimates can be produced by multiplying the two factors and adding back the global mean:

$$\hat{R} = PQ^T + \mu$$

$$= \begin{bmatrix} 5.11 & 4.00 & [\,\mathbf{4.01}\,] & 0.75 & 2.00 & 1.35 \\ 3.94 & [\,\mathbf{2.93}\,] & 3.19 & 1.11 & 1.00 & 1.49 \\ [\,\mathbf{4.31}\,] & 5.03 & 5.19 & [\,\mathbf{2.12}\,] & 3.03 & 2.67 \\ 1.86 & [\,\mathbf{1.61}\,] & 0.94 & 4.30 & 5.01 & 3.71 \\ 1.99 & 2.15 & 1.88 & [\,\mathbf{3.87}\,] & 3.95 & [\,\mathbf{3.51}\,] \\ 1.26 & 1.69 & 1.20 & [\,\mathbf{4.81}\,] & 4.94 & 4.17 \end{bmatrix} \tag{5.105}$$

The results reproduce the known ratings quite accurately and predict the missing ratings in a way that corresponds to our intuitive expectations. The accuracy of the estimates can be increased or decreased by changing the number of dimensions, and the optimal number of dimensions can be determined in practice by cross-validation and the selection of a reasonable trade-off between computational complexity and accuracy.

5.8.3.2   Constrained Factorization

The standard SVD algorithm gives an optimal solution of the low-rank approximation problem, and the factors P and Q produced by the SVD are column-orthogonal. The stochastic gradient descent algorithm 5.1 approximates this optimal solution. If the input rating matrix is complete, algorithm 5.1 converges to the same column-orthogonal outputs as the SVD. The only difference is that the diagonal scaling matrix present in the SVD is rolled into the two factors. However, if the input rating matrix is not complete, the outputs produced by the algorithm are not necessarily orthogonal. This means that the concepts remain correlated in the statistical and geometric senses. Although this does not necessarily impact the quality of the rating prediction, it makes the results less interpretable because of the residual correlations. We can pose the question of how additional constraints, such as orthogonality or non-negativity can be imposed on the latent factors to better define the concept space. Fortunately, the stochastic gradient descent algorithm can be modified to support such additional constraints and provide substantial flexibility and control over the factorization process.

Let us consider the problem of factorization with orthogonality constraints. Similarly to the unconstrained optimization, the objective is to find the latent factors that minimize the squared prediction error, but the additional constraint is that the basis of the concepts has to be orthogonal. This translates into the following constrained optimization problem:

$$\min_{P, Q} \quad \left\| R - P \cdot Q^T \right\|^2$$

$$\text{subject to} \quad P^T P \quad \text{is a diagonal matrix} \tag{5.106}$$

$$Q^T Q \quad \text{is a diagonal matrix}$$

The gradient descent method can be adapted to constrained optimization problems by using a technique called projected gradient descent. The idea of this technique is to apply the constraints at each iteration of gradient descent, so that the updated variable is projected back to the set of feasible solutions. More formally, gradient descent minimizes the cost function by iteratively moving in the negative gradient direction:

$$\min_x \quad f(x)$$

$$\tag{5.107}$$

$$\text{learning rule:} \quad x^{(t+1)} = x^{(t)} - \alpha \cdot \nabla f\left(x^{(t)}\right)$$

The projected gradient descent generalizes this approach to constrained optimization. At each step, we first move in the negative gradient direction and then adjust the solution to stay within the feasible set:

$$\min_x \quad f(x)$$

$$\text{subject to} \quad x \in C$$

$$\tag{5.108}$$

$$\text{learning rule:} \quad z^{(t+1)} = x^{(t)} - \alpha \cdot \nabla f\left(x^{(t)}\right)$$

$$x^{(t+1)} = \underset{x \in C}{\text{argmin}} \ \left\| z^{(t+1)} - x \right\|$$

In the case of orthogonality constraints, the feasible set for concept d is all vectors that are orthogonal to the previously computed concept vectors. This means that we can map the solution updated by gradient descent to the feasible set by subtracting its projections onto the previously computed concepts. For instance, with the assumption that the first user concept vector $\mathbf{p}_1$ (the first column of matrix $\mathbf{P}$) is determined during the first iteration of the outer loop of algorithm 5.1, a candidate solution for the second concept vector $\mathbf{p}_2$ (the second column of matrix $\mathbf{P}$) can be orthogonalized as

$$\mathbf{p}_2 = \mathbf{p}_2 - \text{proj}\,(\mathbf{p}_2, \mathbf{p}_1) \tag{5.109}$$

in which proj $(\mathbf{a}, \mathbf{b})$ is the vector projection of $\mathbf{a}$ onto $\mathbf{b}$ defined as

$$\text{proj}\,(\mathbf{a}, \mathbf{b}) = \frac{\mathbf{a} \cdot \mathbf{b}}{\mathbf{b} \cdot \mathbf{b}} \mathbf{b} \tag{5.110}$$

At the next step, the third user concept vector can be orthogonalized by subtracting its projections onto the previous two

$$\mathbf{p}_3 = \mathbf{p}_3 - \text{proj}\,(\mathbf{p}_3, \mathbf{p}_1) - \text{proj}\,(\mathbf{p}_3, \mathbf{p}_2) \tag{5.111}$$

and so on. This process is essentially an iterative version of the Gram–Schmidt process, a basic procedure in linear algebra that takes an arbitrary set of linearly independent vectors and constructs a set of orthogonal vectors from it. The same approach can be used for the item concept vectors, that is, for the columns of matrix $\mathbf{Q}$. Inserting these orthogonalization operations into algorithm 5.1, we get algorithm 5.2, which uses exactly the same inner loop to update the elements of the latent factors but has an additional projection step to orthogonalize the basis of the concept vectors.

Finally, we conclude this section with a remark about the different types of constraints that can be imposed on the latent factors, other than orthogonality. Algorithm 5.2 produces strictly orthogonal latent factors, even in the case of an incomplete rating matrix. This improves the interpretability of the results to a certain extent, but the relationships between users, items, and concepts can still be difficult to interpret because of the interplay of positive and negative factor values. We can try to address this issue by changing the constraints from orthogonality to non-negativity:

$$\min_{\mathbf{P}, \mathbf{Q}} \quad \left\| \mathbf{R} - \mathbf{P} \cdot \mathbf{Q}^{\mathsf{T}} \right\|^2$$
$$\text{subject to} \quad \mathbf{P} \geqslant 0 \tag{5.112}$$
$$\mathbf{Q} \geqslant 0$$

input   training set $\mathbf{R}$ (sampled from the original rating matrix)

output   matrices $\mathbf{P}$ and $\mathbf{Q}$

initialize $p_{ud}^{(0)} \sim$ random with mean μ_0 $1 \leqslant u \leqslant n,$ $1 \leqslant d \leqslant k$

initialize $q_{id}^{(0)} \sim$ random with mean μ_0 $1 \leqslant i \leqslant m,$ $1 \leqslant d \leqslant k$

for concept dimension $d = 1, 2, \ldots, k$ **do**

> **repeat**
>
> > **for** each rating r_{ui} in the training set **do**
> >
> > > update elements of $\mathbf{p}_d$ and $\mathbf{q}_d$ (see algorithm 5.1)
> >
> > **end**
> >
> > $$\mathbf{p}_d \leftarrow \mathbf{p}_d - \sum_{s=1}^{d-1} \mathrm{proj}\,(\mathbf{p}_d,\ \mathbf{p}_s) \qquad \text{(projection)}$$
> >
> > $$\mathbf{q}_d \leftarrow \mathbf{q}_d - \sum_{s=1}^{d-1} \mathrm{proj}\,(\mathbf{q}_d,\ \mathbf{q}_s) \qquad \text{(projection)}$$
>
> **until**   convergence condition

end

Algorithm 5.2: Matrix factorization with orthogonality constraints by using the stochastic gradient descent algorithm.

This optimization problem, known as *non-negative matrix factorization*, can also be solved by using a variant of the gradient descent algorithm [Zhang et al., 1996; Lee and Seung, 2001]. The advantage of non-negative factorization is better interpretability of the results because each factor element indicates proximity to a concept and each user or item can be represented as an additive linear combination of concepts.

5.8.3.3   *Advanced Latent Factor Models*

The factorization methods we discussed in the previous sections provide a solid framework for the creation of latent factor models. These algorithms, however, are very basic and leave a lot of room for additional improvements and extensions. Such extended models, sometimes very sophisticated, can deliver a substantial improvement in the quality of the top k recommendations, although the incremental improvement in terms of prediction accuracy (i.e., the mean squared error) can be very limited [Koren, 2008]. In this section, we review several advanced models that can be viewed as practical implementations of the latent factors approach. These methods are mainly based on ideas that we have already discussed in connection with other recommendation algorithms, but they have been adapted to the latent factors approach.

REGULARIZATION AND BIASES   As we discussed earlier in section 5.6.1, the user and item biases are important *baseline estimators* that can help to capture and remove the average user and item effects. Because both baseline estimates and latent factors can be determined by using gradient descent, we can combine the two models into one and jointly optimize both bias and latent factor variables. The rating prediction formula for this model will be defined as follows:

$$\hat{r}_{ui} = \mu + b_i + b_u + p_u q_i^\top \tag{5.113}$$

in which μ is the global mean, b_i is the item bias, b_u is the user bias, and the last term corresponds to the latent factors part of the model. Adding a regularization term that helps to avoid overfitting on sparse data, we translate this model into the following optimization problem:

$$\min \quad \sum_{u,i} \left(r_{ui} - \mu - b_i - b_u - p_u q_i^\top \right)^2 + \\ + \lambda \left(b_i^2 + b_u^2 + \|p_u\|^2 + \|q_i\|^2 \right) \tag{5.114}$$

in which λ is a regularization parameter and minimization is done by all bias and latent factor variables simultaneously. This problem can be solved by using a version of basic stochastic gradient descent algorithm 5.1 with the following learning rules:

$$
\begin{aligned}
b_u &\leftarrow b_u + \alpha \left(e - \lambda \cdot b_u \right) \\
b_i &\leftarrow b_i + \alpha \left(e - \lambda \cdot b_i \right) \\
p_{ud} &\leftarrow p_{ud} + \alpha \left(e \cdot q_{id} - \lambda \cdot p_{ud} \right) \\
q_{id} &\leftarrow p_{id} + \alpha \left(e \cdot p_{ud} - \lambda \cdot q_{id} \right)
\end{aligned}
\tag{5.115}
$$

in which α is the learning rate. This model can be considered as a practical version of the basic unconstrained factorization discussed earlier and is often referred to as an SVD model, which is technically not accurate.

IMPLICIT FEEDBACK   The second model that we will consider leverages the observation that the user selects items to rate not at random but in accordance with personal interests and preferences. Consequently, a useful signal is carried not only by the actual rating values but by the positions of the known ratings as well (see section 5.1.1 for details). We can isolate this signal about user–item interactions in the $n \times m$ implicit feedback matrix, which contains ones in the positions of known ratings and zeros in the positions of missing ratings. Normalizing each row to a unit length, we define the implicit feedback matrix $\mathbf{F}$ as

$$
f_{ui} = \begin{cases} |\, I_u \,|^{-1/2}, & \text{if } r_{ui} \text{ is known} \\ 0, & \text{otherwise} \end{cases} \tag{5.116}
$$

in which I_u is the set of items rated by user u. In a general case, the implicit feedback matrix is not necessarily derived from the rating matrix and can be created from a different data source. For example, the implicit feedback matrix can be created based on purchase or web browsing histories, so that each non-zero element indicates an interaction between a user and item.

The idea of the factorized model with implicit feedback is to introduce an additional set of item factors where each factor value y_{id} characterizes *how much the act of rating item i increases or decreases the proximity to concept d.* Let us denote this set of factors as the $m \times k$ matrix $\mathbf{Y}$. The product of the implicit feedback matrix and this new item–factors matrix $\mathbf{FY} = (z_{ud})$ is an $n \times k$ matrix in which rows correspond to users, columns corresponds to concepts, and each element z_{ud} can be interpreted as the incremental proximity of user u to concept d attributed to the implicit feedback, that is, the act of rating. This incremental proximity can be added directly to the main user–factor matrix $\mathbf{P}$, which characterizes the user–concept proximity derived from the rating values; the result is the optimization problem

$$
\min_{\mathbf{P},\,\mathbf{Q},\,\mathbf{Y}} \quad \left\| \mathbf{R} - (\mathbf{P} + \mathbf{FY})\,\mathbf{Q}^{\mathsf{T}} \right\|^2 \tag{5.117}
$$

By adding user and item biases, we get the following rating prediction formula:

$$
\widehat{r}_{ui} = \mu + b_i + b_u + \left(\mathbf{p}_u + |\, I_u \,|^{-1/2} \sum_{j \in I_u} \mathbf{y}_j \right) \mathbf{q}_i^{\mathsf{T}} \tag{5.118}
$$

in which $\mathbf{y}_j$ are the rows of matrix $\mathbf{Y}$. The learning rules for stochastic gradient descent can be straightforwardly derived from expression 5.118 by including regularization terms and taking the gradients:

$$b_u \leftarrow b_u + \alpha (e - \lambda_1 \cdot b_u)$$
$$b_i \leftarrow b_i + \alpha (e - \lambda_1 \cdot b_i)$$
$$p_{ud} \leftarrow p_{ud} + \alpha (e \cdot q_{id} - \lambda_2 \cdot p_{ud})$$
$$q_{id} \leftarrow p_{id} + \alpha \left(e \left(p_{ud} + | I_u |^{-1/2} \sum_{j \in I_u} y_{jd} \right) - \lambda_2 \cdot q_{id} \right) \tag{5.119}$$
$$y_{jd} \leftarrow y_{jd} + \alpha \left(e \cdot | I_u |^{-1/2} \cdot q_{id} - \lambda_2 \cdot y_{jd} \right)$$

in which λ_1 and λ_2 are the regularization parameters. This model, known as the SVD++ model, can offer better accuracy than basic SVD because of more accurate handling of the implicit feedback signal [Koren, 2008]. The SVD++ model is often considered to be one of the most advanced and efficient latent factor models.

FUSING LATENT FACTORS WITH NEIGHBORHOODS   Finally, we consider a model that combines factorization with the nearest neighbor approach. As we discussed in section 5.7.4, neighborhood-based collaborative filtering can generally be considered as a regression problem. This problem can be solved either analytically or by using optimization methods such as stochastic gradient descent. The latter approach enables us to roll the neighborhood model into the factorization algorithm and optimize the latent factors together with the neighborhood model weights. An integrated model can be obtained by combining the latent factor expression 5.118 with the neighborhood expression 5.69 that we discussed previously, which results in the following formula for the rating prediction:

$$\hat{r}_{ui} = \mu + \underline{b_u} + \underline{b_i} + \left(\underline{p_u} + | I_u |^{-1/2} \sum_{j \in I_u} \underline{y_j} \right) \underline{q_i^T} +$$
$$+ | Q_{ui}^s |^{-1/2} \sum_{j \in Q_{ui}^s} \left((r_{uj} - b_{uj}) \underline{w_{ij}} + \underline{c_{ij}} \right) \tag{5.120}$$

in which Q_{ui}^s is the neighborhood of item i in the set of items rated by user u (in other words, the top s most similar items in I_u) and b_{uj} is the baseline prediction. Factors $| I_u |^{-1/2}$ and $| Q_{ui}^s |^{-1/2}$ can be interpreted as the reliabilities of the corresponding terms, that is, the number of ratings that the estimate is based on, so contribution of the terms is scaled up or down accordingly. The rating prediction error is then minimized with respect to all underlined variables simultaneously by using a set of learning rules similar to set 5.119, but with additional rules for weights w_{ij} and c_{ij} [Koren, 2008].

5.9 HYBRID METHODS

Making recommendations is a broad and challenging problem, so an ideal recommender system should leverage multiple data sources and account for a wide range of effects and signals, such as user–item interactions, item content similarities, and many others. Most recommendation methods, however, can use only one type of data and capture only a certain type of effect. Basic collaborative filtering, for example, is focused on the rating matrix analysis and neglects item content; meanwhile, content-based filtering does the opposite. Consequently, each method has its own strengths and weaknesses, and methods can potentially complement each other. The hybrid approach attempts to create superior recommendation systems by combining several basic algorithms together.

We have already seen a few examples of how two or more recommendation methods can be combined together. For instance, user-based and item-based neighborhood methods were blended together by means of regression analysis in section 5.7.4.3, and the basic SVD model was been augmented with implicit feedback data in section 5.8.3.3. These hybrid solutions can generally achieve substantially better performance than could be achieved from any of the constituent algorithms alone. Our next goal is to develop a more systematic and comprehensive framework for hybridization that, ideally, can create the optimal blend from any set of recommendation algorithms. This framework can help us not only to build more powerful recommendation services but also to better and more systematically understand some of the previously described methods. The problem of hybrid recommendation models is closely related to ensemble learning, which focuses on methods that generate and combine multiple classification or regression models to obtain better predictive performance than could be obtained by individual learning algorithms. We use ensemble theory in the following sections to build hybrid recommenders, by starting from very basic methods and gradually increasing the complexity.

5.9.1 *Switching*

One of the most basic ways to combine several recommendation algorithms together is simply to switch between them depending on some condition. For example, we can assume that a collaborative filtering method works well enough unless an item has too few known ratings, in which case content-based filtering is likely to do a better job [Burke,

2002]. Consequently, we can switch between these two algorithms depending on the number of users who rated an item:

$$
\hat{r}_{ui} = \begin{cases} \hat{r}_{ui}^{(\text{collaborative})}, & \text{if } | U_i | > 20 \\ \\ \hat{r}_{ui}^{(\text{content})}, & \text{otherwise} \end{cases}
\tag{5.121}
$$

in which U_i is the set of users who rated item i. This solution can help us to work around the cold-start problem, which is an issue for collaborative filtering, and, at the same time, to improve trivial recommendations produced by content-based filtering whenever possible. A generic schema of such a switching recommender is shown in Figure 5.16. This approach, however, is somewhat rudimentary because it is based on heuristic rules rather than a formal optimization framework. We can definitely achieve better results by leveraging machine learning and optimization algorithms to properly mix the outputs of the individual models.

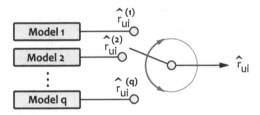

Figure 5.16: A switching recommender.

5.9.2 *Blending*

Let us assume that several recommendation models have been trained for the same set of users and items, so each of these models can estimate rating r_{ui} for a given pair of user and item. Our goal is to combine these estimates together to produce the final rating estimate, which is, ideally, more accurate than the predictions produced by any single one of the models. This can be done by using heuristic rules, as we did in the switching approach described in the previous section, but, at the same time, it is naturally a regression problem that can be efficiently solved by using the machine learning toolkit.

The problem of blending several rating estimates together can be formally defined in the following way. Let us assume that we have s training samples, that is, known rating values in the training set. This set is used to train q recommendation models, each of which can predict the rating for a given pair of user and item. For each training sample j, let us denote the vector of q model outputs (predicted rating values) as $\mathbf{x}_j$ and the true rating value as y_j. The problem of blending the available estimates together can then be defined as finding the blending function $b(\mathbf{x})$ that minimizes the prediction error:

$$\min_{b} \sum_{j=1}^{s} \left(b(\mathbf{x}_j) - y_j\right)^2 \tag{5.122}$$

This view of the problem is illustrated in Figure 5.17. This problem, that is, the combination of the predictions of several learning algorithms by using another learning algorithm, is known as *stacking*, so we use the terms *blending* and *stacking* interchangeably. Stacking is essentially a standard supervised learning problem that can be solved by using a variety of classification or regression algorithms.

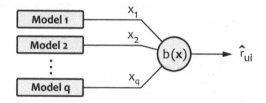

Figure 5.17: A blending recommender.

One of the most basic solutions of problem 5.122 is, of course, linear regression. In this case, the combiner function is a linear function defined as

$$b(\mathbf{x}) = \mathbf{x}^T \mathbf{w} \tag{5.123}$$

in which $\mathbf{w}$ is the vector of model weights. In other words, the final rating prediction is a linear combination of predictions produced by individual recommendation algorithms:

$$\hat{r}_{ui} = \sum_{k=1}^{q} w_k \cdot \hat{r}_{ui}^{(k)} \tag{5.124}$$

The optimal weights for the blending function can be straightforwardly calculated by using ridge regression:

$$\mathbf{w} = \left(\mathbf{X}^T\mathbf{X} + \lambda\mathbf{I}\right)^{-1} \mathbf{X}^T\mathbf{y} \tag{5.125}$$

in which $\mathbf{y}$ is the vector of s known ratings, λ is a regularization parameter, and $\mathbf{X}$ is an $s \times q$ matrix of rating predictions. Each element x_{jk} is the rating predicted by algorithm k for the j-th training sample.

In practice, the best results are often obtained by using non-linear blending models, such as neural networks and gradient boosted decision trees [Jahrer et al., 2010; Koren, 2009; Töscher et al., 2009]. The blend can include dozens of recommendation models that can be of different types (neighborhood-based, factorized, mixed, etc.), and each type can be represented by multiple model variants that are trained with different numerical parameters, such as the number of latent factors. The models can be trained on the entire training set, or this set can be divided into subsets (bins) randomly or according to some criteria and then the individual models can be trained for each bin separately. Blending is a powerful method that can substantially improve the quality of predictions, so many blending techniques have either been adopted from ensemble theory or developed specifically for recommender systems. We review some of these extensions and refinements in the next sections.

5.9.2.1 *Blending with Incremental Model Training*

The basic blending approach assumes that all models in the blend are trained in advance, and the blending function is then learned separately to minimize the overall prediction error. This approach, however, is not necessarily optimal because a set of models, each of which has a low prediction error, does not necessarily produce a blend with the minimal prediction error. To a certain extent, this can be explained by correlation between the models – a good blend not only requires models to achieve low prediction errors individually but also to achieve a certain level of error decorrelation [Töscher et al., 2009]. In fact, an ideal solution would be to merge all models into one big model and simultaneously optimize all parameters with respect to the overall blend prediction error. The hybrid model from section 5.8.3.3 that combines the neighborhood approach with latent factors is actually an example of such a solution. Unfortunately, this approach becomes intractable as the number of models in the blend and, consequently, the number of parameters grows. From this perspective, blending can be viewed as a divide-and-conquer approximation of the globally optimal solution.

Blending can be improved by including the global error function of the blend into the model training process. If it is assumed that individual models in the blend are trained by using gradient descent, which is a fair assumption for many practical applications, one possible solution is to redefine the convergence condition of the gradient descent loop based on the overall prediction error of the blend. This solution is implemented in algorithm 5.3. We initialize the matrix of model outputs $\mathbf{X}$ with a single column of ones that can be interpreted as a constant term in the blend. The recommendation models are then trained and added to the blend one after another. Each model is trained by using gradient descent or stochastic gradient descent in the inner loop of algorithm 5.3. For each iteration, we update the model by using its learning rules, predict ratings for all training samples, assemble a temporary matrix $\mathbf{X}$ by appending a column of newly predicted ratings, re-optimize the blend (the algorithm uses a linear blending function for illustration, but any other blending model can be used), and estimate the blend prediction error. The method does not change the error functions of individual models and learning rules, but it changes the convergence condition so that training stops when the overall prediction error of the blend is minimized. In practice, the blend prediction error can continue to decrease after the model prediction error reaches its minimum and starts to increase.

$\mathbf{X}^{(0)} = s \times 1$ column matrix of ones $\qquad$ (constant component)

for recommendation model $k = 1, 2, \ldots, q$ **do**

$\quad$ **repeat**

$\qquad$ update model k $\qquad$ (one step of model training)

$\qquad$ predict ratings $\mathbf{x}_k$ using model k

$\qquad$ $\mathbf{X} = \left[\mathbf{X}^{(k-1)} \mid \mathbf{x}_k \right]$ $\qquad$ (try adding $\mathbf{x}_k$ to the blend)

$\qquad$ $\mathbf{w} = \left(\mathbf{X}^\mathsf{T} \mathbf{X} \right)^{-1} \mathbf{X}^\mathsf{T} \mathbf{y}$ $\qquad$ (optimize the blending function)

$\qquad$ $\mathbf{r} = \mathbf{X} \cdot \mathbf{w}$ $\qquad$ (calculate prediction of the blend)

$\qquad$ $\mathrm{SSE} = \| \mathbf{r} - \mathbf{y} \|^2$ $\qquad$ (update the overall prediction error)

$\quad$ **until** $\quad$ SSE convergence

$\quad$ $\mathbf{X}^{(k)} = \mathbf{X}$ $\qquad$ (permanently add $\mathbf{x}_k$ to the blend)

end

Algorithm 5.3: Incremental model training by using a linear blending function [Töscher et al., 2009].

5.9.2.2 *Blending with Residual Training*

From the error decorrelation standpoint, it can be beneficial to train some models in the blend by using residual errors of other models as inputs. More specifically, we chain several models so that the outputs of models at the beginning of the chain are used as inputs for the downstream models, as illustrated in Figure 5.18.

The models in the chain are trained sequentially. The first model is trained based on the raw samples, the ratings predicted by this model

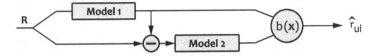

Figure 5.18: Model training on residual errors.

are then subtracted from the raw samples, the second model is trained by using these residual errors as inputs, and so on. The final blend can include predictions produced by models trained on the raw data and predictions created based on the residual errors. Among the previously discussed models, the removal of the global rating average and baseline predictors are basic examples of residual training techniques.

5.9.2.3 Feature-weighted Blending

The accuracy of rating predictions and, eventually, the quality of recommendations can be improved by blending together outputs of several recommendation models. In previous sections, we have discussed how the blending function can be constructed to mix the outputs of models in an optimal way. We can, however, expect that the accuracy can be improved even further if the blending function uses not only the outputs of the recommendation models but also additional signals about model reliability or some external signals about users or items. For example, some models can produce very accurate results if many ratings for a user or item are already known but can become very inaccurate and unstable if the ratings are scarce. The weight of such models in the blend can be increased or decreased depending on the rating statistics. In fact, we can find some traces of this approach in the previously described models. For instance, the discounted similarity technique described in section 5.7.1 mixes the reliability data with the user similarity measures. In the same vein, the latent factor model with implicit feedback from section 5.8.3.3 amplifies certain factors by using an external implicit feedback signal.

The blending framework can take advantage of external signals, sometimes referred to as *meta-features*, in different ways. One possible approach is to admix these signals into the blending function as additional inputs, that is, to append the signals to the vector of the recommender model outputs. Although this approach is generally feasible, it does not work well with linear blending functions and often requires complex nonlinear blending models to be learned, for example, when gradient boosted decision trees are used [Sill et al., 2009]. An alternative approach is to combine several linear models into a pipeline with a predefined structure to mix the signals from recommendation models with the signals from meta-features. This approach allows us to take advantage of the simplicity and stability of linear regression but to achieve much better results than a plain linear model that uses meta-features as additional inputs. We will spend the rest of the section describing the details of this method [Sill et al., 2009].

The idea of feature-weighted blending is to mix the outputs of the recommendation models by using a linear blending function but to calculate the blending weights as functions of the meta-features. Let us assume a set of q recommendation models produces rating predictions $x_1, \ldots, x_q$. In addition, let us assume p meta-features $g_1, \ldots, g_p$ are associated with each rating value. We choose to mix the predictions by using the linear blending function

$$b(\mathbf{x}) = \sum_{k=1}^{q} w_k x_k \tag{5.126}$$

but weights w_k are dynamically calculated based on the meta-features:

$$w_k = f_k(\mathbf{g}) = \sum_{i=1}^{p} v_{ki} g_i \tag{5.127}$$

in which f_k are called feature functions and v_{ki} are static weights. In other words, the feature functions amplify or suppress the signals from the recommendation models, as shown in Figure 5.19. Note that this design is quite similar to the signal mixing pipelines that we discussed in Chapter 4, in the context of search services.

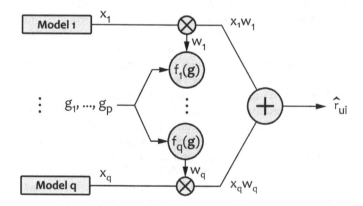

Figure 5.19: Feature-weighted blending.

This model translates into the following optimization problem:

$$\min_{v} \sum_{j=1}^{s} \sum_{k,i} \left(v_{ki} \cdot g_{ji} \cdot x_{jk} - y_j \right)^2 \qquad (5.128)$$

in which the outer sum iterates over all s training samples, x_{jk} is the rating predicted by algorithm k for the j-th training sample, g_{ji} stands for the j-th sample meta-features, and y_j is the true rating value for sample j. To solve this problem, let us first introduce the $s \times (qp)$ matrix **A** that contains the cross-products of predictions and meta-features for each training sample:

$$a_{j,\,p(k-1)+i} = x_{jk} \cdot g_{ji}, \qquad \begin{aligned} & 1 \leqslant j \leqslant s \\ & 1 \leqslant k \leqslant q \\ & 1 \leqslant i \leqslant p \end{aligned} \qquad (5.129)$$

In each row of matrix **A**, the first p elements correspond to the first recommendation model, followed by p elements that correspond to the second model, and so on. In other words, the first segment of p elements is the output of the first model x_{j1}, modulated by each of the feature functions, and so on. Let us also introduce vector **v** with the same structure, created by sequencing weights v_{ki} as a row with qp elements, so that the first p elements correspond to the first model, followed by p elements for the second model, and so forth. The optimal weights can then be found by solving a regression problem that corresponds to the following system of linear equations:

$$\left(A^{\mathsf{T}} A + \lambda I \right) v = A^{\mathsf{T}} y \qquad (5.130)$$

in which λ is a regularization parameter and **I** is a diagonal identity matrix.

Feature-weighted blending provides a relatively simple extension of the basic weighting framework that allows one to modulate model predictions with additional signals or meta-features. Common examples of such meta-features include basic statistics (e. g., the number of times the item has been rated, the standard deviation of the user ratings), time-dependent statistics (e. g., the number of distinct dates on which a user has rated items), and correlation statistics (e. g., the maximum correlation of the item with any other item). These statistics are important for a hybrid recommender because the reliability of the estimates produced by the constituent models depends on the number of available ratings and other similar factors reflected in the statistical signals. Consequently, these features enable the hybrid model to learn how to switch between the models depending on the expected reliability of the estimates.

5.9.3   *Feature Augmentation*

The next class of hybrid methods that we will consider is recommenders with feature augmentation. The feature augmentation technique refers to a design where several recommendation models are chained together in such a way that predictions produced by one recommendation model are consumed by another model as inputs. We already used this approach in blending with residual training, but this idea can be exploited in several other ways.

One possible approach for chaining two recommenders together is to use the first model in the chain to generate completely new features that are not present in the raw data, so that the downstream models can use them as inputs. For example, the content-based Naive Bayes recommender described in section 5.5.2 can leverage item attributes such as *related authors* and *related titles* to recommend books. These attributes can be created by using an item similarity measure computed over the rating matrix, that is, by using collaborative filtering [Mooney and Roy, 1999]. This effectively creates a hybrid recommender with feature augmentation, where collaborative filtering is the first model in the chain that generates new features and the content-based classifier is the second model that consumes them.

The second option for chaining recommenders is to use the first recommender in the chain to enhance the features that are present in the raw data. For example, a content-based recommender can be used to fill missing elements in the rating matrix, and this enhanced matrix can then be used by some collaborative filtering method. This approach can be contrasted with the previous example, which uses collaborative filtering to augment the inputs of the content-based Naive Bayes recommender. Let us flesh out this solution, called *content-boosted collaborative filtering*, in detail, with the assumption that a user-based nearest neighbor recommender is used as the collaborative filtering component of the hybrid [Melville et al., 2002]. The first step is to use a content-based recommender to fill in the missing elements of the rating matrix and create a new pseudo rating matrix, defined as follows:

$$
z_{ui} = \begin{cases} r_{ui}, & \text{if user } u \text{ rated item } i \\ \hat{r}_{ui}^{(c)}, & \text{otherwise} \end{cases} \tag{5.131}
$$

in which $\hat{r}_{ui}^{(c)}$ is the rating predicted by the content-based recommender. The second step is to apply the collaborative filtering part of the hybrid to the pseudo rating matrix to predict the rating for a given pair of user and item. In principle, one can use any out-of-the-box collaborative filtering algorithm to make the final prediction. The challenge, however, is that the ratings filled in during the previous step skew the statistics of the number of known ratings used by many collaborative filtering algorithms. This requires the collaborative filtering part to be modified and several additional factors and parameters to be introduced to fix the statistics:

- The reliability of content-based rating predictions depends on the number of known ratings for a given user. Consequently, predictions that do not have enough support should be devalued when used in collaborative filtering. If we use a user-based neighborhood model for the collaborative filtering step, we can account for the reliability of the incoming ratings by modifying the user similarity measure. Let us first define a normalized support variable that grows proportionally to the number of ratings provided by a user but is limited to one if the number of ratings exceeds the threshold parameter T:

$$q_u = \begin{cases} 1, & |I_u| \geq T \\ |I_u|/T, & \text{otherwise} \end{cases} \tag{5.132}$$

The similarity function can then be redefined by adding a factor that equals the harmonic mean of the support variables for two users:

$$\text{sim}'(u, v) = \frac{2q_u q_v}{q_u + q_v} \cdot \text{sim}(u, v) \tag{5.133}$$

The harmonic mean is chosen because it is biased toward the minimum of two numbers, so the similarity measure will be significantly penalized if either user has provided too few ratings.

- The hybrid system includes content-based and collaborative filtering components that are both capable of predicting the rating for a given user and item, so these two predictions need to mixed together. To manage the balance between the predictions, let us introduce amplification factor w_u for the content-based prediction. This factor is defined as the baseline amplification weight w_{max} multiplied by the support variable in order to penalize unreliable predictions:

$$w_u = w_{max} \cdot q_u \tag{5.134}$$

The final rating prediction formula for the collaborative filtering part can then be defined as follows:

$$\hat{r}_{ui} = \mu_u + \frac{w_u \left(\hat{r}_{ui}^{(c)} - \mu_u\right) + \sum_v \text{sim}'(u, v)(z_{vi} - \mu_v)}{w_u + \sum_v \text{sim}'(u, v)} \tag{5.135}$$

in which μ_u is the average user rating computed over the pseudo rating matrix. This is essentially the basic user-based nearest neighbor model with the content-based estimate $\hat{r}_{ui}^{(c)}$ admixed and the similarity function adjusted to account for the reliability of the content-based estimates. Note that these reliability-related adjustments are fundamentally similar to the feature-weighted blending that we discussed in the previous section: in both cases, the hybrid recommender uses the basic rating statistics to devalue models with low reliability and amplify signals from models with high reliability.

The content-boosted collaborative filtering model defined by expression 5.135 can generally provide better accuracy than either of the two constituent recommendation methods alone. If the raw rating matrix is reasonably dense, the model outperforms both the content and collaborative components by taking advantage of two signals. In the case of a sparse rating matrix, the accuracy of the collaborative filtering component drops and the overall performance of the hybrid model converges to the accuracy of the content-based recommender [Melville et al., 2002].

5.9.4 *Presentation Options for Hybrid Recommendations*

We conclude the discussion of hybrid methods with a brief remark about how a hybrid recommender can leverage the presentation capabilities of the recommendation service. First, it is worth noting that recommendations produced by different models should not necessarily be blended together – a recommender system can simply display several lists of recommended items. Ecommerce web sites, for example, very often display several recommendation bars with different semantic meanings, such as *Customers who viewed this item also viewed*, *Inspired by your browsing history*, *Top rated items*, *Similar items*, and so on. These pieces of content can naturally be created by using different recommendation algorithms, including both personalized and non-personalized methods. Recommender systems that use this approach are typically referenced as *mixed hybrids*.

In certain cases, the recommended items need to meet additional requirements or conditions, depending on how the recommendations are presented and how the user interacts with the recommendation service. For example, a user can explicitly request the recommendation of restaurants in a certain location or more books similar to the selected one. In such cases, the recommender system can be used as a sorting component that postprocesses the results created by a search service or another recommendation model. For instance, a search service can be used to fetch the list of items according to the criteria explicitly specified by the user, and then this list can be sorted by a collaborative filtering unit. This technique, sometimes referred to as *cascading*, can be viewed as an extreme case of blending, where the signal from the first recommender or search service is steeply pitched to sort items into relevant and irrelevent buckets and the second recommender does the secondary sorting within the buckets.

5.10   CONTEXTUAL RECOMMENDATIONS

The majority of recommendation algorithms, including all of the methods we have discussed earlier in this chapter, are based on the assumption that the relevance of a given item for a given user can be predicted by using only the profiles of the item and user. This approach completely ignores the circumstances under which recommendations are made, including time, user location, marketing channel, and other pieces of information about the situation and environment. This contextual information, however, is very important because consumer decisions are almost always contingent on the context of the decision making. Consequently, the relevance of recommendations is unique for each recommendation transaction rather than statistically determined by the item and user profiles. Let us consider several specific cases to better understand the notion of context:

LOCATION Recommendations made by a shoe store for users in Alaska may not be relevant for users in Hawaii. Customers who use a mobile application to find relevant restaurants nearby may receive recommendations that will not be relevant for them when they move to another location.

TIME Movie recommendations that are relevant for a fifteen-year-old user today may not be relevant five years later when that user will be twenty. TV program recommendations relevant in the morning may not be relevant in the evening. Recommendations made by an apparel recommender system in one season may not be relevant in another season.

INTENT The relevancy of restaurant recommendations made for a user can change depending on whom the user dines out with: alone, with their spouse, with co-workers, or with family. Recommendations made for users shopping for themselves can be different from recommendations made if they are shopping for a gift. Hotel booking recommendations for business travelers can be different from recommendations for leisure travelers.

CHANNEL Recommendations made in emails can have a different structure and presentation to recommendations made on a website or in a store.

CONDITIONS Recommendations made by a department store may or may not include umbrellas, depending on the current weather conditions or forecast.

A recommender system should take the contextual information about location, time, intent, and channel into account to deliver relevant real-time user experiences. We will spend the rest of this section discussing how recommendation algorithms can be extended or modified to incorporate these contextual signals.

5.10.1 Multidimensional Framework

Traditional recommendation models predict the relevance of a given item for a given user on the basis of the corresponding item and user profiles. These models can be viewed as functions that take a user and item as arguments and produce rating predictions:

$$\hat{r}_{ui} = R(u, i) \tag{5.136}$$

Context-aware recommender systems extend this framework with additional arguments, each of which represents a certain dimension of the context, such as location, time, or channel [Adomavicius and Tuzhilin, 2008]:

$$\hat{r}_{ui} = R(u, i, \textit{location}, \textit{time}, \ldots) \tag{5.137}$$

In other words, the basic rating function defined over two-dimensional space

$$R: \quad \textit{User} \times \textit{Item} \rightarrow \textit{Rating} \tag{5.138}$$

is replaced by a function defined over a multidimensional space that includes user, item, and context dimensions:

$$R: \quad \textit{User} \times \textit{Item} \times \textit{Location} \times \textit{Time} \times \ldots \rightarrow \textit{Rating} \tag{5.139}$$

This idea is illustrated in Figure 5.20, which shows an example of a three-dimensional recommendation space. In this example, each rating value is a function of a user, item, and time. All known ratings are attributed with a time label and placed in the corresponding cells of a three-dimensional array, instead of a two-dimensional rating matrix. The goal of the recommendation model is, therefore, to predict the rating values in the empty cells of the array. Note that a multidimensional array can be collapsed onto a standard two-dimensional rating matrix by discarding the contextual information. This may require the merging of several rating values that are projected onto one element of the matrix. For example, if a user rated the same item several times on different dates, only the latest value or average value can be kept in the rating matrix. Alternatively, the rating matrix can be obtained by selecting a certain point on the context dimension and cutting out a two-dimensional slice from the multidimensional cube at this point. For example, the array depicted in Figure 5.20 can be viewed as a pile of rating matrices $\mathbf{R}(t)$, one for each time interval. Finally, a rating matrix can be created not for a certain point on the contextual dimension but for a certain range. In the case of the example in Figure 5.20, this would be for a certain time interval.

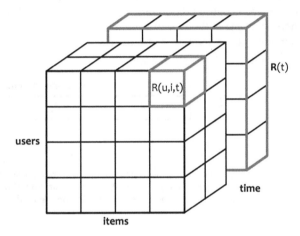

Figure 5.20: Example of a three-dimensional recommendation space.

We generally assume that context dimensions can have a hierarchical structure. For example, each known rating can be attributed with the date it was given, so the time dimension is discrete and contains as many intervals as there are distinct date labels in the rating data. Dates, however, can be aggregated into weekly, monthly, quarterly, or yearly intervals, and the rating matrix $\mathbf{R}(t)$ can thus be cut for a certain week, month, quarter, or year. We can have more than one hierarchy for one dimension. For instance, dates can also be categorized into weekdays and weekends, so that rating matrices for weekdays and weekends can be obtained. In a similar vein, fine-grained location attributes, such as latitude and longitude, can be aggregated into zip codes, cities, states, and countries. Finally, user and item dimensions can also be associated with certain hierarchies. For example, users can be categorized into buckets based on their age and items can be categorized into genres.

Contextual information can be obtained from different sources. Some attributes, such as a rating time stamp or user device location, can be automatically collected by the recommender system or marketing channels that the system is integrated with. Some other attributes, especially intent-related ones, may not be directly available but can be obtained by using special features of the user interface (for example, a *This is a gift order* checkbox on an online order placement form) or inferred by using predictive models.

5.10.2   *Context-Aware Recommendation Techniques*

A non-contextual recommendation service can be viewed as a process that consumes the training data in the form *User × Item × Rating*, creates a model that maps the pair of user and item to rating, and evaluates this model for a given user to produce a sorted list of recommendations. This pipeline is shown in Figure 5.21.

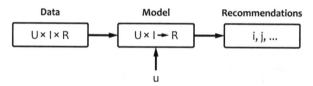

Figure 5.21: The main steps of the non-contextual recommendation process [Adomavicius and Tuzhilin, 2008]. U, I, and R are the dimensions of users, items, and ratings, respectively. Recommended items are denoted as $i, j, \ldots$

The multidimensional framework described in the previous section suggests several ideas for how this pipeline can be modified to incorporate contextual information [Adomavicius and Tuzhilin, 2008]:

CONTEXTUAL PREFILTERING The first possible solution is to create a two-dimensional rating matrix from the original multidimensional data and then apply a standard non-contextual recommendation model or algorithm with this matrix as an input, as shown in Figure 5.22. The rating matrix is a slice of the multidimensional cube selected for a given value of the context. For example, a movie recommendation service that stores ratings with time stamps can make recommendations on the weekdays and weekends by using two different matrices. The matrices are created by selecting all weekday or all weekend ratings, respectively, from the original data cube.

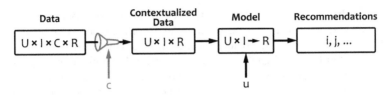

Figure 5.22: Context-aware recommender system with contextual prefiltering [Adomavicius and Tuzhilin, 2008].

One of the key considerations for the prefiltering approach is the trade-off between data sparsity and contextualization accuracy. On the one hand, contextualization of the input data can improve the accuracy of recommendations because the recommendation algorithm uses only the ratings that are relevant for the context. On the other hand, contextualization decreases the amount of data available for the recommendation algorithm, which can negatively impact the quality of recommendations. For example, a movie recommendation service that makes weekend recommendations by using only the ratings submitted on the weekends almost certainly loses some relevant signals carried by the weekday ratings. Contextualization with narrow selection criteria can also result in very sparse rating matrices, which can result in unreliable and skewed rating predictions. The trade-off between data sparsity and context accuracy can be controlled by using the hierarchical aggregation that we discussed in the previous section. For example, the time context can be applied at a days-of-the-week level of granularity (seven buckets in total) or a weekday–weekend level (two buckets in total). Note that, in principle, we can use the controlled precision reduction technique that we discussed in the context of search services in section 4.6.2 to try different granularity levels and select the optimal one for a given value of the context.

CONTEXTUAL POSTFILTERING An alternative approach to contextualization is postfiltering of recommendations, as depicted in Figure 5.23. A recommender system with postfiltering initially discards the contextual information and collapses the rating data cube onto a plain rating matrix, so that a standard recommendation algorithm can be applied to produce non-contextual recommendations. The list of recommended items is then contextualized by using context-aware postprocessing rules that are applied after the main recommendation method. These rules are typically based on user or item attributes and can be either heuristic or driven by a predictive model. For example, an apparel recommender system can create an initial list of non-contextual recommendations by using any content-based or collaborative filtering algorithm and can then filter or re-rank the items according to the current season or weather. For instance, it can push warm clothes to the top in winter. In this case, warm clothes can be determined by using a heuristic rule or content classification model such as a Naive Bayes text classifier.

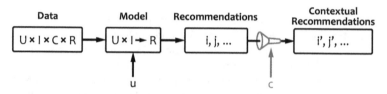

Figure 5.23: Context-aware recommender system with contextual postfiltering [Adomavicius and Tuzhilin, 2008].

CONTEXTUAL MODELING The most generic solution for the contextual recommendation problem is to create a model that can predict ratings directly as a function of multiple arguments, including item, user, and context. This approach is illustrated in Figure 5.24. The key advantage of the contextual modeling approach is that the context-related parameters of the model can be learned and optimized together with other parts of the model. This can lead to better results than heuristic pre- and postfiltering solutions, which, as we have discussed, can filter out relevant data and signals that do not formally meet the context criteria.

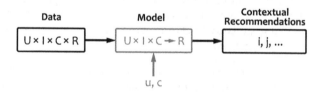

Figure 5.24: Context-aware recommender system with contextual modeling [Adomavicius and Tuzhilin, 2008].

Contextual models can often be obtained by extending standard non-contextual content-based and collaborative filtering models. Let us illustrate this idea with a conceptual example that uses the neighborhood model as a basis. Recall that a non-contextual nearest neighbor model can be expressed as follows:

$$\widehat{r}_{ui} = \sum_{v,j} \text{sim}\left((u,i),(v,j)\right) \cdot r_{vj} \tag{5.140}$$

in which indexes v and j iterate over the neighborhood of users and items, respectively. The similarity measure between user–item pairs (u,i) and (v,i) can be specified in many different ways, as we discussed earlier in the section dedicated to neighborhood-based collaborative filtering. In the case of the user-based neighborhood model, for example, the measure will be reduced to the similarity between two users, which, in turn, can be computed as the Pearson correlation coefficient or some other metric:

$$\text{sim}\left((u,i),(v,j)\right) = \begin{cases} \text{sim}\,(u,v), & i = j \\ 0, & \text{otherwise} \end{cases} \tag{5.141}$$

A time-aware contextual model can extend the notion of similarity and include the time dimension:

$$\widehat{r}_{uit} = \sum_{v,j,s} \text{sim}\left((u,i,t),(v,j,s)\right) \cdot r_{vjs} \tag{5.142}$$

in which index s iterates over the neighborhood of ratings with time stamps close to the target context time stamp t. The multidimensional similarity measure can then be defined as the distance between two cells in the three-dimensional data cube. For example, one can use the Euclidean distance metric:

$$\text{sim}\left((u,i,t),(v,j,s)\right) = \frac{}{\sqrt{\text{sim}^2\,(u,v) + \text{sim}^2\,(i,j) + \text{sim}^2\,(t,s)}} \tag{5.143}$$

This is just a conceptual example that illustrates the approach for incorporating contextual information into a recommendation model, but we will develop more practical solutions in the next section.

Finally, let us note that multiple contextual and non-contextual recommendation algorithms can be combined together into hybrid models. The hybrid approach can help to overcome the limitations of individual methods (for example, sparsity issues caused by overly strict contextualization of the input data) by blending multiple predictions in the optimal way.

5.10.3   *Time-Aware Recommendation Models*

The temporal dimension is one of the most important types of context because of substantial variability in user–item interaction patterns over time. A good example of such variability is item popularity changes over time that can be caused by external factors, such as fashion changes that make certain garments more or less popular, the appearance of an actor in a new movie that boosts the popularity of related movies, or advances in technology that make old electronic devices outdated. Another example is the drift of user preferences over time that can be caused by changes in tastes, social role, or location. For instance, a user who used to rate an average item as 4 stars can become more critical or advanced over time and then give only 3 stars to mediocre products. At the same time, temporal context information is also one of the easiest types to collect because time stamps can be set internally by a recommender system without external dependencies on marketing channels or user interfaces. These factors make time-aware recommendations a low-hanging fruit that can substantially improve the accuracy of rating predictions with relatively low cost.

The multidimensional framework and pre/postprocessing contextualization techniques provide a simple toolkit that can be applied to cases with a periodic temporal context, such as seasonality. This toolkit is, however, very basic, and we will explore how to take advantage of predictive and optimization methods to create more advanced and accurate time-aware recommendation models. We will next discuss how the three main collaborative filtering models – baseline estimates, nearest neighbors, and latent factors – can be extended to account for a temporal dimension. It is worth noting that all three solutions were developed as components for the same hybrid model [Koren, 2009]. However, each model uses its own technique to account for temporal changes.

5.10.3.1   *Baseline Estimates with Temporal Dynamics*

The goal of baseline estimates is to capture the average user and item rating biases, as well as the global rating average. Recall that the standard baseline estimate of a rating is defined as follows (section 5.6.1):

$$b_{ui} = \mu + b_u + b_i \tag{5.144}$$

in which b_u and b_i are the average user and item biases, respectively. With the added assumption that user and item biases can change over time, the time-aware version can be defined as

$$b_{ui} = \mu + b_u(t) + b_i(t) \tag{5.145}$$

in which $b_u(t)$ and $b_i(t)$ are the functions of time that need to be learned from the data. Parameter t can be defined as the number of days measured off from some date zero in the past. In practice, user and item components can have very different temporal dynamics and properties, so one might need two different solutions for these two functions [Koren, 2009]. In many practical applications, item popularity changes slowly over time and each item has relatively many ratings. Therefore, the time range can be split into multiple time intervals (for example, several weeks each), and the item bias can be estimated for each interval independently. This leads to the following simple time-aware model for the item component:

$$b_i(t) = b_i + b_{i,\Delta t} \tag{5.146}$$

in which b_i is the global stationary bias, Δt is the time interval into which t falls, and $b_{i,\Delta t}$ is the item bias estimate for this time bucket. Note that the time-dependent part of the bias can be estimated only for historical dates and has to be set to zero if the entire Δt period is in the future. It may seem strange that this model does not attempt to extrapolate the time trend into the future, but it is important to keep in mind that baseline estimates are used as a component in more advanced models and their goal is to remove the observed trends and refine the signal; extrapolation can be done by the remaining parts of the model.

Although this approach can work well for items, it may not be efficient for users for at least two reasons. First, one user generally has far fewer ratings than one item, so the bias cannot be reliably estimated even for relatively large time intervals. Second, user biases can change much faster than item popularity, and this requires the use of even smaller time buckets. This problem can be solved by modeling the user bias drift as a simple function, instead of point estimates. For instance, one can use the following functional form to model the drift:

$$d_u(t) = \text{sgn}(t - t_u) \, | \, t - t_u \, |^\beta \tag{5.147}$$

in which $\text{sgn}(x)$ is a sign function that equals one when x is positive and equals -1 when x is negative, t_u is the mean rating date, and β is the constant parameter selected by using cross-validation. Roughly speaking, this is a linear function that can be bent down by setting the parameter $\beta < 1$, as shown in Figure 5.25. The time-aware user bias can then be defined as

$$b_u(t) = b_u + w_u \cdot d_u(t) \tag{5.148}$$

in which the stationary part b_u and the scaling factor w_u should be learned from the data for each user u. This model can be improved further by including additional terms that capture the day-specific variability of the user bias, such as the number of ratings provided by a user on a given day.

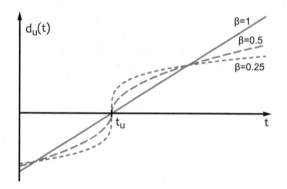

Figure 5.25: The user bias drift function for different values of β. The function is linear when $\beta = 1$.

5.10.3.2 Neighborhood Model with Time Decay

The nearest neighbor model predicts a rating for a given pair of user and item by averaging ratings from similar users or items. The ratings can be averaged by using a heuristic similarity measure or weights learned from the data. For example, one of the basic item-based neighborhood models is defined as follows (we discussed more complete and practical versions of this model in section 5.7.4):

$$\hat{r}_{ui} = b_{ui} + \sum_{j \in Q_{ui}^k} w_{ij} \left(r_{uj} - b_{uj} \right) \tag{5.149}$$

in which Q_{ui}^k is the neighborhood of item i in the set of items rated by the user, b_{uj} is the baseline estimate, and weight w_{ij} is a measure of the similarity between items i and j learned by using gradient descent or, alternatively, defined as some heuristic similarity measure, such as the Pearson correlation coefficient. Regardless of the weight estimation approach, we can generally assert that if a user gives the same ratings to two items i and j, it positively contributes to the corresponding weight w_{ij}, which, in turn, boosts the corresponding rating r_{uj}. It can be argued that ratings can lose their relevancy over time, so the fact that a user equally liked two items in the past should not necessarily contribute to the similarity of these items in the future because of the transient nature of user taste and identity [Ding and Li, 2005; Koren, 2009]. This consideration can be taken into account by adding a time decay factor into the model to discount old ratings:

$$\hat{r}_{ui}(t) = b_{ui} + \sum_{j \in Q_{ui}^k} e^{-c_u|t - t_{uj}|} \cdot w_{ij}\left(r_{uj} - b_{uj}\right) \tag{5.150}$$

Decay rate c_u is generally user specific and should be learned as an additional variable as a part of the gradient descent process.

5.10.3.3 Latent Factor Model with Temporal Dynamics

The latent factor models predict ratings by computing a correlation between user and item representations in the latent factor space. These models can be extended to account for temporal effects by using the techniques we developed earlier for baseline estimates. Recall that the most basic latent factor model is defined as

$$\hat{r}_{ui} = p_u q_i^T \tag{5.151}$$

in which p_u and q_i are the k-dimensional user and item latent factor vectors, respectively. One can account for variability of user tastes by adding a time drift term to each element of the latent factor vector, similar to the corresponding expression 5.148 for baseline estimates:

$$p_{us}(t) = p_{us} + w_{us} \cdot d_u(t), \qquad 1 \leqslant s \leqslant k \tag{5.152}$$

in which p_{us} is the stationary term, $d_u(t)$ is the drift defined by function 5.147, and s is the latent dimension index. Both the stationary and time-dependent parts of this model are estimated from the data by using gradient descent.

In practice, one will most likely use a more advanced latent factor model than basic solution 5.151. Fortunately, the time-dependent user factor defined by expression 5.152 can be utilized in the majority of latent factor models. One particularly important case is the SVD++ model defined in expression 5.118. Inserting the time-dependent user factor into the SVD++ model, we obtain a model called TimeSVD++:

$$\hat{r}_{ui} = \mu + b_i + b_u + \left(p_u(t) + |I_u|^{-\frac{1}{2}} \sum_{j \in I_u} y_j \right) q_i^T \tag{5.153}$$

The TimeSVD++ model is one of the most accurate non-hybrid collaborative filtering models, and it is often considered to be a pinnacle of recommender system engineering [Koren, 2009].

5.11   NON-PERSONALIZED RECOMMENDATIONS

The quality of recommendations is generally determined by the ability of a recommender system to recognize the intent of the user and find offerings that can fulfill this intent. As a result of the wide variability of user intents, recommender systems benefit greatly from accessing and utilizing personal and behavioral data; systems that do not access and use this data are likely to deliver poor quality recommendations. Roughly speaking, we can expect that recommendations created for everybody, that is, for an abstract average user, will actually be good for almost nobody because only a few real users will precisely match the average profile. However, recommender systems have to deal with the fact that the personal and behavioral information may be available, incomplete, or unreliable. For example, online systems often deal with anonymous users who have no interaction history or have only a very limited one collected during the current session. Such cases are very common, so it is important to extend the range of recommendation algorithms with non-personalized methods that can be used in a standalone mode or can be combined with personalized recommenders into a hybrid system. Non-personalized recommendations are not necessarily as accurate as personalized ones, but they can still be an effective solution for certain applications such as product cross-selling.

5.11.1   Types of Non-Personalized Recommendations

Non-personalized recommendation methods can generally be viewed as an extreme case of contextual recommendations where the signals about the target user are completely missing and the recommended items are selected based on the contextual and background information alone. The context, however, can include behavioral data about other users, so the common user–item interaction patterns and item popularity statistics can be known to the recommender. Let us consider several examples of non-personalized recommendations that are frequently used in practice:

POPULAR ITEMS Popular categories and brands are often highlighted in user interfaces to simplify navigation, and popular products are often promoted in sections like *Best Sellers* or *Top 10*. This type of recommendation does not necessarily use any request-level context, but it relies on dynamically updated selling or browsing statistics that can be considered as background context. From the predictive modeling perspective, these methods simply exploit the fact that the most frequent purchasing intents are the best predictions for the purchasing intent of the target user, given that no additional information is known.

TRENDING ITEMS A recommender system can recommend products that are trending upwards, instead of top sellers, based on the assumption that such recommendations can be more serendipitous. This approach, in particular, can better promote long-tail items because even a slow-moving product can have popularity bursts because of advertising or social media activity. A recommender of trending items typically scores items based on some smoothed version of the sales volume change history. For example, the scoring function for item i can be defined as

$$s(i) = 1.00 \cdot \Delta v_1(i) + 0.50 \cdot \Delta v_2(i) \tag{5.154}$$

in which $\Delta v_1(i)$ is the relative sales volume change (in percent) for the previous day and $\Delta v_2(i)$ is the volume change two days ago.

NEW RELEASES Some recommender systems highlight and promote new items or items recently added to the assortment.

SIMILAR ITEMS In online marketing channels, non-personalized recommendations can often be created based on the browsing context. One of the most typical examples is the *More like this* or *You might also like* type of recommendations shown on the product details page, that is, in the context of a certain product. Such recommendations can often be created by using standard search methods. For instance, one can define the distance between two products as the weighted average of the TF×IDF distances between the corresponding product document fields, and the most similar items can be recommended. This strategy relies on the item content and, consequently, tends to produce trivial non-serendipitous recommendations.

FREQUENT PATTERNS Best seller recommendations use only a small fraction of the information available in the purchase and browsing histories, namely, the overall sales statistics. Contextual information such as the currently browsed product or category is also unused, which negatively impacts the cross-selling relevance of the recommendations. More targeted recommendations can be created by analyzing purchasing and browsing patterns and detecting items that are frequently bought together with a given item or set of items. This type of recommendation is often presented on the product detail pages in sections like *Customers who bought this item also bought* or *What other items do customers buy after viewing this item*. We will discuss this approach in detail in the next section.

Although we categorize the above methods as non-personalized, it is important to understand that most of these methods can achieve at least some level of personalization through segmentation and granular contextualization. For example, a news recommender system can ask users to select the topics that they are most interested in (such as politics, science, sports, etc.) and then recommend most popular or trending items within the specified categories, instead of making recommendations based on the global statistics. A recommender system can also filter or re-rank personalized recommendations based on popularity statistics or release dates.

5.11.2 *Recommendations by Using Association Rules*

A non-personalized recommender system can analyze historical transactions from different marketing channels, including stores and online, to discover the typical dependencies between products that can be used to make recommendations. For example, if two items are frequently bought together, it can indicate that the second item would be a reasonable cross-selling recommendation for users who are currently browsing the first item and vice versa. The recommendations are then created in the context of an individual item (e. g., when a user browses a certain product details page) or multiple items (e. g., when a user has already added several products to the shopping basket). It is important to note that the boundary between personalized and non-personalized recommendations is quite blurry in this case. For example, recommendations that are created in the context of a certain product and shown on a product details page can be viewed as an integral static part of this page. It is the same for all users and, consequently, non-personalized. However, if the same context with a single item is persistently attached to a user and their experience is changed based on this context elsewhere, it can be viewed as personalization. A context that includes multiple items can definitely be interpreted as an interaction history or implicit feedback. In this case, recommendations made on the basis of patterns discovered in transactional data can definitely be categorized as collaborative filtering.

If the goal is to make a recommendation based on the currently browsed item or multiple items, we will be most interested in discovering regularities in historical transactions in the form of the following rules:

if a user purchases items $X = \{i_1, i_2, \ldots\}$,

then that user will also purchase items $Y = \{j_1, j_2, \ldots\}$

The sets of items X and Y are called *itemsets*, and the association rule described above is denoted as $X \rightarrow Y$. For example, the rule $\{pasta, wine\} \rightarrow \{garlic\}$ indicates that if users buy pasta and wine together, they are likely to also buy garlic. The number of association rules that have at least some support in data, that is, there exists at least one transaction where itemsets X and Y are bought together, can be very high. The goal of a recommender system, however, is to find rules that correspond to persistent patterns that can be used as predictors of user behavior. We need to introduce more formal rule quality metrics to select such rules.

Let us assume that we have a set of transactions T where each transaction is a collection of items purchased together. *Support* for itemset X can then be defined as the fraction of the transactions that contains all items from the itemset, that is, the empirical probability of X:

$$\text{support}(X) = \frac{|t : X \subseteq t|}{|T|}, \quad t \in T \tag{5.155}$$

Support for an association rule is the fraction of transactions that contains both itemsets of the rule:

$$\text{support}(X \rightarrow Y) = \text{support}(X \cup Y) \tag{5.156}$$

A high support level ensures that the rule corresponds to a persistent pattern where the itemsets are frequently bought together. It can, however, be the case that these itemsets are frequently bought separately as well, so high support merely confirms the fact that both itemsets are popular, even if no dependency between them really exists. This aspect is measured by the *confidence* of the rule, defined as the fraction of transactions containing X that also contains Y:

$$\text{confidence}(X \rightarrow Y) = \frac{\text{support}(X \cup Y)}{\text{support}(X)} \tag{5.157}$$

Confidence can be interpreted as the conditional probability of finding itemset Y in the transaction given that this transaction contains X, that is, $\Pr(Y \mid X)$. Note that support and confidence are defined based on the purchase probability and, consequently, can be linked to monetary measures such as revenue [Ju et al., 2015; Geng and Hamilton, 2006]. For example, one can roughly estimate the expected revenue of the rule (and the recommendation created based on this rule) as follows:

$$\text{revenue}(X \to Y) = \text{support}(X \to Y) \cdot \sum_{i \in Y} \text{price}(i) \qquad (5.158)$$

given that a user is about to buy item X. More accurate estimates of monetary metrics can be obtained by using the uplift modeling techniques that we discussed earlier in the context of promotion optimization. A recommender system typically needs association rules with high support and confidence levels to ensure that these rules are reliable and discriminative. The creation of such rules from a given transaction history is a standard data mining problem, known as frequent itemset mining, affinity analysis, or market basket analysis. This problem can be solved by using a wide range of specialized algorithms, such as Apriory or FP-growth.

EXAMPLE 5.7

▼

Let us consider a detailed example that illustrates how association rules can be used to create recommendations. In contrast with traditional collaborative filtering, association rule learning requires more granular transaction-level data, but the transactions do not need to be linked to individual users (it does not matter which user performed which transaction). We will analyze the sample transaction history for a grocery shop presented in table 5.9.

TRANSACTION ID	ITEMS
1	milk, bread, eggs
2	bread, sugar
3	milk, cereal
4	bread, cereal
5	milk, bread, sugar
6	cereal, milk, bread
7	bread, cereal
8	milk, cereal
9	milk, bread, cereal, eggs

Table 5.9: Sample transaction history.

In order to create recommendations, for example, for milk, we run an association rule learning algorithm on the transaction history with the constraint $X = \{\text{milk}\}$ and sort the rules by the corresponding confidence levels. The result is shown in table 5.10. The confidence level for the milk → cereal rule, for example, is equal to 4/6 because there are four transactions that contain both these items and six transactions that contain milk. The recommended items are then obtained from the right-hand sides of the rules, so that the list of recommendations for milk includes cereal, bread, eggs, and sugar, in order of relevance.

RANK	RULE	SUPPORT	CONFIDENCE
1	milk → cereal	4/9	4/6
2	milk → bread	4/9	4/6
3	milk → eggs	2/9	2/6
4	milk → sugar	1/9	1/6

Table 5.10: Association rules for milk.

Note that although market basket analysis is a method of unsupervised learning, we are essentially solving classification and feature selection problems in this particular setting because the context (milk, in this example) can be viewed as a training label, other items in the transaction can be viewed as features, and the goal is to identify the most predictive features. In the association rule approach, these features correspond to the right-hand side of the rules with high confidence levels.

As we discussed at the beginning of this section, association rules can be used to create personalized recommendations as well, depending on how many items are included in the context (left-hand side of the rule) and the semantic meaning of the context. For usage cases such as anonymous web session personalization, the association rule approach can be an effective alternative to other collaborative filtering methods, such as neighborhood models, both in term of accuracy and computational complexity [Mobasher et al., 2001].

5.12   MULTIPLE OBJECTIVE OPTIMIZATION

All of the recommendation methods discussed above are essentially driven by a single objective – to provide the best semantic match or predicted preference score. However, recommendation accuracy might not be the only concern of the recommender system design: a marketer might also be interested in incorporating multiple competing objectives into the recommendations offered to the customers. For instance, grocers might be interested in boosting perishables with a shorter shelf life, fashion stores might want to promote sponsored brands or seasonal collections, and a wide range of retailers can benefit from recommending products with a higher margin or from taking into account product stock levels to avoid stockouts [Jambor and Wang, 2010].

One possible approach for implementing a multi-objective recommender system is to mix the semantic relevance signals with signals that correspond to the secondary objectives. From this perspective, multi-objective methods can be compared to hybrid models where multiple signals are also mixed together to achieve optimal results. The key difference, however, is that hybrid methods typically use a standard loss function, such as the average rating prediction error, as the optimization goal, whereas multi-objective recommenders use more customized optimization targets. In this section, we will consider a recommender system with multiple objectives that was developed and tested in practice on a large scale by LinkedIn, an employment-oriented social networking service [Rodriguez et al., 2012]. In the case of LinkedIn, the primary objective was to recommend candidates who semantically match a job description and, also, as a secondary objective, display a job-seeking behavior.

We start with the idea that the recommendations produced by the core recommendation algorithm can be re-ranked by using a function that optimizes some secondary objective, with the condition that deviations from the original relevance-based ranking should be penalized. Let us first consider the case with a single secondary objective and define a relatively abstract framework that can be adapted for a wide range of objectives. First, we can use the core recommendation algorithm to rank all m items for each of n users. Let us denote these original recommendations as an $n \times m$ matrix $\mathbf{Y}$, in which each row corresponds to a user, each column corresponds to an item, and each element is a rank of an item in the recommendation lists. We assume that each user is actually presented with only $k \ll m$ recommendations, but all items are scored originally to give enough choice for the re-ranking function. In practice, we do not necessarily need to rank all m items and can limit the number of recommendations by some number that is substantially greater that k. Each recommended item can then be scored according to the secondary objective, and we denote an $n \times m$ matrix of these scores as $\mathbf{X}$. For instance, this matrix can contain product gross margins. Note that the score can be a function of both the item and its position in the recommendation matrix $\mathbf{Y}$, that is, the user and rank. The optimization problem can then be defined as follows:

$$\max_{w} \quad g\left(\varphi\left(\mathbf{Y}, \mathbf{X}, w\right)\right)$$
$$\text{subject to} \quad d\left(\text{top}_k\left(\mathbf{Y}\right), \text{top}_k\left(\varphi\left(\mathbf{Y}, \mathbf{X}, w\right)\right)\right) \leqslant c \tag{5.159}$$

in which

- g represents the utility function that evaluates the quality of the recommendations from the secondary objective perspective.

- φ is a composite ranking function that combines pairs of rows from matrices X and Y into a new list of recommendations that balances the two objectives.

- w is the parameter (weight) that defines the mixing balance between the two objectives. This parameter is the subject of optimization.

- $\text{top}_k(\cdot)$ denotes the first k elements with a maximal ranking score. This operation truncates the original matrices X and Y to the size of $n \times k$.

- d is the distance function that measures the discrepancy between the two recommendation matrices. One possible way to measure the discrepancy between the two score vectors x and y is to calculate the sum of squared errors between their histograms:

$$d(x, y) = \sum_{i=1}^{b} (H(x)_i - H(y)_i)^2 \qquad (5.160)$$

in which the histogram $H(x)$ is a vector with b elements (buckets) and each element corresponds to the number of scores in x that fall into the corresponding range. The overall distance between the matrices is then defined as the sum of distances over all users, that is, rows of the matrices.

- c is a threshold that limits the discrepancy between the original and re-ranked recommendation lists.

The main idea of the optimization problem above is to increase the utility of the re-ranked recommendations that mix the relevance scores with the secondary objective but to penalize the difference between the original relevance-based recommendations and the re-ranked recommendations to make sure that relevance will not be completely sacrificed in pursuit of the secondary objective. The design of function φ should include tunable parameters that control the trade-off between the two objectives and will be the subject of optimization. This approach can be straightforwardly extended to incorporate more than two objectives and multiple divergence constraints. Denoting the number of objectives as q, we can define the following multi-objective optimization problem:

$$\max_{w} \quad g(\varphi(Y, X, w))$$
$$\text{subject to} \quad d_j(\text{top}_k(Y), \text{top}_k(\varphi(Y, X, w))) \leqslant c_j \qquad (5.161)$$

in which X is now the $n \times m \times q$ matrix of scores, w is a vector of q weight parameters, and j iterates over all divergence criteria.

We can illustrate how the optimization model above can be adapted to practical problems by using a couple of examples. First, consider the case of a retailer who wants to incorporate a revenue objective into the recommendation scores. The overall utility function can be defined as the expected gross margin, with the assumption that $M(i) \in [0, 1]$ is a normalized gross margin of item i and the probability of purchase is modeled as a reciprocal to the ranking position (i. e. , the lower the item in the list of recommendations, the lower the probability of conversion):

$$g(\mathbf{z}) = \frac{1}{k} \sum_{i=1}^{m} \frac{M(i)}{z_i} \cdot \mathbb{I}(z_i \leq k) \tag{5.162}$$

in which $\mathbf{z}$ is the vector of ranks produced by the composite ranking function φ and $\mathbb{I}$ is an indicator function that equals one if the argument is true and zero otherwise. As the secondary objective is the expected gross margin, matrix $\mathbf{X}$ is straightforwardly defined as

$$x_{ui} = M(i) \tag{5.163}$$

The composite ranking function can then be specified as the mix of the original relevance score y, produced by the core recommender algorithm, and the margin score x:

$$\mathbf{z} = \varphi(\mathbf{y}, \mathbf{x}) \quad : \quad z_i = y_i \cdot x_i^w \tag{5.164}$$

in which w is the parameter that controls the trade-off between the relevance and pitching of high-margin products. This parameter is the subject of the optimization in problem 5.159.

Our second example of re-ranking according to a secondary objective is the boosting of featured items, such as on-sale products or perishables. The utility function can be specified as the average number of featured products in the short list of k recommendations:

$$g(\mathbf{z}) = \frac{1}{k} \sum_{i=1}^{m} F(i) \cdot \mathbb{I}(z_i \leq k) \tag{5.165}$$

in which $F(i)$ is a feature label that equals one if the item is featured and zero otherwise. The matrix $\mathbf{X}$ is defined as

$$x_{ui} = F(i) \tag{5.166}$$

The composite ranking function combines the relevance score and feature labels with a trade-off parameter w, which is the subject of optimization:

$$\mathbf{z} = \varphi(\mathbf{y}, \mathbf{x}) \quad : \quad z_i = y_i \cdot w^{x_i} \tag{5.167}$$

The ranking function above can be straightforwardly extended to incorporate multiple separate features, each of which contributes to the final ranking score in accordance with its own trade-off parameter (recall that $\mathbf{X}$ can be an $n \times m \times q$ matrix of scores, so that x can be a $q \times m$ matrix):

$$\mathbf{z} = \varphi\left(\mathbf{y}, \mathbf{x}\right) \quad : \quad z_i = y_i \cdot w_1^{x_{1,i}} \cdot w_2^{x_{2,i}} \cdot \ldots \cdot w_q^{x_{q,i}} \qquad (5.168)$$

Optimization problem 5.159 depends on the ranking function, so the standard optimization methods for smooth functions, such as gradient descent, are not directly applicable. In a general case, this problem can be approached by using learning to rank algorithms [Rodriguez et al., 2012]. In many practical applications, however, we can expect to have only one or two parameters w. In this case, the problem can be straightforwardly solved with an exhaustive search over all possible values.

5.13 ARCHITECTURE OF RECOMMENDER SYSTEMS

Thus far, we have discussed a wide range of recommendation models and algorithms, as well as methods that can be used to combine multiple models into a hybrid or adjust recommendations based on contextual information or secondary objectives. A recommender system, however, is more that just the implementation of some algorithm. It is a complex software system that includes multiple components and modules that connect the recommendation model with the outside world and make it function. In this section, we discuss a possible reference architecture of a recommender system, presented in Figure 5.26, as well as some possible variations and trade-offs [Jack et al., 2016].

USER INTERFACE A recommender system can be connected to multiple user interfaces, such as websites, email service providers, mobile notifications, or news feeds. These channels interact with the core recommender system through an interface that receives the contextual information as an argument and returns ranked recommendations. In the most basic cases, the interface of a recommender system can be as simple as a side bar containing recommendations on a web page. Services that heavily depend on recommendations, such as online video services, often provide much more comprehensive interfaces that include multiple sections, such as personalized recommendations, popular items, and latest trends.

DATA COLLECTION The total number of data sources used by a recommender system can be quite high. One reason is that industrial recommender systems often use many different algorithms,

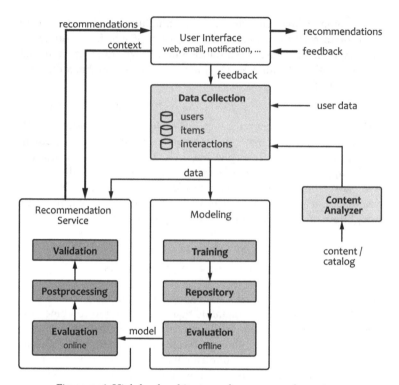

Figure 5.26: High-level architecture of a recommender system.

either for hybridization or experimentation purposes, so the system should consume enough data to support content-based, collaborative filtering, and popularity-based methods. The system may also have access to some external or third party data or signals that can help to refine the recommendations. This often requires the creation of a comprehensive data collection infrastructure that consolidates user profiles (e. g., preferences and personal information), item information that generally requires some sort of content analyzer to be used to parse and transform the raw content data, and the user–item interaction data, which is typically captured by the user interface as ratings and other types of feedback.

MODELING The collected, cleaned, and consolidated data is used to create recommendation models. The models are deployed into a repository and periodically retrained to catch up with data changes. The model can be evaluated in the modeling (offline) tier, service (online) tier, or both. If the model is completely evaluated offline, the output of this process is a set of recommendations for all users. The recommendations can updated on a schedule, for example, on a daily basis, and loaded into the recommendation service. If the model is partially evaluated online, the offline part precalculates only certain data elements, such as item similarity matrices or latent factor vectors. This approach allows one to do the heavy computations offline in batch mode but to keep the flexibility of online recommendations. Industrial recommender systems typically have a repository with multiple recommendation algorithms that are constantly updated and tested.

RECOMMENDATION SERVICE The primary purpose of the recommendation service is to complete the evaluation of the recommendation model and serve the recommendations to the user interfaces. The recommendation service can implement a number of functions related to contextualization and operational control. First, recommendations produced by the core algorithm can be postprocessed to make additional improvements and adjustments. For example, a service can track the recommendations already seen by the user in real time and rotate or randomly shuffle the list of recommendations to make the user experience more dynamic, productive, and serendipitous. Second, the recommendation service can check the quality of recommendations by using validation rules and log issues or can make automatic adjustments in the case of validation failures. Examples of automatic quality checks include validation of the total number of recommendations in the list and monitoring of the algorithm execution time.

5.14 SUMMARY

- Digital channels enable marketers to carry extremely wide and deep assortments with a large number of slow-moving niche products. This is one of the key differentiators in a comparison with traditional distribution channels, where the assortment is limited by distribution costs.

- Extremely wide and deep assortments with a long tail of niche products create a need for efficient discovery services, including search and recommendations.

- The main goal of recommendation systems is to provide customers with relevant offerings when the purchasing intent is not explicitly expressed. This can be viewed as a counterpart to search services, where the intent is explicitly specified as a search query.

- Recommendation systems can generally leverage user–item interaction data, which include explicitly provided ratings and implicitly collected browsing histories, catalog data, and contextual information. The main output of the recommendation service is a ranked list of recommended items.

- One of the main inputs of a recommender system is customer ratings. The ratings are typically represented as a rating matrix, where rows are customers, columns are items, and each element is a numerical rating value. Rating values can also be attributed with contextual information, such as time stamps or the marketing channel that the rating came from. In practice, rating matrices are very sparse.

- The main business objectives of recommender systems include relevance, novelty, serendipity, and diversity of the recommendations. The relevance of recommendations can be measured through rating prediction accuracy and ranking accuracy. Quantitative metrics can also be defined for novelty, serendipity, and diversity.

- The most important families of recommendation algorithms are content filtering and collaborative filtering. These basic algorithms can be extended by using hybridization, contextualization, and admixing of additional objectives and signals.

- Content-based filtering recommends items that are similar to the items that the user liked in the past. Content-based filtering can be viewed as an item classification problem. The key advantages of content filtering are the ability to recommend items based only on a user's own ratings and to recommend new unrated items, as well as the interpretability of the results. The main shortcomings are the complex feature engineering that is required for content classification and the bias toward trivial recommendations.

- Content filtering can use document similarity measures and other search methods, such as latent semantic analysis or latent Dirichlet allocation, to find the most similar items. An alternative approach is to use text classification models, such as the Naive Bayes classifier.

- Collaborative filtering uses the rating matrix to find items or users with similar rating patterns. It generally creates more diverse and serendipitous recommendations than content filtering. Collaborative filtering can be viewed as a matrix completion problem.

- The most important collaborative filtering methods include nearest neighbor recommenders and latent factor models.

- Multiple recommendation models can be combined together into a hybrid model. Hybrid recommenders use the same techniques as signal mixing pipelines in search services. A hybrid recommender can switch between relevance signals from different models, blend them together, or use the outputs from one model as inputs for other models.

- Contextual recommendations use additional attributes such as time or location to make more targeted recommendations. These attributes can be considered additional dimensions that expand the rating matrix into a multidimensional cube. A recommender system can use contextual information to prefilter the input data, postfilter the recommendations, or extend the inputs of the rating prediction model. Contextual recommendations use the same ideas as controlled precision reduction in search services.

- Recommendations for unknown users and users with limited interaction histories and profiles are important usage cases. Recommendation systems can leverage basic sales statistics (best sellers), content (similar items), and purchasing patterns (frequent itemsets) to make non-personalized or partially personalized recommendations.

- The main components of a recommender system include the user interface, data collection tier, modeling tier, and a recommendation service.

6

PRICING AND ASSORTMENT

The problem of price management has a very long history. The fundamental aspects of pricing have been studied for centuries to explain the interplay of supply and demand on a market. This has resulted in the development of a comprehensive theory that describes the strategic aspects of pricing, such as price structures, relationships between price and demand, and others. These methods provide relatively coarse price optimization methods that can, however, inform strategic pricing decisions. The opportunity to automatically improve tactical price decisions was first recognized and seized by the airline industry at the beginning of the 1980s and can be partially attributed to the advancement of digital reservation systems that enabled dynamic and agile resource and price management. This required the development of a totally new set of optimization methods that were later adopted in other service industries, such as hotels and car rentals. This new, truly algorithmic, approach, commonly referred to as *revenue management* or *yield management*, has clearly demonstrated the power of automated price and resource management by multiple cases of late adopters of new techniques being bankrupted or defeated by the pioneers of automated price management.

Price management is closely related to other programmatic services, especially promotions and advertisements. Price management methods can be used both to optimize discount values of promotions and to price advertising and media resources sold to service clients. We will start this chapter with a review of the basic principles of strategic pricing and price optimization. We will then continue with the development of more tactical and practical demand prediction and price optimization methods for market segmentation, markdowns, and clearance sales. We will also briefly review the major resource allocation methods used in service industries to set booking limits. Finally, we will consider the assortment optimization problem, for which we can reuse some of the building blocks developed for price management.

6.1   ENVIRONMENT

As we will demonstrate later in this chapter, price management is a critically important determinant of enterprise profitability and, eventually, survival. Consequently, real-life price management processes often include multiple layers of decision making, which range from strategic executive decisions down to micro-decisions at the level of individual transactions. We are distilling this complexity into the relatively simple model presented in Figure 6.1. This model does not explicitly account for some strategic aspects of pricing, but it captures the major features of the pricing environment that are important for micro-decisioning:

- We generally assume that a company sells some products to its customers and earns the following profit G for each product i:

$$G_i = Q_i (P_i - V_i) - C_i \tag{6.1}$$

  in which Q_i is quantity sold, P_i is price, V_i is variable costs (e. g., wholesale product price), C_i is fixed costs associated with the product, and i iterates over the assortment of products offered to the customers. Most methods considered in this chapter are focused on maximization of the profit G as a function of price, although it is important to keep in mind that this optimization can be a subject of external strategic constraints. For example, a company can choose a competitor-oriented strategy that pursues market share, rather than profits, and restrict the optimization process with a price-match policy.

- The profit is a function of the quantity sold which, in turn, depends on the demand. The key assumption made by the model is the heterogeneity of the demand, that is, the variability of the demand according to one or many dimensions, such as customer segments, store locations, seasons, classes of service, and so forth. This provides an opportunity to differentiate prices according to these dimensions as well and, thus, tune profits at the level of individual customer segments or time intervals. We will spend most of this chapter discussing price structures and price optimization techniques that deal with different aspects of the heterogeneity of the demand.

- The demand is a function of price and other variables that range from competitor prices to weather. In the most basic case, the revenue management system can optimize prices by creating regression models for individual product demands and finding op-

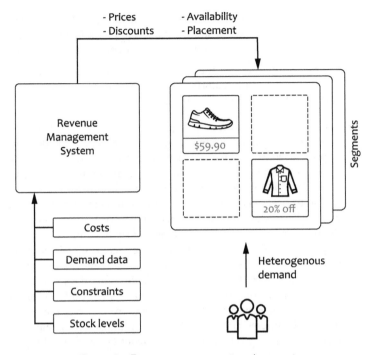

Figure 6.1: Revenue management environment.

timal prices that maximize the profits through maximization of the demand:

$$P_i^{opt} = \underset{P_i}{argmax}\ Q_i\,(P_i) \cdot (P_i - V_i) - C_i \qquad (6.2)$$

in which $Q_i\,(P_i)$ is the demand prediction model for product i. In practice, the problem is typically more complicated than this because of various constraints and interdependencies.

– One notable example is stock level constraint – if a seller has a limited stock of a product, the quantity sold Q is the minimum of the demand and the stock level.

– Another important factor is dependent demands – because products in one category are often substitutable, a change in the price of one product can make customers switch to another product. This makes the optimization problem more complex because product prices have to be optimized jointly, not individually.

– Finally, a seller can pursue additional goals that translate into additional constraints. For example, a fashion retailer can aim at selling out the inventory by the end of the season.

Consequently, the revenue management system has a number of inputs, including historical demand data, fixed and variable costs, stock levels, and other business constraints.

• Although optimization of the price level is a natural task for a revenue management system, many environments provide other important controls. One set of such controls is related to how the price is communicated to the customers. As we will discuss later, it is often more efficient to communicate price changes as discounts and special offers, rather than to change the baseline prices. This establishes a link between price optimization and discount optimization tasks. The second set of controls is related to product availability and classes of service. A classic example is an airline that requires low-cost tickets to be booked in advance and makes this option unavailable a few days before the flight. Finally, the revenue management system can control the assortment of products, their presentation, and the placement options. Examples include shelf-space optimization by removing low-performing products and store-layout optimization by placing related products together to leverage cross-selling opportunities.

The model above outlines the basic areas where programmatic price management methods can be applied. We will spend the next few pages introducing the basic concepts and principles of pricing and will then start to design price optimization methods for the environment described in this section.

6.2   THE IMPACT OF PRICING

Pricing plays a critically important role in the enterprise economy because prices are the key determinants of revenues and profitability. The right pricing decisions can deliver great profitability improvements, whereas the wrong decisions can have grave consequences. One of the reasons is that the price determines how the product or service is positioned on the market and perceived by customers. Prices that are too low undermine a firm's sustainability by leaving unharvested profits and setting the wrong expectations about product value and quality for the customers; prices that are too high harm sales and the firm's reputation, which slows down business growth. Another reason is that the quantitative dependency between prices and profits is very strong in most industries and enterprises, so price often dominates in profit equations. Let us examine an example that illustrates the importance of pricing decisions.

EXAMPLE 6.1

Consider an imaginary apparel retailer that sells 100,000 garments monthly at $40 per item, with a wholesale price of $25 per item and fixed costs of $500,000 per month. We can express the profits of the retailer as a function of price, costs, and sales volume by using the following basic profit equation:

$$G = Q\,(P - V) - C \tag{6.3}$$

in which Q is quantity sold, P is price, V denotes variable costs, and C denotes fixed costs. Consequently, the baseline profit will be

$$G = 100,000 \times (\$40 - \$25) - \$500,000 = \$1,000,000 \tag{6.4}$$

The retailer can choose from several strategies to improve the baseline profit. One alternative is to increase the quantity sold by investing in marketing campaigns or the development of new sales channels. Other approaches are to raise the sale price, change supplier to reduce the variable cost, or cut down the fixed costs. We evaluate all of these strategies in table 6.1 and calculate how a one percent change in sales volume, price, variable cost, and fixed costs will impact profit. It turns out that profits are most sensitive to changes in price, which indicates the high importance of pricing decisions.

	BASELINE	+1% IN Q	+1% IN P	-1% IN V	-1% IN C
Q	100,000	**101,000**	100,000	100,000	100,000
P	$40.00	$40.00	**$40.40**	$40.00	$40.00
V	$25.00	$25.00	$25.00	**$24.75**	$25.00
C	$500,000	$500,000	$500,000	$500,000	**$495,000**
G	$1,000,000	$1,015,000	$1,040,000	$1,025,000	$1,005,000
ΔG%		+1.5%	+4.0%	+2.5%	+0.5%

Table 6.1: Quantitative example that illustrates how changes in prices, costs, and quantity sold influence profits.

Although we have used somewhat arbitrary numbers in this example, this pattern prevails in a huge variety of enterprises across many industries. For example, a study by McKinsey and Associates analyzes the profits of 2,463 companies and comes to the conclusion that a 1% change in price results in 11.1% profit improvement, whereas a 1% improvement in sales volume, variable cost, or fixed costs yields improvements of 3.3%, 7.8%, and 2.3%, respectively [Marn and Roseillo, 1992].

6.3 PRICE AND VALUE

The development of automated price management systems requires us to break down pricing into formal optimization problems that treat profits merely as mathematical functions. On the other hand, price is a complex matter that depends on the nature of the product, the competition, and customer psychology. In this section, we will start to bridge the gap between the fundamental pricing problem and optimization tasks by discussing what the price is and how it can be determined. This discussion is very strategic and gives us very few clues about how automated price management can be implemented, but it provides guidelines that will help us to develop more elaborate methods.

6.3.1   Price Boundaries

Economic theory argues that price is determined by the interplay of supply and demand on the market. Although every product or service has its production cost, which can sometimes be considered as a "fair" baseline for the price, pricing requires us to delve into the valuation logic of both the seller and the buyer.

On the one hand, we can assume that the seller of a product or service has a minimum profitable price point. Selling above this point generates profits; selling below this price incurs losses. In many cases, this price point can be assumed to be equal to the marginal cost of the product.

On the other hand, a buyer extracts a certain *utility* from the purchased product. The utility depends on the functional properties of the product, the customer's ability to achieve useful goals by using these properties, the availability of the product in the right place and at the right time, and other factors. In some cases, a relatively precise estimate of the utility can be obtained. For example, the utility of an industrial electrical generator can be assessed through the price of the electricity it produces. In other cases, only a gross approximation of the utility can be provided. An example of this is innovative medical equipment that may be valued as highly as a human life.

A seller and buyer can commit to a mutually beneficial transaction if the marginal cost is below the utility. If this does not hold, they both will be better off passing on the deal. Consequently, the price is essentially a *range*, not a single point. At a very high level, the goal of a price management system is to dynamically select an optimal point in this range for individual transactions.

The marginal cost and utility often provide very broad price brackets that can be useless in practice. For instance, the purchase of a bottle of soda on a hot day can literally be a question of life and death, which skyrockets the utility, but high competition keeps the price close to the lower boundary. At the other extreme, the negligible marginal cost of software distributions does not prevent the price from staying close to the upper boundary determined by utility. More narrow brackets can often be obtained by comparing a product or service with available alternatives and carefully evaluating the product features.

If a comparable alternative is available, its price can be taken as a baseline. A given product can be superior or inferior relative to the alternative, and the difference in value can be estimated by building a *value exchange model* [Smith, 2012]. A value exchange model estimates the potential difference in price between two products by analyzing and evaluating individual product features that can be advantageous (contribute toward higher price) or disadvantageous (contribute toward lower price), as illustrated in Figure 6.2. The final price, also known as the exchange value, can be obtained by adding this differential value to the baseline price of the alternative.

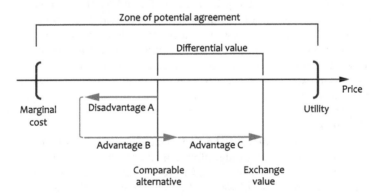

Figure 6.2: Price boundaries and the exchange value.

The exact design of the value exchange model depends on the nature of the products and their differences. In many cases, product features can be evaluated with methodologies, such as *conjoint analysis*, that rely on consumer surveys [Green and Srinivasan, 1978]. In certain cases, the model can be created by analyzing the potential outcomes of choosing one or another product. Let us consider two examples:

- The differential value of a more reliable product relative to a less reliable alternative can be estimated by considering the probability of failure and the potential replacement cost. If the price of the alternative p_A and the replacement cost p_R are known, the price of a new reliable product can be roughly estimated as follows:

$$p = p_R \cdot (1 - \text{Pr(failure)}) + (p_A + p_R) \cdot \text{Pr(failure)} \qquad (6.5)$$

- Accessories and complementary products can incur switching costs that can be incorporated into the value exchange model. For example, manufacturers of razors and blades typically design their products in such a way that blades are not interchangeable between brands, and, consequently, the exchange value of a blade is boosted by the relatively high cost of switching to a razor from a different brand.

Value exchange considerations can be factored directly into price structures, which we will discuss in detail in later sections.

6.3.2   Perceived Value

The concept of utility may suggest that buyers make decisions by comparing their willingness to pay against the price: the product is purchased if, and only if, the price is below the utility. This "rational behavior", however, is not an adequate model of real consumers. Valuation is a subjective process that depends on how exactly the value and price are communicated to the prospect and how the prospect perceives it. Failure to properly communicate the value or price can set the wrong expectations and displace the price boundaries in the undesirable direction. Efficient communication, by contrast, can improve the perceived value of a product or diminish the value of comparable alternatives.

Value communication, at the first glance, might not look very relevant for a discussion of algorithmic methods because it deals with psychological aspects of value and price perception that can probably not be codified in the software. It turns out, however, that analysis of these psychological patterns can produce applicable rules that can be incorporated into price structures and, consequently, can be accounted for in price optimization problems.

One of the most solid frameworks that captures many important aspects of value and price perception is prospect theory [Kahneman and Tversky, 1979]. Prospect theory considers the evaluation process from the risk assessment standpoint and can be characterized by the following propositions:

POINT OF REFERENCE The potential gains and losses associated with a deal are evaluated by comparison with some point of reference. The point of reference is based on past experience (e.g., the last observed price for a given or similar product) or judgement and tends to be persistent once it is set.

DIMINISHING SENSITIVITY Changes in gains or losses are sharply perceived in the zone around the reference point but become less noticeable as the magnitudes of gain or loss increase. The difference between $9 and $19 discounts appears to be substantial, but the same ten dollar difference is not perceived equally valuable for discounts of $719 and $729.

LOSS AVERSION Losses are generally perceived more sharply than gains of the same magnitude. A loss of $100 is typically perceived more important than a gain of $100.

RISK AVERSION FOR GAINS Guaranteed gains are preferred to opportunistic gains of the same magnitude. A prospect who has the choice of getting a guaranteed $450 or of winning $1000 with a 50% chance (and a 50% chance of winning nothing) generally prefers the first option.

RISK SEEKING FOR LOSSES In contrast to gains, potential losses are preferred to guaranteed losses. A prospect who has the choice of definitely losing $450 or of losing $1000 with a 50% chance (and a 50% chance of losing nothing) generally prefers the second alternative.

The propositions above imply a certain shape to the dependency between the real and perceived gains and losses, as shown in Figure 6.3. The slope of the curve in the negative zone is steeper than in the positive zone, in accordance with the loss aversion hypothesis, but the steepness decreases at both ends to follow the principle of diminishing sensitivity.

Prospect theory suggests several important guidelines that can be used to optimize price structures:

- Price rises (surcharges) are viewed much more negatively than price drops (discounts). This is the reason why prices are typically communicated as a list price and discount. This allows the list price to be kept constant and the discount value to be moved in either direction, including personalized pricing, without explicit surcharges.

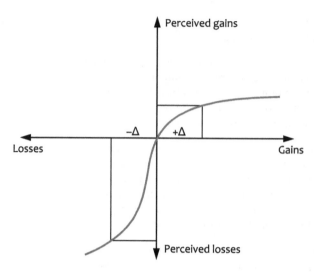

Figure 6.3: A prospect theory value function. The actual value increment of $+\Delta$ can be perceived as a relatively small gain, whereas the actual decrement of the same magnitude $-\Delta$ can be perceived as a huge loss.

- The reference point should be kept at a high level. This complements the previous point about list prices and discounts because reductions in baseline prices can lead to undesired persistent shifts in the reference point.

- It is generally better to subdivide gain into multiple smaller gains. A single gain will be discounted because of diminishing sensitivity, so a price structure with multiple smaller benefits can have a higher perceived value.

- The risk-seeking behavior for losses suggests that some explicit product benefits can be replaced by equivalent potential benefits without substantial loss in perceived value. For example, flat pack furniture requires time and effort to be spent in assembling it, but reduced price and delivery costs can still be perceived as unconditional advantages.

We will use some elements of prospect theory in price optimization to account for behavioral factors that are inconsistent with the basic principle of a rational consumer.

6.4   PRICE AND DEMAND

Utility, value exchange models, and other valuation methods help us to predict the expected willingness to pay for a given product or service. We can also recall that consumer choice theory (see Section 2.6.1 for details) provides us with the tools to predict a consumer choice in the case of multiple available alternatives. Although one can attempt to sell a product to each customer at a price that is derived directly from an individual willingness to pay, we choose to start with the traditional problem of setting a common price structure for all customers. This means that we need to deal with thousands or even millions of individual buying decisions that can be described in probabilistic terms.

Let us define the customer's *willingness to pay* for a given product or service as the maximum price acceptable for a customer. The customer will buy a product if, and only if, the price is less than the willingness to pay. We can describe the population of customers by using the distribution of the willingness to pay $w(p)$: for every pair of prices p_1 and p_2, the fraction of customers $f(p_1, p_2)$ whose willingness to pay is between p_1 and p_2 is

$$f(p_1, p_2) = \int_{p_1}^{p_2} w(p)\, dp \tag{6.6}$$

The demand function $q(p)$, also referred to as the *price–response function*, can be expressed through $w(p)$ as follows:

$$q(p) = Q_{max} \cdot \int_p^\infty w(x)\, dx \tag{6.7}$$

in which $Q_{max} = q(0)$ is the maximum achievable demand for a given seller. The demand function can be viewed not only as an aggregate market metric determined by variance of willingness to pay but also as a model of a single customer behavior, in the sense that a given consumer might be willing to buy different quantities of product at different prices. In the latter case, willingness to pay should be considered as willingness to pay *per unit*.

Mathematical analysis of the demand function can provide us with additional insights and help to define useful metrics and properties. First, let us take a closer look at the derivative of the demand function:

$$\frac{\partial}{\partial p} q(p) = -Q_{max}\, w(p) \tag{6.8}$$

As $w(p)$ is non-negative, the derivative is non-positive for any p, which means that the demand function is downward sloping. The slope of the demand function given by its derivative is a measure of the price sensitivity. A steep slope means that customers are sensitive to price changes and demand rapidly drops as the price rises, whereas a shallow slope means that customers are relatively insensitive to price changes. It is more common, however, to measure price sensitivity not as a slope of the demand function but as the *elasticity of demand*, defined as the ratio of the percent change in demand to the percent change in price:

$$\epsilon = -\frac{\Delta q/q}{\Delta p/p} = -\frac{p}{q(p)} \times \frac{\partial}{\partial p} q(p) \tag{6.9}$$

Although the elasticity in equation 6.9 is a function of price, meaning that it can be different at different points of the *demand curve*, this term is often used more loosely by assuming that the elasticity is roughly constant in the range of interest, so the demand can be characterized by a single value of ϵ. The elasticity of demand does not depend on magnitudes of price or volume, so it provides a convenient way to measure and compare price sensitivities. Elastic markets, with $\epsilon > 1$, respond to a small change in price with a large change in demand. For example, restaurant meals are reported to have an elasticity of about 2.3, which means that a 10% increase in price can drive a 23% decrease in demand. Inelastic markets, with $\epsilon < 1$, respond to price changes with a small change in demand. For example, the price elasticity of motor gasoline in the US was estimated to be around 0.04, which means that it takes a 50% increase in the price of gasoline to reduce automobile travel by 1%. We should, however, distinguish elasticity for a category of goods and for an individual brand in the category. Substitution of one category by another is generally difficult, so category-level demand is relatively inelastic in many industries. A switch between brands is simpler, which makes the demand curves more elastic from a single seller's standpoint.

We will now explore several commonly used demand models by expressing them in terms of $w(p)$ and $q(p)$.

6.4.1   Linear Demand Curve

A simple demand model can be derived under the assumption that the willingness to pay is uniformly distributed in the range from 0 to the maximum acceptable price P:

$$w(p) = \text{unif}(0, P) = \begin{cases} 1/P, & 0 \leqslant p \leqslant P \\ 0, & \text{otherwise} \end{cases} \tag{6.10}$$

The demand function can be obtained by integrating $w(p)$ in accordance with equation 6.7:

$$q(p) = Q_{max} \int_p^P w(x)\,dx$$
$$= Q_{max}\left(1 - \frac{p}{P}\right) \tag{6.11}$$
$$= -\frac{Q_{max}}{P} \cdot p + Q_{max}$$

We can see that the uniformly distributed willingness to pay results into a linear demand function, as illustrated in Figure 6.4. We will assume linear demand curves for the optimization of basic price structures because of their analytical convenience, although this is typically a very gross approximation of real demand functions. One of the shortcomings of the linear demand model is that it assumes that every dollar of price change yields the same increment in demand. This is generally not true because price sensitivity is typically high near the point of reference (e. g., competitive prices) and diminishes as the price moves away from it.

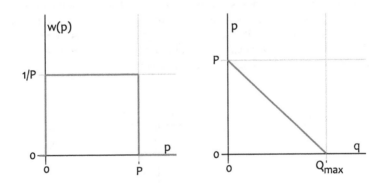

Figure 6.4: Uniform willingness to pay and the corresponding linear demand curve. Note that we follow the traditional economic notation in the right-hand plot by placing price on the vertical axis, although demand is considered as a function of price.

6.4.2 Constant-Elasticity Demand Curve

The constant-elasticity demand function can be obtained from the definition of elasticity under the assumption that the elasticity is globally constant. This means that we need to solve the following equation for $q(p)$:

$$\frac{p}{q(p)} \cdot \frac{\partial}{\partial p} q(p) = -\epsilon \qquad (6.12)$$

This is a differential equation, and its solution is a family of functions given by

$$q(p) = C \cdot p^{-\epsilon} \qquad (6.13)$$

in which $C > 0$ is an arbitrary coefficient. This coefficient is essentially a parameter of the demand function that can be chosen to fit it to known data points, namely, pairs of observed price and corresponding demand. We can calculate the willingness to pay that corresponds to the constant-elasticity demand by substituting 6.13 into 6.8:

$$w(p) = -\frac{\partial}{\partial p} q(p) \cdot \frac{1}{q(0)} = \epsilon \cdot p^{-\epsilon-1} \qquad (6.14)$$

The demand curve $q(p)$ and willingness to pay $w(p)$ with constant-elasticity demand are depicted in Figure 6.5. Similarly to the linear demand function, constant-elasticity demand can be a reasonable approximation for relatively small price changes. The constant-elasticity demand correctly captures a smooth decrease in the willingness to pay as the price grows, but it also implies that the willingness to pay – recall that this is the *maximum* acceptable price – is concentrated near zero, which is not necessarily a realistic assumption.

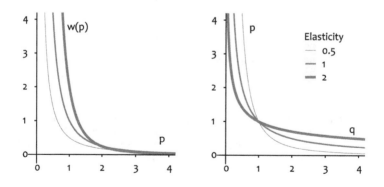

Figure 6.5: The constant-elasticity demand function $q(p) = p^{-\epsilon}$ and corresponding willingness to pay $w(p) = \epsilon p^{-\epsilon-1}$ for different values of ϵ.

6.4.3 *Logit Demand Curve*

The logit demand function attempts to overcome the limitations of the linear and constant-elasticity models by accounting for the fact that the price elasticity reaches its maximum near the point of reference. More specifically, we can expect that demand for a product is persistently low if its price is set much higher than competitive prices and minor changes in the price have very little stimulus, that is, the local demand elasticity is low. In the same vein, prices that are set much below the market are likely to drive persistently high demand that will be relatively insensitive to small price changes – customers will perceive the deal as a bargain anyway. The highest price sensitivity is likely to be in a zone around the competitive prices, where small changes in price can significantly impact the demand. These considerations, as well as empirical support, suggest a sigmoid shape for the demand curve, as depicted in Figure 6.6. The sigmoid demand curve, also referred to as the logit demand function, can be specified as follows:

$$q(p) = Q_{\max} \cdot \frac{1}{1 + e^{a+bp}} \tag{6.15}$$

in which $Q_{\max}$ is the maximum achievable demand, and b is a parameter that controls the steepness of the demand curve. For any a and b, maximum price sensitivity will be achieved at a price numerically equal to $-(a/b)$, so parameter a can be used to shift the point of reference if b is given. The parameters $Q_{\max}$, a, and b can be estimated from data to fit the logistic curve to observed data points.

The willingness to pay function for logit demand can be straightforwardly obtained by differentiating the demand:

$$w(p) = -\frac{\partial}{\partial p} q(p) \cdot \frac{1}{q(0)} = b \left(1 + e^{a}\right) \frac{e^{a+bp}}{\left(1 + e^{a+bp}\right)^2} \tag{6.16}$$

As shown in Figure 6.6, the logistic willingness to pay is a bell-shaped curve that is relatively similar to a normal distribution.

Logit demand is closely related to the multinomial logit (MNL) model that we considered in Section 2.6.1.1. Recall that if a given customer n chooses a product or service among several alternatives $(1, \dots, J)$ and the utility from choosing option i is measured as V_{ni}, then the MNL model states that the probability of choosing option i is as follows:

$$P_{ni} = \frac{e^{V_{ni}}}{\sum_{j=1}^{J} e^{V_{nj}}} \tag{6.17}$$

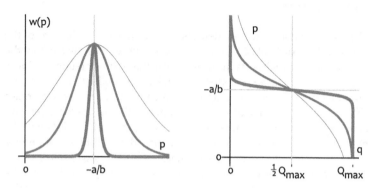

Figure 6.6: Logit demand function for several values of the parameter b and the corresponding willingness to pay. The line thickness is proportional to the magnitude of b.

Utility V_{ni} is typically measured by using a regression model that accounts for the different properties of customers and products. However, if we model it as just a linear function of price $V_{ni} = -b_j p_j$, in which b_j are regression coefficients, then the probability P_{ni} does not depend on individual consumers anymore and becomes equal to the average probability of product selection, which is the market share of the product μ_i:

$$\mu_i(\mathbf{p}) = \frac{e^{-b_i p_i}}{\sum_j e^{-b_j p_j}} \tag{6.18}$$

Equation 6.18 is essentially a new demand model that is even more flexible than our logit demand one because it allows individual competitive prices to be explicitly accounted for. However, if we choose to treat competitive prices as a single parameter that can be defined as

$$c = \sum_{j \neq i} e^{-b_j p_j} \tag{6.19}$$

then we can express the market share of a given product i as follows (note that we use the identity $c^{-1} = e^{-\ln c}$):

$$\mu_i(p_i) = \frac{e^{-b_i p_i}}{\sum_{j \neq i} e^{-b_j p_j} + e^{-b_i p_i}} = \frac{e^{-b_i p_i}}{c + e^{-b_i p_i}} \cdot \frac{c^{-1}}{c^{-1}}$$
$$= \frac{e^{-\ln c - b_i p_i}}{1 + e^{-\ln c - b_i p_i}} \tag{6.20}$$

which is the same as the logit demand model from equation 6.15.

6.5 BASIC PRICE STRUCTURES

A demand curve describes the relationship between the price and demanded quantity. It allows us to express a firm's revenues and profits as a function of price and to solve the optimization problem to determine the profit-optimal price level. Although this approach might look like a precise way to calculate optimal prices, it can rarely produce acceptable results because it is difficult, perhaps impossible, to estimate a globally accurate demand curve that takes into account all of the consequences of a price change, including competitors' responses and other strategic moves. The formal optimization problem, however, can provide useful insights and support decision making, which is an important step towards a programmatic solution. The analysis of demand curves also helps to justify different price structures and their key properties, which is necessary for the more advanced and automated optimizations that we will consider in later sections.

6.5.1 Unit Price

The first price structure we consider is the pricing of individual items or units, such as one book, one shirt, or one pound of oranges. First, let us write down the standard profit equation of the firm by using the demand function $q(p)$:

$$G = q(p) \cdot (p - V) \tag{6.21}$$

in which G is profit, p is price, and V is variable costs. We omit the fixed costs here for the sake of brevity. We then recall that the linear demand curve is defined by

$$q(p) = Q_{max} \cdot \left(1 - \frac{p}{P}\right) \tag{6.22}$$

in which P is the maximum willingness to pay and, consequently, the maximum acceptable price. The price can be optimized by taking a derivative of the profit with respect to the price and setting it to zero:

$$\frac{\partial G}{\partial p} = \frac{\partial q}{\partial p}(p) \cdot (p - V) + q(p) = 0 \tag{6.23}$$

Solving this equation for p, we obtain the optimal price, which is the average of P and V:

$$P_{opt} = \frac{P + V}{2} \tag{6.24}$$

We can substitute the optimal price into equation 6.22 to determine the number of units that the firm is expected to sell at this price:

$$q_{opt} = \frac{Q_{max}}{2P}(P - V) \tag{6.25}$$

Finally, the profit at this price will be

$$G_{opt} = \frac{Q_{max}}{4P}(P - V)^2 \tag{6.26}$$

A geometrical interpretation of the equations above is shown in Figure 6.7. Note that the profit is numerically equal to the area of the rectangle bounded by p_{opt} and V.

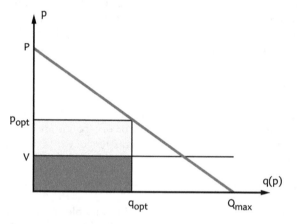

Figure 6.7: Unit price optimization for a linear demand curve.

A similar result can be obtained for the constant-elasticity demand. According to the definition of elasticity we get

$$\frac{\partial q}{p}(p) = -\epsilon \cdot \frac{q(p)}{p} \tag{6.27}$$

Substituting this into equation 6.23, we find the optimal price:

$$p_{opt} = V \cdot \frac{\epsilon}{\epsilon - 1} \tag{6.28}$$

Equation 6.28 is very convenient for demonstrating some weaknesses of strategic price optimization with the basic demand curves. Let us consider the example of a firm that manufactures an item at a cost of $10 and wants to determine the optimal sale price by using the estimated elasticity. If the elasticity estimated from the transactional data is 1.5, the optimal price is $30. However, it is challenging to estimate the elasticity with high accuracy, and it is likely that the estimate is actually more like 1.5 ± 0.4. This leads us to a range of "optimal" prices from $21 to $110, as shown in table 6.2. It is clear that this result has limited practical applicability.

ELASTICITY	1.10	1.20	1.30	1.40	1.50	1.60	1.70	1.80	1.90
OPTIMAL PRICE	$110	$60	$43	$35	$30	$27	$24	$23	$21

Table 6.2: Optimal prices calculated for different values of elasticity and variable costs of $10 with the cost-elasticity demand model.

6.5.2 Market Segmentation

Virtually all markets demonstrate heterogeneity of demand caused by the fact that different customers, and even the same customers at different moments of time, value products differently. This diversity of valuations has numerous reasons. Consumer markets, for example, are fundamentally heterogeneous because the number of human needs, such as meals or clothing, is relatively limited but incomes vary tremendously, which results in very different amounts of money spent on the same needs by different individuals. Customers can use the same or similar products in different ways and derive different values from product features, have more or less information about competitive offerings, and so on. We have already seen how this heterogeneity creates a fertile field for targeted promotions and advertisements, and we can now explore how it influences price decisions. Fortunately, the analysis of unit price optimization provides a very convenient basis for this.

We can see in Figure 6.7 that the maximum achievable revenue is numerically equal to the total area under the demand curve, so the maximum achievable profit can be estimated as

$$G_{max} = \frac{1}{2} P \cdot Q_{max} \tag{6.29}$$

At the same time, any single price p_{opt}, no matter how optimal it is or isn't, represents a trade-off because some customers will not buy a product if they consider it to be too expensive, although they would be willing to buy it at a lower price, in between p_{opt} and V, and would thereby positively contribute to the profit. Moreover, some customers will tolerate prices higher than p_{opt}, although the sales volume that they will generate is relatively small. In both cases, a firm fails to capture additional profits that lie in the triangle in between the demand curve and the variable costs line. Price segmentation is a natural way to overcome the limitations of a single regular price by segmenting customers according to their willingness to pay and offering different prices to different segments. A particular case of this strategy where the regular price has been complemented by a higher premium price and a lower discounted price is shown in Figure 6.8. Note how the profit area increases relative to that in the single-price strategy.

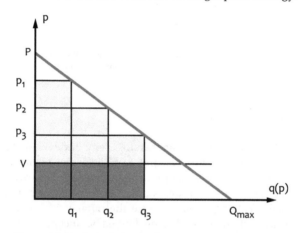

Figure 6.8: Profit optimization by using price segmentation.

This consideration leads to the challenging question of how we can sell the same or similar products to different customers at different prices. Broadly speaking, this requires the setting of fences between customers with different willingness to pay in such a way that customers with higher willingness will not be able to a pay the lower price intended for the lower segments. The fencing mechanisms are multitudinous and vary across industries, although most variations can be reduced to a few basic principles. Let us consider a few examples of price-fencing techniques from the retail industry that demonstrate the remarkable ingenuity in this regard:

STORE ZONE Stores in a retail chain are typically located in different neighborhoods with different demographic and competitive factors, such as average household income, average family size, distance to the nearest competitive store, etc. This naturally separates customers by levels of price sensitivity and ability or willingness to look for an alternative supplier. It enables a retailer to set store-level prices that differ in different zones.

PACKAGE SIZE Fast-moving consumer goods (FMCG), such as soft drinks or toiletries, have high turnover rates and consumers naturally have a choice between buying small amounts of product frequently and stockpiling larger amounts. This trade-off is also impacted by demographic factors, such as household size. This creates fences by willingness to buy large or small packages and enables the setting of different per-unit margins for different package sizes. Quantity-based and purchase-frequency-based offers and discounts also relate to this category.

SALE EVENTS Customers can be differentiated by their willingness to wait for a lower price versus their willingness to buy immediately at the regular price. This type of segmentation is widely used in the apparel domain, where seasonal sales are one of the main marketing mechanisms.

COUPONS Many customers might not be willing to buy a given product at the regular price but might consider buying it at a discounted price. Hence, a retailer can benefit from a discount because it generates additional customers, although the margins are lower relative to the purchasing habits of regular customers. On the other hand, it might be harmful to offer a discount to an excessively wide audience because it will be used even by those customers who would be willing to pay the regular price (in the absence of the discount). The response modeling techniques discussed in Chapter 3 help to solve this problem. However, there is a traditional solution that has been in use since the 19th century – couponing. A coupon represents a price discount that requires some effort to earn or redeem (e. g., the customer has to find it in a newspaper, cut it out, and present at a store), which fences customers by willingness to spend time and effort in getting a discount.

SALE CHANNELS Sale channels naturally represent fences because customers select channels by criteria that strongly correlate with their willingness to pay. For instance, the price sensitivity of liquor store shoppers is consistently lower than that of customers who buy the same wine in grocery stores [Cuellar and Brunamonti, 2013].

DEPARTMENTS Retailers and manufacturers often differentiate markups in accordance with differences in price sensitivity among genders and ages. For example, women's clothing is generally more expensive than men's.

CLUB CARDS Membership helps to differentiate occasional shoppers from high-spending loyal customers for whom private deals outweigh membership fees.

BRANDING Retailers and manufacturers create separate brands that are targeted at higher or lower consumer segments relative to the main brand. The brands can be positioned as inferior to sell products more cheaply without cannibalizing sales from the main brand or as superior to capture additional revenue from consumers with lower price sensitivity.

This list of price fences can be extended with more techniques from other industries, such as airline fare classes or credit card deals. The optimization strategy for price segments can be demonstrated with the setting of prices for n segments in a way that maximizes profits. We can start with the following equation that straightforwardly follows from Figure 6.8:

$$G = \sum_{i=1}^{n} (q_i - q_{i-1})(p_i - V) \tag{6.30}$$

in which p_i and q_i are the prices and quantity sold for a segment i, respectively, and $q_0 = 0$. The quantity sold at price p_i is

$$q_i = Q_{max} \left(1 - \frac{p_i}{P} \right) \tag{6.31}$$

We can find prices that maximize the profit by taking partial derivatives of G and equating them to zero. By inserting equation 6.31 into equation 6.30, setting $p_0 = S$ and $p_{n+1} = V$, and doing algebraic simplifications, we find

$$\frac{\partial G}{\partial p_i} = \frac{Q_{max}}{P}(p_{i-1} - 2p_i + p_{i+1}), \quad 1 \leqslant i \leqslant n \tag{6.32}$$

Equating these partial derivatives to zero, we find a recurrence relationship for segment prices:

$$p_i = \frac{p_{i-1} + p_{i+1}}{2} \tag{6.33}$$

We can easily check that this relationship, as well as initial conditions $p_0 = S$ and $p_{n+1} = V$, are satisfied by the following segment prices:

$$p_i^{opt} = \frac{1}{n+1}\left[(n+1-i) \cdot P + i \cdot V\right] \tag{6.34}$$

Consequently, the optimal prices should be equally distributed in between the variable costs V and maximum acceptable price P. This is illustrated by an example in Figure 6.9.

With these prices, the profit earned can be obtained by inserting equation 6.34 into equation 6.30:

$$G_{opt} = Q_{max} \cdot \frac{n(P-V)^2}{2(n+1)P} \tag{6.35}$$

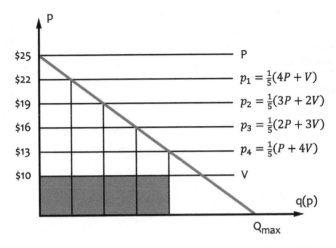

Figure 6.9: Example of optimal prices for four segments with variable costs of $10 and a maximum acceptable price of $25.

This equation is a generalization of the profit equation for unit prices 6.26. We can see that the profit increases proportionally to $n/(n + 1)$ as the number of segments grows and approaches the maximum achievable profit.

Price segmentation is arguably the most powerful and widely used pricing technique. Its power, however, completely depends on the ability to fence segments. Strict segmentation can be achieved in relatively few cases. For example, a theme park can price tickets differently for different age groups by verifying a proof of age. Most segmentations, however, are imperfect and create an opportunity for customers from a higher segment to buy a product marketed for a lower segment at a lower price. For example, online customers are known to have higher price sensitivity than store customers as a result of the ease of price comparisons and other factors, so retailers quite often lower online prices. This creates so-called *showroom behavior* where customers look at objects in a store and then buy them later online. This market *cannibalization* can be quite damaging, as illustrated in the example in table 6.3. The addition of a low-price segment increases the total profits in the case of perfect segmentation, but the leakage of 500 customers to this segment from the higher one completely erases the gains.

		PRICE	DEMAND	REVENUE	PROFIT	TOTAL PROFIT
SINGLE SEGMENT		$19	5000	$95,000	$45,000	$45,000
PERFECT SEGMENTS	A	$19	5000	$95,000	$45,000	$48,000
	B	$13	1000	$13,000	$3,000	
IMPERFECT SEGMENTS	A	$19	4500	$85,500	$40,500	$45,000
	B	$13	1500	$19,500	$4,500	

Table 6.3: Example of segmentation with and without demand cannibalization. The variable costs V are assumed to be $10 per item and Profit = Revenue − V × Demand.

6.5.3 Multipart Pricing

We have seen that segmentation is a powerful method for capturing additional revenues from heterogeneous demand. One popular method of creating fences between customer segments is to leverage the differences in product usage patterns and intensity. For example, manufacturers of photographic cameras typically offer a wide range of products, including entry-level models, advanced enthusiast cameras, and professional cameras. Although these categories are substantially different in image quality and other functional properties, manufacturers also try to capture profits from the more intensive usage of professional equipment by offering better durability and performance. In this regard, the most accurate segmentation can be achieved by charging a camera holder based on the number of shots they will take to capture revenues in direct proportion to usage. Although this approach might not be feasible for cameras because of implementation and competition reasons, variations of this are successfully applied in other industries. The two structurally similar price strategies that exploit this idea are *two-part tariffs* and *tying arrangements*:

TWO-PART TARIFFS A two-part tariff is a price structure with two components – an *entrance fee* and a *metered price*. The entrance fee is charged for access to a product or service. The metered price is a per-unit charge that depends on the consumed quantity. A classic example of two-part tariffs is telecommunication services that charge a connection fee in addition to metered fees for every minute or gigabyte used. Other notable examples include utilities, such as electricity, natural gas, or water, enterprise software, which is often priced in proportion to the number of users, orders, or concurrent connections on top of the baseline price, and amusement parks, which can charge an entrance fee and a price per ride.

TYING ARRANGEMENTS Some products are very closely related to each other, in the sense that a customer cannot extract much value from one product without another. This enables a manufacturer to create tying arrangements that prevent a customer from switching between brands and to rebalance the prices of the related products. Examples of tying arrangements can often be found when a durable product (the tying product) is complemented with a consumable part (the tied product), such as a razor handle and razor blades or a printer and ink cartridges. The revenue contributed by the consumable parts can dominate the total consumer lifetime value, so the durable product can be priced lower or even below its marginal costs.

Let us now consider quantitative models that provide directions on how the entrance price p_e and metered price p_m of a two-part tariff can be optimized. We have previously mentioned that the demand curve can be interpreted both as an aggregate demand of the market determined by the maximum willingness to pay and as the consumption level of a single customer at a given price. Two-part tariffs explicitly depend on the level of consumption and, consequently, require us to account for both the level of consumption and the demand heterogeneity, so we have to use a more complicated model than the one we used for unit pricing and price segmentation [Smith, 2012; Oi, 1971].

Let us first consider the case of a single consumer, for whom the demand curve is shown in Figure 6.10.

Recall that the equation of the linear demand curve is

$$q = Q_{max}\left(1 - \frac{p_m}{P}\right) \tag{6.36}$$

The consumer evaluates the product or service at price P, so the surplus gained by buying a unit at metered price p_m is numerically equal to the area of the triangle under the demand curve bounded by the p_m line. Consequently, we can assume that the optimal entrance fee is equal to this surplus because a lower fee will leave available profits on the table and a higher fee will drive the consumer out of the market. This means that the entrance fee can be expressed as an area under the demand curve:

$$p_e^{opt} = \frac{q}{2}(P - p_m) = \frac{Q_{max}}{2P}(P - p_m)^2 \tag{6.37}$$

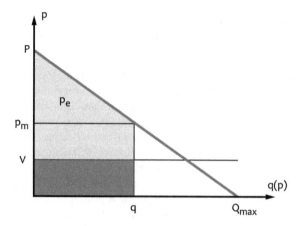

Figure 6.10: Price optimization for a two-part tariff.

The total profit earned for a customer is a sum of the entrance fee and metered charges:

$$G = p_e^{opt} + q(p_m - V) \tag{6.38}$$

The optimal metered price can be obtained by taking the derivative of the profit and equating it to zero:

$$\frac{\partial G}{\partial p_m} = \frac{\partial p_e^{opt}}{\partial p_m} + \frac{\partial q}{\partial p_m}(p_m - V) + q = 0 \tag{6.39}$$

Inserting equations 6.37 and 6.38 into equation 6.39 and solving it for p_m, we find that the optimal metered price should be set equal to the marginal costs:

$$p_m^{opt} = V \tag{6.40}$$

This means that two-part tariff pricing encourages the seller to set the entrance fee as high as possible and lower the metered price to the minimum, so the profit will be extracted exclusively from the entrance fee. This strategy, for example, is widely adopted by amusement parks that tend to charge high entrance fees rather than charge per ride.

The approach with the high entrance fee, however, faces a strong headwind in the case of competition or heterogeneous demand where customers are willing to purchase different quantities of a product at a given price. This situation is depicted in Figure 6.11, where multiple demand curves have the same slope but differ in quantity purchased.

Let us assume that each demand curve corresponds to a certain customer segment. We now cannot set the entrance fee higher than the surplus that corresponds to the lowest demand curve because we would

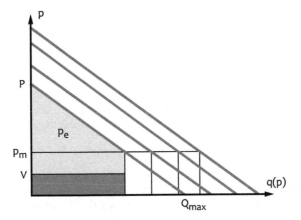

Figure 6.11: Two-part tariff in the case of heterogeneous consumption levels.

lose customers otherwise. Let us denote the ratio between the demand of the i-th segment to the demand of the segment that corresponds to the lowest demand curve as k_i, so the equations for the demand curves can be written as

$$q_i = Q_{max} k_i \left(1 - \frac{p_m}{k_i P} \right), \quad k_i \geq 1 \tag{6.41}$$

The profit can be expressed by summing the entrance fee with the metered charges from each of the segments:

$$G = p_e + \sum_i \mu_i q_i (p_m - V) \tag{6.42}$$

in which μ_i is the share of the segment i, that is, if the total number of customers is N then the segment i contains $N \cdot \mu_i$ customers. The optimal metered price can be found by taking the derivative of the profit with respect to the metered price and equating it to zero:

$$\frac{\partial G}{\partial p_m} = \frac{\partial p_e}{\partial p_m} + (p_m - V) \sum_i \mu_i \frac{\partial q_i}{\partial p_m} + \sum_i \mu_i q_i = 0 \tag{6.43}$$

Equation 6.37 for p_e still holds, under the assumption that P is the maximum acceptable price for the lowest demand curve, so we can insert it into the equation above and, by using the fact that the sum of all μ_i equals one, we derive a simple expression for the optimal metered price:

$$p_m^{opt} = V + P \sum_i \mu_i (k_i - 1) = V + P(\mathbb{E}[k] - 1) \tag{6.44}$$

in which $\mathbb{E}\,[k]$ is the weighted average of the segment demand multipliers. This result demonstrates that heterogeneity in demand levels drives the metered price up and, consequently, decreases the entrance fee, which is already limited by the lowest demand curve. This can reverse the price balance of the original two-part tariff – the metered element can become dominant in the total profit relative to the entrance element. This shift can also be driven by competition, which limits the seller's ability to extract consumer surpluses though the entrance fee.

6.5.4   Bundling

Bundling is often defined in economic texts as the sale of two or more separate products in one package at a single price. This definition is not very precise because virtually any product can be considered as a bundle of its parts, just as a car is a bundle of an engine, wheels, and other components that can be sold separately, at least on industrial markets. From the price optimization standpoint, we are most interested in *price bundling* that offers two or more products at a discounted price relative to the sum of the individual product prices; this discount is the only advantage to the alternative of buying unbundled items.

   Price bundling is a popular price structure that can be found in many industries. Examples of price bundles include sport and opera season tickets, restaurant meals that bundle an appetizer, entree, and dessert, luggage sets with several bags of different size, kitchenware, and software suites. A seller typically has a choice between three options: to sell unbundled products, to sell a group of products only as a bundle, which is known as *pure bundling*, and to offer the individual products as well as the discounted bundle, which is called *mixed bundling*. It is intuitively clear that the discount provided by a bundle should be counterbalanced by capturing more profits than the separate products do. We have seen earlier that complex price structures often accomplish this by exploiting heterogeneity in the willingness to pay. Consequently, we can make the assumption that bundling can leverage the difference in the willingness to pay for different products.

EXAMPLE 6.2

▼ As an example, let us consider an office software suite that includes a spreadsheet application and slide presentation application. The most basic scenario that we can analyze is a single-segment market in which the value of each application is the same for all customers. Let's say that the spreadsheet application is valued at $100 and the presentation application is valued at $150 per user license. We can price the individual products according to this valuation and the bundling of the two products will not be beneficial because any bundle price other than $250 will harm profits. The scenario with two segments shown in table 6.4 is more interesting because the willingness to pay differs between the segments – sales departments highly value the presentation application, whereas accounting departments prefer the spreadsheet. The maximum price levels for the individual products that keep both segments in the market are $100 for the spreadsheet application and $100 for the presentation application. If the two segments are equal in size, these prices are optimal and earn a total profit of $400. The price of a bundle that includes the two products, however, can be set at $250 because both sales and accounting segments value the pair of products at $250. The total profit earned from the two segments will be $500, which is better than the $400 earned with the unbundled pricing.

CUSTOMER SEGMENT	WILLINGNESS TO PAY	
	Spreadsheet	Presentation
Sales	$100	$150
Accounting	$150	$100

Table 6.4: Example of price bundling with two products and two consumer segments.

The example above exploits the asymmetry of willingness to pay between two segments. If all customers consistently value one product higher than another, bundling is not able to capture more profits than unbundled pricing. We can use this observation to build a quantitative model for bundle price optimization. The advantage of this model is that it makes relatively few assumptions about how customer segments are distributed and can take advantage of numerical optimization or simulations to optimize pricing for an arbitrary number of segments or even individual users. Let us consider a scenario where we are selling two products, X and Y, and there are several customer segments in which the maximum willingness to pay P_{ix} for product X is equal or proportional to the willingness to pay P_{iy} for product Y, as illustrated in Figure 6.12. For any product prices p_x and p_y, a consumer segment falls into one of four areas (buy nothing, buy only product X, buy only product Y, or buy two products) depending on the relationship between the willingness to pay and the corresponding price. In our scenario with positively correlated valuations, customers buy either all or nothing, so bundling cannot add value.

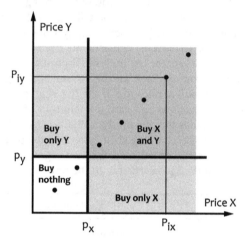

Figure 6.12: Customer segments in which the willingness to pay for two products is positively correlated. The segments are depicted as black dots.

The case with asymmetrical willingness to pay is totally different. For the sake of simplicity, let us assume that all segments have the same aggregate willingness to pay, but segments can allocate it to products differently, as shown in Figure 6.13. This was exactly the case in the example with the office software suite that we just studied.

PURE BUNDLING The price of bundle p_B can be set equal to the aggregate willingness to pay beause it is constant for all segments:

$$p_B = P_{ix} + P_{iy}, \quad \text{constant for all } i \tag{6.45}$$

The profit of selling the bundle will be

$$\begin{aligned}
G_B &= \sum_i n_i \left(p_B - V_x - V_y \right) \\
&= \sum_i n_i \left(P_{ix} + P_{iy} - V_x - V_y \right)
\end{aligned} \tag{6.46}$$

in which n_i is the number of customers in segment i, and V_x and V_y are variable costs for products X and Y, respectively. On the other hand, we find that selling unbundled products earns the following profit:

$$G_U = \sum_{i:\, P_{xi} \geqslant p_x} n_i \left(p_x - V_x \right) + \sum_{i:\, P_{yi} \geqslant p_y} n_i \left(p_y - V_y \right) \quad (6.47)$$

The first and second terms of equation 6.47 are the total profits for product X and Y, respectively. Comparing equations 6.46 and 6.47, we find that G_B is greater than or equal to G_U for any product prices p_x and p_y, so pure bundling is a more effective strategy in this scenario than selling unbundled products.

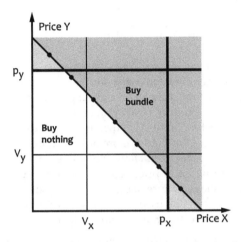

Figure 6.13: Customer segments with a negatively correlated willingness to pay.

MIXED BUNDLING We can try to enhance pure bundling by selling products both separately and in a bundle. This requires us to set prices on separately sold products in a way that does not cannibalize the profits we gain from bundling. We can do this by comparing the bundle profit with the profit of a separate product. Let's take product X as an example:

$$p_x - V_x > p_B - V_x - V_y \quad (6.48)$$

Consequently, we find the prices for individual products to be

$$p_x > p_B - V_y$$
$$p_y > p_B - V_x \quad (6.49)$$

This condition corresponds to the small triangles located at the extreme ends of the bundle price line in Figure 6.13. Customer segments that fall into these areas will choose to buy either product X (rightmost triangle) or Y (leftmost triangle) instead of a bundle, which will generate a higher revenue than that with pure bundling.

The approach above provides relatively high flexibility for the optimization of bundle prices. With the assumption that the willingness to pay is estimated for sample segments or individual consumers, the corresponding points can be pinned on a plane and the optimal prices can be searched by using numerical optimization methods and tessellating the plane into areas with different profits depending on the segment locations and sizes.

6.6 DEMAND PREDICTION

The basic demand models we considered earlier are convenient for strategic analysis but often too coarse for the actual price optimization. The challenge is that the demand on a given product depends on many factors, including a product's own properties such as price or brand, the prices of competing products in the category, sales events, and even the weather. We need to build a more advanced demand model that incorporates these factors and allows one to perform what-if analysis to forecast the response to price changes, assortment extensions and reductions, and shelf-space re-allocation. This model is an important building block that can be used in many applications that depend on quantitative demand estimation, including the following:

STATIC PRICE OPTIMIZATION Baseline prices and markdowns can be customized for different customer segments defined by channels, locations, and propensity models. This requires segment properties to be incorporated into the demand model.

DYNAMIC PRICE OPTIMIZATION Price markdowns, sales event planning, and the pricing of products with constrained supplies require prices to be optimized as a function of time. This implies that the demand model should also take temporal changes into account.

CATEGORY MANAGEMENT Shelf-space optimization and assortment optimization require an understanding of the dependencies between the demands on different products.

STOCK-LEVEL OPTIMIZATION Supply chain management and replenishment benefit from demand modeling. Demand prediction becomes especially important in the case of major sales events and flash-sales business models.

Demand prediction can be considered as a relatively straightforward data mining problem that boils down to the building of a regression model and evaluation of it over historical data. However, the design of the regression model is not so straightforward because the demand is influenced by many factors with complex dependencies. We might need to combine multiple basic demand functions, such as linear demand or logit demand, to assemble a model that is flexible enough to properly capture seasonal changes, consumer choices, price elasticity, and other factors.

The design of demand models is definitely an art because different optimization problems require different demand prediction models, and it is hardly possible to build a universal demand model that incorporates the wide variety of factors that influence demand, such as the following:

- Model usage. A model may or may not include controls for consumer choice, demand changes over time, competitive prices, and so on. The choice of controls depends on the application that the model is created for.

- Available data. The availability, trustworthiness, and completeness of data influence the design of a model and its capabilities.

- Business domain, model, and process. The demand model reflects the terminology, constraints, and structure of a particular business. For example, the demand model can predict the demand rate for individual products or groups that include multiple product variants of different sizes, colors, or flavors.

- Experimentation. Demand models, just like most real-life predictive models, explicitly and implicitly incorporate a lot of domain knowledge and require a lot of experimentation and tuning.

We can, however, learn many useful techniques and design ideas by studying industrial demand prediction models. The structure of models and choice of features provides us with reusable building blocks and hints that can be leveraged for future demand prediction problems. We choose to study two real-life demand models from the retail domain and also to examine the difference between these two examples and a few models reported by other companies. All of these models were created in the context of price and assortment optimization, so they are well aligned with the optimization methods that we will review later in this chapter.

6.6.1 *Demand Model for Assortment Optimization*

The first demand model we will consider was designed for assortment optimization at Albert Heijn, a supermarket chain in the Netherlands [Kök and Fisher, 2007]. It places a strong emphasis on consumer decisions to enable a fine-grained analysis of the factors that influence consumer choice.

A supermarket chain carries a large number of products that are divided into merchandising categories, such as cheese, wine, cookies, and milk. Each category is further divided into subcategories such that products within a subcategory are similar and are often good substitutes for one another but the difference between subcategories is substantial. For example, a fluid milk category can include subcategories such as whole milk, fat-free milk, flavored milk, and so on. Supermarkets typically achieve very high service levels for the products that they carry and stockouts are quite rare, so the model we will consider does not take stockouts into account. At the same time, this demand model was designed for assortment analysis and optimization, so it explicitly accounts for consumer choice, which makes it well suited to the assortment-related problem that we will consider in later sections.

The demand for a single product can be broken down into three separate decisions that apply for every consumer visiting a store:

- First, a consumer purchases or does not purchase from a subcategory. Let us denote the probability that a consumer purchases any product from a subcategory during the visit to the store as Pr(purchase | visit).

- Second, a consumer chooses which product to buy within a subcategory. The probability that a consumer chooses product j among other alternatives when a purchase takes place is Pr(j | purchase).

- Finally, a consumer decides how many units to buy. We can capture this choice by using the mathematical expectation of the quantity (number of units) purchased by the consumer given that product j has been chosen and purchased. Let us denote it as $\mathbb{E}[Q \mid j, \text{purchase}]$.

The demand for product j can then be expressed by using the choice probabilities and expected purchase quantity as follows:

$$
\begin{aligned}
D_j = N &\times \Pr(\text{purchase} \mid \text{visit}) \\
&\times \Pr(j \mid \text{purchase}) \\
&\times \mathbb{E}[Q \mid j, \text{purchase}]
\end{aligned}
\tag{6.50}
$$

in which N is the number of consumers visiting the store within a given time frame (e. g., during the day). All factors in equation 6.50 can be estimated from the transactional data from the stores. The demand generally depends on the date (day of the week, holidays, etc.) and store (size, neighborhood demographics, etc.), so we introduce subscripts t and h to denote date and store, respectively, and estimate the demand as a function of these parameters. Alternatively, store properties, such as size, location, and average consumer's income, can be incorporated into the model as predictive variables. The number of store visitors can be modeled by using a log-linear regression as follows:

$$\log(N_{ht}) = \alpha_1 + \alpha_2 T_t + \alpha_3 W_t + \sum_{i=1}^{7} \alpha_{3+i} B_{ti} + \sum_{i=1}^{N_E} \alpha_{10+i} E_{ti} \quad (6.51)$$

in which T_t is the weather temperature, W_t is the weather comfort index (humidity, cloudiness, etc.), B_{ti} and E_{ti} are 0/1 dummy variables for a day of the week and public holidays, respectively, N_E is the total number of public holidays, and α represent regression coefficients.

The purchase incidence is a binary choice variable (purchase/no purchase), so we can use a standard modeling approach – express the purchase probability as a sigmoid function that approximates the binary decision and estimate its exponential parameter from the data. The sigmoid function can be specified as

$$\Pr(\text{purchase} \mid \text{visit}) = \frac{1}{1 + e^{-x}} \quad (6.52)$$

which is equivalent to

$$x = \log\left(\frac{\Pr(\text{purchase} \mid \text{visit})}{1 - \Pr(\text{purchase} \mid \text{visit})}\right) \quad (6.53)$$

Exponential parameter x is estimated for a given date t and store h by using a regression model with the following structure:

$$x_{ht} = \beta_1 + \beta_2 T_t + \beta_3 W_t + \beta_4 \overline{A}_{ht}$$
$$+ \sum_{i=1}^{7} \beta_{4+i} B_{ti} + \sum_{i=1}^{N_E} \beta_{11+i} E_{ti} \quad (6.54)$$

in which $\overline{A}_{ht}$ is the share of products that are currently on promotion in the subcategory, that is, the ratio between the number of products that are promoted in a given store at a given date to the total number of products in the subcategory. As we will need to build further product-level models, let us express the share of promoted products with indicator variables A_{jth} for individual products that equal one if the product is promoted and zero otherwise:

$$\overline{A}_{ht} = \frac{1}{J} \sum_{j=1}^{J} A_{jht} \qquad (6.55)$$

in which J is the total number of products in the subcategory.

Estimation of the probability of the purchase of a given product in a subcategory is a little bit more tricky. As we have seen earlier, consumer choice can be modeled by using the multinomial logit model (MNL), so we express the probability of the purchase of a product among alternatives as follows:

$$\Pr(j \mid \text{purchase}) = \frac{\exp(y_j)}{\sum_i \exp(y_i)} \qquad (6.56)$$

in which i iterates over all products in a subcategory and y_j is a parameter variable. Similarly to the probability of the purchase incidence, we can build a regression model for parameter variable y_j for a given store and date:

$$y_{jht} = \gamma_j + \gamma_{N+1}(R_{jht} - \overline{R}_{ht}) + \gamma_{N+2}(A_{jht} - \overline{A}_{ht}) \qquad (6.57)$$

in which the regression coefficients γ_{N+1} and γ_{N+2} are shared for all products, R_{jht} and $\overline{R}_{ht}$ are the product price and the average price in the subcategory, respectively, and A_{jht} and $\overline{A}_{ht}$ are the promotion dummy variables and average promotion rate, as described above for the purchase incidence regression model.

Finally, the average number of units sold can be modeled as follows:

$$\mathbb{E}\left[Q \mid j, \text{purchase}\right] = \lambda_j + \lambda_{N+1}A_{jht} + \lambda_{N+2}W_t$$
$$+ \sum_{i=1}^{N_H} \lambda_{N+2+i}E_{ti} \qquad (6.58)$$

in which λ are regression coefficients and the other variables have been defined and explained above. By substituting the individual regression models above into the root equation 6.50, we obtain a fully specified demand prediction model. This model can be adjusted to the retailer's business usage cases by adding more explanatory variables, such as marketing events.

Competing products and their attributes play an important role in demand modeling even if the assortment is not the main concern. For example, the online fashion retailer Rue La La reported that the relative price of competing styles and the number of competing styles are in the top three most important features in their demand prediction model [Ferreira et al., 2016].

6.6.2 Demand Model for Seasonal Sales

The second demand model we will review was developed for Zara, a Spanish fashion retailer and the main brand of Inditex, the world's largest fashion group [Caro and Gallien, 2012]. The model is geared towards sales events optimization and places strong emphasis on the temporal dimension of the demand.

Seasonal clearance sales are an integral part of the business strategy for many apparel retailers. A regular selling season, which is typically biannual (fall–winter and spring–summer), is followed by a relatively short clearance sale period that aims to sell off the remaining inventory and free up space for the new collection for the next season. Some retailers exercise even smaller sales cycles to overrun competitors and get more revenues from customers by offering more diverse and fluid assortment. Price optimization in such an environment requires the creation of a demand model that properly accounts for seasonal effects and stockouts caused by the exhaustion of inventory and deliberate assortment changes.

We describe the demand model in two steps, in accordaance with the original report [Caro and Gallien, 2012]. The first step is to prepare the available demand data for regression analysis by removing seasonal variations and accounting for demand censoring due to stockouts. Next, the regression model itself is specified.

6.6.2.1 Demand Data Preparation

Most clothing items come in multiple colors and sizes, so every stock keeping unit (SKU) can be referenced by using a product number r and size–color variant v. With the assumption that the historical sales and inventory data are available on a store level for individual days, let us denote sales of SKU (r, v) at store h on day d as $S(r, v, d, h)$ and the corresponding inventory level at the beginning of the day as $L(r, v, d, h)$. We also define a function $F(r, v, d, h)$ equal to one if a given SKU was on display at store h on day d and zero otherwise. The on-display information can be available in the data explicitly or one can estimate it from the sales and inventory data by checking if the inventory level or quantity sold is zero for a given item.

First, let us introduce a seasonality factor that incorporates intra-week and inter-week demand variations. We define the following aggregates of the sales data:

- $S_W(d)$ is the total sales volume for a week in which day d falls. This volume is aggregated for all products, size–color variants, and stores.

- $\overline{S}_W$ is the average total weekly sales volume calculated from the historical data.

- $\overline{S}_W(r)$ is the average weekly sales volume for product r calculated from the historical data.

- $\overline{S}_W(r, v, h)$ is the average weekly sales volume for SKU (r, v) at store h calculated from the historical data.

- $\overline{S}_D(\text{weekday}(d))$ is the average sales volume for a given day of the week defined for seven days from Monday to Sunday.

The seasonality factor can then be defined as follows:

$$\delta(d) = \frac{S_W(d)}{\overline{S}_W} \times \frac{\overline{S}_D(\text{weekday}(d))}{\sum_{i=1}^{7} \overline{S}_D(i)} \tag{6.59}$$

The first and second terms account for inter-week and intra-week demand variations, respectively. Next, we introduce the following factor that accounts for both seasonality and on-display information to normalize the demand for product r and week w:

$$k(r, w) = \sum_{h,v} \frac{\overline{S}_W(r, v, h)}{\overline{S}_W(r)} \cdot \sum_{d \text{ in } w} \delta(d) \cdot F(r, v, d, h) \tag{6.60}$$

The fraction in the equation above corresponds to the share of sales at store h relative to all stores, so the contribution of the on-display status variable for the store is properly weighted by the store's sales share. Finally, we define the normalized demand for product r and week w as follows:

$$q(r, w) = \frac{1}{k(r, w)} \cdot \sum_{v,h,d \text{ in } w} S(r, v, d, h) \tag{6.61}$$

6.6.2.2 Model Specification

Our next step is to build a regression model that predicts the normalized demand rate $q(r, w)$. This was achieved by Zara by using a relatively small log-linear model with the following specification:

$$\begin{aligned}
\log(q(r, w)) = \alpha_{0,r} &+ \alpha_1 \log(Q_r) + \alpha_2 A_{r,w} \\
&+ \alpha_3 \log(q(r, w - 1)) \\
&+ \alpha_{4,w} \log\left(\min\left\{1, \frac{1}{T} L(r, w)\right\}\right) \\
&+ \alpha_{5,w} \log\left(\frac{p_{r,w}}{p_{r,0}}\right)
\end{aligned} \tag{6.62}$$

in which α are regression coefficients and the features are defined as follows:

- α_1: Q_r is the quantity of product r purchased by a retailer. Although this value is not directly related to the demand, it is implicitly related to fashion and style because a retailer often purchases large quantities of basic and popular items, whereas niche items are purchased in smaller quantities.

- α_2: $A_{r,w}$ is the number of days since product r was introduced at the stores. The demand for fashion products often depends on their novelty and tends to decrease over time.

- α_3: $q(r, w - 1)$ is the demand rate for the previous time interval. This variable helps to capture demand correlation between adjacent time intervals.

- $\alpha_{4,w}$: The *broken assortment effect* refers to the fact that the demand for a given product can decrease as the inventory level gets low. In the fashion retail context, this can often be attributed to unpopular sizes and colors that remain after the most popular ones have sold out. This effect can be accounted for by introducing a threshold T for $L(r, w)$, which is the aggregated inventory level for product r across all variants and stores.

- $\alpha_{5,w}$: The discount depth is defined as the ratio between the current price $p_{r,w}$ and the regular price $p_{r,0}$. This term is effectively a price sensitivity factor.

We can see that the model is heavily focused on the demand variability over time because it was created for the optimization of seasonal sales events. Demand models reported by other fashion retailers can include more features such as brand, color and size popularity, relative prices of competing styles, and different statistics about past sales events that can shift price sensitivity [Ferreira et al., 2016].

6.6.3 Demand Prediction with Stockouts

The demand models described in the previous sections are merely regression models that are trained to forecast the sales numbers. In practice, the observed sales numbers do not necessarily match the actual demand because of stockout events. If this is the case, the observed sales volume will be lower than the actual demand, that is, the sales volume that could potentially be achieved given an unlimited supply without stockouts. The problem of stockouts can be especially important for business models with seasonal sales or flash sales, where stockouts are very frequent and a demand prediction model created based on the observed sales volume is likely to be biased and inappropriate for optimization of the inventory levels or prices. Therefore, a demand prediction method that explicitly accounts for out-of-stock events and lost sales needs to be developed. This problem has been studied intensively, and a number of methods exist that address demand prediction with stockout events [Anupindi et al., 1998; Musalem et al., 2010; Vulcano et al., 2012]. In this section, we discuss a heuristic technique developed by Rue La La, an online fashion retailer, to account for stockouts that occur during flash sales events, that is, extremely time-limited discounts [Ferreira et al., 2016]. The advantage of this method is the simplicity and ability to work with low inventory levels (if a retailer stocks only a few instances of each SKU) that can be insufficient to fit more advanced models.

On the assumption of a setting where a retailer sells multiple products, let us introduce the following notation:

- d_i is the actual demand for product i

- c_i is the inventory level for product i

- q_i is the actual quantity sold, which can be expressed as follows

$$q_i = \min\{c_i,\, d_i\} \tag{6.63}$$

If a product can be represented by multiple size–color variants, we treat each variant as a separate product and measure the above values for individual variants. Next, we assume that the retailer runs limited-time sale events for individual products. At the beginning of the event, the stock level is equal to c_i. If the product sells out before the end of the event, we can observe that $q_i = c_i$ but we do not observe the true demand d_i. If the product does not sell out, we can assume that we observe the true demand, $q_i = d_i$. The main problem we are trying to solve is how to estimate the expected sales volume q_i given inventory level c_i as a parameter. We can distinguish the following cases:

- If product i has already been on sale and did not sell out, the observed quantity sold q_i can be used as the demand estimate $\hat{d}_i$, and the expected quantity that will be sold given the inventory level c_i^{new} in a new sales event can be predicted based on this estimate. This can be summarized as

$$\hat{d}_i = q_i \quad \rightarrow \quad \hat{q}_i = \min\left\{c_i^{new},\, \hat{d}_i\right\} \tag{6.64}$$

- If the product i has already been on sale and did sell out, we have not observed the true demand. This requires us to perform *demand unconstraining*, that is, to estimate the true demand based on the quantity sold and the historical data for other products.

This unconstrained demand estimate $\widehat{d}_i$ can then be used to predict the expected quantity that will be sold in a new event. This strategy can be summarized as follows:

$$q_i \xrightarrow{\text{unconstraining}} \widehat{d}_i \quad \rightarrow \quad \widehat{q}_i = \min\left\{c_i^{new}, \widehat{d}_i\right\} \quad (6.65)$$

- If the product is new and has never been on sale, the demand needs to be predicted with a regression model that uses product and event properties as features and the unconstrained demand value as the response variable. This problem can be solved by using the methods discussed in the previous section. This case can be summarized as

$$\widehat{d}_i = f(\text{product}, \text{event}) \quad \rightarrow \quad \widehat{q}_i = \min\left\{c_i^{new}, \widehat{d}_i\right\} \quad (6.66)$$

in which f is the predictive demand model. In the case of multiple product variants, the model can be created to predict the demand at product level and then the demands on the product variants can be derived from this based on the observed distribution of demand for different sizes and colors.

In the approach described above, the key task is demand unconstraining. One possible approach is to use historical data for products that did not sell out to estimate the demand for products that did sell out. First, we can create demand curves for products that did not sell out, with each curve describing the percentage of total sales for a given product as a function of time into the event measured in hours or days, as shown in Figure 6.14.

In practice, the number of products and corresponding demand curves can be very high, so we can split the curves into several classes by using standard clustering methods, determine the rules that differentiate the classes (clusters) from one another, and determine the typical demand curve for each class. For example, it can be the case that the key factor that determines the demand curve shape is the event start time, such as morning, early afternoon, late afternoon, and so on. Most events that start, for example, in the morning may have similar demand curves and thus belong to the same cluster. The clustering rule can be more complex and involve multiple properties. Once we have identified the rules that assign products and events to classes and have also determined a typical curve for each class, we can unconstrain the demand for products that sold out based on the curve. First, we use the clustering rules to assign the product and event to a class. Second, we use the demand curve for this class to map the stockout time to the proportion of total sales k, as illustrated

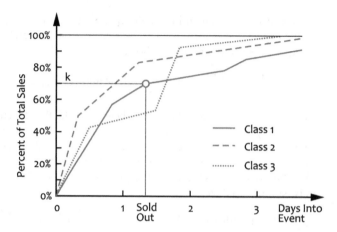

Figure 6.14: Example of demand curves and the determination of the demand-unconstraining proportion [Ferreira et al., 2016]. In this example, there are three classes of events, each of which is represented by a typical demand curve, and the event that needs to be unconstrained falls into the first class.

in Figure 6.14. Once this proportion is determined, the true demand for product i can be estimated by dividing the observed quantity sold by the proportion value:

$$\hat{d}_i = \frac{q_i}{k} = \frac{c_i}{k} \tag{6.67}$$

This estimate can then be used for sales volume prediction, demand modeling, and stock level optimization.

6.7 PRICE OPTIMIZATION

A demand model enables us to search for the optimal price by analyzing how the price changes increase or decrease the profits. We have already seen that this optimization is not particularly difficult for basic price structures and an oversimplified environment that does not account for the special properties of supply, demand, and operations that can be found in real applications. In practice, however, we face numerous constraints and interdependencies that require much more elaborate and specialized optimization models to be developed.

Most of the constraints fall into one of the following three categories: supply constraints, demand constraints, and structural constraints. Supply constraints can be imposed by limited resource capacity, such as the fixed number of seats in an opera house, constrained or expensive replenishment, and product *perishability*, which can take different forms from the limited shelf life of grocery products to the seasonal collections at a clothing store to airline tickets that must be sold before the departure of a plane. Demand constraints are often related to imperfect consumer segmentation, interdependency of the demands on substitutable products, demand changes over time, and demand uncertainty, in the sense that the demand cannot be predicted accurately. Structural constraints are related to operational and legal conditions that might require suboptimal but practicable solutions to be selected.

We will continue this section with price optimization models for different market segmentation strategies and constraints. This group of methods can be considered as static price optimization, although one can repeat the optimization procedures regularly to adjust prices over time or define time-based customer segments, such as weekend and workday cinema tickets. We will then demonstrate that the dynamic pricing that explicitly optimizes temporal price changes is closely related to market segmentation, and we will describe dynamic price management methods.

6.7.1 *Price Differentiation*

The goal of price differentiation, more commonly referred to in economic texts as *price discrimination*, is to find the optimal prices for separate customer segments or individual customers. Price optimization at the segment or customer level requires the creation of a demand model that takes customer or segment properties as parameters or the creation of a separate demand model for each segment. This can be achieved with the demand prediction methods that we have previously discussed. The basic price optimization problem can then be specified as follows:

$$\max_{\mathbf{p}} \sum_s (p_s - v_s) \cdot q_s(p_s) \tag{6.68}$$

in which s is a segment, p_s is the price for segment s, $\mathbf{p}$ is a vector of prices for all segments, q_s is the demand function for segment s, and v_s is variable costs, which can be constant or vary depending on the segment. This optimization problem is separable by segments, so the basic unit price optimization can be applied for each segment separately.

It is often the case that the number and structure of segments is limited by operational constraints, so a programmatic system might need to evaluate the impact of combining several segments together into a group and assigning that group a single price. This can be done by rewriting equation 6.68 for N segment groups S_i as

$$\max_{p} \sum_{i=1}^{N} p_i \sum_{s \in S_i} (p_i - v_s) \cdot q_s(p_i) \tag{6.69}$$

and solving a separate optimization problem for each group to find N optimal prices.

<u>EXAMPLE 6.3</u>

▼

Let us illustrate the optimization models above with an example from the retail domain. Consider a retailer that operates multiple stores and sells a product that comes in several sizes, for example, analgesic tablets that are packaged in bottles of 25 or 50 tablets [Khan and Jain, 2005]. The retailer can offer quantity discounts based on package sizes and set prices separately for each store. Regression analysis of the transactional data has shown that the demand for analgesics is well described by the following model:

$$q(p, s, h) = 2000 - 1400p - 8s - 10s \cdot h \tag{6.70}$$

in which p is the price per tablet, s is the package size (the number of tablets in the bottle), and h is the average household size factor, which is positive when the average household size in the store area is relatively large and negative when the average household is small. The demand is negatively correlated with price, as we expect. It is also negatively correlated with the package size, which indicates that consumers prefer smaller packages to larger ones. The last term is positively correlated with the package size for large households and negatively correlated for small ones, so the demand for large packages is higher in areas with large households, which is also intuitive.

We will optimize prices for a setting with two stores with different values of the household size factor h and two package sizes with different wholesale prices v, as shown in Figure 6.15.

The first scenario we consider is a fine-grained price differentiation that jointly optimizes quantity discounts based on package sizes and store-level prices. The goal is to find four different prices p_{ij}, in which i corresponds to one of two package sizes and j corresponds to one of two stores. The optimization problem can then be stated as follows:

$$\max_{p} \sum_{i=1,2} \sum_{j=1,2} (s_i p_{ij} - v_i) \cdot q(p_{ij}, s_i, h_j) \tag{6.71}$$

This optimization problem is separable and quadratic with respect to prices because the demand function is linear. Solving the problem for

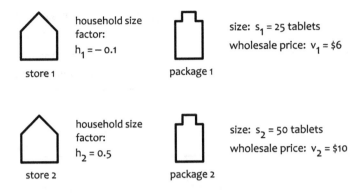

Figure 6.15: Parameters of the price optimization problem for two stores and two package sizes.

the values from Figure 6.15, we obtain the results presented in table 6.5. We can see that the solution justifies quantity discounts and suggests that per-tablet prices are lower for a large package in both stores. It also exploits the higher demand for large packages in the area with large households by raising the price in the corresponding store.

PACKAGE SIZE (TABLETS)	HOUSEHOLD SIZE	PRICE PER TABLET	DEMAND (BOTTLES)
25	SMALL	$0.67	607
25	LARGE	$0.81	794
50	SMALL	$0.49	410
50	LARGE	$0.76	785
TOTAL PROFIT			$45,863

Table 6.5: The optimal prices for a scenario with four segments.

Our second scenario assumes that it is not possible to vary prices at a store level because of operational constraints, so we can only set two prices, for the small and large packages. We change the optimization problem accordingly by following the generic approach from equation 6.69:

$$\max_{p} \sum_{i=1,2} (s_i p_i - v_i) \sum_{j=1,2} q(p_i, s_i, h_j) \tag{6.72}$$

This problem is also separable and quadratic with respect to prices. Solving it, we find that the total profit decreases in comparison with that of the first scenario, as one can see in table 6.6 where the optimization results are shown.

PACKAGE SIZE (TABLETS)	PRICE PER TABLET	DEMAND (BOTTLES)
25	$0.74	1401
50	$0.63	1195
TOTAL PROFIT		$43,038

Table 6.6: The optimal prices for a scenario with two segments.

This analysis allows us to evaluate different segmentation strategies and find the optimal solution under structural constraints.

6.7.1.1   *Differentiation with Demand Shifting*

One of the biggest challenges of price differentiation is imperfect fences between price segments that allow customers to move from one segment to another depending on the price differences. Although it sounds as though this demand shifting is necessarily harmful for a seller, it can actually impact profits both positively and negatively. On the one hand, customers with high willingness to pay can find a way to buy a product at a relatively low price, thereby decreasing the profit of the high-margin segments. On the other hand, the corresponding increase in the segment that the customer migrated to can counterbalance the loss.

The shifting effect is especially important in cases of constrained supply because it can help to achieve a more even demand distribution and reduce stockouts. For example, the supply of seats in an opera house is fixed but the demand can vary significantly, typically reaching its maximum on the weekends and its minimum on weekdays. The opera house can lose potential revenue if the peak demand on the weekends exceeds the capacity. We can expect that setting variable ticket prices for different days of the week can improve profits because the higher demand on the weekends enables the opera house to charge higher prices and make better margins, as we have seen in the previous section. High weekends prices, however, can make some customers buy cheaper weekday tickets, which shifts the demand to days with available seat capacity and improves the revenues even further.

It can be quite challenging to create a demand shifting model. The challenge is partly related to the design and training of a demand model that simultaneously accounts for the prices of all related segments. It is often impossible to measure cross-price elasticities (how the demand in one segment is impacted by the price in another segment) for all possible pairs of segments, so one has to use grosser approximations, such as the ratio between the price in a given segment and the average prices in other segments. Another challenge of demand shifting models is that cross-segment dependencies make the optimization problem inseparable and sharply increase its computational complexity. Assuming that we draw prices from a discrete set of size m and the number of segments is n, we might need to evaluate as many as m^n price combinations if the demand model does not follow any particular functional form that exhibits properties such as linearity or convexity.

One possible approach to price optimization with demand shifting is to make the assumption that the demand shift is proportional to the price difference between the segments. More specifically, if the price for segment i is higher than the price for segment j, then the demand for segment i decreases by $K(p_i - p_j)$ and the demand for segment j increases by the same amount. Parameter K determines the amount of demand transferred between the two segments for every dollar of price difference. The basic optimization problem can then be rewritten as follows to adjust the demand in each segment by the total of the demands shifted from other segments:

$$\max_{\mathbf{p}} \sum_i (p_i - v_i) \cdot \left[q_i(p_i) + K \sum_j (p_j - p_i) \right] \tag{6.73}$$

in which i and j iterate over all segments. Note that this demand shifting model does not change the total demand, in the sense that the sum of all shifts is zero. However, this does not mean that the total quantity sold remains constant for any K because the demand shift causes the optimal prices to change, which, in turn, changes the values of the demand functions.

EXAMPLE 6.4

We can illustrate the impact of demand shifting by continuing our example with analgesic tablets. Inserting the demand shifting terms into equation 6.71, which describes the scenario with four price segments, we get

$$\max_{\mathbf{p}} \sum_{i=1,2} \sum_{j=1,2} (s_i p_{ij} - v_i) \cdot \left[q(p_{ij}, s_i, h_j) + \Delta(p_{ij}) \right] \tag{6.74}$$

in which the demand shift is the sum of the pairwise price differences with other segments, or

$$\Delta(p_{ij}) = K \sum_{x=1,2} \sum_{y=1,2} (p_{xy} - p_{ij}) \tag{6.75}$$

We solve this optimization problem and obtain the prices for the four segments presented in table 6.7. From a comparison with tables 6.5 and 6.7, we find that the demand shifting has increased price sensitivity, so the demand for small packages has decreased but the demand for a large package has increased because of the relatively low price per tablet. This change in demand can be considered positive for a retailer because it increases the total profit.

PACKAGE SIZE (TABLETS)	HOUSEHOLD SIZE	PRICE PER TABLET	DEMAND (BOTTLES)
25	SMALL	$0.75	420
25	LARGE	$0.81	608
50	SMALL	$0.56	535
50	LARGE	$0.69	910
TOTAL PROFIT			$46,170

Table 6.7: The optimal prices for a scenario with four segments and demand shift. The shifting parameter $K = 400$.

▲

6.7.1.2 Differentiation with Constrained Supply

The price optimization models that we have considered so far were focused on setting prices that achieve the highest possible profits allowed by a given demand curve. This view on price optimization assumes perfect replenishment, such that a seller is always able to deliver the quantity of a product demanded at the profit-optimal price. This assumption is reasonably fair for some industries, such as supermarket retail, where it is possible to build a supply chain that almost perfectly replenishes the inventory and stockouts are rare. However, as we have already discussed, it does not hold in many other industries that face different supply constraints. In this section, we will discuss a relatively simple case, in which each market segment has a fixed capacity of a product and we need to find the optimal global price or segment-level prices.

Let us first consider how a product can be priced for a single marketing segment if the available quantity is fixed. This problem is a standard unit-price optimization with the addition of a quantity constraint:

$$\max_{p,x} \quad x\,(p - V)$$
$$\text{subject to} \quad x \leqslant q(p) \tag{6.76}$$
$$x \leqslant C$$
$$p \geqslant 0$$

in which C is the available quantity (capacity), so that a stockout occurs if the demand exceeds C. As usual, we denote the price, demand, and variable costs as p, $q(p)$, and V, respectively. Variable x corresponds to the actual quantity sold.

This problem is quite trivial because the demand is a monotonically decreasing function of price. First, we can find the optimal price, regardless of the constraint and calculate the demand that corresponds to this unconstrained optimal price. Next, we can compare this demand to the available quantity and set the price based on the maximum of these two values. If the demand that corresponds to the unconstrained optimal price is below the available quantity, then this price is the solution because the stock level is less restrictive than the demand. Otherwise, we take the price that corresponds to the maximum available quantity. This price, referred to as the *stockout price*, will be higher than the unconstrained optimal price to slow down sales and avoid stockouts. The latter case is illustrated in Figure 6.16.

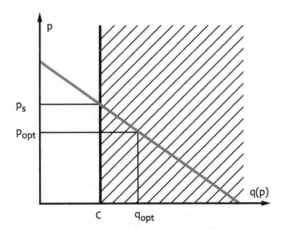

Figure 6.16: Unit price optimization with constrained supply.

The principle above can be combined with the price differentiation and demand shifting considered in the previous sections. However, it is only applicable if the supply constraints are set to each segment separately. Global capacity constraints when all price segments share the same inventory require more advanced optimization methods that we will describe later in this chapter.

EXAMPLE 6.5
_____

▼

As an example, let us take an opera house that optimizes its ticket prices. We assume that the opera gives a performance daily, the capacity C of the auditorium is 1200 seats, and the demand varies over the week in accordance with the following formulas:

$$
q(p, t) = \begin{bmatrix}
1800 - 50p, & \text{Monday} \\
1350 - 50p, & \text{Tuesday} \\
1200 - 50p, & \text{Wednesday} \\
1350 - 50p, & \text{Thursday} \\
1800 - 50p, & \text{Friday} \\
2250 - 50p, & \text{Saturday} \\
3600 - 50p, & \text{Sunday}
\end{bmatrix} \tag{6.77}
$$

in which p is the ticket price and t is the day of the week. We also assume that the variable costs per seat are negligible because the building maintenance costs, cost of the performance, and other expenses are pretty much constant.

The opera house might decide to set a flat price for all days, which would lead to the following constrained optimization problem:

$$
\max_{p,x} \quad p \sum_t x_t
$$
$$
\text{subject to} \quad x_t \leq q(p, t) \tag{6.78}
$$
$$
x_t \leq C
$$
$$
p \geq 0
$$

in which t iterates through the seven days of the week. This problem instance is not particularly difficult because we can assume that the price belongs to a relatively small discrete set, so we can evaluate each candidate solution. We find that the optimal price is $19.80, which corresponds to a revenue of $98,010.

The result above can be contrasted with variable pricing, for which each day is considered as a separate segment and optimized accordingly. We can rewrite the optimization problem for seven different prices:

$$\max_{p,x} \quad \sum_t p_t x_t$$
$$\text{subject to} \quad x_t \leqslant q(p_t, t) \tag{6.79}$$
$$x_t \leqslant C$$
$$p_t \geqslant 0$$

This problem is separable by segments, so we can optimize each day in accordance with equation 6.76. The optimal prices, as well as the number of sold seats x_t, are shown in Figure 6.17, which clearly demonstrates the increased seat utilization. Price differentiation turns out to be extremely efficient in this example and increases the total revenue up to $147,825.

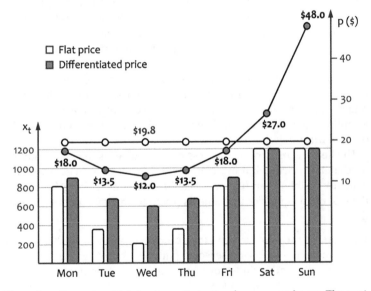

Figure 6.17: Example of ticket price optimization for an opera house. The vertical bars represent the number of seats sold, and the points are the ticket prices for the corresponding days.

6.7.2 Dynamic Pricing

Dynamic pricing is a group of pricing strategies and methods that optimize profits by changing prices over time. As we will see shortly, these methods are structurally similar to other price differentiation techniques, but they offer additional advantages for the algorithmic approach. In particular, dynamic pricing is more focused on incremental continually adjusted pricing decisions that make the problem more tractable than global price optimization. In addition, dynamic pricing typically deals with strict capacity and time constraints that introduce additional complexity, which, in turn, makes automated optimization appealing.

Although it is intuitive that dynamic pricing can be beneficial by providing an additional degree of freedom in comparison with static prices, we need to explore this concept more deeply to understand why one would benefit from changing prices over time.

First, we note that dynamic pricing can be used as a market segmentation technique. Consider a seller who initially offers a product at some baseline price. The product will be purchased by customers whose willingness to pay is above the baseline price and will not be purchased by other customers. Assuming that all customers have made their purchasing decision with regard to the baseline price, the seller can then lower the price. This will generate additional revenue from purchasers whose willingness to pay is in between the baseline and discounted prices. Thus, dynamic pricing is able to create price segments by exploiting only variance in willingness to pay and time without additional segment fences. We will use this concept in the next section to build a quantitative model that provides useful properties for the optimal price trajectories.

The heterogeneity of willingness to pay can be a sufficient condition for dynamic pricing, but in a significant number of business cases, the demand exhibits even higher variability. Dynamic pricing then plays the role of an equalizer that adjusts prices to changing demand conditions:

VARIABLE DEMAND Demand for a product or service can change over time, often following seasonal patterns. Industries that face variable demand include apparel retailers, entertainment businesses, and hotels to name a few.

VARIABLE INVENTORY VALUE Demand changes can often be connected to objective or subjective changes in the inventory value. Fashion products, electronic devices, and automobiles drop their value as newer models enter the market. Perishable grocery products lose their value as the expiration date approaches, whereas airline tickets tend to be more valuable for last-minute buyers.

DEMAND UNCERTAINTY Dynamic price changes can help to find the optimal price by trial and error when a seller is uncertain about the demand [Pashigian, 1987]. For example, an apparel retailer who buys the inventory upfront for the next season might not be able to predict how popular a new fashion garment will be. It can, however, try different markdowns to find a price that maximizes profits and matches the inventory constraints.

From the optimization standpoint, dynamic pricing does not necessarily require specialized optimization methods. Assuming that time is discrete, so that every time interval can be considered as a segment and there are no constraints that make the intervals interdependent, we can optimize intervals separately by similar methods to the price differentiation cases (recall the opera house example). Dependencies between the time intervals might require specialized optimization models to be created, and this is often the case in dynamic pricing. These dependencies are typically related to the supply constraints because all time intervals are typically served from the same inventory resource pool.

We already stated the paradigm that dynamic pricing can be considered as an equalizer of the demand. We can extend this view and say that dynamic pricing equalizes both demand and supply. The main two attributes of a constrained supply are fixed capacity and perishability:

FIXED CAPACITY A global capacity constraint means that a seller sells off a fixed stock of a product that cannot be replenished. A good example is apparel retail, when a retailer buys fixed quantities of inventory upfront. It can also be the case that replenishment is possible but limited in some way.

PERISHABILITY Perishability means that the stock of a product must be sold within a limited time frame. The unsold inventory loses its value or can be sold at a relatively small salvage price. Examples of perishable products include service resources, such as hotel rooms and flight tickets, seasonal collections of apparel, and consumer packaged goods.

The presence of these two constraints in a business is typically a good indicator for dynamic pricing feasibility. These two properties are equally important because we are trying to match the demand rate with the supply rate, which is essentially a ratio of the capacity to the selling time period defined from the perishability.

6.7.2.1   *Markdowns and Clearance Sales*

Dynamic price optimization with a fixed capacity of perishable inventory can be expressed as the following mathematical problem:

$$\max_{p,x} \quad \sum_{t=1}^{T} p_t x_t$$

$$\text{subject to} \quad \sum_{t=1}^{T} x_t \leqslant C \tag{6.80}$$

$$x_t \leqslant q(p_t, t), \qquad \text{for } t = 1, \dots, T$$

$$p_t \geqslant 0, \qquad \text{for } t = 1, \dots, T$$

In the formulation above, we assume that capacity C should be sold out within the time frame that consists of T discrete time intervals. Our objective is to maximize the revenue by setting optimal prices for each of T time intervals. We also assume that the unsold inventory has zero value after point T and variable costs are negligible, although both the salvage inventory price and variable costs can be included into the equation in a relatively straightforward way.

Problem 6.80 models a number of important business cases. In the retail space, markdowns and seasonal clearance sales match this model because the sale period is typically fixed as is the stock to be sold. A wide range of service providers, including airlines, railways, hotels, theaters, stadiums, and freight companies, face conceptually similar optimization problems in selling a fixed capacity of seats, rooms, or freight spaces within a fixed time frame determined by the vehicle schedule, check-in date, or event time. The service industries, however, often face many additional constraints and use different methods of revenue optimization that are based on resource allocation, so we will focus on markdowns and clearance sales in this section. Resource allocation methods will be considered later in this chapter.

The first conclusion we can make from equation 6.80 is that prices can vary over time only if the demand rate varies. If the demand rate is constant, all time intervals are identical, so we can apply the standard unit price optimization and then select the maximum of this unconstrained optimal price and the stockout price determined by the capacity constraint C, in accordance with the logic we described in section 6.7.1.2.

Variability of the demand rate over time can be attributed to different factors, such as seasonality or changes of the product value. In a general case, the demand changes over time can take different shapes, including increasing and decreasing trends, as does the price. We can, however, show that markdown prices tend to follow a certain pattern by considering a finite population of customers [Talluri and Van Ryzin, 2004]. Let us assume that one sells a durable product to a finite number of customers, such that a customer does not buy a product more than once during the sale period. If a seller sets a certain price p_t for time interval t, it means that all customers with willingness to pay higher than or equal to p_t will buy the product and become inactive until the end of the sale period. The seller, however, can decrease the price to attract customers with a lower willingness to pay. This indicates that markdown prices should be set close to the customer valuation at the beginning of sales and then monotonically decrease.

To build a quantitative model, let us also assume that customers' willingness to pay is uniformly distributed between 0 and some maximum price P:

$$w(p) = \text{unif}(0, P) = \begin{cases} 1/P, & 0 \leqslant p \leqslant P \\ 0, & \text{otherwise} \end{cases} \tag{6.81}$$

Recall that uniform willingness to pay implies a linear demand curve, which, in this context, can be interpreted as the number of customers who buy a product at a given price and become inactive until the end of the sale. Consequently, we can visualize the markdown process as sliding down the demand curve, as shown in Figure 6.18. Note that the optimization of markdown prices in this interpretation is almost identical to the market segmentation problem that we studied earlier, so the equations below are structurally similar to the equations for market segmentation but have different meanings.

We find that the quantity sold during period t is

$$Q_t = Q_{max} \left[\left(1 - \frac{p_t}{P} \right) - \left(1 - \frac{p_{t-1}}{P} \right) \right]$$
$$= \frac{Q_{max}}{P} (p_{t-1} - p_t) \tag{6.82}$$

Consequently, the total sales revenue is

$$G = \sum_{t=1}^{T} p_t \frac{Q_{max}}{P} (p_{t-1} - p_t) \tag{6.83}$$

We take partial derivatives of the revenue to find the revenue-maximizing prices:

$$\frac{\partial G}{\partial p_t} = \frac{Q_{max}}{P} (p_{t-1} - 2p_t + p_{t+1}) \tag{6.84}$$

Equating these derivatives to zero, we find that

$$p_t = \frac{p_{t-1} - p_{t+1}}{2} \tag{6.85}$$

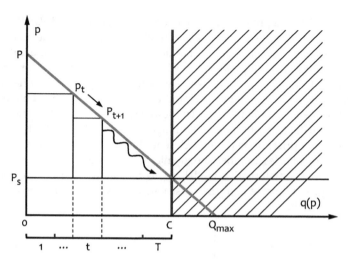

Figure 6.18: Markdown optimization model for uniformly distributed willingness to pay.

The initial conditions for this recurrence equation should be set to
meet the capacity constraints, so that the markdown prices are distributed in the range between the maximum price P and the stockout
price P_S:

$$p_0 = P$$
$$p_{T+1} = P_S \qquad (6.86)$$

The markdown prices that meet relationship 6.85 and conditions 6.86
are given by

$$p_t^{opt} = P_S + (P - P_S)\left(1 - \frac{t}{T+1}\right) \qquad (6.87)$$

This result suggests that markdown prices should be evenly distributed between the list price and stockout price. Although this is an
interesting conceptual insight, the finite population model is too gross
for applicable pricing decisions, so we need to return to basic optimization problem 6.80 and solve it directly for arbitrary demand functions.
This approach provides more flexibility because demand prediction
models are able to incorporate various patterns observed in the past,
including the effects related to the finite population.

6.7.2.2 *Markdown Price Optimization*

Optimization problem 6.80 plays a very important role in algorithmic pricing, so we will spend this section discussing how it can be solved efficiently and working through a numerical example.

Let us assume that the set of allowed prices is discrete, which is the case in most practical applications where prices are integer values of cents or dollars. If the set of allowed prices has K price levels and the number of markdown rounds is T, then we can find the optimal prices for each round by evaluating K^T possible price combinations. This approach is computationally feasible for business cases with small K and T values. For example, it is common for many discount retailers to set prices that end in 4.90 or 9.90, such as \$34.90 or \$59.90, so the total number of price points is relatively low. However, the problem becomes intractable even if we only have twenty price levels and optimize daily prices for a horizon of two weeks, which would require us to evaluate 20^{14} price combinations.

One possible solution is to approximate the original non-linear optimization problem with a linear programming relaxation [Talluri and Van Ryzin, 2004]. Let us denote the set of allowed price levels as $\{P_1, \ldots, P_K\}$ and introduce weight variables z that control the price levels selected for each time interval, such that

$$p_t = \sum_{i=1}^{K} z_{it} P_i \tag{6.88}$$

The optimization problem can then be restated as finding $K \times T$ revenue-maximizing variables z, such that, for any time interval t, one z_{it} is equal to one and the other z variables are equal to zero. Let us relax the zero-or-one constraint for variables z and just require them to sum to one for each time interval:

$$\sum_{i=1}^{K} z_{it} = 1, \qquad \text{for } t = 1, \ldots, T$$

$$z_{it} \geqslant 0 \tag{6.89}$$

This effectively means that we allow fractional prices, that is, two or more prices from the discrete set can have non-zero weights in the same time interval. We assume this to be acceptable, which means that a markdown round can be broken down into smaller intervals. For example, if we have two price levels with non-zero weights 0.2 and 0.8, then the first price level should be set for one fifth of the round duration and the second price level should be set for the remaining four fifths of the round. This relaxation allows us to rewrite the dynamic price optimization problem as follows:

$$\max_{z} \sum_{t=1}^{T} \sum_{i=1}^{K} z_{it} \cdot P_i \cdot q\left(P_i, t\right)$$

$$\text{subject to} \quad \sum_{t=1}^{T} \sum_{i=1}^{K} z_{it} \cdot q\left(P_i, t\right) \leqslant C \tag{6.90}$$

$$\sum_{i=1}^{K} z_{it} = 1, \quad \text{for } t = 1, \ldots, T$$

$$z_{it} \geqslant 0$$

Problem 6.90 is a linear program: if we arrange all variables z in a flat vector with $K \times T$ elements and calculate the vectors of revenue and demand values for the corresponding pairs of time t and price level i, then the objective function and capacity constraint can be expressed as vector products. This formulation allows us to use standard optimization software for linear programming.

EXAMPLE 6.6

▼

Let us now consider an example of a retailer who plans a four-week sale campaign for a single product. The set of allowed prices includes five levels: \$89, \$79, \$69, \$59, and \$49. Demand functions are estimated for each week of the sale as follows:

$$q(p, t) = \begin{bmatrix} 1800 - 10p, & \text{week 1} \\ 1300 - 15p, & \text{week 2} \\ 1200 - 15p, & \text{week 3} \\ 1100 - 18p, & \text{week 4} \end{bmatrix} \tag{6.91}$$

We substitute these parameters into problem 6.90 and solve it for different values of product capacity C. These solutions are presented in the small tables below. Each solution is a price schedule with 20 values of z: each column corresponds to one of the four weeks, and each row corresponds to one of the five price levels, with the topmost row corresponding to the highest price and the lowermost row corresponding to the lowest price. For example, the optimal price is \$89 for the first, third, and fourth weeks when the capacity is 700 items. For the same capacity, the price is fractional for the second week, which means a mix with 22% at \$89 and 78% at \$79.

C = 700, G = $61,400

1.00	0.22	**1.00**	**1.00**
0.00	**0.78**	0.00	0.00
0.00	0.00	0.00	0.00
0.00	0.00	0.00	0.00
0.00	0.00	0.00	0.00

C = 1000, G = $81,507

1.00	0.00	0.00	**1.00**
0.00	**0.27**	0.00	0.00
0.00	**0.73**	**1.00**	0.00
0.00	0.00	0.00	0.00
0.00	0.00	0.00	0.00

C = 1300, G = $96,778

1.00	0.00	0.00	0.00
0.00	0.00	0.00	0.00
0.00	**1.00**	0.00	0.00
0.00	0.00	**1.00**	**0.60**
0.00	0.00	0.00	**0.40**

C = 1600, G = $109,218

1.00	0.00	0.00	0.00
0.00	0.00	0.00	0.00
0.00	0.00	0.00	0.00
0.00	**1.00**	**0.72**	0.00
0.00	0.00	**0.28**	**1.00**

C = 1600, G = $116,198

0.58	0.00	0.00	0.00
0.42	0.00	0.00	0.00
0.00	0.00	0.00	0.00
0.00	0.00	0.00	0.00
0.00	**1.00**	**1.00**	**1.00**

C = 2200, G = $117,242

0.00	0.00	0.00	0.00
1.00	0.00	0.00	0.00
0.00	0.00	0.00	0.00
0.00	0.00	0.00	0.00
0.00	**1.00**	**1.00**	**1.00**

We can see that the prices generally decrease over time, which reflects the decreasing trend in the demand rates. Another tendency is that tight capacity constraints generally diminish and delay markdowns, which is also expected.

▲

6.7.2.3   Price Optimization for Competing Products

One of the main challenges of price optimization is the dependencies between the products. In many business domains, especially in retail, customers constantly make a choice between competing or substitutable products by using the price of one product as a reference point for another product, so the demand for a given product is usually a function of both the product price and the prices of the competing products. If this is the case, the prices cannot be optimized for each product in isolation, and the prices for all competing products need to be optimized jointly instead. The number of competing products can be as high as several hundreds in some applications, so the optimization problem can become computationally intractable. In this section, we dive into this problem and discuss the framework developed by Rue La La, an online fashion retailer, which can significantly reduce the computational effort [Ferreira et al., 2016].

Let us assume that a retailer is selling n distinct products. Let us denote the set of products as N, so $|N| = n$, and the set of possible price levels as P, so $|P| = k$. In practice, the set of prices is often relatively small because it is a common practice to use prices with certain endings, such as \$9.95 and \$14.95. We also assume that the retailer has a demand prediction model that estimates the demand for a given product as a function of the product price and the prices of competing products. In the case of an unlimited inventory, the model can predict the true (unconstrained) demand. If the retailer has a fixed quantity of product in stock, the model can predict the expected quantity sold, which is the minimum of the true demand and the available quantity, as we discussed earlier in section 6.6.3.

The optimization goal is to assign a price to each product in a way that the total revenue is maximized. This problem statement is applicable both in the case of static and dynamic pricing. In the case of dynamic pricing, for example, multiple concurrent sales events, this optimization problem needs to be solved repeatedly. For example, a retailer can start n sales events for all n products at the same time with a certain quantity of each product in stock. The initial prices are assigned by solving the optimization problem for the initial settings. The next day, the prices are updated by solving the problem once more with the latest stock levels, and so forth. A naive solution for the problem is to try all k^n possible price assignments and evaluate the demands and revenue for each assignment. This problem can be formally defined as

$$\max_{\mathbf{p}} \quad \sum_{i \in N} p_i \cdot q_i(\mathbf{p}) \tag{6.92}$$
$$\text{subject to} \quad p_i \in P, \quad \text{for } i = 1, \ldots, n$$

in which $\mathbf{p}$ is an n-dimensional vector of product prices, p_i is the price of product i, and q_i is the demand model for product i that uses all prices, including the product price p_i and the prices of all competing products, as inputs. Both the number of products n and the number of possible prices k can be relatively large, so this approach is inappropriate in many practical applications. One possible way to work around this problem is to predict the demand not as a function of all individual product prices but as a function of some aggregate that has a smaller number of possible states than vector $\mathbf{p}$. For example, one can use the sum of the prices for the competing products as an aggregate:

$$Q = \sum_{i=1}^{n} p_i \tag{6.93}$$

It is easy to see that the total number m of possible values of Q is

$$m = n(k-1) + 1 \tag{6.94}$$

For example, if the number of products is 10 and the set of possible prices includes 10 levels $P = \{\$1, \ldots, \$10\}$, the value of Q will be in the range from \$10 to \$100 with steps of \$1. The assumption that the demand depends mainly on the sum of the prices and not on the individual prices may or may not be true in practice, but there is evidence that this works in at least some applications [Ferreira et al., 2016]. This assumption essentially reduces the search space from k^n price combinations to $O(nk)$ possible values of Q. The optimal price assignment can then be found by solving m optimization problems for each possible value of Q and selecting the best solution. To define the optimization problem, let us denote the j-th element of the set of price levels P as $p^{(j)}$ and introduce binary variables $z_{ij} \in \{0, 1\}$, such that z_{ij} equals one if product i is assigned price $p^{(j)}$ and zero otherwise. With the assumption that the value of Q is given, the optimization problem can then be defined as the following integer program:

$$
\begin{aligned}
\max_{z} \quad & \sum_{i \in N} \sum_{j \in P} p^{(j)} \cdot q_i(p^{(j)}, Q) \cdot z_{ij} \\
\text{subject to} \quad & \sum_{j \in P} z_{ij} = 1 \\
& \sum_{i \in N} \sum_{j \in P} p^{(j)} \cdot z_{ij} = Q \\
& z_{ij} \in \{0, 1\}
\end{aligned}
\tag{6.95}
$$

The first constraint ensures that each product has exactly one price, and the second constraint guarantees that all product prices sum up to Q. The demand function q_i has to predict the demand for product i as a function of the price assigned to the product and the sum of the prices Q, so the sum of the prices is used as one of the features for model training. The demand function, as we have already discussed, can take into account the available inventory, so the predicted demand level can be bounded by the product stock level. This can be especially important if the model is used for sales events and markdown price optimization when the goal is to sell off the stock.

Integer programming problem 6.95 has substantially lower computational complexity than the naive exhaustive search approach, but it can still be challenging if the number of products and prices is high. If this is the case, the linear programming relaxation of the problem (where z_{ij} is not binary but is a continuous variable, such that $0 \leqslant z_{ij} \leqslant 1$) can be used to approximately evaluate all possible values of Q, and the exact optimal solution can then be found by solving integer programming problem 6.95 for only a subset of Q values [Ferreira et al., 2016]. This approach can greatly reduce the computational complexity and make the problem tractable, even for a large number of products and price levels.

6.7.3   *Personalized Discounts*

The price optimization methods that we discussed earlier leverage the diversity of willingness to pay by setting different discounts for different customer segments or time intervals. Eventually, we would like to combine these two approaches to manage both the monetary and temporal properties of a discount at a segment level. Moreover, we can attempt to improve the efficiency of price differentiation by replacing segmentation with personalized discount levels. At this point, pricing methods converge with the promotion methods discussed in Chapter 3: pricing services can take advantage of targeting techniques to make pricing decisions based on individual customer profiles, and promotion services can optimize the monetary aspects of a promotion, such as discount depth, by using price optimization methods. We spend this section developing a method that optimizes the depth of the discount and tries to find the optimal time and duration for the offer of a discount to a given user [Johnson et al., 2013]. The idea of temporal properties optimization comes from the assumption that a customer's probability to purchase is not uniform and varies over time, so there is an optimal discount time window for each user.

In order to model the temporal properties of a discount, we will decompose the probability of the purchase of brand k by customer u at time t with discount value d into two multipliers: the brand purchase probability and the probability to make a purchase at time t:

$$p_{ktud} = p(\text{brand} = k \mid u; d) \cdot p(\text{time} = t \mid u; d) \qquad (6.96)$$

Now we need to model the probability density functions $p(\text{brand} = k \mid u; d)$ and $p(\text{time} = t \mid u; d)$ separately. Nevertheless, we will use a common approach for both of them. First, we define the form of probability distribution and describe it with an utility function as a parameter. Second, we build a regression model to estimate the utility function from the data.

The probability density function of the purchase of a given brand $p(\text{brand} = k \mid u; d)$ is a typical case of a multiple choice model because the consumer chooses a brand from several alternatives (let us denote the total number of competing brands as K) that can substitute for one another. Consequently, we can use the multinomial logit (MNL) model to define the distribution:

$$p(\text{brand} = k \mid u; d) = \frac{\exp(x_{kut})}{\sum_{i=1}^{K} \exp(x_{iut})} \tag{6.97}$$

The utility function x_{kut} can be learned from the data by building a regression model such as the following:

$$x_{kut} = \sum_{w=1}^{W} \beta_{uw} F_{kutw} \tag{6.98}$$

in which F_{kutw} are W explanatory variables that include discount d and other features like loyalty and price, and β_{uw} are W regression coefficients.

The probability density function of a purchase at time t is modeled in [Johnson et al., 2013] in the form of an Erlang distribution:

$$p(\text{time} = t \mid u; d) = y_u^2 \cdot t \cdot \exp(-y_u t) \tag{6.99}$$

in which the parameter variable y_u can be estimated by means of a regression model that, similarly to the model for the parameter variable x in equation 6.97, includes the discount value as an explanatory variable, so it can later be a subject of optimization.

The probability of purchase defined above enables us to model the sales volume for a given customer Q_u as a function of the discount value in dollars d, discount start time t, and discount duration T:

$$Q_u(d, t, T) = \int_{t}^{t+T} p_{ktud} \, dt \tag{6.100}$$

This leads us to the following optimization problem for the gross margin:

$$\max_{d,t,T} \sum_{u} m \cdot (Q_u(0,0,t) + Q_u(d,t,t+T) + Q_u(0,t+T,\infty)) \\ - d \cdot Q_u(d,t,T) \tag{6.101}$$

in which m is the margin at the regular price. The first term in the equation above corresponds to the revenue, which, in turn, consists of three components – revenue received before the promotion, during the promotion, and after the promotion – and the second term corresponds to promotional costs. Figure 6.19 illustrates this breakdown.

The plot at the top shows the probability density of purchase by customer u when the expected sales volume for a given product at the regular price corresponds to the S_0 area. A flat permanent discount

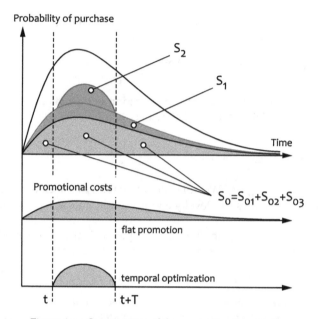

Figure 6.19: Optimization of the promotion time frame.

will lift this volume by adding area S_1, so the total revenue and promotional costs (shown in the middle plot) will both be proportional to $S_0 + S_1$. A time-optimized promotion will make the revenue proportional to $S_0 + S_2$, and its costs will be proportional to $S_{02} + S_2$ (the plot at the bottom). This difference between a flat promotion and an optimized promotion shows the potential to take advantage of temporal optimization in the case of certain quantitative properties of probability density functions.

6.8 RESOURCE ALLOCATION

In a nutshell, dynamic pricing provides a way to segment customers by their willingness to pay and a way to optimize the prices for each segment given that the total capacity is limited. As we discussed earlier, one of the greatest advantages of this approach is that it does not require predefined price segments and is able to create and tune them dynamically. On the other hand, it requires the business model and operational environment to be flexible enough in how prices are set and updated. This flexibility varies across industries. For example, the retail and eCommerce environments typically provide good capabilities for dynamic pricing, whereas service industries, such as airlines, hotels, and freight distribution, might be less flexible in that regard. This difference can be partly attributed to historical reasons, namely the practice of setting fixed fares for different classes of service. This has resulted in the development of a large group of methods that are based on an alternative interpretation of the problem. These methods first appeared in the airline industry and historically preceded dynamic pricing, as well as most programmatic methods in general.

Assuming that a seller has operational, legal, or business constraints that limit the ability to vary prices arbitrarily, we can turn the dynamic price optimization problem upside down and consider an alternative approach. The idea is to define a set of fixed price segments, typically referred to as *fare classes*, and allocate a fraction of the total capacity to every class in a way that maximizes profits. Consequently, the subject of optimization is the capacity limits allocated for each class. A classic example of this problem is an airline that offers three fare classes (e. g., economy, business, and first class) and decides how many seats of each class should be reserved, given that the total airplane capacity is fixed.

6.8.1 Environment

We discussed earlier that dynamic pricing is feasible for environments that exhibit certain properties, such as variability of demand and fixed resource capacity. These fundamental considerations are generally also applicable to resource allocation because it is essentially a different solution for the same problem. Many resource allocation methods, however, were developed primarily for service applications and address a number of constraints that are specific for this domain. We confine our discussion to the basic environment described below and only briefly review additional challenges that exist in the theory and practice of resource allocation.

- A seller offers a product or service to several market segments at different fares. The segments can be defined based on the level of service, such as economy or business classes in the airline industry, or can be based on more complex and fine-grained business rules that aim to improve fencing between the classes. For example, a hotel chain or airline might be willing to sell their services to business customers at a higher price than to leisure customers. To prevent business customers from buying the service at the lower price, the service provider can set a condition that low-price offerings must be booked a few weeks in advance or not include overnight Saturday stays.

- All fare classes are served from the same fixed capacity of a resource, and the booking limits for classes can be changed dynamically. For example, an airline can allocate different percentages of standard economy and discounted economy seats for different flights, although the total number of economy seats remains fixed.

- An optimization system analyzes historical and ongoing demand data to set or update booking limits for each fare class. The booking limits are loaded into a reservation system, which is a transactional application that receives booking requests. A booking request is a request to reserve a unit of capacity for a specified fare class, such as a request to reserve one discounted economy seat. The reservation system either accepts the request if the corresponding booking limit is more than zero, subsequently decrementing the limit counter, or rejects the request if the capacity is exhausted.

- The basic optimization models that we will consider make several important assumptions about the demand. First, the demand for each fare class is assumed to be a random variable with a known distribution. Secondly, it is assumed that all demand variables are independent. In particular, the demand for a given class does not depend on the availability or unavailability of other fare classes. This is a very gross approximation because a customer who has a request for a certain fare class rejected can consider other fare classes and increase the corresponding demands, just as in other cases with imperfect segmentation. Finally, it is assumed that the requests arrive sequentially from the lowest class (the cheapest one) to the highest class (the most expensive one). This assumption is also a relatively gross approximation, but it is widely accepted in practice and often matches the real demand patterns – for example, fencing rules for low-fare leisure travelers often include a condition that the booking should be done in advance.

It should be noted that many applications of resource allocation require two major requirements that are not included in our basic environment model to be addressed. First, resources are often allocated not as single units but as products that include multiple units. For example, a hotel booking is a product that includes one or more room nights, and an airline itinerary may be a chain of flight legs. This requires a network of resources to be jointly managed and optimized. Secondly, booking requests are eligible for cancellation in many industries, including airlines and hotels, and the share of canceled requests can be significant. American Airlines has reported that about half of reservations are canceled or become no-shows [Smith et al., 1992]. This results in the practice of *overbooking*, when a service provider allows resources to be booked beyond the capacity with the anticipation that some of these reservations will be canceled in the future. Overbooking also requires the development of specialized methods that adjust booking levels according to the expected cancellation rates.

As we already mentioned, resource allocation considers booking limits as the subject of optimization. A straightforward way to define a booking limit is to assign a capacity for each fare class separately. The major issue with this approach is that the capacity for a higher class may be exhausted when lower classes remain available. Consequently, a reservation system can reject a request for a higher class to preserve the capacity it could use for future low-fare requests. This behavior is obviously damaging from the profitability standpoint. A better approach, accepted as a standard in most theoretical models and practical applications, is *nested limits*. The idea of nesting is to set limits not for a given fare class individually but for all classes higher or equal to a given one, as illustrated in Figure 6.20. We can see that these limits, commonly called *protection levels*, are set in such a way that the first limit is equal to the capacity reserved for the first class and the last limit is equal to the total capacity.

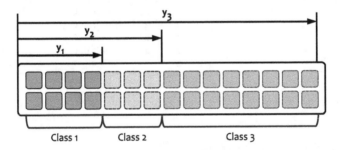

Figure 6.20: Three fare classes and protection levels y_1, y_2, and y_3.

The reservation system accepts or rejects a request in accordance with the following logic:

- A request for class i is accepted only if $y_i > y_{i-1}$. This is intuitive because the reservation limit for class i is the difference between y_i and y_{i-1}.

- If the request is accepted, y_n is decremented and all protection levels greater than the new value of y_n are set equal to y_n. This can visualized in Figure 6.20 as the right-hand boundary of y_n being moved to the left as more and more capacity is reserved; the right-hand boundaries of the other protection levels are bumped on the way.

The reservation process is illustrated in table 6.8. Initially, we have 2 units allocated for the first class, 2 units for the second class, and 4 units for the third class, which totals the capacity to 8. Any request is accepted until round 5, when the total capacity decreases to 4 units. The difference between y_3 and y_2 is zero, so class 3 closes. Note that the process is irreversible – once the difference between y_i and y_{i-1} becomes zero, class i remains permanently closed. Requests for the second class are accepted until round 7, and only requests for the first class are accepted after that.

	PROTECTION LEVELS			UNITS SOLD			RESERVATION REQUEST	ACTION
	y_1	y_2	y_3	C_1	C_2	C_3		
1	2	4	8	0	0	0	1 unit in C_2	ACCEPT
2	2	4	7	0	1	0	1 unit in C_3	ACCEPT
3	2	4	6	0	1	1	1 unit in C_3	ACCEPT
4	2	4	5	0	1	2	1 unit in C_1	ACCEPT
5	2	4	4	1	1	2	1 unit in C_3	REJECT
6	2	4	4	1	1	2	1 unit in C_1	ACCEPT
7	2	3	3	2	1	2	1 unit in C_2	ACCEPT
8	2	2	2	2	2	2	1 unit in C_2	REJECT
9	2	2	2	2	2	2	1 unit in C_3	REJECT
10	2	2	2	2	2	2	1 unit in C_1	ACCEPT
11	1	1	1	3	2	2	1 unit in C_1	ACCEPT
12	0	0	0	4	2	2	—	REJECT

Table 6.8: Example of the reservation process with nested booking limits.

6.8.2 Allocation with Two Classes

The allocation problem is challenging, so we start with the most basic scenario with two fare classes. Let us assume that we have a capacity of C units and denote prices for the first and second classes as p_1 and p_2, respectively, so $p_1 > p_2$.

In accordance with our assumptions about the environment, the demand for each of the two classes is a random variable Q_i and its cumulative distribution function F_i is known. We receive allocation requests sequentially and, according to another assumption, the requests for the second, less expensive class come first. Consequently, our goal is to determine the optimal value of the protection level y, such that we accept no more than $C - y$ requests for the second class and reserve the remaining y units for the first class requests.

Any time we receive a request for the second class, we have the choice of accepting it or rejecting it and switching the space to the first class. This decision can be easily analyzed in terms of expected outcomes, as illustrated in Figure 6.21. If we accept the request, we earn revenue of p_2. If we reject the request, close the second class, and switch to the first class, then two outcomes are possible. On the one hand, if the demand for the first class will eventually exceed the remaining capacity y, we will book this unit at price p_1. On the other hand, if the demand for the first class is lower than the remaining capacity, the unit would not be booked at all and we would earn zero revenue. Consequently, the acceptance condition for the second class can be written as follows:

$$p_2 \geqslant p_1 \cdot \Pr(Q_1 \geqslant y) \tag{6.102}$$

which is the same as

$$p_2 \geqslant p_1 \cdot (1 - F_1(y)) \tag{6.103}$$

Inverting the cumulative distribution function, we find the optimal protection level for the first class:

$$y_{opt} = F_1^{-1}\left(1 - \frac{p_2}{p_1}\right) \tag{6.104}$$

Equation 6.104 is known as Littlewood's rule [Littlewood, 1972]. The optimal protection level does not depend on the demand distribution for the second class because we are looking for the larger quantity to be reserved in the first class and assume that whatever remains is booked in the second class, regardless of the distribution.

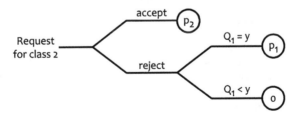

Figure 6.21: A decision tree for a two-class allocation problem.

EXAMPLE 6.7

▼

Let us illustrate the optimization of two fare classes with the following example. Consider a service provider that has 20 units of a resource and sells them at a full price of \$300 and a discounted price of \$200. The demand for the full price service is estimated to be normally distributed with a mean of 8 and a standard deviation of 2. Consequently, the probability that the demand for the full price offering will exceed y units can be expressed by using the cumulative distribution function Φ of the standard normal distribution

$$Pr(Q_1 \geq y) = 1 - \Phi\left(\frac{y - 8 - 0.5}{2}\right) \tag{6.105}$$

Note that we have added a shift of 0.5 because of the discrete nature of the reservation units – the probability that the demand is exactly y units can be approximated by integrating the cumulative distribution function over the interval from $y - 0.5$ to $y + 0.5$. Given that we reserve y units to be sold at full price, the marginal revenue for a full-price unit can be defined as

$$r_1(y) = \$300 \times Pr(Q_1 \geq y) \tag{6.106}$$

In other words, the marginal revenue is the difference between the expected revenue from the full price segment, given that y units are allocated for this segment, and the corresponding revenue, given that only $y - 1$ units are allocated. The total expected revenue from the full-price segment is the sum of the marginal revenues:

$$R_1(y) = \sum_{i=1}^{y} r_1(i) \tag{6.107}$$

The revenue from the discounted segment is simply the number of remaining units multiplied by the discounted price:

$$R_2(y) = \$200 \times (C - y) \tag{6.108}$$

The total revenue earned by a provider is the sum of the revenues for the full price and discounted segments. Let us now calculate these metrics for all possible values of the protection level y and put them into table 6.9.

We can see that the highest revenue is achieved when the protection level is 7, that is, 7 units are allocated for the full price segment and 13 units are allocated for the discounted segment. Littlewood's rule leads us to the same result – the marginal revenue $r_1(y)$ that corresponds to the right-hand side of equation 6.102 goes below the discounted price of \$200 from protection level 8 onwards.

▲

y	$r_1(y)$	$R_1(y)$	$R_2(y)$	$R_1(y) + R_2(y)$
1	\$299	\$299	\$3800	\$4099
2	\$299	\$599	\$3600	\$4199
3	\$299	\$898	\$3400	\$4298
4	\$296	\$1195	\$3200	\$4395
5	\$287	\$1483	\$3000	\$4483
6	\$268	\$1751	\$2800	\$4551
▶ 7	**\$232**	**\$1983**	**\$2600**	**\$4583** ◀
8	\$179	\$2163	\$2400	\$4563
9	\$120	\$2283	\$2200	\$4483
10	\$67	\$2351	\$2000	\$4351
11	\$31	\$2383	\$1800	\$4183
12	\$12	\$2395	\$1600	\$3995
13	\$3	\$2398	\$1400	\$3798
14	\$0	\$2399	\$1200	\$3599
15	\$0	\$2399	\$1000	\$3399
16	\$0	\$2400	\$800	\$3200
17	\$0	\$2400	\$600	\$3000
18	\$0	\$2400	\$400	\$2800
19	\$0	\$2400	\$200	\$2600
20	\$0	\$2400	\$0	\$2400

Table 6.9: Example of the protection level optimization for two fare classes.

6.8.3 *Allocation with Multiple Classes*

Littlewood's rule provides a compact expression for the capacity allocation problem with two classes. In practice, however, the problem typically has to be solved for more than two classes. The determination of an optimal solution is quite challenging in this case, but there are several ways to cope with it. One possible approach is to solve the problem recursively by using the assumption about sequentially arriving demand classes, so a decision about the protection level for one class leads to a problem of smaller dimensionality. This method allows us to express and solve the allocation problem in terms of dynamic programming. A different approach is to extend the probabilistic analysis that we did for Littlewood's rule and use simulations to find the optimal protection levels [Brumelle and McGill, 1993; Talluri and Van Ryzin, 2004]. We choose to follow this latter approach here.

We have shown that, for the two-class problem, the optimal protection level for the first class is given by

$$p_2 = p_1 \cdot \Pr\left(Q_1 \geq y_1^{\text{opt}}\right) \tag{6.109}$$

Let us take one step forward and consider a decision tree for a third class, as shown in Figure 6.22.

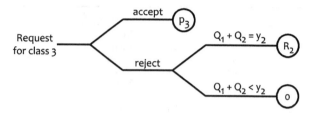

Figure 6.22: A decision tree for a three-class allocation problem.

Similarly to the two-class problem, a request for the third class can be either accepted, which earns us the revenue of p_3, or rejected. The latter action means that the third class will be closed and all further requests will be handled in the two-class mode. This can result in two possible outcomes:

- If the total demand for the first and second classes is below the protection level y_2, the unit will be lost – we closed the third class too early.

- Otherwise, the rest of the requests will be handled as a standard two-class problem. As we have shown in the previous section, the average revenue per unit R_2 is equal to p_2 in this case, given that the protection level y_1 is set optimally, that is, in accordance with Littlewood's rule.

Consequently, the optimal value for y_2 can be expressed as follows:

$$p_3 = p_2 \cdot \Pr\left(Q_1 + Q_2 \geq y_2^{opt} \mid Q_1 \geq y_1^{opt}\right) \tag{6.110}$$

We can compare equations 6.109 and 6.110 and apply the decision tree approach recursively to find the following relationship for the optimal protection levels:

$$\frac{p_{j+1}}{p_j} = \Pr\Big(Q_1 + \ldots + Q_j \geq y_j^{opt} \mid$$

$$Q_1 \geq y_1^{opt} \text{ AND } \ldots \text{ AND } Q_1 + \ldots + Q_{j-1} \geq y_{j-1}^{opt}\Big) \tag{6.111}$$

Although equation 6.111 does not look as simple as Littlewood's rule, it provides a relatively simple way to estimate protection levels by using simulations. Let us consider an example with three classes for the sake of convenience, although the method can be straightforwardly applied to any number of classes. We assume that the distributions of demands Q_1 and Q_2 are known, so we can generate a relatively large number of two-dimensional points with the coordinates defined as Q_1 and $Q_1 + Q_2$.

The optimal value for protection level y_1 can be estimated by using equation 6.109 – we need to find a line that splits the points by the first coordinate in such a way that the number of points on the left and the number of points on the right are in the same proportion as p_1 and p_2. This is illustrated in Figure 6.23. The points on the right satisfy the condition $Q_1 \geq y_1^{opt}$ from equation 6.110, so we split them by the second coordinate in such a way that the number of points in the bottom section and the number of points in the top section are in the same proportion as p_2 and p_1 to estimate protection level y_2.

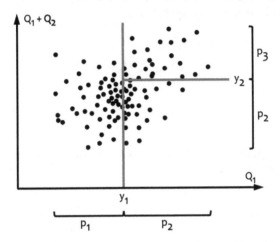

Figure 6.23: Optimization of the protection levels for three classes by using simulations.

6.8.4 Heuristics for Multiple Classes

Although the optimal protection levels can be calculated by using the simulation method considered in the previous section, as well as alternative algorithms, many implementations use simpler heuristic methods that give suboptimal solutions but are known to be very close to optimality in most practical applications. The most important method of this kind is the expected marginal seat revenue (EMSR) algorithm, which has two versions: EMSRa and EMSRb [Belobaba, 1987, 1989]. Both versions attempt to adapt Littlewood's rule to multiple fare classes heuristically.

6.8.4.1 EMSRa

Recall that the protection level for class j is the total capacity reserved for classes from j down to 1. If we have already calculated the protection levels for the cheaper classes from n down to j + 1, the protection level for j determines how to split the capacity between class j + 1 and the more expensive classes. The idea of EMSRa is to approximate this protection level by the sum of the protection levels obtained by applying Littlewood's rule for class j + 1 and each of the classes from j down to 1 separately. This means that we first calculate j pairwise protection levels from the following equations:

$$p_{j+1} = p_j \Pr\left(Q_j \geq y_{j+1}^{(j)}\right)$$

$$p_{j+1} = p_{j-1} \Pr\left(Q_{j-1} \geq y_{j+1}^{(j-1)}\right)$$

$$\vdots$$

$$(6.112)$$

$$p_{j+1} = p_1 \Pr\left(Q_1 \geq y_{j+1}^{(1)}\right)$$

The final protection level is calculated as a sum of the pairwise levels, as illustrated in Figure 6.24.

$$y_j = \sum_{k=1}^{j} y_{j+1}^{(k)} \qquad (6.113)$$

Comparing equations 6.112 and 6.113 with the optimal solution 6.111, we see that EMSRa uses the probabilities that separate demands exceed the levels determined by the corresponding price ratios to approximate the probability that the sum of demands exceeds a certain level. As a result, EMSRa tends to be excessively conservative, in the sense that it reserves too many units for the higher classes and, thereby, rejects too many low-fare bookings.

6.8.4.2 EMSRb

The alternative approach to the problem is to merge the classes from j to 1 into one virtual aggregate class that has its own demand and price and to then apply Littlewood's rule. The demand for an aggregate class can be estimated as the sum of demands for the included classes:

$$\overline{Q}_j = \sum_{k=1}^{j} Q_k \qquad (6.114)$$

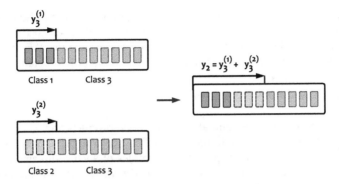

Figure 6.24: Example of EMSRa for three fare classes.

The "price" of the aggregated class can be defined as the weighted average price of the included classes:

$$\overline{p}_j = \frac{\sum_{k=1}^{j} p_k \mathbb{E}\left[Q_k\right]}{\sum_{k=1}^{j} \mathbb{E}\left[Q_k\right]} \tag{6.115}$$

The protection level for class j can then be estimated by applying Littlewood's rule to the aggregated class and the previous class j + 1, that is

$$p_{j+1} = \overline{p}_j \cdot \Pr\left(\overline{Q}_j \geqslant y_j\right) \tag{6.116}$$

It is generally accepted that both EMSRa and EMSRb provide approximations that are very close to the optimal solutions. EMSRb was developed to improve EMSRa and is sometimes said to perform better that EMSRa, but the experimental results with both real data and simulations show that neither method consistently outperforms the other [Talluri and Van Ryzin, 2004].

6.9 ASSORTMENT OPTIMIZATION

The customer's willingness to pay for a given product or service is almost always influenced by alternative options, that is, the ability to choose a competing or substitutable offering. The impact of these forces on demand functions and, eventually, profits can be more or less significant depending on the particular industry and business case. We have already discussed that pricing decisions for multiple products or customer segments might need to be jointly optimized in the case of demand shifting or dependent demands within a category. This problem grows more challenging in retail industries that deal with tens or hundreds of thousands of products, so not only prices but also other marketing and enterprise resources should be optimized to take demand dependencies and substitution effects into account. We devote this section to examining this type of optimization task in detail.

6.9.1 Store-Layout Optimization

Demand dependencies and affinities between products and categories suggest an opportunity to cross-sell related or complementary offerings to buyers of certain products. Examples of such complementary products include coffee and sugar, cosmetics and handbags, and even beer and diapers. One possible way to leverage these opportunities is to identify products that customers tend to buy together and optimize the store layout or placement of content items on a media site to simplify navigation and encourage customers to buy product sets instead of single products.

The first part of this strategy, the identification of items that are frequently bought together, can be accomplished by using a basic market basket analysis. Let us assume that we have a history of sales transactions where each transaction t is represented as a set of items r purchased in this transaction:

$$t_n = \{r_{n1}, r_{n2}, \ldots, r_{nk}\} \tag{6.117}$$

The *support* for an item or item set is the fraction of transactions in the history that contain that item or item set. In other words, it is the empirical probability that a randomly selected transaction contains a given item or item set. The *lift* is defined for a pair of items as the ratio of the support for the pair divided by the product of the supports for each item separately:

$$\lambda(r_a, r_b) = \frac{\text{support}(r_a \text{ AND } r_b)}{\text{support}(r_a) \times \text{support}(r_b)} \tag{6.118}$$

In other words, the lift is the ratio between the observed probability of two items co-occurring and the co-occurrence probability calculated under the assumption that the items are independent. Consequently, a lift higher than one indicates affinity of the items (assuming statistical significance of the results, of course). We can measure the lift not only for pairs of products but for pairs of categories as well, by mapping each item in the transaction history to its category and evaluating expression 6.118 with the assumption that r_a and r_b are categories.

Let us now return to the store-layout optimization problem. We have n product categories and n product locations, such as aisles or shelves. The optimization problem can then be stated as the assignment of all categories to different locations with the goal of placing categories with high pairwise affinity close to each other. First, let us calculate the matrix of pairwise lifts for the categories:

$$L = \{\lambda_{ij}\}, \quad i,j = 1,\ldots,n \tag{6.119}$$

Next, we need some sort of a distance matrix for locations:

$$D = \{d_{ij}\}, \quad i,j = 1,\ldots,n \tag{6.120}$$

in which d_{ij} is the distance between locations i and j. The distance can be defined in different ways, for example, it can be a binary variable that is equal to one if the locations are adjacent and zero otherwise. The optimization problem can then be defined as

$$\max_{\pi} \sum_{i=1}^{n} \sum_{j=1}^{n} \lambda_{ij} d_{\pi(i),\pi(j)} \tag{6.121}$$

in which $\pi(i)$ is a permutation function that maps categories to locations, that is, $\pi(x)$ equals y when category number x is assigned to location y. Problem 6.121 is an instance of the quadratic assignment problem[1] (QAP). It is a well-studied combinatorial optimization problem that, however, is fairly difficult computationally. Nevertheless, it has been reported that this method has been used in practice to optimize layouts for convenience stores [Winston, 2014].

EXAMPLE 6.8
_____

The following example illustrates store-layout optimization. Consider ▼ a grocery store that offers six categories of products: dairy, deli, bakery, drinks, produce, and frozen food. The matrix of pairwise lifts for these categories is estimated from the historical data:

		DAIRY	DELI	BAKERY	DRINKS	PRODUCE	FROZEN
	DAIRY	1.00	0.80	1.30	0.90	1.00	0.90
	DELI	0.80	1.00	1.20	1.10	1.30	0.80
L =	BAKERY	1.30	1.20	1.00	1.30	1.20	0.90
	DRINKS	0.90	1.10	1.30	1.00	1.20	1.50
	PRODUCE	1.00	1.30	1.20	1.20	1.00	0.80
	FROZEN	0.90	0.80	0.90	1.50	0.80	1.00

$$\tag{6.122}$$

_____

1 QAP was first introduced in the context of operations research to model the following real-life problem. There is a set of facilities and a set of locations. The objective is to assign each facility to a location such that the total cost is minimized, with the assignment cost being a product of the distance between locations and the flow between the facilities.

The floor plan is the 2×3 grid shown in Figure 6.25, in which each placement represents a display shelf. In total, we have six available placements for six categories.

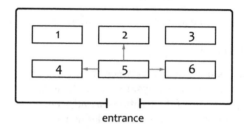

entrance

Figure 6.25: Store floor plan.

The distance matrix for this layout is defined as follows:

$$
\mathbf{D} = \begin{array}{c} \\ 1 \\ 2 \\ 3 \\ 4 \\ 5 \\ 6 \end{array} \begin{array}{c} \begin{array}{cccccc} 1 & 2 & 3 & 4 & 5 & 6 \end{array} \\ \left[\begin{array}{cccccc} 0 & 1 & 0 & 1 & 0 & 0 \\ 1 & 0 & 1 & 0 & 1 & 0 \\ 0 & 1 & 0 & 0 & 0 & 1 \\ 1 & 0 & 0 & 0 & 1 & 0 \\ 0 & 1 & 0 & 1 & 0 & 1 \\ 0 & 0 & 1 & 0 & 1 & 0 \end{array} \right] \end{array} \qquad (6.123)
$$

We assume that the distance is only equal to one between adjacent placements and is zero otherwise. For example, placement number five has a distance of one to cells two, four, and six. By solving optimization problem 6.121 for the matrices specified above, we find the optimal layout presented in Figure 6.26. This small example can be easily solved by evaluating all $6! = 720$ possible permutations, but larger problems require the use of optimization software that can handle QAP or one of its relaxations.

▲

6.9.2   *Category Management*

The problem of category management appears when a seller needs to optimize the overall performance of a product category as opposed to the performance of a single product. This problem is very typical in the retail industry because a retailer can change product assortment within a category relatively easily and the primary goal is to utilize the available resources, such as shelf space, in the most efficient way.

A category represents a relatively cohesive set of products that have a lot in common such as "dairy desserts" or "women's jeans", so it is

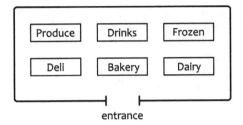

Figure 6.26: One of the optimal store layouts for the example with six categories.
Alternative optimal layouts can, of course, be obtained by mirroring
this grid horizontally or vertically.

generally possible that customers might be willing to substitute one
product with another if the product of their choice is not available for
some reason. The reasons for product unavailability can include both
deliberate assortment changes and temporary stockouts. One of the
main goals of category management is to find a subset of products
that meets physical constraints, such as available shelf space, and maximizes the profit by taking advantage of the substitution effect in the
optimal way. Alternatively, this problem can be stated as the identification of the least significant products, those that can be excluded from
the assortment and substituted by other products without a negative
impact on the profits. The outputs of this analysis can then be applied
in the optimization of several different controls:

- Product stock levels can be optimized to account for substitution
  effects and potential losses caused by stockouts.

- Shelf layouts can be optimized to adjust the relative product
  shares on a shelf.

- Assortment can be optimized by the introduction or removal of
  products from the assortment.

From an econometric perspective, the problem of category management arises from the law of diminishing returns or, more specifically,
the fact that revenues and costs depend on the category size in different
ways. The general tendency is that consumer buying capacity comes to
saturation at some point, whereas costs continue to grow because of
the increasing selling area and other operational costs, as shown in
Figure 6.27. This tendency leads to the category optimization problem.
It is a very challenging problem because it requires the modeling of an
entire category with the interdependencies between the products in it
accounted for. However, despite these challenges, a practically feasible
assortment optimization model has been developed and evaluated at

Albert Heijn, a supermarket chain in the Netherlands [Kök and Fisher, 2007]. We spend the rest of this section studying their solution.

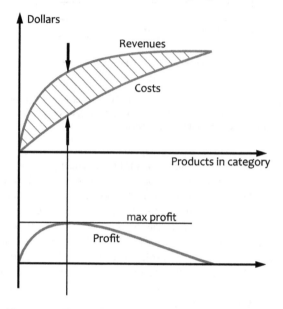

Figure 6.27: Diminishing returns in category management.

Consider a supermarket store chain that operates multiple stores. Each store sells many categories of products, but, as we discussed above, demands are assumed to be dependent only within a category and categories are considered to be independent. Consequently, a retailer solves an assortment optimization problem for each category in each store independently. Let us first introduce the following notation that applies to a single category in a single store:

- $N = \{1, 2, \ldots, J\}$: the maximal set of products in a category that a retailer offers to its customers, that is, the full assortment.

- $f_j \in \{0, 1, 2, \ldots\}$: the stock level for product j. A retailer optimizes its assortment by choosing f to be zero (product is not present in the assortment) or non-zero. Let us also denote the vector of stock levels for all J products as $\mathbf{f} = (f_1, \ldots, f_J)$.

- F_0: the total inventory capacity measured in the same units as stock levels. It is assumed that the sum of stock levels for all products cannot exceed F_0. The total capacity can be constrained by warehouse space or available shelf space in a store.

- $N_h \subset N$: the assortment in store h, a subset of the full assortment.

- d_j: the original demand rate for product j, that is, the number of customers who would select product j if presented with full assortment N. We also denote the vector of demands for all products as $\mathbf{d} = (d_1, \ldots, d_J)$.

- D_j: the observed demand rate for the products, that is, the actual number of customers per day who selected product j because of their original intention or substitution. The observed demand for a given product depends on the original demand and the availability of other products because of the substitution effect, so it can be thought as function $D_j (\mathbf{f}, \mathbf{d})$.

With the above notation, the assortment optimization problem for a given store and a given category can be specified as follows:

$$
\max_{\mathbf{f}} \quad \sum_{j \in N} G_j \left(f_j, D_j (\mathbf{f}, \mathbf{d}) \right)
$$
$$
\text{subject to} \quad \sum_j f_j \leq F_0
$$

(6.124)

in which G_j is a function that describes the profit for a given product and corresponding observed demand. This function heavily depends on a retailer's business model, so we can outline a few generic templates that can be customized for practical usage. The simplest way to model profit is to multiply the observed demand by the product margin m:

$$
G_j(f_j, D_j) = m_j \cdot D_j
$$

(6.125)

Equation 6.125 implicitly assumes perfect replenishment and the absence of stockouts. This might be the case for fast-moving consumer goods like groceries, but other retail domains such as apparel should probably take stockouts into account by taking the minimum of the demand and the actual stock levels:

$$
G_j(f_j, D_j) = m_j \cdot \min(D_j, f_j)
$$

(6.126)

Retailers of perishable goods should also take into account the losses owing to disposed-of inventory, which can be modeled by introducing a per-unit disposal loss L that applies to unsold inventory:

$$
G_j(f_j, D_j) = m_j \cdot \min(D_j, f_j) - L_i \cdot \left(f_i - \min(D_j, f_j) \right)
$$

(6.127)

For the sake of brevity, we hereafter assume that all products are perfectly replenished, so stockouts are not possible or are negligible.

This allows us to treat $f_j \in \{0, 1\}$ as a binary variable that indicates the presence of a product in the assortment.

To solve optimization problem 6.124, one needs to define the observed demand function. With the stockout-free assumption that we made above, the demand function can be modeled as follows:

$$D_j (\mathbf{f}, \mathbf{d}) = d_j + \sum_{k:f_k=0} \alpha_{k \to j} \cdot d_k \tag{6.128}$$

in which $\alpha_{k \to j}$ is the probability of substitution of product k by product j. Formula 6.128 is relatively straightforward: the first term is the original demand and the second term corresponds to the cumulative substitution effect from all products that are evicted from the assortment set.

Equation 6.128 requires the estimation of the substitution probabilities $\alpha_{k \to j}$ and original demand rates d_j. In order to do this estimation, let us assume that the following variables are known (we already discussed demand prediction in Section 6.6):

- Q_{jh}, $j \in N_h$: the demand for product j per customer at store h. If K_h is the number of customers who visit store h during the day, $D_j = K_h \cdot Q_{jh}$.

- Q_{jh}^0, $j \in N$: the demand for product j per customer at store h with a full assortment (let us assume that stores with full assortments exist). Q_{jh}^0 corresponds to the original demand because no substitution happens at stores with the full assortment.

Substitution rates $\alpha_{k \to j}$ are challenging to estimate because up to J^2 different rates can exist for the assortment of J products. It is unlikely that a retailer has enough data to estimate this variety of rates reliably. However, there is empirical evidence that the following simplistic model of customer behavior is sufficiently accurate in practice and requires the estimation of just one variable instead of J^2: if product k is not available, customers either select their second-choice product j as a substitution with the probability δ, which is the same for all products in a category, or no purchase takes place, with the probability $(1 - \delta)$. This model leads to the following simple equation for the substitution rate:

$$\alpha_{k \to j} = \delta \frac{1}{|N|} \tag{6.129}$$

In order to estimate δ, let us define the total demand at a given store as the sum of Q_{jh} values, which can be estimated from the data:

$$S_h = \sum_{j \in N_h} Q_{jh} \tag{6.130}$$

On the other hand, the same value can be estimated according to expression 6.128 as follows:

$$\hat{S}_h(\delta) = \sum_{j \in N_h} \left[Q_{jh}^0 + \sum_{k \in N \backslash N_h} \alpha_{k \to j} Q_{kh}^0 \right]$$

$$= \sum_{j \in N_h} Q_{jh}^0 + \sum_{j \in N_h} \sum_{k \in N \backslash N_h} \frac{\delta}{|N|} Q_{kh}^0 \qquad (6.131)$$

Now δ can be estimated by solving the following optimization problem, which minimizes the discrepancy between the observed and predicted values of the total demand:

$$\delta_0 = \underset{0 \leqslant \delta \leqslant 1}{\mathrm{argmax}} \ \sum_h \left(\hat{S}_h(\delta) - S_h \right)^2 \qquad (6.132)$$

The next step in solving optimization problem 6.124 is to compute the original demand rates that are used in equation 6.128. We first note that the total demand for all products in N at store h can be computed as follows:

$$T_h = V_h \cdot \sum_{j \in N} Q_{jh}^0 \cdot \frac{S_h}{\hat{S}_h(\delta_0)} \qquad (6.133)$$

in which V_h is the total number of customers visiting store h per day. In equation 6.133, the sum of all Q_{jh}^0 multiplied by V_h represents the total demand given a full assortment. However, values Q_{jh}^0 are estimated for stores with a full assortment, so the specifics of a given store h (e.g., location, store size in square feet, etc.) are not modeled. This is compensated for by scaling the ratio of estimated category demand from equation 6.130 to the predicted demand from equation 6.131.

In a store with a restricted assortment, the total demand T_h is the sum of two components: the demand that comes from the products included in the assortment of a given store and the demand for other products in N. The ratio between these two components can be expressed via Q_{jh}^0 as follows:

$$r_h = \frac{\sum_{j \in N_h} Q_{jh}^0}{\sum_{j \in N} Q_{jh}^0} \qquad (6.134)$$

Consequently, $T_h \cdot r_h$ represents the fraction of the demand attributed to the products in the assortment, and $T_h \cdot (1 - r_h)$ represents the remaining fraction attributed to the products that are not in the assortment. Finally, we compute the demand for a single product as a fraction of the total demand proportional to the estimated per-product demand:

$$
d_{jh} = \begin{cases} T_h \cdot r_h \cdot \dfrac{Q_{jh}}{\sum_{j \in N_h} Q_{jh}}, & \text{if } j \in N_h \\[3ex] T_h \cdot (1 - r_h) \cdot \dfrac{Q_{jh}^0}{\sum_{j \in N \setminus N_h} Q_{jh}^0}, & \text{if } j \notin N_h \end{cases}
\tag{6.135}
$$

All coefficients in equations 6.135 and 6.132 can be estimated from the data, so we can roll up all formulas to original optimization problem 6.124, which can be solved by using numerical methods.

Equation 6.124 will produce a set of presumably optimal stock levels f_j for all products. These levels can be used to adjust inventory and optimize shelf layout. It is important to note that the model enables a retailer to perform what-if analyses to evaluate how changes in assortment and stock levels might impact the gross margin. In particular, a retailer can plot curves that show the expected gross margin as a function of stock levels for a given product or group of products. Such curves are especially descriptive for perishable products because the gross margin is a convex function that is zero when the stock level is zero and also zero when the stock level is too high, which leads to losses from expired products, with a maximum in between these two extremes.

6.10 ARCHITECTURE OF PRICE MANAGEMENT SYSTEMS

Although the design and implementation of algorithmic price management systems can vary significantly across industries, price management typically includes several principal processes that can be thought of as functional components in the reference logical architecture. A high-level diagram that depicts these key components and their relationships is presented in Figure 6.28 and includes three major subsystems.

TRANSACTIONAL SYSTEM The purpose of the transactional system is to execute the pricing decisions received from the optimization system. In certain environments, the optimized prices and pricing rules can be loaded into multiple transactional systems that calculate final prices independently. For example, a retailer can refresh prices in store point of sales (POS) nightly or weekly, as well as updating prices in its eCommerce platform. Each store or eCommerce platform then operates independently. In many other environments, a single transactional system, which can be

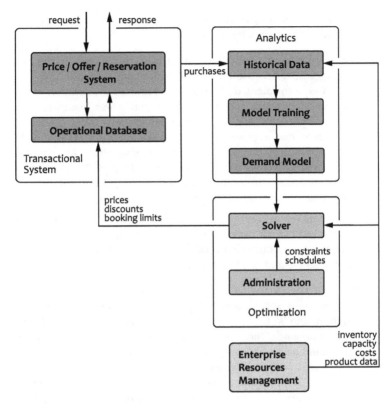

Figure 6.28: High-level architecture of a price management system.

centralized or distributed in technical terms, processes real-time requests for prices or resource quotes. This approach is generally preferable because complex pricing decisions can be made in a consistent way. For example, a retailer often calculates the final price for every transaction based on the list prices, active discounts, customer loyalty number, entered or scanned promotion codes, and other factors. The reservation systems in service industries, such as airlines or hotels, are even more interactive because they not only apply the pricing rules but also keep track of booked resources and update records in the operational database after each transaction.

A transactional system can be owned by a seller or can be a shared resource provided a third-party. For instance, airline tickets are typically reserved through global distribution systems

(GDS) operated by dedicated companies, and the airlines set the booking limits directly in the GDS.

ANALYTICS Demand prediction plays a mission-critical role in price management because it enables quantitative evaluation of pricing and assortment decisions. This requires the creation of an analytical infrastructure that collects and stores historical data and supports training and evaluation of predictive models. We have seen that demand prediction models can use quite a wide range of information, including product data, discounts, competitive prices, weather data, and holiday calendars. Many of these data elements can be pulled from the enterprise resource management systems and third-party data providers.

The demand model training pipeline is often automated and works in a loop or incrementally to refresh the model as new data arrive. This ensures that models are up to date with changes in the business and competition landscapes.

OPTIMIZATION SYSTEM The main component of the optimization system is a solver, which typically uses numerical optimization methods to find the price schedule or booking levels that maximize the revenue. The solver is configured from the administration component to set optimization parameters and constraints. In certain applications, such as airlines, the optimization process can be administered by a team of analysts who monitor system performance and can correct the decisions in special cases, such as large public events.

Similarly to the demand modeling process, optimization is also executed in a loop to recalculate prices or booking limits as the sales and inventory data are updated. The optimization process, however, is typically executed more frequently than analytics to catch up with rapidly decreasing capacity levels. This continual optimization is almost always used for dynamic pricing and resource allocation, as well as other price optimization methods that may not model temporal changes directly but that continually adjust prices when applied repeatedly and, thus, become dynamic.

6.11 SUMMARY

- Pricing decisions are extremely important for firm competitiveness and profitability. Improvements in pricing often have much more impact on profits than comparable improvements in quantities sold (advertising and sale channels), variable costs (supply and production), or fixed costs (operations and asset management).

- Price is a monetary measure of value. Boundaries for a good price can be determined by estimating consumer utility and comparable alternatives. The perceived surplus of a product or service, however, depends on how exactly the product information and price is communicated. In particular, price drops and multiple unbundled gains are known to be efficient. This provides fundamental justification for markdowns and discounts.

- Demand is determined by customers' willingness to pay. Different distributions of willingness to pay result in different demand curves. The basic demand curves include linear, constant-elasticity, and logit functions.

- The basic price structures include unit price, segmented price, two-part tariffs, tying arrangements, and bundling. All of these structures can be optimized if a global demand curve is accurately estimated.

- The basic demand curves do not account for seasonality, competition, and product properties. Algorithmic price optimization requires more powerful demand models to be developed. A significant number of such models can be found in the literature for different industries.

- Price optimization typically requires the solution of a numerical optimization problem that is tailored for specific structural, supply, and demand constraints. The two major business cases for price optimization are price differentiation, which aims to optimize prices for multiple market segments, and dynamic pricing, which can also be considered as a market segmentation technique. The main constraints accounted for in price optimization include interdependent demand functions, limited capacity, and perishable inventories.

- Service industries, such as airlines, hotels, freight transport, and sports, can reserve fractions of their capacity for different fare classes. This resource allocation approach can be considered as an alternative to dynamic pricing. The most basic resource allocation methods allow booking levels to be optimized for individual units of constraint capacity, such as seats in an airplane, but a large number of more advanced methods exist that are able to optimize networks of resources and handle booking cancellations.

- Assortment optimization is closely related to price management because both problems are based on demand prediction. Assortment optimization focuses on modeling dependencies between demands on different products and categories, thereby enabling the analysis of assortment changes and enterprise resource reallocation that could impact profits.

- Price, booking limits, and assortment can be considered as different controls that a seller can use to execute pricing decisions. All optimization methods related to these controls use demand prediction as a basic building block but perform different business actions to accommodate this prediction.

APPENDIX: DIRICHLET DISTRIBUTION

Dirichlet distribution is a relatively advanced topic, especially in the context of marketing applications, so we will provide a brief introduction here. We use the Dirichlet distribution in Chapter 3 where we discuss observational studies and Chapter 4 where the Dirichlet distribution is used in topic modeling.

In most marketing applications, we deal with probability distributions of random variables, such as events or counts. Although the Dirichlet distribution can be viewed in this way, it also has a substantially different meaning that is important for our purposes. Let us consider a simplistic example that illustrates this aspect [Frigyik et al., 2010]. A six-sided die can be viewed as a discrete probability distribution that generates numbers from one to six. With a perfect die, all of the numbers have the same probability, equal to one sixth. The probability distribution of a real die, however, would deviate from the uniform one because of imperfect manufacturing and other physical factors. If we take a bag of 100 dice, each die corresponds to its own *probability mass function* (PMF), and the bag of dice corresponds to the distribution of PMFs. The properties of this distribution depend on the quality of the dice: the PMFs can substantially deviate from the uniform distribution in the case of low-quality dice or can be almost identical to it in the case of precisely manufactured ones. This distribution of PMFs can be described by using the Dirichlet distribution.

A more practical and relevant example is a collection of text documents. Given that documents contain m distinct words in total, each document can be viewed as a PMF that can be estimated by counting frequencies for each word in the document. A collection of documents is then a collection of PMFs, and we can choose the parameters of a Dirichlet distribution to fit this collection. More formally, each document d can be modeled as a vector of m word probabilities that must add up to one:

$$p_{d1} + \ldots + p_{dm} = 1, \qquad p_{di} \in [0, 1] \tag{A.1}$$

Geometrically, this equation describes an $(m - 1)$-dimensional simplex in an m-dimensional space. For example, a collection of documents with three distinct words corresponds to a two-dimensional triangle (simplex) in a three-dimensional space, as illustrated in Figure A.1. Each point on the simplex corresponds to a valid PMF, whereas all other points in the space do not match any valid PMF. We can generate a collection of m documents by specifying a distribution over the simplex, drawing m PMFs from this distribution, and then generating the m-th document by drawing terms from the corresponding PMF.

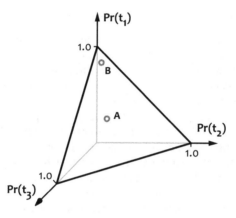

Figure A.1: A three-dimensional probability simplex. Point A corresponds to a document with a uniform distribution of terms; point B corresponds to a document where term t_1 is much more probable than the other two terms.

The Dirichlet distribution is the probability distribution over the simplex. Assuming m dimensions, each instance drawn from the Dirichlet distribution is an m-component probability mass function:

$$\mathbf{p} = (p_1, \ldots, p_m), \qquad \sum_i p_i = 1 \tag{A.2}$$

The distribution itself is specified by a vector of m parameters:

$$\boldsymbol{\alpha} = (\alpha_1, \ldots, \alpha_m), \qquad \alpha_i > 0 \tag{A.3}$$

in which each parameter can be thought of as a weighting of the corresponding component. The probability density function of the Dirichlet distribution is then defined as

$$\mathrm{Dir}(\boldsymbol{\alpha}) = \frac{1}{B(\boldsymbol{\alpha})} \prod_{i=1}^{m} p_i^{\alpha_i - 1} \tag{A.4}$$

in which $B(\alpha)$, the normalization constant, is given by

$$B(\alpha) = \frac{\prod_{i=1}^{m} \Gamma(\alpha_i)}{\Gamma\left(\sum_{i=1}^{m} \alpha_i\right)} \tag{A.5}$$

If all of the elements making up the parameter vector have the same value, the distribution is completely specified by this single value, called the *concentration parameter*. Probability density functions for the Dirichlet distribution in a three-dimensional space are visualized for different parameter values in Figure A.2.

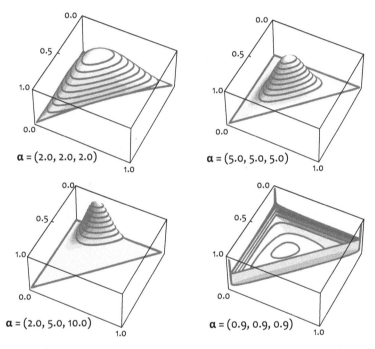

Figure A.2: Density plots for the Dirichlet distribution over the probability simplex in a three-dimensional space.

The density function is completely flat when $\alpha = (1,1,1)$. The density function is bell-shaped and symmetric about the center of the simplex when the parameter vector is flat. If the parameter vector is not flat, the bell is shifted in the direction of the parameters with the biggest magnitudes. Finally, the important thing to note is that the Dirichlet distribution is sparse for the parameter elements with small magnitudes, in the sense that the density is concentrated in the corners, and, consequently, the PMFs drawn from such a distribution tend to have a strong bias towards a small subset of terms [Telgarsky, 2013].

Adomavicius, G. and Tuzhilin, A. (2008). Context-aware recommender systems. In *Proceedings of the 2008 ACM Conference on Recommender Systems*, RecSys '08, pages 335–336, New York, NY, USA. ACM.

Aggarwal, C. C. (2016). *Recommender Systems: The Textbook*. Springer Publishing Company, Incorporated.

Almon, S. (1965). The distributed lag between capital appropriations and expenditures. *Econometrica*, 33(1):178–196.

Anderson, C. (2008). *The Long Tail: Why the Future of Business is Selling Less of More*. Hyperion.

Anupindi, R., Dada, M., and Gupta, S. (1998). Estimation of consumer demand with stock-out based substitution: An application to vending machine products. *Marketing Science*, 17(4):406–423.

Artun, O. and Levin, D. (2015). *Predictive Marketing: Easy Ways Every Marketer Can Use Customer Analytics and Big Data*. Wiley.

Asuncion, A., Welling, M., Smyth, P., and Teh, Y. W. (2009). On smoothing and inference for topic models. In *Proceedings of the Twenty-Fifth Conference on Uncertainty in Artificial Intelligence*, UAI '09, pages 27–34. AUAI Press.

Bell, R. M. and Koren, Y. (2007). Scalable collaborative filtering with jointly derived neighborhood interpolation weights. In *Proceedings of the 2007 Seventh IEEE International Conference on Data Mining*, ICDM '07, pages 43–52. IEEE Computer Society.

Bellogín, A., Castells, P., and Cantador, I. (2014). Neighbor selection and weighting in user-based collaborative filtering: A performance prediction approach. *ACM Trans. Web*, 8(2):12:1–12:30.

Belobaba, P. (1987). Air travel demand and airline seat inventory management. Technical report, Cambridge, MA: Flight Transportation Laboratory, Massachusetts Institute of Technology.

Belobaba, P. P. (1989). Application of a probabilistic decision model to airline seat inventory control. *Operations Research*, 37(2):183–197.

Bergamaschi, S., Po, L., and Sorrentino, S. (2014). Comparing topic models for a movie recommendation system.

Berger, P. and Nasr, N. (1998). *Customer Lifetime Value: Marketing Models and Applications*, volume 12.

Berry, M. (2009). *Differential Response or Uplift Modeling*.

Bishop, C. M. (2006). *Pattern Recognition and Machine Learning*. Springer-Verlag New York, Inc., Secaucus, NJ, USA.

Blattberg, R. C. and Deighton, J. A. (1996). *Manage Marketing by the Customer Equity Test*, volume 74.

Blei, D. M., Ng, A. Y., and Jordan, M. I. (2003). Latent dirichlet allocation. *J. Mach. Learn. Res.*, 3:993–1022.

Bradford, R. (2008). An empirical study of required dimensionality for large-scale latent semantic indexing applications. In *Proceedings of the 17th ACM Conference on Information and Knowledge Management*. ACM.

Breese, J. S., Heckerman, D., and Kadie, C. (1998). *Empirical Analysis of Predictive Algorithms for Collaborative Filtering*. UAI'98. Morgan Kaufmann Publishers Inc., San Francisco, CA, USA.

Breslow, N. E. (1972). Discussion following "regression models and life tables". *Journal of the Royal Statistical Society*, 34:187–220.

Breslow, N. E. (1974). Covariance analysis of censored survival data. *Biometrics*, 30(1):89–99.

Broadbent, S. (1979). One way tv advertisements work. *Journal of the Market Research Society*, 23(3).

Brumelle, S. L. and McGill, J. I. (1993). *Airline Seat Allocation with Multiple Nested Fare Classes*, volume 41.

Burges, C., Shaked, T., Renshaw, E., Lazier, A., Deeds, M., Hamilton, N., and Hullender, G. (2005). Learning to rank using gradient descent. In *Proceedings of the 22Nd International Conference on Machine Learning*, ICML '05.

Burges, C. J. C. (2010). From RankNet to LambdaRank to LambdaMART: An overview. Technical report, Microsoft Research.

Burke, R. (2002). Hybrid recommender systems: Survey and experiments. *User Modeling and User-Adapted Interaction*, 12(4):331–370.

Cao, Z., Qin, T., Liu, T.-Y., Tsai, M.-F., and Li, H. (2007). Learning to rank: From pairwise approach to listwise approach. In *Proceedings of the 24th International Conference on Machine Learning*, pages 129–136. ACM.

Caro, F. and Gallien, J. (2012). *Clearance Pricing Optimization for a Fast-Fashion Retailer*, volume 60.

Carpenter, G. S. and Shankar, V. (2013). *Handbook of Marketing Strategy*. Elgar original reference. Elgar.

Catalina Marketing (2014). *Catalina Category Marketing*.

Chalasani, P. and Sriharsha, R. (2016). *Monte Carlo Simulations in Ad Lift Measurement Using Spark*.

Chapelle, O. and Chang, Y. (2011). Yahoo! learning to rank challenge overview. *Journal of Machine Learning Research - Proceedings Track*, 14:1–24.

Chickering, D. M. and Pearl, J. (1996). *A Clinician's Tool for Analyzing Non-compliance*.

Cossock, D. and Zhang, T. (2006). Subset ranking using regression. In *Proceedings of the 19th Annual Conference on Learning Theory*, pages 605–619. Springer-Verlag.

Cox, D. R. (1972). Regression models and life-tables. *Journal of the Royal Statistical Society*, 34(2):187–220.

Cox, D. R. (1975). Partial likelihood. *Biometrika*, 62(2):269–276.

Crammer, K. and Singer, Y. (2001). Pranking with ranking. In *Advances in Neural Information Processing Systems 14*, pages 641–647. MIT Press.

Cremonesi, P., Koren, Y., and Turrin, R. (2010). Performance of recommender algorithms on top-n recommendation tasks. In *Proceedings of the Fourth ACM Conference on Recommender Systems*, pages 39–46. ACM.

Crocker, C., Kulick, A., and Ram, B. (2012). Real user monitoring at walmart.

Cuellar, S. S. and Brunamonti, M. (2013). *Retail Channel Price Discrimination*, volume 21.

Dalessandro, B., Perlich, C., Hook, R., Stitelman, O., Raeder, T., and Provost, F. (2012a). *Bid Optimizing and Inventory Scoring in Targeted Online Advertising*.

Dalessandro, B., Perlich, C., Stitelman, O., and Provost, F. (2012b). *Causally Motivated Attribution for Online Advertising.*

Debreu, G. (1960). *Review of R. D. Luce, Individual Choice Behavior: A Theoretical Analysis.*

Deerwester, S., Dumais, S. T., Furnas, G. W., Landauer, T. K., and Harshman, R. (1990). Indexing by latent semantic analysis. *Journal of the American Society for Information Science*, 41(6).

Devooght, R., Kourtellis, N., and Mantrach, A. (2015). Dynamic matrix factorization with priors on unknown values. In *Proceedings of the 21th ACM SIGKDD International Conference on Knowledge Discovery and Data Mining*, pages 189–198. ACM.

Ding, Y. and Li, X. (2005). Time weight collaborative filtering. In *Proceedings of the 14th ACM International Conference on Information and Knowledge Management*, CIKM '05, pages 485–492, New York, NY, USA. ACM.

Duhigg, C. (2012). *How Companies Learn Your Secrets.*

Efron, B. (1977). The efficiency of cox's likelihood function for censored data. *Journal of the American Statistical Association*, 72(359):557–565.

Ekstrand, M. D., Riedl, J. T., and Konstan, J. A. (2011). Collaborative filtering recommender systems. *Found. Trends Hum.-Comput. Interact.*, 4(2):81–173.

Falk, K. (2017). *Practical Recommender Systems.* Manning Publications Company.

Ferreira, K. J., Lee, B. H. A., and Simchi-Levi, D. (2016). *Analytics for an Online Retailer: Demand Forecasting and Price Optimization*, volume 18.

Freund, Y., Iyer, R., Schapire, R. E., and Singer, Y. (2003). An efficient boosting algorithm for combining preferences. *J. Mach. Learn. Res.*, 4:933–969.

Frigyik, B., Kapila, A., and Maya, G. (2010). Introduction to the dirichlet distribution and related processes. Technical report, University of Washington.

Funk, S. (2016). Netflix update: Try this at home.

Ge, M., Delgado-Battenfeld, C., and Jannach, D. (2010). Beyond accuracy: Evaluating recommender systems by coverage and serendipity. In *Proceedings of the Fourth ACM Conference on Recommender Systems*, pages 257–260. ACM.

Geman, S. and Geman, D. (1984). *Stochastic Relaxation, Gibbs Distributions, and the Bayesian Restoration of Images*, volume 6. IEEE Computer Society, Washington, DC, USA.

Geng, L. and Hamilton, H. J. (2006). Interestingness measures for data mining: A survey. *ACM Comput. Surv.*, 38(3).

Ghani, R. and Fano, A. (2002). Building recommender systems using a knowledge base of product semantics. In *In 2nd International Conference on Adaptive Hypermedia and Adaptive Web Based Systems, Malaga*.

Ghani, R., Probst, K., Liu, Y., Krema, M., and Fano, A. (2006). Text mining for product attribute extraction. *SIGKDD Explor. Newsl.*, pages 41–48.

Giunchiglia, F., Kharkevich, U., and Zaihrayeu, I. (2009). Concept search. In *Proceedings of the 6th European Semantic Web Conference on The Semantic Web: Research and Applications*, ESWC 2009 Heraklion. Springer-Verlag.

Goldberg, D., Nichols, D., Oki, B. M., and Terry, D. (1992). Using collaborative filtering to weave an information tapestry. *Commun. ACM*, 35(12):61–70.

Google Inc. (2011). *The Arrival of Real-Time Bidding*.

Gormley, C. and Tong, Z. (2015). *Elasticsearch: The Definitive Guide*. O'Reilly Media.

Green, P. E. and Srinivasan, V. (1978). *Conjoint Analysis in Consumer Research: Issues and Outlook*, volume 5.

Grigsby, M. (2016). *Advanced Customer Analytics: Targeting, Valuing, Segmenting and Loyalty Techniques*. Marketing Science Series. Kogan Page, Limited.

Hall, R. E. (1967). Polynomial distributed lags.

Heckerman, D. and Shachter, R. D. (1995). *Decision-Theoretic Foundations for Causal Reasoning*.

Herbrich, R., Graepel, T., and Obermayer, K. (2000). Large margin rank boundaries for ordinal regression. In *Advances in Large Margin Classifiers*, pages 115–132. MIT Press.

Herlocker, J. L., Konstan, J. A., Borchers, A., and Riedl, J. (1999). An algorithmic framework for performing collaborative filtering. In *Proceedings of the 22Nd Annual International ACM SIGIR Conference on*

Research and Development in Information Retrieval, SIGIR '99, pages 230–237, New York, NY, USA. ACM.

Herlocker, J. L., Konstan, J. A., Terveen, L. G., and Riedl, J. T. (2004). Evaluating collaborative filtering recommender systems. pages 5–53.

Hofmann, T. (1999). Probabilistic latent semantic indexing. In *Proceedings of the 22Nd Annual International ACM SIGIR Conference on Research and Development in Information Retrieval*, SIGIR '99, pages 50–57, New York, NY, USA. ACM.

Hu, Y., Koren, Y., and Volinsky, C. (2008). Collaborative filtering for implicit feedback datasets. In *Proceedings of the 2008 Eighth IEEE International Conference on Data Mining*, ICDM '08, pages 263–272. IEEE Computer Society.

Hughes, S. (2015). Implementing conceptual search in Solr using LSA and Word2Vec.

Jack, K., Ingold, E., and Hristakeva, M. (2016). Mendeley suggest architecture.

Jahrer, M., Töscher, A., and Legenstein, R. (2010). Combining predictions for accurate recommender systems. In *Proceedings of the 16th ACM SIGKDD International Conference on Knowledge Discovery and Data Mining*, KDD '10, pages 693–702, New York, NY, USA. ACM.

Jambor, T. and Wang, J. (2010). Optimizing multiple objectives in collaborative filtering. In *Proceedings of the Fourth ACM Conference on Recommender Systems*, RecSys '10, pages 55–62, New York, NY, USA. ACM.

Järvelin, K. and Kekäläinen, J. (2000). IR evaluation methods for retrieving highly relevant documents. In *Proceedings of the 23rd annual international ACM SIGIR conference on Research and development in information retrieval*.

Jo, B. (2002). *Statistical Power in Randomized Intervention Studies With Noncompliance*.

Johnson, J., Tellis, G. J., and Ip, E. H. (2013). *To Whom, When, and How Much to Discount? A Constrained Optimization of Customized Temporal Discounts*, volume 89. Elsevier.

Ju, C., Bao, F., Xu, C., and Fu, X. (2015). A novel method of interestingness measures for association rules mining based on profit. In *Discrete Dynamics in Nature and Society*.

Kahneman, D. and Tversky, A. (1979). *Prospect theory: An analysis of decisions under risk.*

Kamotsky, D. and Vargas, M. (2014). System and method for performing a pattern matching search. US Patent App. 14/292,018.

Kane, K., Lo, V. S., and Zheng, J. X. (2014). Mining for the truly responsive customers and prospects using true-lift modeling: Comparison of new and existing methods. *Journal of Marketing Analytics*, 2(4):218–238.

Kaplan, E. L. and Meier, P. (1958). Nonparametric estimation from incomplete observations. *Journal of the American Statistical Association*, 53(282):457–481.

Khan, R. J. and Jain, D. C. (2005). *An Empirical Analysis of Price Discrimination Mechanisms and Retailer Profitability*, volume 42.

Khludnev, M. (2013). Concept search for eCommerce with Solr.

Kleinberg, J., Papadimitriou, C., and Raghavan, P. (1998). *A Microeconomic View of Data Mining*, volume 2. Kluwer Academic Publishers, Hingham, MA, USA.

Kohavi, R. and Longbotham, R. (2007). Online experiments: Lessons learned.

Kök, A. G. and Fisher, M. L. (2007). *Demand Estimation and Assortment Optimization Under Substitution: Methodology and Application*, volume 55. INFORMS.

Koren, Y. (2007). How useful is a lower rmse?

Koren, Y. (2008). Factorization meets the neighborhood: A multifaceted collaborative filtering model. In *Proceedings of the 14th ACM SIGKDD International Conference on Knowledge Discovery and Data Mining*, pages 426–434, New York, NY, USA. ACM.

Koren, Y. (2009). The bellkor solution to the netflix grand prize.

Koren, Y. and Bell, R. M. (2011). Advances in collaborative filtering. In Ricci, F., Rokach, L., Shapira, B., and Kantor, P. B., editors, *Recommender Systems Handbook*, pages 145–186. Springer.

Koyck, L. M. (1954). Distributed lags and investment analysis.

Lauterborn, B. (1990). *New Marketing Litany: Four Ps Passe: C-Words Take Over.*

Lee, D. D. and Seung, H. S. (2001). Algorithms for non-negative matrix factorization. In Leen, T. K., Dietterich, T. G., and Tresp, V., editors, *Advances in Neural Information Processing Systems 13*, pages 556–562. MIT Press.

Li, P., Burges, C. J. C., and Wu, Q. (2007). Mcrank: Learning to rank using multiple classification and gradient boosting. In *NIPS*, pages 897–904. Curran Associates, Inc.

Linden, G., Smith, B., and York, J. (2003). Amazon.com recommendations: Item-to-item collaborative filtering. *IEEE Internet Computing*, 7(1):76–80.

Littlewood, K. (1972). *Forecasting and Control of Passenger Bookings*.

Liu, T.-Y. (2009). Learning to rank for information retrieval. *Foundations and Trends in Information Retrieval*, (3):225–331.

Liu, T.-Y. and Qin, T. (2010). Microsoft learning to rank datasets.

Lo, V. S. (2002). The true lift model: a novel data mining approach to response modeling in database marketing. *ACM SIGKDD Explorations Newsletter*, 4(2):78–86.

Manning, C. D., Raghavan, P., and Schütze, H. (2008). *Introduction to Information Retrieval*. Cambridge University Press, New York, NY, USA.

Marn, M. and Roseillo, R. (1992). *Managing price, gaining profit*.

McCarthy, E. J. (1960). *Basic Marketing. A Managerial Approach*.

Melville, P., Mooney, R. J., and Nagarajan, R. (2002). Content-boosted collaborative filtering for improved recommendations. In *Eighteenth National Conference on Artificial Intelligence*, pages 187–192. American Association for Artificial Intelligence.

Mikolov, T., Chen, K., Corrado, G., and Dean, J. (2013a). Efficient estimation of word representations in vector space.

Mikolov, T., Sutskever, I., Chen, K., Corrado, G. S., and Dean, J. (2013b). Distributed representations of words and phrases and their compositionality. In *Advances in Neural Information Processing Systems 26*. Curran Associates, Inc.

Miyahara, K. and Pazzani, M. J. (2000). Collaborative filtering with the simple bayesian classifier. In *Proceedings of the 6th Pacific Rim International Conference on Artificial Intelligence*, PRICAI'00, pages 679–689. Springer-Verlag.

Mobasher, B., Dai, H., Luo, T., and Nakagawa, M. (2001). Effective personalization based on association rule discovery from web usage data. In *Proceedings of the 3rd International Workshop on Web Information and Data Management*, WIDM '01, pages 9–15, New York, NY, USA. ACM.

Mooney, R. J. and Roy, L. (1999). Content-based book recommending using learning for text categorization. In *Proceedings of the SIGIR-99 Workshop on Recommender Systems: Algorithms and Evaluation*.

Murphy, K. P. (2012). *Machine Learning: A Probabilistic Perspective*. The MIT Press.

Musalem, A., Olivares, M., Bradlow, E. T., Terwiesch, C., and Corsten, D. (2010). Structural estimation of the effect of out-of-stocks. *Management Science*, 56(7):1180–1197.

Oi, W. Y. (1971). *A Disneyland Dilemma: Two-Part Tariffs for a Mickey Mouse Monopoly*.

Oneata, D. (1999). Probabilistic latent semantic analysis. In *Proceedings of the Fifteenth conference on Uncertainty*, pages 1–7.

Park, L. A. and Ramamohanarao, K. (2009). Efficient storage and retrieval of probabilistic latent semantic information for information retrieval. *The VLDB Journal*, 18(1):141–155.

Pashigian, P. (1987). *Demand Uncertainty and Sales: A Study of Fashion and Markdown Pricing*.

Pennington, J., Socher, R., and Manning, C. D. (2014). Glove: Global vectors for word representation. In *Conference on Empirical Methods on Natural Language Processing*, volume 14, pages 1532–1543.

Perlich, C., Dalessandro, B., Raeder, T., Stitelman, O., and Provost, F. (2013). *Machine Learning for Targeted Display Advertising: Transfer Learning in Action*.

Peter, G. and Eugene, S. (2015). Deep data at macys: Searching hierarchical documents for ecommerce merchandising.

Pfeifer, P. and Carraway, R. (2000). *Modeling Customer Relationships as Markov Chains*.

Porter, M. F. (1980). An algorithm for suffix stripping. *Program*, 14(3):130–137.

Radcliffe, N. J. and Simpson, R. (2007). Identifying who can be saved and who will be driven away by retention activity.

Radcliffe, N. J. and Surry, P. (1999). Differential response analysis: Modeling true response by isolating the effect of a single action. *Credit Scoring and Credit Control VI. Edinburgh, Scotland.*

Radcliffe, N. J. and Surry, P. D. (2011). Real-world uplift modelling with significance-based uplift trees. *White Paper TR-2011-1, Stochastic Solutions.*

Radlinski, F. and Joachims, T. (2005). Query chains: Learning to rank from implicit feedback. In *Proceedings of the Eleventh ACM SIGKDD International Conference on Knowledge Discovery in Data Mining*, pages 239–248. ACM.

Rodriguez, M., Posse, C., and Zhang, E. (2012). Multiple objective optimization in recommender systems. In *Proceedings of the Sixth ACM Conference on Recommender Systems*, RecSys '12, pages 11–18, New York, NY, USA. ACM.

Rohde, D. L. T., Gonnerman, L. M., and Plaut, D. C. (2006). An improved model of semantic similarity based on lexical co-occurence. *Communications of the ACM.*

Rong, X. (2014a). wevi: Word embedding visual inspector.

Rong, X. (2014b). Word2Vec parameter learning explained.

Rubin, D. (1974). *Estimating causal effects of treatments in randomized and nonrandomized studies.*

Sarwar, B., Karypis, G., Konstan, J., and Riedl, J. (2001). Item-based collaborative filtering recommendation algorithms. In *Proceedings of the 10th International Conference on World Wide Web*, pages 285–295. ACM.

Shao, X. and Li, L. (2011). *Data-driven Multi-touch Attribution Models.*

Sill, J., Takacs, G., Mackey, L. W., and Lin, D. (2009). Feature-weighted linear stacking.

Smith, B., Leimkuhler, J., and Darrow, R. (1992). *Yield Management in American Airlines.*

Smith, T. (2012). *Pricing Strategy.* South-Western Cengage Learning.

Spangher, A. (2015). Building the next new york times recommendation engine.

Su, X. and Khoshgoftaar, T. M. (2006). Collaborative filtering for multi-class data using belief nets algorithms. In *Proceedings of the 18th IEEE International Conference on Tools with Artificial Intelligence*, ICTAI '06, pages 497–504, Washington, DC, USA. IEEE Computer Society.

Su, X. and Khoshgoftaar, T. M. (2009). A survey of collaborative filtering techniques. *Adv. in Artif. Intell.*, pages 4:2–4:2.

Su, X., Khoshgoftaar, T. M., Zhu, X., and Greiner, R. (2008). Imputation-boosted collaborative filtering using machine learning classifiers. In *Proceedings of the 2008 ACM Symposium on Applied Computing*, SAC '08, pages 949–950, New York, NY, USA. ACM.

Talluri, K. and Van Ryzin, G. (2004). *The Theory and Practice of Revenue Management*. International Series in Operations Research & Management Science. Springer.

Telgarsky, M. (2013). Dirichlet draws are sparse with high probability.

Terry, D. B. (1993). A tour through tapestry. In *Proceedings of the Conference on Organizational Computing Systems*, COCS '93, pages 21–30, New York, NY, USA. ACM.

Töscher, A., Jahrer, M., and Bell, R. M. (2009). The bigchaos solution to the netflix grand prize.

Train, K. (2003). *Discrete Choice Methods with Simulation*. SUNY-Oswego, Department of Economics.

Turnbull, D. and Berryman, J. (2016). *Relevant Search. With applications for Solr and Elasticsearch*. Manning Publications.

Vasigh, B., Tacker, T., and Fleming, M. (2013). *Introduction to Air Transport Economics: From Theory to Applications*.

Vulcano, G. J., van Ryzin, G. J., and Ratliff, R. (2012). Estimating primary demand for substitutable products from sales transaction data. *Operations Research*, 60(2):313–334.

Walker, R. (2009). *The Song Decoders*. The New York Times Magazine.

Wierenga, B. (2010). The interface of marketing and operations research. In Kroon, L., Zuidwijk, R., and Li, T., editors, *Liber Amicorum in Memoriam Jo van Nunen*.

Winston, W. L. (2014). *Marketing Analytics: Data-Driven Techniques with Microsoft Excel*. Wiley Publishing, 1st edition.

Xia, Z., Dong, Y., and Xing, G. (2006). Support vector machines for collaborative filtering. In *Proceedings of the 44th Annual Southeast Regional Conference*, ACM-SE 44, pages 169–174, New York, NY, USA. ACM.

Xu, J. and Li, H. (2007). Adarank: A boosting algorithm for information retrieval. In *Proceedings of the 30th Annual International ACM SIGIR Conference on Research and Development in Information Retrieval*, pages 391–398, New York, NY, USA. ACM.

Zaki, M. J. and Meira, W. (2014). *Data Mining and Analysis: Fundamental Concepts and Algorithms*.

Zhang, A., Goyal, A., Kong, W., Deng, H., Dong, A., Chang, Y., Gunter, C. A., and Han, J. (2015). adaqac: Adaptive query auto-completion via implicit negative feedback. In *Proceedings of the 38th International ACM SIGIR Conference on Research and Development in Information Retrieval*, pages 143–152. ACM.

Zhang, H. (2004). The optimality of naive bayes. In Barr, V. and Markov, Z., editors, *Proceedings of the Seventeenth International Florida Artificial Intelligence Research Society Conference (FLAIRS 2004)*. AAAI Press.

Zhang, S., Wang, W., Ford, J., and Makedon, F. (1996). Learning from incomplete ratings using non-negative matrix factorization. In *In Proc. of the 6th SIAM Conference on Data Mining*, pages 549–553.

CPSIA information can be obtained
at www.ICGtesting.com
Printed in the USA
BVHW040953210720
584232BV00008B/171